Plato and Nietzsche

Also available from Bloomsbury

Heidegger and Nietzsche, Louis P. Blond
Nietzsche and Political Thought, edited by Keith Ansell-Pearson
Nietzsche as a Scholar of Antiquity, edited by Anthony K. Jensen and Helmut Heit
The Continuum Companion to Plato, edited by Gerald A. Press

Plato and Nietzsche

Their Philosophical Art

Mark Anderson

B L O O M S B U R Y

LONDON • NEW DELHI • NEW YORK • SYDNEY

Bloomsbury Academic

An imprint of Bloomsbury Publishing Plc

50 Bedford Square	1385 Broadway
London	New York
WC1B 3DP	NY 10018
UK	USA

www.bloomsbury.com

Bloomsbury is a registered trade mark of Bloomsbury Publishing Plc

First published 2014

© Mark Anderson, 2014

Mark Anderson has asserted his right under the Copyright, Designs and Patents Act, 1988, to be identified as Author of this work.

British Library Cataloguing-in-Publication Data
A catalogue record for this book is available from the British Library.

ISBN: HB: 978-1-4725-2204-7
ePDF: 978-1-4725-2874-2
ePub: 978-1-4725-3289-3

Library of Congress Cataloging-in-Publication Data
A catalog record for this book is available from the Library of Congress.

Typeset by Fakenham Prepress Solutions, Fakenham, Norfolk NR21 8NN
Printed and bound in Great Britain

Contents

Preface

Think of this book as a scholarly work not restricted to scholars. I have outfitted the text here and there with traditional academic impedimenta, textual references and the occasional quotation of a Greek word or phrase. But I do this only to illuminate particular points, and only those points that the thoughtful general reader will appreciate along with the scholar. Additional details and arguments are in the endnotes.

As for the book's content, it is an exploration of those of Plato's and Nietzsche's ideas that can be joined in dialogue or debate. These include many of their most representative ideas, so one result of my study is a general survey of their work. And as the particulars of the relationship between these two thinkers provide material for reflection on the nature of philosophy and wisdom, I explore these matters too, and I conclude that in exceptional cases this apparent duality might be a unity, especially when a third element, artistry, is present.

Finally, with this book I tell a story. Some parts of my narrative are traditional and will therefore be familiar and uncontroversial, others are less conventional. In any case, it is on the whole my own version of Plato and Nietzsche, and of wisdom and the love of wisdom. As particularly my own, the story I tell is somewhat idiosyncratic, but I trust it will engage and inform a few curious readers.

Acknowledgments

My thanks to Sally Holt for her patient assistance and enthusiastic support, also to Francesca Muccini, Theron Spiegl, Ronnie Littlejohn, Andrew Davis, Noel Boyle, Mike Awalt, Ginger Osborn, Anthony Kaldellis, Paul Loeb, Patrick Lee Miller, Paul Bishop, Greg Whitlock, Cameron Smith, Mason Marshall, Bronwen Wickkiser, Scott Aikin, Trey George, Charles Ives, Scott Hawley, Nathaniel Greeson, Mark Migotti, Paige Carter, and Liza Thompson.

Conventions

Translations

All translations from the Greek are my own. Editions are listed in the bibliography under the author's name.

The majority of Nietzsche translations are borrowed from published works, which are listed in the bibliography under Nietzsche's name. Selections from Nietzsche's early lectures and notes on Plato (*KGW* II.4) are by Andrew Davis. A few unattributed quotations from Nietzsche's notebooks and letters are my own.

Abbreviations

Plato's works:

Ap.	*Apology*
Cra.	*Cratylus*
Euthphr.	*Euthyphro*
Grg.	*Gorgias*
Ion	*Ion*
Lg.	*Laws*
Men.	*Meno*
Phd.	*Phaedo*
Phdr.	*Phaedrus*
Phlb.	*Philebus*
R.	*Republic*
Sph.	*Sophist*
Sts.	*Statesman*
Smp.	*Symposium*
Tht.	*Theaetetus*
Ti.	*Timaeus*

Nietzsche's works:

KGW	*Nietzsche Werke: Kritische Gesamtausgabe*
KSA	*Sämtliche Werke: Kritische Studienausgabe*
KGB	*Briefwechsel: Kritische Gesamtausgabe*

A	*The Antichrist*
BGE	*Beyond Good and Evil*
BT	*The Birth of Tragedy*
EH	*Ecce Homo*
GS	*The Gay Science*
GM	*On the Genealogy of Morals*
HH	*Human, All Too Human*
HL	"On the Uses and Disadvantages of History for Life"
P	"The Philosopher"
PHT	"Philosophy in Hard Times"
PPP	*The Pre-Platonic Philosophers*
PTG	*Philosophy in the Tragic Age of the Greeks*
SE	"Schopenhauer as Educator"
TI	*Twilight of the Idols*
TL	"On Truth and Lies in a Nonmoral Sense"
UM	*Untimely Meditations*
WP	*The Will to Power*
WS	*The Wanderer and His Shadow*
Z	*Thus Spoke Zarathustra*

Other works:

DK	Diels and Kranz: *Die Fragmente der Vorsokratiker*
DL	Diogenes Laertius: *Lives of Eminent Philosophers*
WWR	Schopenhauer: *The World as Will and Representation*

Citations

I refer to passages in Plato's works by title abbreviation and line number. Regarding the transliterated Greek as it appears in my text, sometimes when making a general point by way of the mention of a word, or when I want the reader to see the word in its primary form, I put the word in the nominative case regardless of its form in the cited location.

I refer to passages in Nietzsche's works by title abbreviation, chapter or part title when necessary, and aphorism or section number. I refer to *PPP* and *PTG* by page number, and to *TL* by page number of Breazeale 1990.

Introduction

There is a tradition going back to the ancients of evaluating a philosopher according to the way he lived his life and how he met and managed his death. Plato died naturally while revising a work that he must have known would be his last, the final summit in a long life of intellectual mountaineering. Nietzsche died most unnaturally, his mind passing away a full decade before his body finally expired, during a period that should have been the prime, not the end, of his career as a thinker and author. As for their lives, Plato at birth (c. 428 BCE) was given the name "Aristocles," the "Plato" being a nickname derived from a word meaning "broad" and applied to him, according to one ancient account, from his robust physique; he was reputed to have been a wrestler. He was born into a noble family, and many of his relatives were active in Athenian political life—on his mother's side he descended from the same family as the sage, poet, and lawmaker Solon, and he was related as well to Critias and Charmides, two notorious anti-democrats active especially in the aftermath of the Peloponnesian War. As a young man he composed poems and aspired to be a tragedian, but when he met Socrates everything changed: he burned his tragedies and dedicated his life to the love of wisdom. In the turmoil following Socrates' trial and execution (in 399 BCE), Plato fled Athens for a time but eventually returned and began to write the dialogues for which eventually he was designated "divine." Sometime later, and perhaps following the first of three trips to Italy and Sicily, where he made the acquaintance of everyone from Pythagorean philosophers to Dionysius I, tyrant of Syracuse, he commenced teaching in a public park approximately a mile beyond Athens' city walls and near to a property he purchased and on which he established a residence. The park was sacred to an Athenian hero named Hekadêmos, and it is from this name that we have the word "Academy." In later years at the request of a friend Plato sailed again to Sicily, this time in order to educate young Dionysius II, who from his father had inherited rule of Syracuse. The idea was to produce a philosopher-king, but this was not to be. Dionysius was mercurial and peevish; he made neither ethical nor intellectual progress and eventually sent Plato brusquely away. Later still, after a final fruitless effort in Sicily, Plato disengaged from political affairs and settled exclusively into a life of the mind. He lived into, or close to, his eightieth year, and to judge from his late works, including his last work the *Laws*, his mind was sound until the day he died.[1]

Nietzsche's life was very different. Born in 1844 to a Lutheran minister who died young from "softening of the brain," Nietzsche suffered throughout his life from a variety of debilitating ailments, and he lived in fear of succumbing to a fate like his father's. As a child he was pious, quiet, small and serious—and also remarkably bright. In 1858 he earned a scholarship to attend a prestigious boarding school called Pforta, where for the next six years he received an excellent classical education. From Pforta he went to university with the intention of studying theology, but soon he abandoned his faith and turned his attention exclusively to classical philology, which is to say to the meticulous study of the languages, literature, history, and culture of the ancient Greeks and Romans. He was early on recognized as a brilliant young scholar, and at the age of twenty-four, before he had even completed his doctorate, he was hired by the University of Basel in Switzerland as Professor of Classical Philology. Around this time he made the acquaintance of the composer Richard Wagner, with whom he enjoyed a close, indeed almost a filial relationship for several years. The men bonded in particular over a common admiration for the philosopher Arthur Schopenhauer, whose masterwork, *The World as Will and Representation*, Nietzsche had discovered in a bookstore by chance only a few years earlier. It was his first serious exposure to contemporary philosophy, and he was captivated.

As a young professor with a passion for the Greeks and a steadily intensifying interest in philosophy, Nietzsche studied, taught, and wrote at length about the Presocratic philosophers and Plato. Once he even applied to fill the university's vacant chair of philosophy, but he was passed over for not being officially credentialed in the subject. Despite this particular lack of academic training, Nietzsche began eventually to publish works of philosophy, and in 1879 he retired from Basel and spent the rest of his active life living and writing as a philosopher, surviving on a small inheritance and a pension, these funds supplemented by the occasional kindness of friends. He withdrew from teaching primarily because he was too sick to continue (his eyesight in particular was abysmal, and for a time there was fear that he might go blind), and his various disorders dogged him the rest of his days. Convinced that his physical and mental health depended on the appropriate atmospheric-meteorological conditions, he resided most winters in northern Italy and summers in Switzerland. He lived alone in rented rooms, maintaining contact with friends and relatives through the mail. He sent them his books as they appeared, and these associates were among the few who read them. In the late 1880s Nietzsche at last began to attract a small audience, and in 1888 a highly regarded intellectual-literary historian and critic, Georg Brandes, delivered a series of lectures on Nietzsche's philosophy at the university in Copenhagen, Denmark. But this was all too late; Nietzsche was doomed.

In December of 1888 while lodging with a family in Turin, Italy, Nietzsche posted several bizarre notes to various friends and strangers (including the German Kaiser and the King of Italy), signing them "The Crucified" and "Dionysos." Then, on the third day of the new year, he suffered a fit and collapsed in a local piazza. A few days later a friend from Basel arrived in Turin to find the philosopher in his rooms unmistakably out of his mind. The man took Nietzsche to a psychiatric clinic in Switzerland, and from there Nietzsche's mother took him to a clinic in Germany. For some time after his breakdown Nietzsche cycled in and out of semi-lucidity, but eventually he ceased almost altogether to talk or to exhibit any signs of a normal mental life. From 1890 he stayed with his mother in Naumburg until she died seven years later, at which point his sister installed him in Weimar under her own care, where he remained until his death in August 1900.

So what can we learn of philosophical significance from the lives and deaths of Plato and Nietzsche? It is evident that Plato was the healthier of the two, psychologically as well as physically; he lived a long, full life, as rich in action as in thought. There is no indication of morose withdrawal from the world, nor of any shallow or naive optimism. As even Nietzsche would admit—as perhaps he *does* admit when he writes that Plato had "the greatest strength any philosopher so far has had at his disposal" (*BGE* 191)—Plato possessed and exercised the power to mold the western world in his image, which form it has held for more than two millennia.

Nietzsche was not so fortunate physiologically. He recognized this himself, and he acknowledged in print that he was decadent, at least to a degree (*EH* "Wise" 1). But this was so through no fault of his own, no rash decisions or reckless behavior. Nietzsche's problems were more fundamental, elemental, and they may have been inherited.[2] More striking than his debilitated condition was his capacity to accomplish so much in spite of it. That a man so sick and often unhappy could compose a hymn of affirmation as profound as *Thus Spoke Zarathustra* was to Nietzsche's way of thinking the surest sign of his fundamental health; and if we think of this as a spiritual or philosophical health, then I for one believe that he must have been right. *Zarathustra* is most definitely the work of a man who has attained to the condition of Yes-sayer and world creator, even if only temporarily.

As different as their lives were, Plato and Nietzsche walked the same path. Plato set out first, and Nietzsche was the upstart who insisted on walking beside him. Under normal circumstances such a man would be only obnoxious, a nuisance the great man must ignore to press forward on his own. But Nietzsche was that rarest of latecomers, one who actually merits the respect he claims for himself.

* * *

Quite apart from the problem that we lack secure biographical information, Plato is nearly impossible to know. His decision to adopt the dialogue form is simultaneously an election never to address his audience directly. Plato nowhere unambiguously states that "this is who I am, and *this* is what I believe." We are left guessing, and nothing is ever finally settled. A Platonic dialogue is a labyrinth, and Plato presents us with no Ariadne for aid. So although in this book I attribute to him a variety of beliefs and philosophical commitments, the truth is that no one has any idea what Plato thought about specific matters. I am sure it is reasonable to suppose, for example, that he believed in a soul under some description, and that he thought it somehow more valuable than the body, for the general idea recurs so often in his writings that the claim that he believes something like this is at least *prima facie* plausible. But only plausible; never certain. And as to how exactly he conceived the substance of this soul, and what he thought of its fate after the death of the body: I cannot say with confidence, nor can anyone else. Plato addresses these matters on more than one occasion, but often in the context of what appear to be myths or allegories, and usually with differences in the details. All labyrinth, no thread.

For a different perspective on this same problem, consider the question whether Plato intends his creation story in the *Timaeus* literally or figuratively.[3] There was disagreement even among his own students. Xenocrates, who knew Plato personally, maintains that he described an act of creation merely in order to facilitate understanding of his analysis of ontological principles that are conceptually distinct but that never have in actual fact existed independently one from the other. Aristotle, on the other hand, writes as if he takes the creation story literally, and he even argues against it. Aristotle also knew Plato well. Here we have two of Plato's personal acquaintances, each with his own interpretation of a matter of great import for understanding the master's ideas about the nature of the universe. How can there be such confusion? Could these men not approach Plato and ask him what he meant? If not, why not? Or did they query him but receive the sort of reply one sometimes hears from poets and artists—"I meant what I wrote exactly as I wrote it. Had I meant something different I would have written something different"—which is to say a reply that amounts to a refusal to elaborate or explain? If so, why would Plato speak this way? Was he as secretive in person as he is in his texts?

We know just as little about the chronology of Plato's composition of the dialogues. We are told that he left the *Laws* unfinished at his death, which leads most scholars to identify this as his final work; and since this work exhibits certain stylistic features in common with some dialogues but not with others, many scholars conclude that he wrote the stylistically similar dialogues in the same period as the *Laws*, which is to say late in his life. This line of reasoning, if not conclusive, is at least plausible; but it accounts for only a handful of dialogues. As for the others, it is often assumed that Plato intended those that stress uncertainty, indecision, and lack of knowledge (aporia) to be more or less accurate depictions of Socrates, but we cannot be sure, for Xenophon's Socrates seems to know quite a lot, and even Plato's Socrates makes broad claims to knowledge from time to time.[4] If these dialogues are authentically "Socratic," then it might make sense to date them early in Plato's career, before he developed his own independent ideas to any great degree of complexity and depth. But it is *not* plausible to conclude that every aporetic dialogue *must* be early, for presumably there was nothing preventing Plato from later in life composing a work in the mode of his early style.[5] Finally, then, there are the so-called "middle-period" dialogues, which exhibit a mature and refined artistic sensibility (both of prose style and dramatic-narrative construction) and a well-developed metaphysical system usually involving the theory of Forms. The artistry and the metaphysics seem to distinguish these works from the less ambitious "early" dialogues, in which the Forms do not explicitly appear, and also from the technical and frequently dense "late" dialogues, which seem to some to reject or at least to minimize the theory of Forms and to introduce different (or additional) metaphysical principles. Platonic chronology has always been controversial, and today many scholars regard these three divisions with suspicion,[6] but as the terminology is still more or less standard, I shall refer in this book to "early" dialogues, which depict specifically Socratic practice and that stress aporia; "middle" dialogues, in which we encounter Plato's own thoughts in their first full blossom and early maturity; and the "late" dialogues, which are more complex, obscure, and whose central problems and methodologies are of course related to, but also somewhat different from, the middle works.[7] I myself am not committed to these divisions, and while I think it important to familiarize readers with terms that they are likely to encounter in the secondary literature, I consider it equally important to stress that scholarly consensus and practice are always subject to change, and that this is so because in the end we just do not know the truth about these matters, and in many cases we *cannot* know it. In the nineteenth century it was common to identify the *Phaedrus* as Plato's first work,[8] and although nearly no scholar active today accepts this, I would not insist that it is impossible.[9] Plato, as I have mentioned, wrote no work in his own voice; he speaks to us only through his characters, and sometimes he stresses his authorial absence by, for example, framing a dialogue as the report of a report of a conversation overheard. In short, he goes out of his way to distance himself from us, or from the ideas he is relating, or both. But which is it, and why? As usual, we do not know.

We know much more about Nietzsche's activities as a writer. It is standard to divide his works, too, into early, middle, and late, though in his case the chronology is undisputed. But his *intentions* as a writer are somewhat more obscure. Determining exactly what he meant to say, what ideas, if any, he advocated and why, where he stood with respect to certain specific matters (the generalities are usually relatively clear)—it can be as difficult to sort through all this as it is in Plato's case. Nietzsche makes nothing easy for us. This is so in part because, unlike many traditional philosophers, he seems not to have ranked consistency among the highest of his aspirations as either a thinker or a writer. In *Human, All Too Human* he advises philosophers against maintaining "a *single* mental posture, a *single* class of opinions, for all the situations and events in life." Better, he suggests, to "listen to the soft voice of different situations in life," and to resist "treating ourselves as fixed, stable, *single* individuals" (*HH* 618). But please do not mistake me here: I do not maintain, with some philosophers and many a literary theorist, that Nietzsche was so playful, so self-deconstructive, that in his texts he intentionally undermines and contradicts his own words and ideas. No: it is clear to me that Nietzsche maintains a uniform intellectual approach to a recurrent set of problems throughout much of his work, at least in a general sense. But when it comes to specifics he was, I believe, perfectly content to entertain a thought and to put it into print whether or not it was strictly consistent with other thoughts expressed in other works, or even with material in other sections of the same work, so long as the idea struck him as insightful, provocative, or intellectually fertile.[10] He once wrote that "[o]ne does not only wish to be understood when one writes; one wishes just as surely *not* to be understood" (*GS* 381). Nietzsche got his wish, for he is often misunderstood, as much by those who exaggerate the significance of his "playfulness" as by those who impose their personal ideal of a rigorous consistency on the riotous flow of his ideas.

The free-spiritedness of Nietzsche's intellectual life is manifest in his practical activities as an author. He loved to write while walking in the open air, a fact that doubtless inspired his observation that "[o]nly thoughts reached by walking have value" (*TI* "Maxims" 34). We know from a letter that he wrote *The Wanderer and His Shadow* in several small notebooks while walking around St. Moritz,[11] and in *The Gay Science* he mentions his "habit to think outdoors—walking, leaping, climbing, dancing, preferably on lonely mountains or near the sea where even the trails become thoughtful" (*GS* 366). More than one account of his daily activities in Sils-Maria has him strolling thoughtfully around the local lakes or hiking high into the mountains, pencil and notebook in hand.[12] Nietzsche came alive when thinking and writing while walking outdoors, pursuing through the clear sky of his mind an endless flight of ideas, the most appealing of which he caught and pinned down in prose. This approach is well suited to one who would assemble a fascinating collection of thoughts, and although the singularity of a man's taste will give to his collection a recognizable unity of style, it will not necessarily eliminate every idiosyncrasy, including a mischievous attraction to a diversity of surprising and apparently incompatible ideas.

In the section of *The Gay Science* from which I have quoted just above, Nietzsche remarks on his habit to "approach deep problems like cold baths: quickly into them and quickly out again." He insists that this approach does not necessarily hinder one from thinking deeply about deep problems, and at least in his case I am sure he is right. Nietzsche is often profound, but his way of thinking and writing also leads to the "inconsistencies" at issue here. He who dives and resurfaces repeatedly rarely approaches his treasure from the same angle of descent. We might judge this imprudent if the treasure were a lockbox full of gold, but if it is a tangled knot of philosophical problems, then approaching from different directions to view it from a shifting variety of perspectives may well be the most appropriate method. Such problems are multifaceted in and of themselves, and one's thoughts about them probably ought to reflect this diversity.

* * *

While on the topic of what to make of Nietzsche's way of writing, I should mention the vexed question regarding the proper use of his unpublished notes (his *Nachlass*), particularly the collection of notes available today under the title *The Will to Power*. Nietzsche did not prepare this book for publication himself; rather, his sister Elisabeth Förster-Nietzsche assembled the manuscript after his death with the help of editorial assistants. The group worked from one of many drafts (though not the most recent) of proposed contents for a book that Nietzsche sometimes thought to call *Der Wille zur Macht*. But this draft amounts to only four general subject headings, so the selection of specific excerpts from Nietzsche's notebooks, the distribution of his notes under the four headings, and the arrangement of these notes relative to one another are the result of decisions made by Förster-Nietzsche and her editorial team. In at least one sense, then, *The Will to Power* is not a book. It certainly is not a book by Nietzsche. However, so long as one keeps this in mind I see nothing illicit in making use of the work. It is after all a vast and convenient collection of Nietzsche's notes available in an English translation, and Walter Kaufmann in his commentary helpfully indicates instances of editorial malfeasance (as when Nietzsche's text has been altered or, inexplicably, carved up and scattered throughout the work). The careful reader will disregard the headings and order of presentation, attend to the indicated dates of composition, and always keep in mind that the work is a selection of excerpts from Nietzsche's notebooks rather than an intentional, polished, and finalized work. The unpublished notes are available in their entirety in Mazzino Montinari and Giorgio Colli's edition of Nietzsche's complete works (the *Kritische Gesamtausgabe*), and the "student edition" of this work (the *Kritische Studienausgabe*) is gradually appearing in translation by way of Stanford University Press's *The Complete Works of Friedrich Nietzsche*.

Some scholars have taken Nietzsche's unpublished material to reveal the true core of his thought, while others dismiss it as material that Nietzsche either benignly abandoned or quite intentionally discarded. Still others strive for a *via media*; they find much fascinating material in the notes (including, for example, Nietzsche's reflections on nihilism, a subject on which he promised in print eventually to publish, but never did), and much they believe to illuminate or supplement the published matter, but they would never ground significant and controversial assertions regarding Nietzsche's "true doctrines" on material that occurs only in the notes and that has no support whatever in the published works. Bernd Magnus, in an article on the notes of 1888 in particular, distinguishes between those who regard Nietzsche's *Nachlass* as unproblematically legitimate and who, therefore, are supposedly eager to "move Nietzsche squarely into the wax museum of the great dead philosophers" by attributing to him quite definite moral, ontological, and epistemological views, and those who mind the sharp line between published and unpublished material and insist "that Nietzsche's philosophy cannot be divorced from his style, that the mode of expression and what is expressed are in some sense inseparable."[13] Magnus argues that the latter approach (which is his own) "ought to situate [Nietzsche] as the first full-blooded postmodern, non-representational thinker, the fountainhead of a tradition which flows from him to Heidegger, Derrida, Foucault, Rorty, and much recent literary theory."[14] Whatever the value of Magnus's philological insights, I cannot concur with his interpretive glosses. I count myself among the moderate types I described above, for I make use of Nietzsche's notes, which I regard as rich, full of surprising thoughts and conjectures, and invaluable for gaining insight into the workings of Nietzsche's mind; but I am particularly interested in, and most comfortable relying on, those notes Nietzsche wrote between 1885 and 1888, the last four active years of his life. This is so because, although we may with reason conclude that Nietzsche "discarded" ideas that he recorded in his notebooks in, say, 1882 but never developed (though his neglecting to develop them tells us nothing by itself about *why* he discarded the ideas, and it may have had nothing at all to do with his ceasing to believe them); nevertheless, given his tendency to write out, abandon, and revisit and revise ideas, I would not like to insist that he had rejected any particular note he wrote between 1885 and 1888 but failed to publish. We simply cannot say what he might have done with these notes had he not lost his mind. Nietzsche's early notes and plans make it clear that he frequently dreamt up ideas, titles, outlines, and even drafts of content which he then set aside, modified, or even apparently rejected only to return to the original or a similar idea. His intentions to produce a work on the pre-Socratic philosophers, for example, cycled through a variety of phases over the course of more than three years—he developed plans, altered them, allowed them to languish, returned to original intentions, modified these; he announced a title to friends, later wrote to others of different titles, then wrote later still with reference to the previous title; he wrote and revised long sections but then seemingly abandoned the project to write and publish another book altogether, only later to return to his original notes, some of which he incorporated into other works and some of which he finally abandoned.[15]

In his final period Nietzsche removed several passages from the material that would later become *Twilight of the Idols* and made of them the beginning of *The Antichrist*.[16] With this in mind, ask yourself: had Nietzsche suffered his breakdown before incorporating these passages into the later manuscript, or before sending this work off to the printer, would scholars today insist that we must count them among his "rejected notes"? If so, they would be mistaken.

In any case, it is at least plausible to suggest that Nietzsche "discarded" those early notes and drafts that he left undeveloped for a very many years, for we can say with confidence that he had every opportunity to return to them but decided against it. Yet few scholars raise the alarm at the publication of Nietzsche's early work on Homer, Greek history, or the pre-Socratic philosophers. They object only (or for the most part) when the unpublished material includes ideas that they themselves reject and so would rather not associate with Nietzsche, whom they admire. Thus the early essay "On Truth and Lies in a Nonmoral Sense" is controversial among those who want a Nietzsche friendly to knowledge and the pursuit of truth, and Nietzsche's ruminations on the eternal return as cosmology or the will to power as ontology are unpopular among members of two different camps, among those who judge contemporary science the proper measure of all that is true and good, and also among those who have little use for the pronouncements of scientists or of anyone else who claims to know some truth about the world.

Having said all this, I should point out that I do not base any significant claims exclusively on Nietzsche's notes. Yet I do make some use of them, and I am sure that we may gain occasional insights into, and even important elaborations on, his published thoughts by way of material from the *Nachlass*. But to return to Magnus's classification of approaches to Nietzsche based on the use scholars make of his notes, I do not regard Nietzsche as a typical, traditional philosopher, and certainly not as ready for any wax museum. I believe, with Magnus, that Nietzsche's artistry is essential to his work and his life as a philosopher, yet I regard the postmodern tradition with which Magnus would like to identify Nietzsche as (for the most part) a deviation from his thought, a deviation that in both form and content Nietzsche would repudiate. But this is not to say that I approach Nietzsche from the perspective of analytic philosophy—not, anyway, if this is taken to mean a style of philosophy that emphasizes logical rigor above all else and that makes every effort to conform to the latest substantive claims and methodological standards of the natural sciences.

No text in the received Platonic corpus is as problematic as Nietzsche's *Will to Power*. It is true that scholars dispute the authenticity of this or that work (the so-called *First Alcibiades*, for instance), but as to the authorship of the major dialogues there is near universal agreement. Along with the dialogues there come down to us several letters, most of which scholars are inclined to dismiss. The "Seventh Letter," however, is believed by many to be authentic. Unfortunately, there is no direct evidence on which to ground any judgment, and I must say that despite every argument in its favor I cannot resist the thought that the letter is just too good to be true. It is very nearly exactly the sort of document one would like to have from Plato (one could wish for more, I suppose; but I doubt that one could reasonably *expect* more), and this seems to motivate much of the passion in its favor. Scholars support their passion with arguments, but in this case no argument can secure anything more than probability, and probabilities of this sort depend far too much on subjective opinion to sway me one way or the other. Therefore I try to suspend judgment, though I admit to inclining toward doubt. In any case, as with my occasional use of Nietzsche's unpublished notes, my not making use of the "Seventh Letter" does not affect my interpretation in any particularly controversial manner.

* * *

Every text produced by a serious thinker who is also a gifted writer is difficult to the extent that the author expresses complex ideas in a lush style, and sometimes even profound ideas in a sublime style. This is true of Plato and Nietzsche, who unlike most other philosophers, but in common with the greatest of poets and creative writers, are challenging primarily because their work is often much richer than is evident from the easily accessible surface meanings. The edifices of their works conceal cellars beneath even their hidden basements. So, for example, Plato's *Phaedo* addresses many subjects simultaneously, some of them more obviously than others: we must take seriously the arguments for the immortality of the soul, but we will overlook much if we ignore the possibility (which Plato himself calls to our attention) that the arguments are incomplete, unsound, or dependent on unproven hypotheses. The dialogue is also about, and *as much* about, the nature of philosophy and the life of a philosopher, a life that involves purification, from which notion there radiates a multiplicity of connotations and implications, from the mystic frenzy of Bacchic rites to the ethereal stillness of serene divinity. Then there are the dreams, the charms, the condemnation of misology beside the praise of ungrounded belief. All this is to say that Plato is capable of addressing many matters simultaneously, from a variety of perspectives and in different modes as well; and in the best of his works his skills are often on display. Nietzsche is like this too. To take just one example, consider the essay "What is the Meaning of Ascetic Ideals?" from *On the Genealogy of Morals*: here Nietzsche examines the deep background of western asceticism from such a variety of perspectives that this ostensibly singular phenomenon fractures into a multiplicity of meanings, many of them active simultaneously in one and the same man, class of men, or social-cultural tradition. Running through all this, sometimes on the surface, sometimes submerged but moving resolutely through the undercurrents, are reflections on the nature and practice of the philosopher.[17]

I do not claim to have mined in this book the secret core of Platonic or Nietzschean doctrine. My intentions are rather more modest. I have tried to represent the work that I do with Plato and Nietzsche in the classroom as a professor and in my head as a thinker. As a result of this approach some readers might find certain of my interpretive choices idiosyncratic, but I suppose this is unavoidable in any case. I have not written with the aim of expressing The Truth About Plato And Nietzsche; rather I intend to present a generally informative and engaging account of the lessons I have taken from my long relationship with these men and their ideas. Others no doubt have different relationships with them, but I hope that interested readers will profit from my work despite the occasional disagreement or disappointment.

In the first four chapters of this book my primary goal is to present a general account of those of Plato's and Nietzsche's views on art, reason, ontology, epistemology, and ethics broadly construed that, as I have written in the preface, may be brought together in dialogue or debate. For this purpose I need not cover every aspect of either man's philosophy, nor even every element of, or perspective on, the aspects that I do cover. Any such undertaking must involve judgments as to selection and presentation, judgments dependent at times on argument, and here and there throughout this work

I move beyond the bare presentation of my subjects' views to take account of, or to remark on, current debates. Still, whatever I have to offer by way of original insight I reserve by and large for the final chapter, in which I draw on Plato and Nietzsche, the men as well as their work, to reflect on wisdom and the love of wisdom.

From time to time in the body of this work I object to Nietzsche's reading of Plato, which may seem to indicate a preference or bias; but I do not value either one of these thinkers above the other, and I hope no one will read any such judgment into my commentary. It would be impossible to object to Plato's reading of Nietzsche, for there is no such reading; and as for my occasional animadversions on Nietzsche's remarks, notice that I reserve them for those of his criticisms directed specifically against Plato. I say little against either man's ideas in and of themselves. If I criticize Nietzsche, it is only to disarm his attempts to prejudice readers against Plato, and thereby in favor of himself, and I do this because I would like to generate in readers' minds an equipollence of evaluation. For me the greatest good to be had from observing the struggle between Plato and Nietzsche is in the experience of the struggle itself, the constant interplay between the two with neither one ever dominating the other—and not only in observing all this, but in wrestling with them intellectually, participating in this agon in which no victor is ever declared, nor any quarter asked. I strive for equipollence also because I believe there is much to be learned from the commonalities between Plato and Nietzsche, especially the similarities in their approach to philosophy, for I do believe they are similar in this regard, although I admit that this is not quite evident. I attempt to bring out these commonalities at least indirectly in the first chapter of this book, and I do so quite explicitly in the last.

* * *

I have long been absorbed by questions regarding the nature of philosophy and the proper activities of the philosopher, and usually I am moved, and find it fruitful, to reflect on these matters with reference not only to Plato's and Nietzsche's explicit statements about philosophy, but with reference as well to their manner of manifesting philosophy in their own lives and practices. But given the lack of agreement today as to the meaning of the term "philosopher," and considering also that the popular meanings diverge from anything that either Plato or Nietzsche would have recognized as the term's true substance, it does us no good to refer to them as philosophers. But neither should we refer to them as "wise men" or "sages," for in an age when even adolescents may be characterized as "wise," we must regard these words as presently devoid of meaning. I would like to rediscover the proper substance of these words, but without assuming a shared understanding of either their connotations or denotations. Therefore I will avoid them—at least when addressing this subject specifically—and employ instead an expression that I believe captures something of Plato's wisdom as well as Nietzsche's philosophy, namely, the expression "thinker-artist."

By "thinker" here I mean to indicate one whose primary activity is intellectual, a pondering man who reflects deeply on the sort of questions that Dostoevsky called "accursed" and that Melville, borrowing from Milton, liked to sum up as revolving around "Fixed Fate, Free-will, fore-knowledge absolute," which questions inevitably introduce the related problems of God (or God's absence), human suffering, and meaning. For such men the "interesting" but ultimately shallow cogitations of the political man, the scholar, and the scientist are, even in their ripest maturity, little more than the raw material and seeds of thought. As for the "artist" in this expression, with this term I intend to designate one who thinks about these deep matters *creatively*, which is to say unconstrained by contemporary standards of either substance or methodology, one so disinclined to restrict the freedom of his intellectual spirit that he is happy to engage even in what Nietzsche once characterized as "*indemonstrable philosophizing*" (P 61). He may draw on logic or science if he is moved to do so, but if he is not so moved he will suffer no pangs of conscience from ignoring or flouting them for the sake of beauty or profundity, provocation or the sublime.

Plato died while writing his *Laws*, a philosophical work that hints at being in the tradition of wisdom literature. Wise men write poems and legislation (which is not to say that every poet or legislator is wise), and the anonymous Athenian in this work not only formulates laws but he refers to the work itself as a sort of poem. But Plato, sage though he may have been, never wrote explicitly *as* a sage. Why this is, why he chose always to write from behind the mask of the philosopher—this is only one of the many veils that hide him from our view.

Nietzsche does not immediately strike one as a sage. The wise man is serene, is he not? But Nietzsche was forever agitated. He understood that he was something like an explosive in human form, that he was, as he wrote, dynamite, or as I would put it, a depth charge. He insisted on more than one occasion that his demolitions were meant to clear the ground for the greater and more serious task of creative affirmation, and I for one am willing to take him at his word. His *Zarathustra* alone confirms this. But he did not live long enough to transition from destruction to sustained creation.[18] He was forever *thinking through* his problems, an intellectual activity characteristic of the philosopher still only on his way to wisdom. I adapt this idea from Plato's "Divided Line," and although I know that Nietzsche would reject the epistemology and the ontology associated with this schematic, the notion of *dianoia*, of thinking through, captures something of Nietzsche's intellectual life: he was bound to certain first principles, even if bound only in the sense of continually working to undermine them.

Nietzsche wrote poems, to be sure, and we may even say that he formulated laws through his second-self, Zarathustra. But if Plato was a sage writing in the mode of a philosopher, Nietzsche-Zarathustra, though writing occasionally in the mode of a wise man, was perhaps the eternal philosopher. But wise man or philosopher, Plato and Nietzsche both acted as thinker-artists, which is to say that they lived, thought, and wrote, in brief that they *created* as this type.

If philosophy and wisdom are distinct, as they are on most accounts, even so they must each involve the thinking and the artistry that I have described above, and to which I will return in the final chapter of this book. If they are not distinct, as may be implied by an ancient anecdote involving Pythagoras as well as by an implication of Diotima's speech in Plato's *Symposium*, then in that case we may characterize them identically. In any case, this expression "thinker-artist" will, I hope, serve to unsettle the clichéd connotations of the words "philosopher" and "sage" and so provide a clearing for an unobstructed consideration of their proper meaning, or anyway of a meaning, proper or not, that Plato and Nietzsche perhaps held in common.

1

Art and Reason

Plato or Socrates

Attentive readers will have remarked that in the Introduction I have much more to say about Plato's life and works than about Socrates. So it is, and to borrow a phrase that Nietzsche once aimed at Plato: I am a complete skeptic about Socrates. This is not to say that I doubt the man's existence. Although it is true that the Socrates we encounter in Plato's dialogues never lived, that he is a character fashioned by Plato's creative genius, it is no less true that Plato drew inspiration for his character from the life of a real man, Sôkratês the son of Sôphronsikos. This Socrates was born in 470 BCE, matured in Athens during the city's Periclean golden age, trained as a stonemason, fought as a hoplite in the Peloponnesian War, grew famous and then infamous as a rationalizing intellectual (a philosopher or a sophist—many could see no distinction between the types), was charged after the war with religious heterodoxy and corrupting the city's youth, then tried, convicted, and executed in 399 BCE. I do not doubt that this man was an impressive, even an inspirational human being and philosopher; the existential and intellectual influence he worked on those who knew him, and even on those who only occasionally encountered him, is testament to his uniqueness and merit. Nietzsche is surely right to regard him as having had a decisive influence on world history.[1] But this man, as remarkable as he was, was not identical to the Socrates whose words and ideas we know through Plato's dialogues. He may have resembled the Socrates of Plato's early aporetic works, but really we have no good way to verify this. Evidence culled from the writings of Aristophanes, Plato, and Xenophon is so inconsistent that it may be naive even to count it as evidence.[2] It is, at best, difficult to know what to make of the conflicting testimony, each item individually as well as the collection taken together. I do not mean to imply that other scholars thoughtlessly identify the historical Socrates with Plato's Socrates. No one would equate the two without any qualification whatever. Most would likewise resist any attempt to sever them utterly, as would I. My eccentricity is that in the expression "Plato's Socrates" I put the stress on "Plato" whereas others tend to stress the "Socrates." Scholars of ancient philosophy too often neglect in practice the distinction they admit in theory between Socrates and Plato; they slide from the formula "Plato's Socrates," through the expressions "Socrates as he appears in Plato's dialogues" and "the Socrates Plato wrote about" to, finally, "Socrates," without qualification. Thus they often write of "Socrates" as if the word denoted Socrates the man, the historical figure who lived and died before Plato had even begun to write his dialogues, all the while attributing to this man ideas and qualities that so far as we know belong only to the character that Plato created.

Of course there are scholars who when analyzing doctrine—that is, when attempting to determine what the ancient philosophers believed—are careful to mind the distinction between Plato and Socrates,[3] but even these scholars tend to neglect the implications of this distinction. If we admit that the Socrates who moves and inspires us is the character who appears in Plato's dialogues, then we should reflect on the fact that this character would lack the resonance that so deeply affects us if he were abstracted from the dialogues as artistic wholes. To me this suggests that Plato is the primary source of Socrates' power. It is standard practice to dismiss or diminish Xenophon's Socratic works on the grounds that the man was just too simple, too shallow, to comprehend a mind as restless and original as Socrates'.[4] This may well be right, but I would add from the other direction that Plato was in turn more profound than Socrates; so some measure of the depth that we criticize Xenophon for failing to fathom in Socrates was not actually present in the man to begin with. It was carved out later by Plato. Nietzsche seems to have acknowledged this in at least one place, namely when he asked whether "the Platonic Socrates" is anything other than "Plato in front and Plato behind and Chimaera in the middle" (*BGE* 190).[5] Plato fashioned the Socrates we know by drawing the character as he did, but also by situating this character in the context of the specific interlocutors he interacts with, the resonant settings in which they converse, and the subtle undercurrents of hidden significance of the order of their discourse and their language, even down to their vocabulary and syntax. In short, Socrates is nothing without the dialogues that contain him, and these dialogues are nothing without their creator, Plato.

Although I mentioned "doctrine" in the previous paragraph, the point I am insisting on here is distinct from a structurally parallel concern with the doctrinal content of the dialogues. Early in the twentieth century it was common among Anglo-American philosophers working in the analytic tradition to rifle Plato's work for arguments relating to their own specific interests. If they were concerned with proving or disproving the proposition that the soul is immortal, for example, then they might extract the relevant arguments from, say, Plato's *Phaedo* and subject them to logical analysis. The fact that these arguments appear in a dialogue with a meticu- lously particularized dramatic setting was of no consequence to them. They were not interested in Plato or his work, but only in the soundness (or otherwise) of arguments for and against some specific position. But even those with a genuine interest in Plato have all too often mined his works primarily for arguments and doctrine. This approach goes back to the ancients themselves, to Aristotle first of all and later to the Neoplatonists, who were more systematic and analytical than literary (though Plotinus himself manages often to combine logical rigor with lyrical beauty). The same is true even of the great Renaissance Platonists. Many of Marsilio Ficino's writings on Plato read more like scholastic commentaries than poetically informed interpreta- tions.[6] This narrow doctrinal approach was first challenged on a grand scale early in the nineteenth century when Friedrich Schleiermacher published the "General Introduction" to his series of German translations of Plato.[7] Schleiermacher called his contemporaries' attention to Plato's magnificent artistry, and he argued at length that to understand the dialogues' content one must attend to their form. Schleiermacher's influence was apparent in the late nineteenth and early twentieth centuries, but a plurality of scholars began to attend to the dialogues' literary qualities especially in the second half of the twentieth century.[8] Unfortunately, many of these scholars follow Schleiermacher also in exploring the form, not at all in order to appreciate its natural wonders, but from a steely determination to discover the secret path to the heart of Platonic doctrine. They approach Plato's works as artistic wholes, to be sure; but attending to the art is for them only a means of acquiring a proper conception of the argument. In one sense, then, they are not so different from their hermeneutic opponents. They share with them a similar end, disagreeing only about the means.

I myself am less interested in Platonic doctrine than in Plato the man as a paradigm of the philosophical life. I study the dialogues as artistic wholes, not for the light this approach may shed on a dialogue's argument or arguments, but rather for insight into Plato's activity *as a philosopher and as an artist*. Socrates has long been our model of the philosophical life, but it seems to me that when thinking about the nature of philosophy and the activity of the philosopher we would do well to attend more closely to Plato. The differences between the two men are rarely discussed—the existential-philosophical differences, I mean, *not* the doctrinal differences—but they are striking. Socrates conducted impromptu dialectical investigations into the nature of virtue in the streets and the public areas of Athens.[9] Plato spent hours alone in silence plotting and composing complex dramatic ruminations on an astounding variety of subjects, from the nature and fate of the human soul to the creation of the cosmos and early human history, that read at their best like prose poems. Presumably Plato taught in the Academy, but we have no idea what form this activity took. And presumably his students read and discussed the dialogues, but according to what hermeneutical principles and to what end? Again, we have no idea.[10] We know what we have, and we have the dialogues. We know that Plato elected to write *these* works in *this* style (or rather in *these* styles, for Plato was a master stylist), and we know that in both form and content the dialogues are anything but simple and straight philosophy. Whatever else Plato may have done as a philosopher, his activity as author, as artist, to which he must have devoted prodigious amounts of time and energy, has as much in common with the tragedians as it has with Socrates. It is often said that the Socrates we encounter in an early work like the *Euthyphro* is a more or less faithful representation of the man himself, and the aporetic works certainly do not depict anyone engaged in Plato's most characteristic philosophical activity: Socrates was a talker, but Plato was a creative writer. Moreover, if Plato's Socrates were always only the Socrates of the aporetic dialogues, then he would be impressive but ultimately limited. But ever faithful to his muse, Plato over the years matured into a deeper thinker and a more gifted writer than he had been when he conceived and executed his early works. His fully articulated version of Socrates is an endlessly surprising source of insight and inspiration, and this has less to do with his character's historical exemplar than with Plato's philosophical-artistic genius.

Again, most every scholar active today would accept at least some part of what I have just written, but even so it strikes me that many would rather not confront the consequences, for the consequences suggest a revision of our traditional notion of the ideal philosopher. If for once we could look around Socrates to see Plato clearly for what he was in himself, and for what he accomplished as himself, we might acquire insight into philosophy and the philosopher quite different from that generated by attending exclusively to Socrates, or to Plato's Socrates, or to Plato as only an adjective in the phrase "Plato's Socrates." We certainly will not agree with Alexander Nehamas that "it is just in being shown to fail to change the mind and life of those who talk to him that Socrates has succeeded in changing the mind and life of all those who have read the Platonic dialogues … ."[11] Rather, insisting on a point that Nehamas himself acknowledges, namely that Plato "created the Socrates with whom we have all become more or less familiar,"[12] we will say that it is in *showing* Socrates to fail to change the mind and life of those who talk to him that *Plato* has succeeded in changing the mind and life of all those who have read *his* dialogues. And when contrasting Socrates as a conversationalist with Nietzsche as a writer, we will not designate the latter "the most writerly of philosophers"[13] without simultaneously applying the description to Plato. For, to whatever extent Nehamas is right that for Nietzsche "writing is also the most important part of living,"[14] we might make the same claim respecting Plato.[15]

I shall reflect on philosophy in light of Plato's (and Nietzsche's) work in the final chapter, but let me state at the outset that if in this book I refer to Socrates in my own voice, then unless I am writing explicitly about the historical man, I intend nothing else than the *character* Socrates as created by Plato, and any interest or excellence I attribute to this Socrates belongs solely to his creator, Plato.

Apollo and Dionysus

To say that Nietzsche was obsessed with Socrates might well be an overstatement. But if so, it is no greater hyperbole than Nietzsche himself often indulged in. Still, if we would psychologize the man in this manner, I think a more accurate diagnosis would be that he was obsessed with *contradicting* Socrates. In an early notebook Nietzsche jotted down the following telling remark: "Simply to acknowledge the fact: *Socrates* is so close to me that I am almost continually fighting with him."[16] This is revealing, but the confession would have been more honest still had Nietzsche admitted that he almost always picks these fights himself, going out of his way to initiate the conflict. This, anyway, is how it appears to me when I consider the fact that if Nietzsche at some time believes *x*, then he criticizes Socrates for denying or undermining the influence of *x*, and if later he comes to believe not-*x*, then he attacks Socrates for affirming and promoting *x*. Consider, for example, his critical characterization of Socrates in *The Birth of Tragedy* as the "archetype and progenitor" of Alexandrian culture, the paradigmatic theoretical optimist who naively believes that with knowledge acquired through science we humans one day will "heal the eternal wound of existence" (*BT* 18). Now set beside this the fact that he immediately followed up his *Twilight of the Idols*, in which work he devotes an entire chapter to analyzing "The Problem of Socrates," with *The Antichrist*, in which he *praises* science and "Alexandrian training" (*A* 47).[17] Is Socrates, then, culpable as the spiritual source of Alexandrian scientific culture, or is he to blame for being its greatest opponent? Either one, it seems, depending on Nietzsche's own position at the relevant moment: if he disapproves of Alexandrianism and science, then Socrates must affirm them, and if later he admires them (or allies with them as the enemy of his enemy), then Socrates, naturally, must oppose them.

It is true that Nietzsche occasionally expresses admiration for Socrates, particularly in the writings of his middle period, when he was somewhat friendlier than in his early and late periods to reason and science.[18] Yet in the works of his maturity he is regularly (if not quite exclusively) hostile. The pattern began with his first published work, *The Birth of Tragedy Out of the Spirit of Music* (1872), which he wrote under the twin influences of Richard Wagner and Arthur Schopenhauer. Though Nietzsche was already well educated in the facts of ancient Greek history and culture, having received the best philological training available in contemporary Germany, he learned much about the *interpretation* of the Greeks in conversation with Wagner. Wagner's influence, however, was on the whole more inspirational than substantive.[19] The real philosophical force of the book Nietzsche borrowed from Schopenhauer.

Arthur Schopenhauer was born to a prosperous German mercantile family in 1788. Unhappily ordained to apprentice and work in the family business, his father's death (possibly by suicide) in 1805 liberated the young man from a life of shallow drudgery. Studying thereafter with private tutors as well as in the universities of Göttingen and Berlin, Schopenhauer developed remarkably quickly. In 1813 he composed a dissertation entitled *On the Fourfold Root of the Principle of Sufficient Reason*, with which he laid the groundwork for his masterpiece, *The World as Will and Representation*. In this latter work, published in 1818, Schopenhauer appropriates Kant's philosophy of Transcendental Idealism, develops and modifies the original system, and supplements it even with elements of Platonic metaphysics. Over the course of many years he brought out three editions of the book: in 1844 he issued a modest revision of the first edition accompanied by an entire second volume of supplementary chapters, and in 1859 he issued a third edition expanded by over 100 pages of fresh material. The most remarkable feature of the later editions must be the extent to which Schopenhauer augmented his original argument and analysis with references to the Buddhist literature he had in the interval come to admire, but his primary concepts remain unaltered. For our present purposes an exhaustive account of Schopenhauer's philosophy is unnecessary. In this section I need only explain those of his ideas that are relevant to Nietzsche's *Birth of Tragedy*. I shall return to his work in later chapters whenever it is—and it often is—in the background of Nietzsche's thought.

To understand Schopenhauer we should know at least this much about Immanuel Kant (1724–1804): in his *Critique of Pure Reason* and *Prolegomena to Any Future Metaphysics* Kant argues that our knowledge of the nature of reality is not exclusively *derived from* the world through experience; much of our knowledge is rather *imposed on* the world by those faculties of our mind that generate experience.[20] Consider, for example, our knowledge of the world's spatial properties. Prior to Kant it was widely believed that the world in and of itself is spatial, which is to say that things like trees and suns are extended in space as three-dimensional objects and located in space at specific distances from one another, and that these spatial properties exist independently of anyone's experiencing them. Even if there were no minds to perceive the world, the world would exist and its contents would have spatial properties and stand in spatial relations to one another. It was supposed that the same is true of temporal and causal relations. Events in the world really are earlier than, simultaneous with, or later than other events, and some of these events really do cause others—the two instances of "really" in this sentence stressing the point that these temporal and causal relations are features of the world as it is in itself independent of any and every perceiving mind. Kant rejects this way of thinking and argues that spatial, temporal, and causal relations are *not* properties of the world as it is in itself but are rather necessary features of our way of experiencing the world. Our minds impose these features on the world as it enters into our experience. So it is not the case that the world is independently characterized by spatial, temporal, and causal properties that we take in and come to know by experiencing the world; rather, the preconditions for a thing's having these properties exist in our minds, and we bestow these properties on the world through the medium of our experience.

Think of it this way: space, time, and causality are like filters on the apertures of our minds, through which the world as it is in itself must pass in order for us to experience it, and by which the world in its passage is stamped with spatial, temporal, and causal properties. Or, to employ another analogy, imagine a child's toy, a small plastic box in which we may place an unformed blob of clay. The box has a star-shaped opening on one side and on top a lever attached to a pressure plate. When you push down on the lever the plate squeezes the clay through the hole, and the clay emerges from the box in the shape of a star. Now reverse this procedure just a little and imagine the box (the inside of the box) as a human mind, and set the unformed clay outside of the box to represent the external world independent of mind. Instead of a star-shaped opening our mind-box has space-, time-, and causality-shaped openings, so when we push and squeeze the unformed clay (representing the world as it is in itself) into the mind-box, it enters in the form of a well-defined spatial-temporal mass causally related to other such masses (which have entered the mind in the same way). Strange as they may be, these two images effectively illustrate Kant's notion that space, time, and causality do not exist "out there" in the world itself, but only in our experience of the world. According to this scheme, then, in a very real sense the mind with its spatial, temporal, and causal filters *constructs* the world around us.

Schopenhauer adopted this idea from Kant, but not without making a few significant changes. Kant sometimes suggests that things in themselves cause our experiences. Schopenhauer objected to both the subject and the predicate of this proposition. He objected, specifically, to the plural noun, which implies that the world in itself is or contains a plurality of things, and to the verb, which suggests that these things are causally efficacious. To deal with the first objection first, Schopenhauer argued that there can be no plurality without either space or time, which he referred to together as the *principium individuationis*, the principle of individuation, for space and time are forms of sensibility that divide reality into distinct individuals. For two or more objects to be two or more objects rather than a simple unity, they must occupy either different spaces at the same time or the same space at different times. Two objects in exactly the same space at precisely the same moment of time are—well, they are not two objects; they are one and the same. If, then, the world's spatial and temporal features are products of the *principium individuationis*—products, that is, of our way of experiencing the world rather than properties of the world as it is in itself—then there can be no real divisions between or among things, in which case it makes no sense to refer to things in themselves, in the plural. Independent of our experience, reality must be one, an undivided unity. Similarly, if causality is exclusively a product of our cognitive faculties, then we cannot believe that the world independent of our experience acts causally on us to produce this experience. The world as it is in itself must indeed be related *in some way* to our experience, for it is this world that our perceptual-cognitive apparatus (our senses and our brain, which language Schopenhauer prefers to Kant's talk of "mind") transforms into the spatial, temporal, causally interconnected reality in which we live, move, and act—the reality that we *experience*—every day of our lives. But the world cannot be *causally* related to this experience. Causality exists only *within* experience; hence it cannot obtain *between* experience and the world independent of experience.

All this is to say that Schopenhauer insists on following through to the end the idea that space, time, and causality are, and are *only*, modes of our experience having no reality whatever in the world as it is in itself. The world of experience, this plurality of objects that occupy distinct times and places and act causally on one another, which Kant had labeled the *phenomenon*, Schopenhauer prefers to call the *representation*. The word "phenomenon" derives from a Greek word meaning, literally, "the thing that appears," so we can accept "representation" as an appropriate synonym, for with this word Schopenhauer means to indicate the world as it is shown, displayed, or represented to us in experience through the medium of our perceptual-cognitive apparatus. The world as it is in itself, independent of our experience, Kant had called the *noumenon*. Schopenhauer objects to this usage, for the original meaning of the word is "that which is thought" or "that which is the object of abstract knowledge," whereas Kant had employed it to designate that side of reality to which thought and knowledge necessarily cannot attain.[21] Schopenhauer refers to the world in itself as *will*, the reason for which I explain more fully in Chapter 3 (specifically pp. 86–8). For now it suffices to remark that Schopenhauer conceives of the world in itself as a unified entity perpetually striving toward no particular end. It strives because striving is of its essence, and that which essentially strives is *will*. So the world as it is in itself is identical to that which we know in ourselves under the name "will." Its striving is not an act it performs as distinct from what it is, for it just *is* a striving, and nothing besides. And since it is nothing besides—nothing, for example, like a mind that could formulate a goal for its striving—it is a blind, aimless, purposeless striving.

This world as it is in itself, as I have said, does not cause our experience, as if it were one thing and our experience another, the two being related as cause to effect. Rather, it *objectifies* itself *as* the representation. It is, as it were, the "behind" or the "inside" of the world of our experience. In other words, the will and the representation are one and the same, absolutely identical, the relevant difference having to do not with them (or, rather, with *it*) but with our relation to it. Reality independent of our experience is will, and this same reality as experienced by us is representation.

And then there is music, which I introduce at this point because music is central to Nietzsche's appropriation of Schopenhauer and because, as odd as this may sound, music for Schopenhauer is essentially metaphysical. In the third book of the first volume of *The World as Will and Representation* Schopenhauer writes that music is "quite independent of the phenomenal world," that it is "as *immediate* an objectification and copy of the whole will as the world itself is" (*WWR* 1:52). In music the kernel of the world (known to us most directly as will) is made manifest to our senses, precisely as it is manifest also as the spatial, temporal world of our daily experience. Nietzsche later mocked this view as making of the composer "a kind of mouthpiece of the 'in itself' of things, a telephone from the beyond" (*GM* 3.5), but this is what Schopenhauer believed, and Nietzsche for a time agreed. A great musician like Richard Wagner (with whom Nietzsche was on intimate terms during the period he wrote *The Birth of Tragedy*[22]) is a conduit through whom the thing in itself reveals itself, his various melodies exhibiting in disembodied form the strivings, anticipations, exaltations, doubts, withdrawals, frustrations, and sufferings that appear also in the phenomenal world in human form. In a human life these states are always bound by spatial, temporal particularities, which is to say that the phenomenal world always only *partially* reveals the will. The composer, on the other hand, evokes through his music the universal, for music expresses not merely this or that person's specific instance of (for example) suffering, but the essence of suffering in general. Music, in short, is as direct a revelation of the metaphysical ground of physical reality as the human brain can either conjure or experience.

These elements of Schopenhauer's metaphysics inform Nietzsche's analysis throughout *The Birth of Tragedy* and are particularly relevant to the book's famous thesis that "the continuous development of art is bound up with the *Apollinian* and *Dionysian* duality" (*BT* 1).[23] The two terms of this duality were originally "artistic energies which burst forth from nature herself," the Apollinian energy being most immediately manifest in "the image world of dreams," the Dionysian in "intoxication and mystical self-abnegation" (*BT* 2). Apollo in this scheme represents an orderly and serene world of beauty, Dionysus a frenzied insight into the natural terrors of existence. Greek culture, Greek art, the whole of the Greek psyche itself, were infused with and informed by these opposed tendencies. Homer represents the highest manifestation of the Apollinian artist; the lyric poet Archilochus was the paragon of Dionysian poetic force. Homer was active most likely in the second half of the eighth century BCE, Archilochus not long thereafter, and the Apollinian and Dionysian energies remained distinct and in tension until the second half of the sixth century BCE when Greek cult and certain Greek artists managed to effect a "mystery of union" between them (*BT* 5). From this reconciliation Greek tragedy emerged, flowering in the first half of the fifth century BCE, withering miserably away in the second.

But what has all this to do with Schopenhauer? Quite a lot, actually, for Nietzsche models his conception of the nature and significance of the Apollinian and Dionysian energies specifically on Schopenhauer's two-sided account of the world as representation and as will. The Apollinian dream image is a symbolical *representation* of the world's Dionysian essence of *will*. Recall that Schopenhauer describes the world as it is in itself, which he calls "will," as an undifferentiated, ceaseless, and goalless striving force or impulse. Now add to this his insight that this will is beastly and terrible, the source of all the world's suffering and pain. Every being in the world, whether it be a force of nature, a chemical compound, or an animal, maintains its existence by overpowering and in some sense devouring other beings in its environment; and since these beings are one and all objectifications of the will, Schopenhauer infers that the will is ghastly, violent, and ultimately even self-tormenting. Nietzsche contends that the Dionysian artist knows this truth about the world's heart, or rather that he experiences the reality of this in a manner beyond knowing. In mystical states of furious ecstasy he breaks free from the *principium individuationis* and, liberated from the spatial-temporal properties that individuate him, that bound, delimit, and determine him as a distinct individual separate from the totality, he sinks into the whole, dissolves and becomes one with the whole, and thereby acquires immediate insight into the nature of fundamental reality, the will. It is a thrilling and alarming glimpse into "the terror and horror of existence" (*BT* 3), an ephemeral experience that on a personal level corresponds to the Dionysian energy that pervades Greek culture in general. By this route the Greeks came to understand the "wisdom of Silenus," according to which the best thing for humans is never to be born and second best is, having suffered the misfortune of birth, to die as soon as possible. The Dionysian artist carries this truth in his bones.

The Apollinian artist has an altogether different psychology: he is at home in the world as fashioned by the *principium individuationis*, resting comfortably in the spatially and temporally circumscribed world of the representation. This is the realm of "measured restraint," of Doric architecture and dactylic hexameter verse (*BT* 1–2). In this realm also are the Olympian gods, deities who by conquering the titans, the giants, and a grotesque variety of ravaging monsters brought harmony and order to the world. The Olympians mediate between suffering man and the menacing wildness of nature; they justify our lives by living similar lives themselves (*BT* 3). I wrote just above that the Apollinian dream image is a symbolical representation of the Dionysian element of will, and now I can clarify the thought by explaining that in Greek tragedy the appalling Dionysian truth that the world at its core is a ceaselessly and aimlessly striving will that feeds forever on itself and its own is revealed through the soothing Apollinian medium of beautiful dramatic symbolism. The dithyrambic chorus, in its Schopenhauerian role as musical medium of metaphysical truth, expresses in song the disquieting vision of reality that the action and dialogue manifest through speech and structured form. This is what Nietzsche has in mind when he insists, for example, that we must understand "the essence of tragedy" as "a manifestation and projection into images of Dionysian states, as the visible symbolizing of music, as the dream-world of a Dionysian intoxication" (*BT* 14).

Greek tragedy, then, is a revelation of the metaphysical will whose life-blood infuses the physical world that exists as representation. Oedipus's suffering his abominable fate is a symbolical image of the metaphysical reality that is the essence of the world in itself. The Greeks at their best, according to Nietzsche, were able to confront such awful truths, to hold them up to view in their myths and on their public stages, because they were healthy and powerful enough to endure them. They could acknowledge the wisdom of Silenus—not merely abstractly to concede the point, but to feel it, experience it, indeed to have summoned it themselves from the depths of their own abysmal souls[24]—without succumbing to suicidal despair.

Such was the mentality and vigorous nature of the Greeks who lived during the period that Nietzsche in his early work refers to as the Tragic Age, a period we might date roughly to between 600 and 400 BCE, though during the last half century of this span tragedy and the tragic worldview more generally were in decline. Tragedy itself finally died by suicide (*BT* 11), or we might say by assisted suicide, the assistant being a man whom many contemporaries mistook for a cultural physician.

The suicidal agent himself was Euripides, the last of the three great Athenian tragedians, whose commitment to the tragic worldview has been doubted since antiquity. Euripides, it is often said, debased the tragic stage by populating his plays with common men rather than heroes—and not just with common men but with women and slaves as well. Nietzsche sums up this view by writing that through Euripides "the everyday man forced his way from the spectators' seats onto the stage; the mirror in which formerly only grand and bold traits were represented now showed the painful fidelity that conscientiously reproduces even the botched outlines of nature" (*BT* 11). But Nietzsche, as usual, thinks his way beyond this standard account. The truth as he sees it is that Euripides altered tragedy as he did because he himself did not appreciate it, and that he did not appreciate it because he could not *understand* it. The emphasis on understanding, on rationalism and the misguided longing for critical knowledge, is central to Nietzsche's analysis of tragedy's demise. The tragic effect depends in part on inscrutability, the inscrutability of a human life, its relation to the gods and to fate, certainly, but also the obscurity and ambiguity of language, which mirrors and transmits to the audience the spirit of the broader existential mysteries. Euripides rejected this aspect of tragedy, as even his contemporaries suspected. Aristophanes, a younger comic poet, depicts in his *Frogs* a debate in the underworld between Euripides and Aeschylus. Aeschylus's tragedies are permeated by an ominous spirit of enigmatic darkness, not just in the action but in the language as well, and Euripides complains in Aristophanes' comedy that Aeschylus's works are incomprehensible. Aeschylus, for his part, blames Euripides for contributing to the decline of vital cultural traditions, insisting that under his leveling influence the youth of Athens abandoned the virtues of physical activity to indulge in chatty conversations and disputations with their superiors. Here Aeschylus fingers the flaw that Nietzsche attributes to Euripides: under the influence of late fifth-century rationalism, he composes plays that all too often read less like tragic myths than transcripts of a philosophical debate.

But as much as Euripides' critical spirit did to destroy tragedy, the medicine man who brewed the intellectual poison the poet drank, the assistant at the suicide, was none other than Socrates. Socrates *inspired* Euripides' suicidal impulse; the Socratic spirit working through the man raised the poison to his lips. Euripides was "only a mask," as Nietzsche puts it, through which Socrates acted (*BT* 12).

Socrates, too, was a mask, though in a sense only a very thin one. Nietzsche admits the existence of "an anti-Dionysian tendency operating even prior to Socrates," but he insists that this tendency "received in [Socrates] an unprecedentedly magnificent expression" (*BT* 14). In *Twilight of the Idols* he characterizes the philosopher as having been marked by a "hypertrophy of the logical faculty" (*TI* "Socrates" 4), and this formulation captures nicely the thrust of his point in *The Birth of Tragedy*.[25] Above all else Socrates sought knowledge, knowledge accessible to the rational mind that rational agents can compress into precise definitions and communicate in words. He aspired to bring light to the darkness, to carry the torch of reason into those labyrinths of history and life in which others saw only the shadowy operations of chance or fate. As Nietzsche puts it, "Socrates conceives it to be his duty to correct existence" (*BT* 13), and he will do so by forcing what he can of the world into the confines of logic and dismissing the rest as misunderstanding and illusion.

Reason equals virtue equals happiness. This equation, which Nietzsche regards as the axis around which the Socratic worldview revolves, is quintessentially anti-tragic.[26] He who regards the world from a tragic perspective understands (as a result of intuition or naked insight) that truth is obscure and suffering ultimately ineradicable. Bad things happen to good people, unavoidably and for no reason. This is the way of the world, and there is nothing to be done about it. Nothing, that is, by way of changing it. But if we can do nothing about it, we can at least do something with it. We can acknowledge and accept it, and perhaps even aspire to a condition of exuberant wellbeing from which to affirm it. This tragic affirmation Nietzsche refers to, especially in the books of his maturity, as Dionysian—simply Dionysian, with no distinct reference in these late works to the Apollinian element.[27] The fundamental antagonism is not that between Apollo and Dionysus—the *union* of these two gods is the procreative force out of which tragedy was born. The real opposition is between Dionysus and Socrates, the god of unreason versus the idolator of dialectic.

Socratic rationalism can never accept an image of the world as inaccessible to intellect at its core. But this is precisely what Nietzsche's Dionysian version of Schopenhauer's metaphysics postulates (and Nietzsche here is in fundamental agreement with Schopenhauer himself[28]). And since a human is one more part of this world, a representation carved out from the will by the sorting and categorizing activities of the *principium individuationis*, and therefore in a sense an ephemeral appearance and illusion, there is no independent identifiable self for a man to know in compliance with the Apollinian maxim, "know thyself," to which Socrates was especially dedicated. In short, the world as a whole, ourselves included, is a representation of the will inaccessible to reason as embodied in logic and science, or accessible only on the surface, for reason itself necessarily generates the representation and so can never reach beneath this to the world as it is in itself. If it be possible at all to attain to a deeper insight, it must come by way of a Dionysian dissolution of the individual (a rupturing of the *principium individuationis*) resulting in a "mystic feeling of oneness" with the eternal, infinite, metaphysical will at the root of all things (*BT* 2). Losing oneself in this way is doubtless a disorienting event, and the insight one attains in consequence is most definitely disturbing. But this, as we have seen, is precisely why we need art: science is impotent to understand or to address this sort of metaphysical-existential mysticism; art alone has the affirmative, redemptive, transformative power to guide men safely through these obscure and haunted realms.

Art and life

When Nietzsche writes that "it is only as an *aesthetic phenomenon* that existence and the world are eternally *justified*" (*BT* 5), he assumes a metaphysical account of reality such as we have just gone through—he assumes, that is, that we humans are representations of the will, representations that in this and other passages he imagines as living artistic creations through which the will as the one true artist contemplates, redeems, and entertains itself (*BT* 3, 4, 24). The immediate context of the line makes it clear that Nietzsche is imagining Schopenhauer's great metaphysical will as an unconsciously creative artist that projects the phenomenal world of empirical reality (the representation) as an artist paints a picture. We may therefore regard the world as we know it, and every item within it, as analogous to images on a painter's canvas. On this view we are, quite literally, phenomena, appearances, which according to Schopenhauer, and to Nietzsche as well during this period, is the precise ontological status of everything empirical; and with the addition of only the slightest metaphorical note, we may regard ourselves as appearances generated by an artist, as art-objects, and hence as aesthetic phenomena. Ten years later, when Nietzsche writes in *The Gay Science* that "[a]s an aesthetic phenomenon existence is still *bearable* for us" (*GS* 107), he no longer accepts Schopenhauer's metaphysics. Humans are humans, products of nature and natural forces, not phenomenal objectifications of the metaphysical will. But even though a full decade intervened between Nietzsche's formulating these different accounts of life as an aesthetic phenomenon, during which time he revolutionized his approach to metaphysics, there is underlying both passages the idea that humans bereft of assistance tend to suffer from the burden of their lives. In *The Birth of Tragedy* Nietzsche identifies as the "very first philosophical problem" the human experience of guilt, and the suffering consequent on this, deriving from the necessary act of satisfying basic needs—the need for fire, for example, which early humans imagined they satisfied by theft (*BT* 9). Thus Nietzsche assumes that we humans require, or at least desire, a justification of the world and our existence. Given our alleged history of transgression and a Dionysian insight into "the terrible destructiveness of so-called world history as well as the cruelty of nature" (*BT* 7), we require a theodicy. Art, and for the Greeks an art-world populated by gods and heroes acting and suffering very much like humans, who through the nobility of their splendor show life to be eternally good—art like this is a theodicy in and of itself. In *The Gay Science*, despite his rejection of Schopenhauer's metaphysics, Nietzsche continues to conceive of humans as somehow strangers in the world, or to the world, sunk in untruth, at a loss and suffering. But art can still help us, can make our lives bearable, even if it cannot *save* us. Through art we gain a perspective above our troubled lives, a view from mountain peaks to contemplate our own grave moods and moodiness with a light heart; observing our lives with the clarity of distance, regarding ourselves as an artistic spectacle, we delight in the action below, the comedy as well as the tragedy of existence. There is no redemption; no theodicy is possible. But with the aid of art we can learn to endure, persevere, and perhaps at long last to enjoy.

When Nietzsche reissued *The Birth of Tragedy* in 1886 he was even more consumed by the problem of suffering than previously, and the new subtitle he affixed to the book reveals his mood: *Hellenism and Pessimism*. In the freshly composed "Attempt at a Self-Criticism," with which the new edition begins, Nietzsche reflects on two different versions of pessimism as responses to an awareness of "everything underlying existence that is frightful, evil, a riddle, destructive, fatal" (*BT* "Attempt" 4). There is what he labels the "pessimism of *strength*" (*BT* "Attempt" 1), and there is the degenerate Christian pessimism of weakness. The former affirms even the ugly and terrifying sides of life; the latter denies them and longs to escape into an airy and comforting beyond. But the differences between these two reactions are less my concern here than Nietzsche's formulation of the problem, which reveals something of his state of mind during his last intellectually active years, and something as well of the concerns he projected onto Socrates and Plato. In the fifth book appended to the second edition of *The Gay Science* (which appeared in 1887) Nietzsche writes that art and philosophy always "presuppose suffering and sufferers," and once again he distinguishes the Dionysian pessimist who affirms life, however nasty and harsh, from Christian and romantic pessimists who long for healing and salvation (*GS* 370). Which variety of pessimist was Nietzsche himself? It seems to me that he wavers. He denies that the death of God has made the world worth less than we formerly believed (*GS* 346), yet he acknowledges that the decline of the Christian-moral interpretation of the world confronts us with the unsettling question whether our lives have meaning (*GS* 357). And although he advocates fighting against the religious types who "brood … about the value of existence and also about their own value" (*GS* 350), it is obvious that Nietzsche frequently engaged in these gloomy meditations himself. This, I believe, is why he had to strive, to struggle, to *aspire* to be a "Yes-sayer" (*GS* 276),[29] and why he had so often to remind himself of this aspiration.[30]

The problem of suffering is in the background (and occasionally in the foreground) of Nietzsche's account of the ascetic ideal in the "Third Essay" of *On the Genealogy of Morals* (from 1887). Here Nietzsche returns to man's need to justify and affirm himself given the undeniable fact of human suffering and the dispiriting possibility that our suffering is meaningless.[31] What can we make of a life that seems so flawed, and so *essentially* flawed, as always to suffer from itself? Worse, what can we make of such a life when we recognize this life as none other than *our own*? Observing himself, man senses that he is somehow malformed, and some men attain to the grim understanding that the malformation and their awareness of it together results in psychological-spiritual suffering. Here I am reminded of Dostoevsky's insight that "[t]he tragic lies in one's awareness of being misshapen."[32] This is not quite Nietzsche's account of the tragic, but with this line Dostoevsky captures the gloom of the mood of one who knows himself to be an organism whose roots are rotten. In the relevant sections of the *Genealogy* Nietzsche is concerned with the priestly manipulation of metaphysics and morality as a response to suffering, but in other places, as we have seen, he himself regards *art* as among the noblest responses to human ills. A late note is representative here: "The *profundity of the tragic artist* lies in this … that he affirms the *large-scale economy* which justifies the *terrifying*, the *evil*, the *questionable*—and more than merely justifies them" (*WP* 852). The final clause is indicative of a tendency that emerges especially at the end of Nietzsche's active life, a tendency to conceptualize the artistic impulse as more than merely a means for justifying or making life bearable, but additionally as an indication of overabundant health and strength—and more than an indication, but actually a manifestation of the power one possesses to affirm and to stride with boldness into the shadow-sides of life that induce in weaker men shivers of suffering and fear.[33]

Nietzsche believes that Socrates was aware of the morbid truth of his own malformation. He interprets Socrates' last words, as reported in Plato's *Phaedo*, as a veiled admission of his misshapenness, or to employ Nietzsche's preferred terminology, of his decadence.[34] Relying on this interpretation, he takes Socrates to have judged that life is no good, that human existence is worthless. In *Twilight of the Idols* (1888) he objects to philosophical estimates of "the value of life," for, he says, life's value cannot be determined, neither by the living, who are "an interested party," nor by the dead, for obvious reasons (*TI* "Socrates" 2). But this logical scruple is not Nietzsche's main concern. Far more important to him is the observation that the very act of raising the question of the value of life must call the inquirer himself into question. And the man who answers his questionable question by concluding that life has little or no value—this man only condemns himself, exposes himself as infirm and corrupt. A man is just a piece of life, as it were, so to suffer from life to such an extent that one finds one's existence problematic is to admit to being a problem oneself. What sort of man suffers from life, suffers from himself? A man who has "come to grief," which is to say a decadent man (*A* 15).

In the case of a decadent like Socrates, art is of no use. Decadence is incurable. In his last works Nietzsche does not treat art as a possible solution to "the problem of Socrates." Art may serve for some as a bulwark against a certain type of suffering and the threat of nihilism, but a hyper-rational metaphysician (a decadent type) has an improper relation to art. Art will do him no good, and he is no good for art. In this connection Nietzsche specifically identifies Plato as "the greatest enemy of art Europe has yet produced" (*GM* 3.25). I leave it to readers to judge for themselves the soundness of this estimation, remarking only that it differs from Nietzsche's assessment of Socrates and Plato in *The Birth of Tragedy*, in which work he suggests that even though Plato was seduced by Socrates' optimistic rationalism, his dialogues as art bear some relation to tragedy. He even speculates as to the possibility of an "artistic Socrates" (*BT* 14), and although he does not make the connection himself, I would argue that in Plato this possibility was actualized. When Nietzsche imagines Socrates asking himself whether there might be "a realm of wisdom from which the logician is exiled," and whether art might be "a necessary correlative of, and supplement for science" (*BT* 14)—when I read this I cannot resist thinking of Plato himself as this wise artist.[35]

Nietzsche doubtless would disagree.

I have noted Nietzsche's early observation that he is often fighting with Socrates. Later in life he reflected in a postcard to a friend that "perhaps this old Plato is my true great adversary?"[36] He certainly has much to say against Plato. The question is whether we should take his criticisms seriously or, rather, which ones we should seriously consider, and which we may permit ourselves to shrug off. Plato understood that art in itself aims at the beautiful, which is why his account of *mousikē* in the *Republic* ends where "it is necessary to end," namely, with a consideration of "desire for the beautiful" (*ta tou kalou erôtika*, 403c6).[37] Plato knew the poets well; he cites them throughout his works, and it is impossible to believe that he failed to appreciate their aesthetic value.[38] In the *Republic* he has Socrates say (on his—Plato's—behalf, I am sure) that he has "a certain amity and respect from childhood for Homer" (595b9–c1), which is consistent with the Athenian's expression of admiration for Homer and Hesiod in the *Laws* (658d–e). Yet, as we have just seen, Nietzsche labels Plato Europe's greatest enemy of art. As for Plato's own artistry, most unbiased critics will I think agree that Plato was an artist of tremendous power, one of the most astounding, mesmerizing artists ever to have created in any medium. Yet in *Twilight of the Idols* Nietzsche claims that "Plato is boring." More, he condemns Plato as a "first-rate decadent in style" on the grounds that he "throws all stylistic forms together" (*TI* "Ancients" 2). Here Nietzsche aligns himself with the judgment of certain unnamed ancients, which he does also in his early unpublished lectures on Plato, in which he writes that "the verdict of the ancients was quite bitter (veering between styles, hyperbolic, dithyrambic, etc.)."[39] In this passage Nietzsche is almost certainly relying on Dionysius of Halicarnassus who, in a chapter treating of Plato's style in his treatise on Demosthenes, complains in connection with the *Phaedrus* (which Nietzsche mentions in his lecture notes just prior to the passage I have quoted) that when Plato switches from a plain to a lofty style he often "disturbs the purity of his expression and exhibits a tasteless poetic style."[40] But though Dionysius reports that Plato's contemporaries censured him for the same failing, he obviously judges Plato to have ranked among the preeminent masters of style. He opines that Plato's failings are minimal at worst and not really deserving of censure,[41] and he notes that Plato himself calls attention to the dithyrambs in the passage from the *Phaedrus* at issue.[42] Dionysius's primary objections apply to Plato's attempts at oratory, but he acknowledges that some consider Plato the "most daimonic" (*daimoniôtatos*) stylist of all the philosophers and orators,[43] and later he adds that others have remarked that if the gods speak a human language, then their king (Zeus) surely speaks in a Platonic style.[44]

There were among the ancients many other critics of Plato's style, but the dominant view was that Plato was a stylist of the first order. Longinus mentions a minor stylistic flaw, but he introduces it by remarking that Plato was "divine in other respects."[45] He even identifies Plato as the most Homeric of writers (*Homêrikôtatos*), which, he says, the philosopher accomplished not by plagiarism but by emulation, as an impression molded from the beautiful forms of statues or craft-works.[46] In brief, then, Longinus regards Plato as an artist, as a writer who creates as an artist.

But be these facts as they may, as Holger Thesleff notes, "the views taken by the ancient critics were mostly based on conventional rhetorical theory and concerned what we are used to calling Plato's late style."[47] The ancient critics, to expand Thesleff's point, were less attuned than we are today to the possibility that Plato sometimes employs unexpected, unsettling, and even tortuously frustrating constructions (as in his "late style") specifically for philosophical ends. So an ancient critic might, say, take Plato to be striving for elegance (and failing to attain it) when we would take him to be affecting a tragic tone in order to exploit the ironic potentialities of an expression or situation.[48]

In the *Republic* as well as the *Laws* Plato writes at some length specifically concerning the value of uniformity of style. He, too, opposes what Nietzsche terms "decadence in style." While analyzing the decline of Athens into a unmanageable state of excessive freedom, the Athenian in the *Laws* remarks that when ancient legislation was maintained music was divided into certain specified forms, namely, prayers to the gods, hymns, dirges, paeans, dithyrambs, and songs sung to the cithara. Once these and other classes were distinguished, it was not permitted to mix styles. Eventually, however, certain poets yielded to a Dionysian frenzy and a possession by pleasure beyond the necessary limit, and as a result they jumbled the styles together. This undermined musical standards and, in the end, standards in general, which led to a sort of relativism of judgment under the reign of which the commoners regarded their opinions as in no way inferior to the opinions of their superiors. Cultural chaos ensued and was followed by social and political decline (*Lg.* 700a–701b). So Plato was well aware of the dangers of decadence in style, and of the specific sort of stylistic decadence that troubled Nietzsche.

In the *Republic* Plato identifies three distinct styles of what we might call poetic presentation (392c–398b). Poems are presented either as pure narrative, pure imitation, or as a combination of the two. In a narrative poem the poet speaks always and only in his own voice, reporting indirectly the words and deeds of others. The narrative poet says, for example, "Chryses begged Agamemnon to release his daughter, but the king rebuffed him." This, we are told, is the style of early dithyrambic poetry in particular. In an imitative poem the poet hides behind the words of his characters, as when the author of a drama writes the characters' names followed by their dialogue, thus: "Chryses: King, I beg you to release my daughter. / Agamemnon: I will not!" This is the style of tragedy and comedy, in which the poet himself does not appear and no one other than the characters speaks. In a poem of the mixed type the poet sometimes narrates in his own voice while at other times he speaks in the voices of his characters. In this style of poem the poet might say, for example, "Chryses begged Agamemnon to release his daughter, but the king rebuffed him, saying 'I will not!'" This is the style of the Homeric epics.

It cannot have escaped Plato's notice that his own dialogues are classifiable according to this scheme, and he seems on occasion to make a point of calling attention to these stylistic elements of his work. No dialogue throughout is presented in a purely narrative form—and in fact every one of the dialogues is a pure imitation (more on this below)—but through much of the *Symposium* the narrative element is stressed by way of indirect discourse;[49] and the work concludes with a narrative report of Socrates' claim that one and the same man should be skilled in the purely imitative arts of tragedy and comedy (223c–d; cf. *R.* 395a). Here Plato must be intending some reference to himself, as he certainly is also in the *Theaetetus*. In the introductory frame of this latter dialogue we learn that Euclides has produced a transcript of a conversation between Socrates and Theaetetus, but that he was not present for the talk himself, which he heard after the fact as narrated by Socrates. But Euclides did not write it out as Socrates delivered it, as a narrative-imitative blend (epic style), but omitting all the instances of such narrative devices as "I said" and "then he replied," he composed the work as pure imitation (tragedy-comedy style).

Plato did not write in iambic trimeter, the standard poetic meter of the non-choral sections of tragedies and comedies,[50] but he did elect to present his dialogues as pure imitations. Plato hides away behind the words of his characters in all of his works, every bit as much as Aeschylus conceals himself in his. Dialogues with a direct, dramatic presentation—*Euthyphro*, *Gorgias*, and *Meno* are examples—are unambiguously pure imitation. But even those dialogues that lack the standard dramatic structure of the imitative style are pure imitations nonetheless.[51] The *Republic*, for example, is a monologue delivered by a single character, Socrates. It is, therefore, a pure imitation from Plato's perspective as author. But the monologue of which it is an imitation is Socrates' report of an earlier dialogue presented in the mode of an imitative-narrative blend. Sometimes Socrates *narrates* details of the prior conversation in his own voice, and at other times he *imitates* his own words as well as the words of his interlocutors. The *Republic*, then, is Plato's presentation in the style of a tragedy of Socrates' presentation in the style of an epic of a previous conversation that itself concluded with Socrates' presentation of the "Myth of Er" in the style of a dithyramb.

Plato's last work, the *Laws*, has a reputation for being dry, yet in Book 7 the Athenian surveys the course of the preceding conversation and comments that all that he and his interlocutors have said so far appears to him "to have been spoken altogether very nearly like some poem," even if their words have been "poured out in a flood" and "in prose" (811c–e). Later he even imaginatively addresses the tragedians and claims, with reference to the conversation that constitutes the text of the *Laws* itself, that "[w]e ourselves are authors of a tragedy, the noblest and best we are capable of: our entire constitution has been set up as an imitation (*mimêsis*) of the noblest and best life, which we say is really the truest tragedy. So you are poets, and we too are poets of the same things, your rivals and competitors of the noblest drama" (817b).

And while on this subject of poets and tragic competitions, I note that in the *Critias* Socrates refers to Timaeus as a poet and to themselves as delivering their discourses in the theater (108b). None of Plato's dialogues is a traditional poem, to be sure, and I doubt that anyone would classify the *Laws* or the *Timaeus* as a prose poem (as I myself would classify the *Phaedrus*, for example). Still, on this matter I take Plato at his word, even if that word is spoken by one of his characters. Plato understood that he was more than a thinker; he understood that he was a thinker and an artist as well.

Given the evident self-referentiality of Plato's literary-critical analyses, we must conclude that he was well aware of the status of his own works and that he played with their form and style intentionally for substantive ends. Thus Plato is one of those writers whom it is good to imagine as having total control of his every stylistic choice. I admit that he may nod from time to time, but I admit this only as a possibility. Whenever I suspect I have caught him napping, I pause to consider whether it isn't more likely *I* who am asleep. I approach Nietzsche this way as well, for his mind often operates so subtly that he demands of readers a meticulous and wary attentiveness. But for this very reason I am often baffled by his attitude toward Plato. Nietzsche more than most practiced the art of reading behind the words on a page, yet he seems always to have read only the foregrounds of Plato's dialogues; it is as if he were determined to read historical Platonism *back* into Plato. When confronted with Plato Nietzsche's touch for nuance deserted him, or he intentionally set it aside. But in his defense we may conjecture that as a good philologist Nietzsche, too, knew what he was up to, and that if he ignored Plato's self-reflective insights into the dialogue form, he did so for substantive ends. This may have been unfair, but I do not recall Nietzsche ever insisting that fairness is a trait essential to a great philosopher. Late in life he even wrote in a note, specifically in reference to his opposition to Plato as "moralist," that "Plato … becomes a caricature in my hands" (*WP* 374).

Why would Nietzsche manipulate Plato in this way? Surely by now it is obvious that Plato was no philistine. The problem, I think, is that Plato's perspective on art was just too different from Nietzsche's. Nietzsche could not, or would not, consistently acknowledge either the depth of Plato's appreciation of art or the magnitude of his artistic gifts because he was disconcerted and confused by the fact that Plato stood in an altogether different relation to art than he did himself. And here I do not mean to stress Plato's ethical-political relation to art, but rather his *existential* relation. He does not seem to have been *dependent* on art in the specific ways that Nietzsche required it. Earlier in this section we surveyed, though admittedly only impressionistically, the role of suffering in Nietzsche's works beginning in the early 1880s. Throughout his career Nietzsche maintained that art is born of suffering, art as redemption, art as solace, art as encouragement or a discharge of power through which a fundamentally healthy organism combats and overcomes every onslaught of illness and depression. Art arises through other channels as well, and humans have developed other responses to suffering than art, so I do not mean to suggest that for Nietzsche suffering and art necessitate one another. Yet it is true that the two are regularly associated in his mind, and this is so, I believe, as a result of Nietzsche's self-observations. He understood these functions of art because he himself at various times employed aesthetic resources for each of these ends.[52]

In Nietzsche's case "art" means, first and foremost, his own books.[53] Consider, for example, *Thus Spoke Zarathustra*, his great prose poem of the mid-1880s. Looking back on *Zarathustra* in his autobiographical *Ecce Homo* (from 1888), Nietzsche associates the work with suffering, illness, melancholy, distress, and lonely isolation. Yet he also refers to "the Yes-saying pathos," which, he says, "was alive in me to the highest degree" in the period leading up to his writing the first of *Zarathustra*'s four books (*EH* "Z" 1). Almost certainly Nietzsche is recalling the events surrounding his acquaintance with Lou Salomé, a brilliant young Russian émigré whom he hoped to have for a student and disciple, and perhaps even for a wife. Their relationship began well enough but soon degenerated into a torturous ordeal of misunderstanding, confusion, and sorrow. Although Nietzsche was 37 when they met, he was innocent of romance; he does not seem to have understood his own emotions. Lou's attachment to Nietzsche's friend Paul Rée complicated the situation further. When these two took up together Nietzsche at times imagined that they had abandoned him, that perhaps they were even mocking him, and he could barely understand what was happening. Brooding on the situation, he frequently succumbed to ugly bouts of self-pity, bitterness, and rage. He had lived a wandering, solitary life since resigning his university post in 1879, but in the aftermath of this affair he felt alone as he never had before; he suffered terribly and regarded himself thereafter as a sort of pagan hermit.[54] When in later years he wrote of suffering excessively his whole life long, of his unendurable solitude, of being attacked by a "black despair," and of being "absurdly alone," he was giving vent to emotions similar to those stirred up during his tumultuous involvement with Lou Salomé, whose companionship moved him to write to a friend that "I have lived in solitude too long."[55]

Nietzsche was well aware of his own physiological and psychological depressive states, in fact he insisted on them, for he took his ability in spite of them to say Yes in works like *Zarathustra* as evidence that at bottom he was sound, healthy, and strong (*EH* "Wise" 1–3).[56] In contrast to his own fundamental health Nietzsche would like to cast Plato as physiologically degenerate. Just above I noted his identification of Plato as Europe's greatest enemy of art. In doing so he associates Plato with the scientific impulse. But science, Nietzsche says, presupposes "a certain *impoverishment of life*," and because Plato was thus impoverished he was "the great slanderer of life." We know that Nietzsche takes Plato (by way of "Plato's Socrates") to privilege dialectic over instinct, but here he fills out his characterization with such traits as a depressed affect, a sluggish "tempo of life," and an exaggerated seriousness resulting from a "labored metabolism" and a "laborious life" (*GM* 3.25). Nietzsche's explicit target in this section is science, but since he has in the previous paragraph carefully—or recklessly—assimilated Plato to science, we may take him as offering a description of Plato as well. There is certainly no ambiguity in his portrait of Plato in *Twilight of the Idols*, in which he condemns Plato for having been "a coward before reality" whose philosophy represents "the decadence of the Greek instinct" (*TI* "Ancients" 2). In this Nietzsche is merely reiterating a criticism from earlier in the book, namely, that Plato (like Socrates) was a symptom of Greek degeneration, "anti-Greek" (*TI* "Socrates" 2). This last claim he makes in the context of his account of those who question the value of life and judge it to be no good. Given his reference to Socrates' last words in the immediately preceding section, Nietzsche clearly has the *Phaedo* in mind, in which work Plato most definitely denigrates the body, describing it as a prison from which the soul must escape in order to attain purity. But this dialogue is set on the day of Socrates' death, and the philosopher's reflections on immortality are meant at least in part to comfort his grieving friends. So the dramatic setting may account for the dialogue's more radical elements. It is true that Plato *always* privileges the soul over the body, but he rarely does so to this extreme. So unless we grant Nietzsche the authority to decree by fiat that metaphysical thinking in and of itself is sufficient to demonstrate physiological degeneration, we shall require evidence before agreeing that Plato was decadent. Yet when I read the dialogues, even the dense, complex, argument-laden works of Plato's later period, I see no signs of a morose, labored life, of undue seriousness or a peevish lack of humor, of cowardice, weakness, bitterness, or resentment. Plato was known to the ancients as "the divine" for many reasons, not least for the miraculous touch of his artistry, for what we might with reason describe as the *joyfulness* of his wisdom.

So I find no evidence that Plato suffered from life, nor that he was given to brooding morosely on the value of existence. This seems rather to have been Nietzsche's particular obsession. But if I call attention to the occasional morbid heaviness of Nietzsche's heart, the weight of his spirit that dragged him down into pits of loneliness and despair, I do so not to discredit him. To the contrary, I accept his assertion that his works, with their rare combination of a restlessly searching profundity and light-hearted cheerfulness, are indicative of a physiological-psychological foundation of affirmative power. I do, however, intend to undermine those of his criticisms of Plato that are founded on his dubious backward inferences from Christian theology and ethics to Platonic metaphysics, and from Platonic metaphysics to Plato's decadence. Despite his later distaste for Plato, and his attempts to obscure his earlier expressions of (admittedly qualified) admiration, Nietzsche recognized Plato's nobility, and occasionally he had the good will to acknowledge it (as in *BGE* 14 and 190). Nor was he always blind to Plato's artistic genius, as we have seen in *The Birth of Tragedy*, and as comes out in *Beyond Good and Evil* when he calls Plato "the most audacious of all interpreters" of Socrates because, like a master composer, he turned the elder man's little tunes into "infinite and impossible" variations (*BGE* 190). Earlier I quoted from a letter in which Nietzsche identifies Plato as his true adversary, but I omitted the following line: "But how proud I am to have such an adversary!"

I like to imagine that if Nietzsche had lived to think and to write for the two or three decades that might still have been his had he been healthy, he would have disentangled Plato from his disdain for Christianity and felt free to revive his early acknowledgment that Plato was "a richly gifted prose stylist: highly versatile, a master of all kinds of tone, the most completely cultivated [man] of the most cultivated time."[57] He might even have disentangled Plato from Socrates and pursued the implications of his insight, as expressed in *Beyond Good and Evil*, that Plato was "too noble" for the "Socratism" that in *The Birth of Tragedy* he denounces as anti-tragic, and that the morality of Socrates "does not really belong to Plato" but is something of an alien presence in his work (*BGE* 190).

Having said all this, I do admit that Plato had his quarrels with art, and with poetry in particular. And although I believe that Nietzsche exaggerated the relevant facts as well as their implications for Plato's thought and character, we must not neglect to examine the matter for ourselves. Plato wrote about the uses and abuses of poetry throughout his long career, and his attitudes were not at all one-sided or simplistic. As we shall see, he wrote of art primarily in the context of its cultural impact and its ethical influence on individuals. He is, it is true, mostly critical in this regard; but whenever I consider these matters, I find myself inevitably returning to a thought that strikes me as undeniable: Plato was too powerful an artist to have been mastered by himself as a moralist.

Plato and the poets

Plato's *Republic* is often mistaken for an account of an ideal city.[58] It is in fact an account of a second best city. (It is also much else besides this.) The account is initiated in the drama by Socrates' attempt to demonstrate that justice is superior to injustice, a problem put to him by his interlocutors Glaucon and Adeimantus (Plato's older brothers). He proceeds by explaining the nature of justice and injustice and their effects on the human soul, and this he does analogically by likening a soul to a city and then investigating the origins, nature, and consequences of justice and injustice in a city.[59] In short, then, Socrates and his friends discuss the nature and value of justice by, as it were, founding a city in speech. The city is only second best because

Glaucon is not satisfied with Socrates' early description of "the true city," a city that makes do with the necessities of life and is "healthy." Instead, he desires a city that Socrates calls "luxurious" and "inflamed," a city stuffed with delicacies and amusements (372c–e). This is Plato's accommodation of theory to practical reality, and as a result of this approach his great "Kallipolis" is not so much an ideal city as ideal under the circumstances.[60]

Given the nature of the city under consideration, and particularly given its citizens' desires for unnecessary pleasures, the city requires more land than would have been necessary to accommodate the needs of the minimal city of necessity that Socrates initially proposes. This luxurious city will have to appropriate land from neighboring *poleis*, and this leads to the expansion of the citizen body to include a new class of men, the warriors. The introduction of this class generates new problems. To be successful in battle the city's soldiers must be harsh to their enemies; but to prevent internal bloodshed they must be gentle to their fellow citizens. A dual nature of this sort is hard to come by in men, and when found it must be nurtured by a specific pedagogical regime, a regime that will encourage a warrior's violence in one direction while taming it in another. To this end the city's soldiers must receive both a musical education (i.e. an education involving those arts overseen by the Muses) and rigorous physical training. Our present concern is with the "musical" element, for it is in this context, and specifically in the second and third books of the *Republic*, that Plato issues his infamous denunciation of the poets, including of course the tragedians (376c–398b). Plato worries that many traditional poems project images of men and gods that associate a good life with injustice and other vices. This is a serious concern, for the men whose educational regime he is devising are potentially very dangerous— they are inclined by nature to be violent. If such men are reared on tales that teach that even the gods cheat, deceive, and fight with their friends, then they may see nothing wrong in harming one another or treating the citizens under their protection as they should treat only their enemies. This is the concern that motivates Plato's censorship of poetry.

In Book 2 of the *Republic* Socrates argues that since the young are impressionable and malleable, the city's children must be reared on stories that will improve rather than degrade their characters. Therefore, when providing for their education it is necessary to supervise those who fashion myths for the children's consumption, accepting those myths that are noble and rejecting those that are not (377a–c). Children must not hear, for example, about strife between fathers and sons. The stories told of conflict between Ouranos and Kronos, and between Kronos and Zeus, together constitute "the greatest falsehood concerning the greatest matters," for they mislead the young into thinking that behaving this way toward one's elders is an unexceptional imitation of the actions of the first and greatest of the gods (377e–378b). Children quite simply should hear nothing at all about the gods at war with or plotting against one another, for they must be raised to believe that antagonism among citizens is most shameful and, worse, unholy (378b–c).

The founders of a city are not poets, so they should not themselves fashion myths, but it is proper to them to know the patterns according to which poets should tell their tales (*muthologein*, 378e–379a). Socrates explains two such patterns, all the while citing examples of poetic passages that deviate from the ideal. First, one must always describe the god as he is, namely, good; and since god is good he cannot be the cause of all things but only of those that are good. It must not be said, for example, that the god punishes anyone unjustly, or that a man justly punished is not benefitted, for this is likely to impede the proper functioning of a city's system of law (379a–380c). The second pattern has two parts, the first being that the gods do not alter their form. It is impossible for them to want to do so, for since each god is the noblest and best it is possible to be, to change would be to assume an inferior form, which neither man nor god would wish to do. The gods, therefore, always retain their own proper shapes (380d–381e). The second part is that the gods do not mislead us by falsehoods in word or deed. The gods have no need of lies, for they are ignorant of nothing about which they might want to appear knowledgeable, nor do they have need to deceive either enemies or friends. Teaching otherwise would undermine the warriors' reverence for the divine and their own aspiration to a mortal approximation of this condition (382a–383c).

Socrates continues to cite the poets' depictions of the gods in Book 3, contrasting them with his account of the patterns to which they ought to adhere instead. Since those who fear Hades will fear death, and whoever fears death will lack courage, warriors must hear nothing bad about the underworld. Nor should they hear of men mourning the death of friends or lamenting other misfortunes, for such stories will teach them to fear death themselves and to smart at even minor inconveniences (386a–388e). These men should not love laughter (388e–389b), and they must regard truth as of great consequence (389b–d). They must practice self-control (*sôphrosunê*), especially by being obedient to the rulers and by ruling their own desires for pleasure (389d–390d). They must not be allowed to be venal or lovers of money (390d–391a), nor should they display arrogant contempt for gods or humans (391a–c). Finally, regarding the gods, no poet should depict them daring to perform appalling and impious acts, such as rape (391c–392a). And as for humans, neither poets nor prose-writers should be permitted to say that unjust men are happy, that just men are wretched, or that injustice is profitable so long as one is not caught (392a–b).

In Book 10 Socrates returns to his critical analysis of the poets, and at this point he mentions "an ancient quarrel between philosophy and poetry" (607b6–7).[61] It may be that he has in mind attacks on the poets by early philosophers like Xenophanes and Heraclitus. Xenophanes objected in particular to Homer's and Hesiod's depictions of the gods as often engaging in immoral activities, as well as to their anthropomorphisms, and in this he anticipates those of Plato's own criticisms that we have just examined. In Book 10, however, Socrates' objections to poetry are not primarily social-political, not at first anyway. Here he objects to the poets' activities on theoretical grounds, though even these ultimately resolve into practical political and ethical considerations. He states as a belief held in common by himself and his interlocutors that although there are many instances of any particular type of physical object—many tables, for example—there exists only a single metaphysical exemplar of the type—one metaphysical Form of *table*.[62] This metaphysical Form is created by god.[63] It is, also, ultimately real; it *is* in the fullest sense of the verb *to be*.[64] The physical tables with which we have commerce in our daily lives are imitations of these

Forms fabricated by carpenters. They are, therefore, at one remove from ultimate reality; they are less than fully real. But there are yet other tables around as well, for example the tables that appear in paintings. These are imitations of the physical tables and so are imitations of imitations. These tables, then, are two removes distant from ultimate reality; they are less real even than physical tables, third on a three-tiered scale of reality. In fact, since painters never imitate physical objects as they are in their fullness, but rather only as they appear from a single perspective, their products may be even further removed from reality. In any case, they occupy the lowest rung on the declining hierarchy of reality. But paintings are not alone on this rung; also here at this lowest level are tragedies. The tragedians, like painters, imitate the works of imitators.[65] They are, therefore, naturally "third from the king and from the truth" (597e).

For Plato reality and truth are intimately related, so that which is less than fully real is less than true as well. Therefore, the ontological objections to the tragedians' works imply an epistemological critique. Tragedians lack authentic knowledge of the subjects they write about. This is so fundamentally because the subjects of their poetry, being less than fully true, are not proper objects of knowledge. But the poets' ignorance can be demonstrated in practical terms as well. Consider Homer, for example, whom Socrates calls (oddly perhaps) the leader of tragedy and first of the tragedians.[66] Homer sang about war, about kingly rule, generalship, and the conduct of battle. Yet no one believes that any man ever ruled well or waged war successfully with Homer as his personal advisor. Homer did not grasp the truth about the specific subjects of his poems (their content); rather, like all good imitators of imitations, he possessed a certain knack for poetic composition that enabled him to appear knowledgeable to those who are ignorant of the truth themselves.

Whoever lacks knowledge of the truth of a subject must also fail to understand what is good and bad in relation to that subject. Therefore, the epistemological critique of imitation implies corresponding moral objections. Imitators like Homer and the tragedians, being ignorant—not ignorant of the techniques required to compose beautiful poems, but ignorant of the subjects that constitute the content of the poems—and therefore incapable of distinguishing the good from the bad, imitate only what appeals to the fancy of the equally ignorant crowds. Their imitations bypass reason and work on that part of the human soul that desires pleasure and shuns pain with no thought to proper measure. This is the irrational element of a man, and because it is irrational it thoughtlessly inclines toward outrageous and dangerous deeds. It represents a human's baser self, and by catering to it the poets embolden and strengthen it, inspiring it to resist the dictates of reason. The man in whom this lowest part of the soul is conditioned from youth to usurp the power of the highest is gravely harmed, for he will act solely as moved by impulses directed toward pleasures and away from pains rather than as motivated by considerations of the good and the bad, justice and injustice. Even the best of men can be injured this way, for they too may be moved by beautiful poetry and so actually enjoy portrayals of men and actions that in real life they would deplore. Poets, in short, have a way of making everyone approve more or less of base behavior. In this way they have the power to corrupt entire cities. And since, as we have seen, they are ignorant of good and bad, they do not know the difference between corruption and improvement—worse, they may very well mistake their corruption of a city for its improvement. Here we confront a standard Platonic worry: ignorance conjoined with power is dangerous, and if the power manifests as influence, then the danger is compounded.[67]

So the poets produce potentially harmful imitations of imitations, and their works—their tragedies, for example—are dangerous because through their power and beauty they conjoin in the souls of their viewers (or readers) pleasant feelings with the vicious or irrational acts of bad men. In Nietzschean terms, they associate the good conscience with ignoble deeds. But imitation plays another role in the corruption of character, imitation of a sort we might call existential. After concluding his account of the patterns poets should follow when discoursing of the gods, Socrates develops the three-fold analysis of poetic presentation that we considered in the previous section.[68] The purely imitative style of poetic presentation is particularly worrisome, he says, because when men perform it on stage (and presumably even when they perform it in their own minds while reading, though Plato does not specify this) they take on, if only temporarily, the characters of the men they are imitating. They literally speak and behave as the characters themselves speak and behave. But imitations engaged in from youth eventually solidify as one's habits and nature in body, speech, and thought. In short, one becomes like the man one regularly pretends to be. Considering, then, that pure imitation is the style of tragedy and comedy, and also that characters in tragedy and comedy are often vicious, disturbed, gloomy, crass, or ridiculous, in light of these facts it is evident that tragedies and comedies condition men to become vicious, disturbed, gloomy, crass, or ridiculous themselves. This is clearly unacceptable, and no reasonable legislator would permit it. Thus Socrates says that although a gifted imitative poet merits reverence as a holy, wondrous, and pleasant sort of man, he must not be allowed to enter the city that he and his interlocutors are constructing in speech, nor should any such man born in this city be permitted to stay (398a).

Here we have the first instance of Plato's so-called "banishment of the poets." But in fact the poets are not banished *en masse* at this point. Socrates states quite explicitly that cities may benefit from poets who imitate good men and who adhere in their work to the patterns of discourse previously established (398a–b). Strangely, however, Plato begins Book 10 by having Socrates remark in reference to the conversation in Book 3 that they have agreed not to admit into their city any form of imitative poetry (595a). He then launches into the analysis of the ontological status of imitation (with its epistemo-logical and practical consequences) that we examined above, at the conclusion of which he reiterates that they had acted reasonably when earlier they banished (*apestellomen*) poetry from the city (607b). Here, then, are the only explicit references to all of the poets being excluded from the city. But they did not in fact banish all the poets in Book 3, as we have seen. Moreover, immediately following this talk of universal banishment in Book 10, Socrates insists at some length that they must give a fair hearing to any poet or lover of poetry who wishes to argue that pleasant and imitative poetry ought to be present in a well-regulated city by demonstrating its benefit to the city's social-political structure (*politeia*) and to human life in general (607c–608a). Having defended itself in this way, Socrates says, poetry may justly return to the city (607d).

So Plato's infamous banishment of the poets is not nearly so unambiguous, or so crude, as the standard caricature portrays it. It certainly does not expose Plato as a man who hated or was incapable of appreciating poetry. As I have said, Plato was no philistine. Stephen Halliwell has designated him a "romantic puritan" on the ground that his "fear of the imagination is that of a thinker and writer who does not simply stigmatize certain kinds of art as dangerous or corrupting but who claims to appreciate, to know *from the inside*, just how seductive the transformative experience of art can be."[69] This, I think, is right. The fact is that Plato understood poetry's power to affect men's characters, for good as well as for ill; and he lived in a society so relatively small (approximately 30,000 citizens in Plato's time, with perhaps as many as 100,000 free resident aliens) that the corruption of even a few influential individuals could ultimately bring about its downfall.[70] Surely it is neither irrational nor aesthetically backward to reason that however beautiful a work of art may be, there will be no one to admire it if the work itself, or other works of art, contribute to the production of a populace so vicious that their actions undermine the stability of the very society that supports the production and appreciation of art. I have no doubt that Plato, like Nietzsche, had a deep appreciation of the beautiful, as spectator as well as creator. But he was not so naive as to believe that art is everything, that art is All. There is more to life, and more to a city capable of supporting life, than art; and if the art is to flourish, the city must survive.

Wine and song

If at the beginning of the previous section I seemed to suggest that Plato's critique of poetry in the *Republic* is relevant only to the education of a warrior class in an ideal (or nearly ideal) city, then I should stress here that this is not the case. Evidence from other dialogues demonstrates that Plato's objections to poetry apply in various contexts and extend over many domains. Nevertheless, I admit that if anyone was temporarily misled, I do not regret the fact. A superficial version of Plato's position is today so prevalent that I am happy to unsettle presuppositions that might hinder readers from giving the man a fair hearing. It just is not true that Plato despised art without qualification, could not appreciate the sublimity of Homer and the dark power of tragedy, and advocated a ban on all music and poetry for every citizen in all circumstances. Yet this is the impression many people have, for all they know—or think that they know—is that "Plato banished the poets." In this connection I repeat a thought I expressed earlier, for it is good to remind ourselves of Plato's many sides and talents: Plato was too powerful an artist to have been mastered by himself as a moralist.

Having said this, however, it is important to acknowledge the fact that Plato was indeed a moralist, or if "moralist" is too pejorative a word (and in this instance I believe that it is), then let us call him a social-political thinker with an interest in guiding and regulating the behavior of citizens.[71] In his theoretical role as legislator (a primary function of a genuine philosopher, according to Nietzsche) Plato was determined to have control of the arts, for he understood that "the modes of music cannot change without the modes of the greatest political laws changing," as Socrates puts it in the *Republic*, on the authority of Damon, a fifth-century BCE Athenian philosopher of music (424c). In the *Laws*, too, the Athenian insists that alterations in children's entertainments, particularly in their songs and dances, undermine the stability of laws and traditions (797a–798d). With this in mind, Plato dedicates the second book of the *Laws* to the proper musical education of citizens.[72]

But before attending to Book 2 I note a surprising theme introduced in the first book: drunkenness. The Athenian assumes that a stable city depends on stable citizens, citizens with the virtue of *sôphrosunê*, which in this context we may translate as self-control. Yet too many cities focus obsessively on inculcating primarily the virtue of courage. The Spartans, for example, train their citizens to confront and endure every shade of terror and pain, but like other cities they neglect to train their men to resist the temptations of pleasure. This is a problem because anyone innocent of pleasure is easily seduced by it, and lacking the resources to resist its charms a man may eventually become its slave. A city populated by men in thrall to pleasure will be weakened by a debauched citizenry, and a city thus undermined may collapse or be overrun by invaders. But how to train men to deal properly with pleasure? The answer, according to the Athenian, requires a theory of education with a place for drunkenness. Education, he says, is training in virtue (*aretê*) from childhood (643e), and a proper education tests and strengthens a man's resistance to pleasures as thoroughly as it tests and strengthens his endurance of pain. Drunkenness is relevant because taking wine at a symposium under the supervision of a sober leader is an ideal way to experience pleasure in a controlled environment. Both the inebriation and the oversight are essential to the pedagogical end, for when we are drunk our souls are temporarily debased; we become silly, shameless, and recklessly over-confident; but to experience these states in a setting designed to teach us how best to manage them, to learn, that is, how to manage ourselves while in this uninhibited condition, is a great benefit. Controlled drunkenness, then, is pedagogically beneficial.

Drunkenness serves another educational role in the city, this one having to do with the pedagogical uses of song and dance. In Book 2 of the *Laws* the Athenian modifies his definition of education (training in virtue) by adding that education is the proper rearing of children with respect to pleasures and pains (653b–c), and later he clarifies his position by explaining that to experience pleasures and pains correctly is to be pleased and pained by the same things as please and pain the city's oldest citizens, for these men abide by the city's laws (659d–e). A proper relation to pleasures and pains is inculcated in youth and maintained in adults through songs and dances: a man nobly (*kalôs*) educated will sing and dance nobly (*kalôs*)—so long, that is, as he sings noble (*kala*) songs and dances noble (*kala*) dances (654b–c), which is to say songs and dances that represent good men and virtuous actions. And since men adopt the characters of that which they enjoy, if citizens are taught through song and dance to delight in the actions of virtuous men, they will strive to be virtuous themselves.

At this point Plato takes up the theme, so prominent in the *Republic*, of the legislation of music. The Athenian claims that the Egyptians have maintained for thousands of years a strict uniformity in songs and dances, and he would like through his legislation to accomplish the same feat. Songs, he says, are actually charms (*epôidai*) for the soul that associate pleasures with virtue and pains with vice. Songs and dances are this serious, which is why the correct legislator will persuade his city's poets to compose their poems correctly by producing rhythms that represent the bearing, and harmonies that represent the songs of virtuous men—and if he cannot persuade them, he will force them to do so (660a).

The poets' charms and incantations will be performed by the citizens themselves, whom the Athenian proposes to divide into three choruses, according to age classifications, to sing and dance one after the other at certain unspecified festivals. The first is a chorus of children dedicated to the Muses. The second chorus, dedicated to Apollo, will comprise adults up to the age of 30. The last chorus, composed of "old men" from over 30 to 60 years of age, will be dedicated to Dionysus.[73] There will also be a group of men over the age of 60 who no longer have the strength to sing, but who will by way of "divine speech" deliver mythical tales (*muthologoi*) similar to the choruses' (664b–d). The Athenian never specifies the precise nature of the songs the choruses will sing, but in Book 7 he says that many ancient songs and dances are noble and appropriate for the sort of city he and his interlocutors are discussing (802a–b). So here, at any rate, we see that Plato has no intention of obliterating the Greeks' cultural heritage. As to the general content of the songs, the Athenian in Book 2 reasons that since men tend to adopt the lifestyle they find most pleasant, the prudent legislator will reinforce through music the idea that the just life is most pleasurable (660d–663d). No city will long survive whose citizens learn from youth to associate pleasure with injustice. The citizens' songs and tales, therefore, must be such as to promote the idea that the just life is best and most pleasant while the unjust life is bad and painful. The Athenian formulates an argument to demonstrate that this is in fact the case (661d–663d), but he insists that even if it were not so, a thoughtful lawmaker would spread the lie that it is, for nothing is more advantageous to a city than that its citizens be voluntarily just (663d–e).

When the Athenian's interlocutors express their incredulity that men as old as 60 should sing and dance in honor of Dionysus, he returns to his earlier theme of drunkenness. No one in the city under the age of 18 shall be permitted to drink wine. Adults up to the age of 30 will be allowed to drink in moderation. Men approaching 40[74] will feast and entertain themselves at common meals[75] where they will "call the other gods and summon Dionysus in particular to their mystic rite (*teletê*) and play of old men." Thus relaxed and cheerful, the old men will readily sing and offer up their incantations (666b). This Dionysian chorus of old men is the best element of the city and its members are the most competent to draw the young men toward virtue. The Athenian advises that the choruses' songs be constantly updated and varied, for this will ensure that the singers derive pleasure from singing them. But the changes must conform to the purpose of the songs with respect to pleasure and justice, and they will presumably be supervised by the old Dionysian men who, according to the Athenian, are the proper judges of musical correctness (667b–671a, 812b–c).

Plato's dedicating the first two books of a major work of his old age to the educational benefits of inebriation has long struck commentators as most unusual.[76] But when one follows his argument it makes sense as coming from a septuagenarian who after years of reflection has come to acknowledge that the irrational elements of human nature cannot be eradicated or suppressed, though they may be managed and channeled in healthy directions. The elderly Plato is much less optimistic than the younger man who wrote the *Republic*, and the evidence of the *Laws* has suggested to some that Plato in the end was a pessimist. In Book 1 his Athenian describes human beings as the living playthings of the gods with no idea whether our makers fashioned us as their toys or for some serious end. We are as puppets constructed with cords of pleasures and pains that function like sinews to drag us this way and that. It is a haunting image of a force affecting us from within, at least partly beyond our control, which manipulates our muscles and thereby even the very movements of our bodies. Fortunately, the divinities who made us have supplied us also with a "golden and holy leading-chord of calculation," which is known as the "common law of the city." In cooperation with this we humans may gain a proper perspective on pleasures and pains, which will in turn enable us to distinguish more clearly between virtue and vice (644c–645c).

But our cooperation is essential, for unlike the other animals we do not incline by nature toward our highest and best potentialities. We are in fact a species that naturally suffers. Fortunately, however, the gods have taken pity on us and established festivals in honor of the Muses, Apollo, and Dionysus, which on regular occasions provide temporary relief from our sufferings (653c–d); and Dionysus himself has given us his frenzy, his mad dances, and his wine, that we might acquire reverence in our souls and health and strength in our bodies (672b–d). I suppose it would be misleading to suggest that Plato in the end came around to a philosophy of Dionysian pessimism, for despite his tragic insights and his recognition of the benefits of madness, he was no Nietzschean. Still, the pessimism does bleed through now and then; and the recognition, or we might even say the *celebration* of madness is often quite explicit.

Divine madness

Plato in the *Ion* makes the case that poets are ignorant, that they have no knowledge of the subjects of their poems (532c–533d). Homer, for example, knew nothing of the arts of kingly rule and generalship, however movingly he versified about royalty and war. In this the poets are like sophists, who know nothing of the just and unjust even though they regularly speak and write about judicial and legislative matters. In the *Gorgias* the sophists are said to possess opinion acquired through experience that enables them to speak persuasively to crowds of ignorant men (458e–459c). But how to account for the poets? Whence comes *their* power? For they do possess a power, a *dunamis*, to employ the Greek word. In the *Ion* Socrates readily acknowledges this, and he identifies the source of their power. The poets, he says, operate from a *theia dunamis*, a divine power (533d3), and in one of his most striking images, Plato likens poets, rhapsodes (professional reciters of poems, like Ion himself), and their audiences to links in a magnetized chain. A god, more specifically a divine Muse, is the magnet itself. Attached to this is the poet, and to the poet the rhapsode is attached. The final links in the chain, bonded to the rhapsode, are individual members of the audience. Dangling from the sides of this chain are choral dancers, trainers, and various production assistants. As a magnet infuses whatever clings to it with a magnetic attraction of its own, so the Muse transmits a divine power through the links in the chain that descends from her. The real poet is the divinity; the man we call "poet" is in fact only the god's interpreter (*hermêneus*). And the rhapsode, who does not himself compose but merely learns by heart and recites the poet's words, is an interpreter of an interpreter (533c–536d).

The idea that the rhapsode is an interpreter of an interpreter is reminiscent of Socrates' account in the *Republic* of the poet as an imitator of an imitation. But in the *Republic* there is no suggestion that the imitators are divinely inspired; instead they are portrayed as imitators of mundane physical objects. In the *Ion*, on the other hand, poets are said to interpret the gods. Moreover, the poets' relation to the divine is closer even than the word "interpreter" suggests. It is not that a poet receives a message from a god and then undertakes to translate its substance into words comprehensible to humans. There are far too many opportunities for misunderstanding and errors of transmission in a process like this, and it is precisely this sort of separation between representer and represented that in the *Republic* makes poetic activity objectionable on ontological and epistemological grounds. The poets misrepresent the truth because they have no direct connection to reality. Poetry as presented in the *Ion* is a remarkably different phenomenon: it is a medium through which divine truth is communicated to humans. In this work Socrates claims that the poets are "possessed" (*katechomenoi*, 534e5) by the Muse to whom they are devoted, and by this he means (among other things) that "the god himself … speaks to us" through the poet. Like "the chanters of oracles and the divine seers," poets are the mouthpieces of the gods (534c–e). From this we may infer that even the rhapsode, a more distant link in the divinely magnetized chain, by faithfully repeating the poet's words, accurately transmits the divine discourse. And this means that we in the audience in one sense hear directly from the god.

But is this really the message of the *Ion*? The conversation is motivated by Socrates' inquiries into Ion's knowledge of Homer. Soon the poet's knowledge along with the rhapsode's is explicitly called into question, and Socrates argues that neither type has expertise or knowledge.[77] The notion that poets compose and rhapsodes recite under the influence of inspiration (*entheoi ontes*, 533e6–7) is introduced to explain the poets' undeniable ability to produce beautiful poems and the equally undeniable fact (as revealed through the sort of interrogation to which Socrates subjects Ion) that they do not understand the subjects about which they sing. It may be, then, that the true substance of the work is the claim that the poets are ignorant, while the suggestion that they are divinely inspired is merely another way of expressing our own ignorance of how they manage to do what they do.

But the *Ion* is not the only dialogue in which Plato writes about poetic inspiration. He does so in the *Phaedrus* with no stress at all on the poets' ignorance. In both works it is denied that good poets are good through expertise and affirmed that they are possessed by a Muse; in both works poets are said to be overcome by Dionysian frenzy (*bacheuousi*, *Ion* 534a4; *ekbakcheuousa*, *Phdr.* 245a3). In the *Ion* the idea that the poet is out of his mind dominates,[78] whereas in the *Phaedrus* the recurrent idea is madness,[79] but in both the poet is as he is because of divine activity—inspiration in the *Ion* is a "divine allotment" (*theia moira*, 534c1); madness in the *Phaedrus* is "from the gods" (*apo theôn*, 245b2). In brief, then, we ought not dismiss the idea of poetic possession as merely a colorfully expressed confession of ignorance of the source of a poet's genius; divine possession plays too significant a role in other dialogues, and in contexts other than considerations of poetry, to believe that Plato employed it only as a literary device or an intellectual flourish.

In the *Meno* we hear once again of the poet's divinity and inspiration, also of the divinity of chanters of oracles and seers (99c–d). But, surprisingly, Socrates suggests at the end of this work that even political men (Themistocles, for example, or Pericles) lack understanding but act correctly in the many great things they do and say because they are divine, inspired, and possessed (99b–c). Virtue, he says, is present in men by a "divine allotment" (*theia moira*, 99e6), echoing the phrase we have just encountered in the *Ion*. In one sense this is an unexpected conclusion to the dialogue, which has in parts been a sober investigation into whether virtue comes to be in men by nature or by education. Regarding the dialogue from this perspective, we might linger over Socrates' remark that the conclusion that politicians are divinely inspired follows *if* the arguments earlier in the dialogue are sound, and we might infer from this that Plato is subtly encouraging his readers to assume and seek out a flaw in some previous section of the argument. We might also suspect that Plato is being ironic at the expense of Athens' lauded political figures by way of Socrates' irony at the expense of one of his interlocutors, Anytus, who in real life joined with Meletus and Lycon to prosecute Socrates because he was angry "on behalf of … the politicians" (*Ap.* 23e). On the other hand, we might regard the dialogue from a perspective that attends to its less than sober elements, for example Socrates' reference to initiation into mystic rites (76e) and his relating certain "true and noble" statements that, he says, he has heard from wise priests and priestesses concerning the immortality of the soul, reincarnation, and the fact that what we call knowledge is actually recollection of "the truth of the beings" that is always present in our souls (81a–86b). With these latter elements of the dialogue in mind we might at least take seriously the possibility that Plato means what Socrates says about the divinity of virtuous men. It is consistent with ideas expressed in other works. From a famous passage in the *Theaetetus*, for example, we learn that virtue and understanding in man constitute a likeness to god (*homoiôsis theôi*, 176b1), and this idea is repeated in the *Republic* (613a–b). Now it may be that this talk of divine inspiration is only an image representing the fact that a philosopher's virtue is a consequence of his knowledge of the Forms, which activity in the *Republic* Socrates describes as "keeping company with the divine" (500c–d); but, as I say, we should at least take seriously the evident fact that Plato is drawn to this way of conceptualizing the matter. Even staid Aristotle proposes in his *Nicomachean Ethics* that humans should strive to imitate the divine through a life of contemplation, which is dependent on the intellectual virtues and at least indirectly on the virtues of character as well.[80]

So oracles and prophets, poets and politicians may all be divinely inspired, possessed by a god, perhaps even by Dionysus himself, in which case these men are out of their minds and frenzied. Attending to Nietzsche's stress on Socratic and Platonic rationality, we might take Plato's talk of inspiration and possession as his way of comparing all these types invidiously to the rational philosopher. But poets, prophets, and politicians are not the only ones who stand divinely beside themselves. Returning to the *Phaedrus* we learn that philosophers too are possessed. In this work Socrates identifies himself as a seer (*mantis*, 242c4), which gift, he says, enables him to know that the speech he delivered about Eros earlier in the dialogue offended the divinity. Therefore he must, he says, purify himself with another, more appropriate, speech. This new speech he begins with the declaration that "the greatest of good things come to us through madness, if it is given as a divine gift" (244a). He then proceeds to identify four types of madness. One of these, as we have seen, is the madness of the poet, for which the Muses are responsible (245a, 265b). Another is the madness of prophetesses, priestesses, and various oracles who through oracular (mantic) inspiration have done many noble things for the Greeks. Employing a bit of playful etymology, Socrates claims that although their practice is called "mantic," it was originally called "manic," which means "mad" or "frenzied," for "the ancients who established the names (of things)" understood that madness is noble when given by the gods.[81] Apollo is responsible for this sort of madness (244a–d, 265b). Dionysus is responsible for a madness related to mystic rites[82] that through purification liberate (*apallagê*, *lusis*) a family from illnesses and sufferings arising from ancient crimes (244d–245a, 265b). The vocabulary here is reminiscent of the *Phaedo*, in which Plato associates purification with the soul's separation (*apallagê*, 64c5) and release (*lusis*, e.g. 67d4) from the body, also with mystic rites and *Bakchoi* (69c–d). In any case, Socrates devotes most of his speech in the *Phaedrus* to elaborating on the madness of the philosopher, which he associates with Aphrodite and Eros (245b–257b, 265b). This is the madness of one who encounters beauty in the physical realm and is thereby reminded of the Form of *beauty*—the true and real immaterial essence of beauty, of which every beauty here is a pale imitation—which the soul beheld before descending into its body. Moved by this vision, the soul of a man longs to return to the metaphysical source of everything physical and so disdains and ignores the things of this world. Men in this condition are, like madmen, driven outside of themselves, yet theirs is the greatest of all forms of inspiration (literally, divine indwellings: *enthousiaseôn*, 249e1). Describing the soul's original experience of seeing the Form of *beauty*, Socrates employs a vocabulary borrowed from rituals of initiation into mystery cults, such as the one at Eleusis just north of Athens proper (centered on Demeter and Persephone, queen of the underworld). He also, and once again, recalls the *Phaedo* by describing properly initiated souls as experiencing a vision in pure light when they are pure themselves and not fettered to their bodies (250c4–6; cf. *Phd*. 67d–e).

It is true that later in the *Phaedrus* Socrates says that much of his speech was delivered in play,[83] and it is also true that in Book 2 of the *Republic* he says that no one thoughtless or mad is dear to god (382e3), but we need not take either of these passages to imply that Plato did not believe what he wrote about poetry, philosophy, and madness. Play in the *Phaedrus* does not amount to irony or deception. In writing, play may function as a reminder of the truth for those who know—not as serious, perhaps, as a discourse grounded in knowledge delivered directly to the soul of a learner, but by no means false (275c–278e). And the comment on madness in the *Republic* is consistent with Socrates' identification of two varieties of madness in the *Phaedrus*, one arising from "human disorders," the other from "divine release from customary standards" (265a). Moreover, the initiatory language at *Phaedrus* 250b–c echoes Diotima's characterization of the philosophical activity of the erotic lover of beauty as related by Socrates to Phaedrus and others at *Symposium* 210a. Later in this same work Alcibiades says that people upon hearing Socrates' *logoi* are driven outside of themselves and are possessed (215d), and in this same context he refers to the "madness and Dionysian frenzy of philosophy."[84]

Finally, in the *Timaeus* there is a curious section on the liver as an organ given to humans by the gods and employed by the soul to practice divination (*manteia*). The gods made the liver the seat of an internal oracle, and the sleek and shiny surface of this organ gleams with apparitions and images, reflections as in a mirror of the impressions made by "the power of the thoughts borne down (on the liver) from the intellect."[85] These images, in other words, are communications from the higher, divine soul encased in the head;[86] and when the mortal soul housed in the region below the midriff gazes on the reflective surface of the liver when a man is asleep, the images it encounters amount to oracular visions. When out of his mind and altered this way through sleep, sickness, or divine inspiration, a man by consulting this oracle might "in some way lay hold of truth,"[87] even in that part of his soul that has no share of reason. But the visions and voices he receives when mad (*manentos*, 72a3) appear in the form of riddles that must be interpreted by a prophet in possession of his senses—presumably either the frenzied man himself upon coming to, or some other sensible prophetic man. This divine gift of physiological-spiritual oracular power has been granted to mortals that our sorry condition may be ameliorated as much as possible (71a–72b).

Timaeus's description of the liver-oracle reads like a microcosmic version of Apollo's oracle at Delphi;[88] it is another source of contact with "inspired and true divination" (71e4). And thinking of Apollo, oracles, and dreams, one is reminded of Socrates in the *Phaedo* struggling to understand the meaning of a dream's command that he practice music (*mousikê*), and one wonders who was the prophet-interpreter of the riddle in this case, Socrates himself or Plato.

Near the beginning of the *Phaedo* Socrates tells his visiting friends of a recurring dream that urges him to "compose and practice" *mousikê*, which is to say to engage in those activities overseen by the Muses (60e). At first, he says, he assumed the dream was encouraging him to continue his usual practice of philosophy, for philosophy itself is the "greatest music" (61a). But just in case he had misunderstood, he began in prison to compose poems. He produced a hymn to Apollo and then set to verse some familiar tales of Aesop (60d–61b). While discussing these matters Socrates comments on the differences between philosophy and poetry. The practices are not identical because the philosopher produces *logoi* whereas the poet produces *muthoi*; and as a philosopher himself, he says, he is not a teller of *muthoi* (*muthologikos*, 61b5). Yet almost immediately following this remark he insists that it is appropriate for him, as a man soon to die, to produce *muthoi* about the journey to Hades (*muthologein*, 61e2). Later he introduces his arguments for the immortality of the soul *not* with a verb that means, say, "to prove," but with *diamuthologômen*, which means "to relate by way of *muthoi*" (70b6). And near the conclusion of the dialogue he refers to his previous remarks as a *muthos* (114d8).[89]

In the *Phaedrus* Socrates describes a hierarchical scheme of reincarnation based on the amount of truth a soul has seen in its disembodied state. Poets are ranked sixth out of nine, the ninth place being the lowest (occupied by tyrants). At the summit of the hierarchy is the philosopher, who would appear from this ranking alone to be other than, and superior to, the poet. But the poet in sixth place is described as being "concerned with imitation" (*mimêsis*, 248e), so the inferiority of poets may have less to do with poetry than with mimesis. The philosopher as described in this section shares features in common with the poet, for besides being a lover of wisdom he is called a "lover of beauty" and "musical and erotic" (*philokalou … mousikou … kai erôtikou*, 248d3–4). The mention of beauty and eros brings to mind the *Symposium*, and the "musical" we have just encountered in the *Phaedo*; but the language in general is also related to the poetic practice of composing *muthoi*. So in the *Phaedrus*, as in the *Phaedo*, Socrates associates his activities with poetry. The first speech he delivers in the *Phaedrus* he refers to as a *muthologia* (243a4); and his second speech (in which the hierarchical account of reincarnation appears) he terms a "palinode"—the word means literally a "second-" or a "to the contrary-" song, and he borrows it from a poem by Stesichorus, who was *mousikos* (243a–b). So it seems that according to Plato there are genuine commonalities between philosophical and poetic activity, which at least suggests that there may be a form of poetry that is not essentially, and merely, mimetic. And in fact, at the end of the *Phaedrus* Socrates suggests that there may be a type of poetry based on knowledge of the truth whose author may properly be called a philosopher (278b–d). The implication is that no previous poet has managed to produce such a work of philosophical poetry, but it also seems to be implied that the *Phaedrus* itself is such a work. The description of the man who ought to be called a philosopher (278c–d) is, I believe, transparently meant to apply to Plato as the author of the *Phaedrus*. For one of the marks of such a man is the ability to demonstrate that his writings are ultimately trivial, which is precisely what Plato has done from 274c to 278b.[90]

All this is to say that Plato often associates the arational and the explicitly irrational with the proper practice of philosophy.[91] This is noteworthy in itself, but it also suggests that we should not mistake the assertion that poets are mad for a simple denunciation of their moral or epistemological standing. Throughout the second half of this chapter we have surveyed examples of Plato's philosophical poetry; we have seen him through his characters refer to his own works as poems—not only indirectly (as in the account of mimesis in the *Republic*), but quite explicitly as well (in the *Laws*). To judge according to the standards that he laid down in the *Phaedrus*, then, Plato was philosophical and musical simultaneously. He was, I believe, and as I suggested earlier, Nietzsche's "artistic Socrates."

Walter Kaufmann writes that Nietzsche's depiction of the "Socrates who practices music" (*BT* 15) is "an idealized self-portrait,"[92] and he may well be correct: Nietzsche wrote about art, artistry, and artists throughout his career, and his own creative gifts are evident not only in his writing but in his ideas as well. His *Thus Spoke Zarathustra* is a prose poem, and he seems at times to have conceived of the work as the product of a rapturous inspiration, and of himself in relation to it as an ecstatic poet in the tradition of the ancients (*EH* "Z" 3–4). He included verses in some of his philosophical works (in *The Gay Science*, for example, and *Beyond Good and Evil*); in 1882 he published a collection of poems as the *Idylls from Messina* in a journal owned by his publisher; and he prepared his *Dithyrambs of Dionysus* for publication just prior to his final collapse in 1889. He even composed music for the piano. But we must not overlook Plato's own devotion to *mousikê*. His works alone demonstrate his artistic enthusiasm to my satisfaction, but there are other indications as well: reports that he wrote poetry go back at least as far as to Aristotle's student Dicaearchus, and several epigrams have come down to us under his name. The attribution is uncertain, but there may be some bedrock of historical fact in this vicinity. Diogenes Laertius in his life of Speusippus says that Plato erected a shrine to the Muses on the grounds of the Academy,[93] and I can easily imagine him raising this structure, grounding it on the broad foundation of his poeticism.

Despite their differences, then, Plato and Nietzsche are alike in being thinkers and artists simultaneously. I have already noted that I prefer not to call them "philosophers," for philosophy today is rarely regarded as a creative endeavor; the highest aspiration of many a contemporary philosopher seems for all the world to be to attain to the status of "scientific" (as opposed to, say, *wise*). Plato and Nietzsche respected science, at least occasionally and in some of their moods, but they never limited themselves to a single perspective; art was never far from their minds. This rare combination of intellect and artistry is perhaps their greatest distinction, and it makes of them something other than mere "philosophers."

2

Being

Metaphysics

There is no undisputed account of the origin and specific meaning of the word "metaphysics." It does not appear in Plato, who has no special term for the undertaking we refer to by this name. The standard story is that an ancient editor of the works of Aristotle grouped the writings that we refer to as the philosopher's *Metaphysics* after his *Physics* and, not knowing quite what to title a collection of treatises addressing such a multiplicity of unusual topics, he labeled it simply *The Matters Following* (*Ta Meta*) *the Physical Matters* (*Ta Phusika*), hence, in short, *Ta Metaphusika*. According to this account, then, the *Metaphysics* takes its name from the philosophically irrelevant fact that it happened to sit on the shelf, as it were, next to a volume entitled *Physics*. Others have suggested the title communicates a substantive doctrinal meaning understood by Aristotle's students and later followers, the idea being that metaphysical considerations must come after (*meta*) the study of the physical world (*phusika*) because this study generates problems unanswerable by its own resources and therefore leads one to postulate the existence of non-physical principles. Some have gone further and argued that the Greek preposition "*meta*" is used in this instance to suggest an idea of transcendence, in which case *Ta Meta Ta Phusika* would indicate the study of those principles or beings that transcend mere physical, material reality. Whether or not Aristotle himself would have understood or intended the preposition this way, this interpretation does capture at least some part of the content of the writings in question, and it corresponds as well with contemporary philosophical usage.

The term "metaphysics" may be used broadly to indicate the study of the nature of reality in general, on which reading the word is compatible with any account of the world whatever, from a robust essentialism to a bare physicalism, and every position in between. Construing the word this way, we may say that even a notorious anti-Platonist like Nietzsche has a metaphysics. However, the word is commonly used to refer specifically to transcendent, non-physical (or "supra–physical") reality. It is this latter sense that we usually have in mind when speaking of Plato's metaphysics, and it is precisely to Plato's musings on transcendent reality that Nietzsche particularly objected.

Essence and existence

Plato almost always couches his account of reality—his "metaphysics" in the broad sense of the word—in terms of Being and Becoming. Being refers to the "metaphysical" in the strict, transcendent sense, to that which "always is but never comes to be" (*Ti.* 27d) and which, moreover, is invisible, unchanging, non-composite, and indissoluble (*Phd.* 78c–80b)—think here of God or the human soul traditionally conceived. Becoming, on the other hand, refers to physical reality, to that which "comes to be and passes away but never really is" (*Ti.* 28a) and which, moreover, is visible, constantly changing, composite, and dissoluble (*Phd.* 78c–80b)—think here of material substances like a human body or a tree. Nietzsche employs these same terms when writing about Plato (*Sein* and *Werden*), and it will be convenient if we do so as well, taking Being and Becoming as shorthand for the Metaphysical and the Physical respectively, and also for their correlative properties as listed above (and to be further developed below). It is important to note that with respect to these terms Nietzsche's usage is for the most part identical to Plato's; the disagreement is rather that Nietzsche denies that the term "Being" has any actual referent.

But before considering Nietzsche's critical analysis of Platonic metaphysics, we should explore further Plato's notion of Being, and anterior even to this I must obviate a misunderstanding that this word, Being, is likely to engender. The Greek I am translating as Being is τὸ ὄν, which we transliterate as *to on*. The *to* here is the definite article, and the *on* is the neuter singular participial form of the verb "to be." In cumbrous language, then, we could translate *to on* as "the is-ing thing," or in more felicitous language as "the existing thing." Acceptable as well would be "that which is" or "what-is." Now since "what-is," obviously, exists, or *be-s*, we can say that it is existing, that it is *be-ing*, and from this we generate the noun "Being." This is all very strange, no doubt, but the point is to bring out the closeness of Plato's term Being to the notion of existence, for the semantic proximity of these terms is the source of the potential misunderstanding at issue.

Philosophers today are accustomed to distinguish a thing's essence from its existence, the former designating *what* a thing is, the latter *that* it is. Now given the stress that Plato's formulation *to on* places on the "is," we may be inclined to take his Being to be identical with existence and to conclude, therefore, that it must be distinct from essence. But this would put the relationship precisely backwards, for with his term Being Plato consistently refers, *not* to the bare fact or phenomenon of a thing's existence, but rather to its existing *as* something or *in* some particular manner. It is perhaps the majority opinion that neither Plato nor any other ancient thinker possessed a clear and well-developed conception of Being as existence. Of course even the average non-philosophical Greek knew the difference between, say, Socrates existing (Socrates alive) and Socrates not existing (Socrates not yet born or Socrates dead),[1] but the idea is that not even the philosophers had attained to an abstract notion of existence in and of itself—of existence, that is, as an activity distinct from the existing thing.[2]

It is all well and good to insist that we not read Plato's Being existentially, but we have seen that in the *Timaeus* Plato says of Being that it "always is," and this certainly appears to be an existential use of the verb "to be." But it may be that when Plato writes that "something is" he always has in mind that "something is *x*," which is to say that his apparent existential uses of "is" are shorthand expressions for the "is" appropriate to the designation of essence, which is known as the predicative "is." To be clear: to use "is" existentially is to state simply that something exists; to use "is" predicatively is to attribute to a thing some property, to state that something is green or tall or a tree—and the scholarly consensus is that in conceptualizing Being Plato did not employ the existential "is."[3] But despite their consensus we may wonder whether the scholars are correct, and to think through this question it may help to introduce the predecessor to whom Plato was most indebted for his notion of *to on*.

The first western philosopher to write about that which we have referred to as Being was Parmenides, a Greek from Elea in southern Italy, who lived sometime between 540 and 440 BCE. Parmenides composed an enigmatic poem in which he relates the details of his visit to a goddess who spoke to him the truth of the nature of reality. Parmenides—or the goddess—is coy when it comes to announcing the precise subject under consideration, for the relevant section of the poem begins with reference to an "it" that has no clear antecedent. There are, however, occurrences in the poem of the noun *to eon* (*eon* is an earlier form of Plato's *on*), and this is the best candidate for the poem's primary subject. Regarding this *to eon* we learn first and foremost that it is and cannot not be. We learn as well that it neither comes to be nor perishes, that it is nontemporal, that it is uniform and undivided, motionless and unchanging. Near the end of this section of the poem *to eon* is said to be spherical, and some ancients (Aristotle for one) inferred from this and other indications that it is physical, and that Parmenides, therefore, was a materialist.[4] If he was, then this would be surprising in itself (for it is at least not obvious that something physical could be, for example, nontemporal and unchanging), but it would also be inconsistent with Plato. Nothing requires that these two philosophers be consistent on this point; Plato could well have developed ("improved," he might have said[5]) Parmenides' account. But the contemporary consensus is that "spherical" is best taken as an image of the wholeness and uniformity of *to eon*. Be that as it may, Parmenides' catalogue of properties seems to describe a necessarily existing unalterable unity—a great cosmic One. But we should not take this One for a supreme divinity above and apart from the cosmos. Parmenides is suggesting that whatever there is—*everything* there is—is one. He is, in short, denying plurality: he is a monist. We experience reality as composed of a multiplicity of changing, contingent, ephemeral, particular individuals; but according to Parmenides, this is an illusion. There is only the One. This, anyway, is how Parmenides has typically been understood in the tradition, and by Platonic philosophers in particular.

For a literal translation of Parmenides' *to eon*, then, we may employ the expression "what-is," and we should take Parmenides to be more interested in demonstrating the essential properties of what-is (indivisible unity in particular) than in concentrating on the fact of its existence. That something exists is uncontroversial; it is rather the predicates that Parmenides applies to what-is that are original and disconcerting. So even though it is common to translate Parmenides' *to eon* as Being, the subject of his poem is not the existence of any entity abstracted from the entity itself, which would be Being in the strictest sense, Being as existence; the object of his inquiry is rather everything that exists, and his goal is to reconceptualize what-is as a single unified entity. For our purposes, then, we need not solve without remainder the problem whether Parmenides could have conceived of the existential "is," for it is evident that in his poem he is interested primarily in communicating a truth for which the predicative "is" is best suited.[6]

These same considerations we may apply to Plato, for although he writes in many places of "what is," of "what completely is," or of "what absolutely is" (see, for example, *R*. 477a–478d), which certainly appear to be existential uses of "to be," there are textually grounded reasons to believe that these expressions are his way of attributing to *to on* a specific property, namely, its always being the same as itself in every respect (*aei kata tauta hôsautôs onta*, *R*. 479e6–7), and this is a predicative use of the verb. The textual evidence is clearest in Plato's account of Becoming, which word we recall is his preferred designation for physical reality, this reality comprising what are often referred to as "the many particulars" (individual physical objects). Of these particulars Plato says that they both are and are not, which expression appears on the surface to employ an existential use of "to be." But there is no reason whatever to believe that in writing this way Plato means to imply that a tree, say, both exists and does not exist, or that it is forever blinking out of and back into existence. He is rather adverting to the fact that a beautiful object is both beautiful to one person and ugly to another, or beautiful at one time but ugly at another; or, similarly, that a collection of six stones is both a double of a collection of three stones and a half of a collection of twelve; or, again, that an apple is heavy compared to an ant but light compared to a man (*R*. 479a–d). In these instances, then, the object both is and is not beautiful, the collection of stones both is and is not a double, the apple both is and is not heavy; and these are all evidently predicative rather than existential uses of "to be."[7]

Here we may deal with Plato as we dealt with Parmenides: we need not adopt a specific opinion with respect to whether he could have conceived of the existential "is." For our purposes it is enough to show that in developing his metaphysics he was more interested in distinguishing that which is always the same as itself from that which both is and is not self-identical. The former sort of thing is an essence, the latter a physical particular. The essence of beauty, or of double or heavy, always is what it is, whereas any particular beautiful, double, or heavy thing is also ugly, half, or light. This is a notable difference between things (or types of thing), but it is not a difference between what does and what does not exist. The essence of beauty and the beautiful object both exist; the difference is in *how* they exist. Essences exist unchangingly; particular physical objects exist in a constant state of change. Readers of Plato should not, therefore, be misled by the existential connotations of our word "Being," which they should take to signify essence rather than existence.[8]

Having said this, however, I would like to note one instance in the dialogues of Plato's perhaps intending to stress the phenomenon of existence. Near the end of Book 6 of the *Republic*, in the course of his famous discussion of the Good (505a–509b), Socrates compares the Good to the sun, and at 509b he says that as the sun provides for visible things their generation, growth, and nourishment, so the Good provides for knowable things their *einai* and *ousia*. The latter word, *ousia*, is, like *on*, derived from the verb "to be," and may here be translated as "essence." But this word we can set to one side, for I would like now to attend to the former word, *einai*, which is itself the infinitive verb "to be." Since here in the text this verb is coupled with a definite article (*to einai*), we may translate it literally but clumsily as "the to be." But this translation will not do, and the noun-form "being" would be both more accurate and more elegant. In this instance, however, "being" is not an alternative translation of our by-now-familiar term *to on* (Being as "what-is"), for in this context *ta onta* (the plural of *to on*) have been identified with knowable things (476d–477a), and the "being" now under consideration designates, not *ta onta* themselves, but rather *a property provided to them* by the Good. In sum, then, what-is (*to on*) is knowable (*gnôston*)—more, only what-is, as defined above as that which is always the same as itself in every respect, is knowable[9]—and to this object of knowledge the Good supplies the property of being (*to einai*). Now since Socrates has introduced this property of being by comparing it to the generation, growth, and nourishment of living visible things, it seems reasonable to infer that *to einai* here is being as that power which causes what is to exist—it is, in short, being as existence.

That this inference is reasonable I would insist, but unfortunately we have no way of knowing whether it is correct. We cannot read Plato's mind. And even if by this *to einai* Plato intended to designate existence, this would be only a first step toward a fully developed abstracted notion of being as existence, a notion corresponding to Subsistent Being, which notion Aquinas developed from his reflections on the Latin infinitive *esse* (to be) and which he identified with the Christian God.[10]

Forms

In general, then, the term Being, when employed with reference to either Plato or Nietzsche, designates the metaphysical; with reference to Plato in particular it designates more specifically *to on*, or "what-is." And now that the distinction between Being as what-is and Being as existence has been clarified, we may proceed to consider what Plato thinks this "what-is" is. We have seen that Being (as what-is) is always the same as itself in every respect, ungenerated, unchanging, and indestructible. But since nothing of this sort forms any part of our daily experience, it may help if I state outright from the beginning just what we are dealing with and then back up to provide the relevant context and explain the motivating assumptions. I wrote above that if we take Plato's Being for existence rather than for essence, we will put the matter the wrong way round, and this is so because Being (*to on*, what-is) just is Plato's expression for essence—or anyway for essence conceived according to a particular metaphysical understanding of the term.

The essence of a thing, without putting too fine a point on it, is the collection of properties that make the thing what it is as opposed to something else. A human is a human and not a tree; a square is a square and not a triangle; a mineral is a mineral and not a drop of water—and all this is so because man, tree, square, triangle, mineral, and water possess different properties. A human is characterized by (among others) the property *animality*, but a tree is not; a square is characterized by (among others) the property *four-sided*, but a triangle is not; a mineral is characterized by (among others) the property *solidity*, but water is not. So the complete collection of properties that characterizes a thing as *this* rather than *that* is its essence. There is an abstruse question as to what sorts of things have essences—most of those who believe in essences would agree that there are essences of natural kinds of things, for example the six items mentioned above; but there is less agreement whether there are essences of, say, a clump of dirt or this individual man—but we need not concern ourselves with this question, for the dispute between Plato and Nietzsche regarding essences does not concern their precise distribution but rather their very existence.[11] Nietzsche quite simply did not believe in essences, at least not as the metaphysical entities that Plato imagined them to be.

The unusual thing about essences as conceived by Plato is that they are independent entities existing apart from the things whose essences they are. They are not merely verbal descriptions of certain significant facts about things, nor are they conceptions of the human mind. Platonic essences are rather substances in and of themselves, but substances of a sort quite different from the physical objects with which we are familiar. Platonic essences do not exist in either space or time, and being unconstrained by spatial-temporal limitations they operate in many places and times at once. The essence *man* (one and the same essence) relates in some way to me here and now precisely as it related to Socrates there and then. This is part of what we mean by designating a Platonic essence *metaphysical*.

I say that the essence *man* "relates" to me and to Socrates both, and the standard expression for this relationship is "participation"—Socrates and I "participate" in the form *man*. Yet Plato never clarifies the precise nature of this relationship, and in the *Phaedo* (believed by many to be the dialogue in which he first introduces these ideas) Socrates declines to affirm any specific account of participation (100d). This is a problem, to be sure; but I will now present what I hope is at least a workable (if not exhaustive) description of what Plato had in mind. Consider the following image:

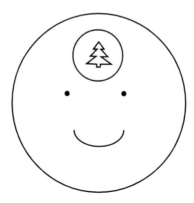

This is an image of God, God's mind, and the mental image God has in his mind whenever he creates a tree (any type of tree that either has existed, does exist, or will exist). I realize that no one reading this book actually believes in anything like this picture or the following narrative, but this is not the point. My intention is only to call to mind a certain set of ideas that may facilitate understanding.[12]

Imagine, then, that God has decided to create trees with which to adorn our planet. He must have an idea of the object he intends to create; and since he will create a variety of different species of tree, his idea must be sufficiently general to apply to each of these species. His idea serves as the paradigm or blueprint according to which he will model his trees, so if his idea of a tree were an idea specifically of an oak tree, then he would create only oak trees. Similarly, his idea should be of a tree of no definite age, size, number of leaves, location, or date (to list only a few of the properties that must remain indeterminate), for if his idea specified these facts, then he would create nothing but trees that are, say, 30 years old, 20 feet tall, with 2,000 leaves, in New York City's Central Park in the year 1916. If I ask you to form in your mind an abstract representation of *tree*, not any particular tree but rather the idea of *tree* in general, it may be that in your mind you will "see" a particular dogwood of a certain height with a determinate hue to its leaves, and this is perhaps inevitable given the way the human mind operates. As a result of this phenomenon, in thinking of your general idea you will have to ignore a number of properties represented by your image (its height and age, for example)—you will have to look beyond them, as it were, and concentrate on only those properties that make your idea the idea of a tree rather than of a dogwood. But God is capable of greater feats than any mere mortal can perform, and so even though in the image I have drawn above God has in mind what appears to be the idea of a pine tree, we can agree that in reality the image in his mind is a purely general idea—a representation of nothing more determinate than those properties that characterize a tree as a tree (of no particular variety) and nothing besides.

Now let's imagine the sequence of actions by which our deity actually creates a tree, concentrating in this paragraph on his ideas and in the next on his application of these ideas to matter. In the first stage of his creative act, then, God imposes on his raw materials the general properties of his idea of *tree* (one of these properties specifying even the nature of his material, for a tree cannot be made from paper or iron), at which point he generates a general, species-less tree. In the second stage he introduces the specific properties that make this tree an oak, and to do so he employs as a paradigm another general idea—general because it represents those properties that make any and every oak tree an oak tree rather than a sycamore, a birch, or any other species of tree—but this second idea is a degree less general than the first, for it is specified by those properties that transform a general, species-less tree into a tree of this rather than that species (an oak rather than a sycamore). At the conclusion of this stage there appears before God not only a tree, but an oak tree. But the oak tree is still no particular oak tree, for it possesses only those properties that make it a tree and an oak, but none of those that would make it *this* individual oak (no particular height, coloring, location in space or time, etc.). To individuate the oak tree God must add to it these latter sorts of properties, which he does in the third stage of his creative act, thereby producing an actual individual oak tree, *this* one as opposed to *that* one, this tall, flourishing thirteenth-century oak in a meadow north of London as opposed to that stunted twentieth-century oak with brownish leaves beside an interstate near Baltimore. During this final stage of creation God has in mind an idea of what he is doing as he produces this individual tree, but his idea is not general, for it applies to one tree and one tree only.

Now let's inspect more closely God's manipulation of matter, picking up the process at a very early stage. Imagine the deity hovering over an undifferentiated sea of matter (left over, let's say, from his creation of the earth). This is Prime Matter in Aristotelian terms, which is to say the pure potentiality of thinghood not yet become any particular type of thing, not even any particular type of matter. With the thumb and forefinger of his right hand, then, God pinches off a portion of this Prime Matter and sets it in the palm of his left hand. Then he rolls it around between his hands to form it into a ball. Next he molds and shapes this ball until it takes on the characteristic form of wood, at which point he pinches off another bit of Prime Matter and casts it into the form of leaf. (Yes, to keep it simple we are imagining the tree as composed solely of wood and leaves.) In creating these two types of matter God is guided by his ideas of *wood* and *leaf*, which are ideas in precisely the same sense as the idea of *tree* with which we are by now familiar. Having created his raw materials, God makes of them a wood-leaf compound and then, calling to mind his idea of *tree*, he rolls this compound round and around, squeezes it here and smooths it off there until, at last, he shapes it into a tree (as opposed to some other wood-leaf compound like a bush). A touch more manipulation and he forms his tree into an oak. Then, finally, he reaches forth from his abode on high, penetrating with a divine arm our transient realm of space and time, and plants this tree somewhere and somewhen on the earth, at which moment his oak tree becomes an individual oak tree, the very sort of oak tree we encounter in our daily lives. The process that began with a metaphysical idea in the mind of God has culminated in a physical object before our eyes.

This account of God's creation is wildly fantastical, I know. But through it we have encountered a number of relevant facts, which I would like now to review. First, God's idea of *tree* is a general idea, general in the sense that it covers anything and everything that is a tree (it is, as we say, a One over Many). But it is not so general that it covers everything that exists; it is specified sufficiently to cover all trees and nothing that is not a tree. His idea, in short, is the idea of that collection of properties necessary and sufficient to determine a thing as a tree (and only a tree). Second, God's idea is eternal, for since it represents any and every tree, he need not reimagine the idea for each new tree he creates, which is to say that his idea of *tree* abides; and since his idea applies to every possible as well as to every actual tree, and since, moreover, for God the creation of trees is eternally possible, his idea of *tree* abides eternally. Third, God's idea of *tree* is immutable, for if it were to change, then two or more completely different kinds of things would be trees, or those physical objects that once were trees would no longer be so but instead something utterly different would be a tree. Fourth, God's idea of *tree* is perfect, is perfectly a tree, and every individual tree is an imperfect copy or image of this divine paradigm. Fifth and finally, to bring out facts that may well be implicit in all that has so far been said, God's idea (like God himself) transcends both space and time.

God's idea of *tree*, then, is a general, unified, eternal, unchanging, perfect, nontemporal, nonspatial entity—which is to say, a metaphysical entity—that serves as a paradigm for any and every individual tree. And this account holds generally, for *all* of the ideas in the divine mind that serve as paradigms for natural kinds of things are characterized by these properties of unity, eternality, perfection, and so on.

Recall that I introduced the topic of God's ideas in order to explain (or to begin to explain) the Platonic notion of essence. What I have been calling an idea of God is very much like a Platonic essence, though Platonic essences are not usually taken to exist in the mind of a deity.[13] At this point, then, we may introduce the standard term by which we refer to Platonic essences. At the beginning of this chapter I explained that the term Being refers to "what-is," which translates the Greek *to on*, which is one expression Plato employs for essence (*ousia* is another)—and now I can add that the technical term we employ for the metaphysical entity that is the bearer of essence is Form (*eidos*, *idea*, or *morphê* in the Greek). So the story we have been telling about God and his ideas is one way to introduce and to take the first few steps toward the clarification of Form.

I have acknowledged that no one reading this book believes the creation account just provided, but many early Christians accepted a version of God's activity at least similar to it, particularly those influenced by the later Platonic tradition. The tradition I have in mind here has come to be known as Neoplatonism, which is the label modern scholars have appended to the version of Platonism developed and disseminated by Plotinus, a philosopher born in Egypt in 205 CE who, after years of study in Alexandria, moved to Rome where he taught and wrote until his death in 270.[14] Plotinus's student Porphyry gathered his master's works into six groups of nine treatises, which arrangement has given the collection its name, the *Enneads* (*ennea* being the Greek word for the number *nine*). Plotinus wrote (or so he would have said) as a faithful follower of Plato, neither altering nor adding to his great predecessor's philosophy in any significant way, but rather only making explicit and elaborating on ideas that appear implicitly in the dialogues. The aspect of Plotinus's philosophy that interests us here is his treatment of the Forms. We have seen the philosophically inclined early Christian account according to which the Forms are ideas in the mind of God; we may now transition from this to the earlier Neoplatonic account by erasing the figure of God from the image with which we have been operating, leaving only a Mind and its Forms:

This Mind in which according to Plotinus the Forms reside is not quite the mind *of* any being, human or divine, not anyway in the sense in which we normally understand the relationship between a being and its mind. Mind in Plotinus's system is one of three fundamental ontological principles, collectively known as the three hypostases (a hypostasis being quite literally that which "stands under" something as a support—hence the word "substance" in Latin—or, in this case, a metaphysical ground of reality). Mind is the second of these hypostases and is dependent on the first, known as the One, and on Mind the third hypostasis, the World Soul, depends.[15] Despite the drawing above, it would be a mistake to insist on too sharp a distinction between Mind and its Forms, for Mind is exclusively a thinking thing and the Forms are its thoughts which are themselves intellectually active. Nor are these thoughts in any way separate from Mind (though they are distinct), for if they were external to or independent of Mind, then Mind could grasp them only indirectly by way of a representation, in which case it would not fully know them. We may therefore picture the Mind-Form complex as a buzzing hive of rational activity in which not only the hive as a whole but each of its cells thinks unceasingly of the whole and of every part of the whole simultaneously. Plotinus identifies Mind and its Forms so closely that he is often as comfortable referring to this hypostasis as *to on* (Being, as in Form) as he is referring to it as *nous* (Mind).[16]

Forms in Plotinus's system have the same properties as those in the Christianized Platonism we examined earlier (generality, eternality, perfection, etc.), but they are not bestowed on particulars through the activity of any intentional, personal deity. Rather, Plotinus's account of what Plato names "participation" involves the third hypostasis, the World Soul, contemplating the second, Mind, and imprinting an image of the Form resident in Mind on the particular through the activity of its *logos*.[17]

I mentioned above that Plotinus is explicit about much that in Plato is implicit, and I suspect it is now apparent that this makes Plotinus's work in many places exceedingly complex. Fortunately, for our purposes we need not grasp every nuance of Plotinus's metaphysics, for our aim is not to understand Neoplatonism in itself, but rather to employ later developments of Platonism as means to understanding Plato's metaphysics of Form. The first problem one encounters when presented with Plato's theory of Forms involves nothing having to do with comprehending the details of their causal activity (which is a problem, but a later one), but rather quite simply trying to "picture" the objects Plato has in mind. But it is easy to conjure up an image of general ideas in the mind of God and to move toward Plato by first removing from our image the figure of God (as we have just done to introduce Neoplatonism) and by then removing even the Neoplatonic Mind, as we shall now do to introduce Platonism.

Here, then, we have a representation of the Platonic Form of *tree*. It is something like an idea in the mind of God as explained above—for it is the general, perfect, eternal, and immutable paradigm that plays a causal role in any tree's being a tree by embodying the essential properties of a tree—but it is not the thought of any deity, nor does it exist in a mind or Mind. Where does it exist? It is common to reply that it exists in a "Realm of Forms," but this expression is meant as an elementary image to facilitate understanding, precisely as my image of Forms as ideas in the mind of God.

In truth, Platonic Forms do not exist anywhere—not because they do not exist, but rather because they are nonspatial entities and so are not the kind of thing that might exist here rather than there; nor do they exist now rather than then (or vice versa), for they are nontemporal. All this is to say that Platonic Forms are metaphysical; they are the beings (*ta onta*) Plato has in mind when contrasting Being (*to on*) with Becoming (*genesis*), this latter term designating all that is physical.

It may be useful here to recall Parmenides, for, as I noted above, his understanding of *to eon* ("what-is") influenced Plato's own account of *to on* (Being).[18] Parmenides argues that "what-is" is one, by which he means that one and one thing only exists. This One Parmenides describes as eternal, indivisible, and immutable, which properties we have seen are shared by Plato's Forms, for each Form (the Form of *tree* or *human* or *equality*) is itself an eternal, indivisible, immutable unity. No Form is a unity in precisely the same sense as Parmenides' One, for if it were it would be the one and only existent reality. But each Form is a One with respect to the Many particular individuals of which it is the Form—the Form of *tree*, for example, is the singular and self-identical metaphysical essence that somehow causes the plurality of individual physical trees to possess those properties through which they exist *as* trees. I have explained that Plato never quite specifies the nature of the causal agency involved (whereby the particular "participates" in the Form), and I think all scholars would agree that at least it is not clear that he does. It is true that in his *Timaeus* he provides an account of something like a craftsman god,[19] which he calls *ho dêmiourgos*—the Demiurge—that enforms matter in accordance with the metaphysical essences to which he looks as paradigms (29d–34b); and it is also true that this account inspired the Neoplatonic and Christian accounts that we have examined (the activity of the World Soul's *logos* and the activity of God, respectively). But there is, and has been since antiquity, widespread disagreement concerning whether Plato intended his account literally. Xenocrates, the third head of the Academy, argued that Plato depicted the Demiurge in the act of constructing the cosmos moment by moment and piece by piece as a convenient way to illustrate the eternally composed metaphysical principles that ground physical reality. Aristotle, on the other hand, writes in his *Physics* as if he takes Plato's account of creation in time literally.[20] Fortunately, we need not adjudicate this dispute, for all parties agree at least to the basics as we have presented them, namely, that Plato taught the existence of Forms as perfect and eternal metaphysical entities that are more real than, more valuable than, and somehow responsible for the nature of the imperfect and ephemeral physical particulars.

The Forms are also objects of knowledge—they are, moreover, the *only* objects of knowledge, for the many physical particulars are objects of mere belief.[21] This is so because to Plato's mind (and this position was common—though by no means universal—among ancient philosophers) only that which is stable is knowable, but physical objects are notoriously unstable, always coming into and passing out of existence, always changing. One can know the Form of *double* because it always is what it is and is never anything else, whereas any particular double will simultaneously be also a half. The Form of *tree* is eternally the Form of *tree*, but every particular tree at some time does not exist, and even when it does exist it is constantly changing.[22] Physical objects may be perceived or believed in, but never known. If there is any sense in saying that the physical world is at all intelligible, it is so only to the extent that it participates in the metaphysical—its intelligibility is derived, dependent, and indirect, for the physical world is not intelligible in and of itself, but only insofar as it is an image of the intelligible Form.

Please note well the radical nature of this claim. It is precisely the reverse of our way of thinking. We are sure that we have knowledge of objects like trees and tables, even planets and atoms, whereas with respect to the metaphysical we imagine we must believe or "have faith." It is common even among the religious to insist that we cannot know God or the fact of God's existence, their standard reason being that knowledge in this instance would leave us no room to exercise the virtue of faith. But these same people generally also accept the modern view that such knowledge is impossible because claims regarding that which supposedly transcends the physical are insusceptible of either "evidence" or "proof," these terms being defined according to a naive but popular understanding of scientific method. For Plato, something about the nature of the objects themselves determines their knowability or otherwise; for us moderns, it is rather something about the nature of the objects as subject to investigation by our five senses, which we take to be a human's only paths to knowledge. We have, in short, accepted the inversion of Being and Becoming that began among the ancients (the atomists and some of the sophists in particular), gained widespread currency with the rise of modern empirical science, and reached its zenith in Nietzsche's philosophy. But prior to the modern era (the beginning of which we may date, roughly, to around AD 1500) metaphysical thinking was not uncommon, and many philosophers and theologians were sure that humans can attain to knowledge of metaphysical truth. The greatest source for the philosophical elaboration of this position was Plato.

Closely related to the idea that the Forms are objects of knowledge is an argument for the existence of Forms, which it may be helpful to introduce at this point.[23] Plato assumes that knowledge is possible, even that it is actual, that we do in fact have knowledge. We know, for example, that every point on the circumference of a circle is equidistant to the center. This is not a mere belief: this is a *truth*, and we *know* it to be true. Nor is this a truth about our use of words or our concept of a circle. Vocabulary and meaning evolve; concepts depend on the minds that think them; but the truths of circularity are fixed and eternal. In short, the truth that every point on the circumference of a circle is equidistant to the center is in no way contingent on the changeable phenomena of a particular culture's language games or human psychology. The object of our knowledge is external to the human mind and human social conventions; when we come to know it we enter into a cognitive relation to it, but in itself it exists independently of any and all human activities.

What, then, is the *object* of our knowledge of the nature of a circle? Circles, obviously. But *which* circles? This may seem an odd question, but consider the "circles" around you. The shape of a quarter, for example: is this a circle? Loosely speaking, it is. It is certainly more nearly a circle than it is a square or a triangle. But we are not now concerned with whether the shape of a quarter approximates a circle, but with whether it precisely meets the definition of a circle and so is a circle in fact. To determine this we must examine the quarter up close and judge whether every point on its surface is equidistant to the center. Quarters have reeded edges, incorporated into their design in the days when they were made of precious metals, to prevent people shaving their edges to collect the valuable filings. Because of this reeding, some points on the circumference of a quarter are further from the center than others. But if this is so, then the shape of a quarter is not a circle. It is approximately a circle, to be sure; but strictly speaking it is not a circle. Consider, then, the rim of your drinking glass or the cap of your fountain pen. Their edges are much smoother than those of a quarter. They are smooth to the naked eye, anyway. But remember: the definition of a circle has to do with the *points* on the circumference of a circle, and a point is not a segment on the circumference measuring a centimeter, millimeter, or one one-thousandth of a millimeter: a point is infinitesimally small. We know therefore that we can never actually locate a point to measure its distance from any other point, but we must come as close as we can in order to verify whether we have before us a circle (or at least to conclude that we cannot disconfirm the possibility). The fact that every segment measuring one one-thousandth of a millimeter along the perimeter of a shape under investigation is equidistant from the center does not suffice to determine the shape as a circle, for there may be inequalities of distance at the level of segments that measure one ten-thousandth of a millimeter or smaller. So imagine putting your glass or the cap of your pen under a powerful magnifying glass. Their rims are ridged and uneven, not so pronounced as the ridges along the circumference of a quarter, which is why one requires a magnifying glass to detect the fact; but the fact itself is sufficient to rule them out as circles. Imagine, then, a figure drawn with a fine tip marker and compass on a smooth, new dry-erase board. Well, again, one need only examine the line under a magnifying glass to detect irregularities, caused in this case by the compound micro-structure of the silicon polymer ink and the texture of the board itself. So let's imagine a shape inscribed by a computer-guided micro-fine laser on a surface composed of a specially designed, ultra-smooth material. This is more promising, but ultimately we must confront the same problem we encountered with the dry-erase board. If our laser and board are physical, material objects, then however smooth they may be, they are composed of molecules composed of atoms; and since molecules are compound structures and atoms have moving components, it cannot be the case that every point on the circumference of the line formed of them is equidistant to the center. Relative to the scale involved, the differences will be great. And the obstacle is not, for example, the state of contemporary laser technology. The problem is with matter itself, which is composed of compound moving parts that may, in some cases, even pass into and out of existence; certainly they can and do compose and decompose and so cause the higher-level structures constituted by them to pass into and out of being. A circle is a shape that perfectly conforms to, or instantiates, the definition of a circle, but the nature of matter prevents any material object from meeting this standard. Matter, in short, is the principle of imperfection.

All this is to say that there are no circles in nature. There are shapes that approximate circles, and these we encounter and work with every day. But never in our experience do we meet with a figure every point on the circumference of which is equidistant to the center. What, then, is the object of our knowledge of the definition of a circle? The definition is true, so it must be true *of* something. If this something is not a natural object, and *cannot* be a natural object given the facts of physical reality, then it must be a metaphysical object. This, anyway, is Plato's inference. The metaphysical circle, being nonspatial, is non-material. It is unburdened by the principle of imperfection and so may perfectly instantiate the definition of a circle. The reality that corresponds to the definition of a circle, then, the objective correlative of this definition and the object of our knowledge of the truths of circularity, is a metaphysical entity—it is the Circle itself or the Form of *circle*.

Most people have in mind some version of this account of the Forms when they think of Platonic metaphysics. Nietzsche was no different. He makes no attempt to deal at length or in any detail with Plato's metaphysical principles in their fullest development and complexity; he is generally content to sum it all up in the word "Being" and declare this a fiction. But there is in fact much more to Platonic metaphysics than the Forms. This much more, however, is all rather obscure and for the most part confined to the late dialogues. And since Nietzsche was not particularly interested in Plato's late ontology, I will here provide only a sketch of what we know, or think that we know.

In the late dialogues Plato modifies his account of dialectic to include the method of collection and division (which first appears in the middle-period *Phaedrus*, at 265c–266d). By employing this procedure the dialectician is able to identify kinds by gathering like things together into genera and then separating them out according to their specific differences. So, for example, the Stranger in the *Sophist* identifies the angler by gathering up human types into a larger collection of experts, which class he then divides according to types of expertise—expertise in production and expertise in acquisition. Identifying the angler as an expert in acquisition, he divides this class into acquisition through exchange and acquisition through taking. Identifying the angler as an expert in acquisition through taking, he continues with such divisions until he identifies the angler as an expert in taking by hunting living, swimming, underwater-dwelling animals by striking them from below with hooks (218e–221c). Later in this same work the Stranger employs this technique to identify the "greatest kinds" of Forms and to specify their interrelations.[24] That there are greatest kinds of Form—*unity, being, sameness, difference, motion, rest*, and perhaps others—and that Forms participate in one another, are other late developments, as is the idea (also in the *Sophist*) that we must admit change into the "realm" of Being since souls (which are classified as Being rather than Becoming) change whenever they come to know an unchanging Form.[25]

Then there is the matter of ontological principles whose relation to the Forms is unclear. In the *Philebus* Socrates introduces the unlimited, the limit, the mixture of these two, and the cause of this mixture (23c–27c). These principles are obscure in themselves, and they are introduced in the *Philebus* only incidentally (for the dialogue is concerned with ethics rather than ontology), so we do not quite understand either their nature or their function. There is also the problem that in the *Metaphysics* Aristotle provides an account of Plato's ontology that adds to our confusion. He identifies two principles, the-great-and-the-small and the One, and says that the-great-and-the-small participates in the One and thereby generates numbers, which are the causes of the substance of other things. He identifies this with the tradition of Pythagoreanism, but says that Plato was original in believing that the infinite is generated from the-great-and-the-small and that the numbers exist independently of sensible particulars.[26] He goes on, but it is clear from this much that we have waded into deep and murky waters. There is no consensus among scholars regarding any of these matters. Aristotle's account is particularly problematic, and his testimony has led some to attribute to Plato unwritten doctrines, metaphysical teachings presented in person to his students but never committed to writing for publication, on which Aristotle draws in his account.[27] Other scholars, arguing that Aristotle misunderstood Plato's ontology, see no reason to postulate the existence of unwritten doctrines to explain the discrepancy between Aristotle's account and what we find in the dialogues.[28] At least one scholar has attempted to resolve the problem by arguing that Aristotle's account corresponds (albeit with different terminology) to the ontology of the *Philebus*.[29]

Finally, in the *Timaeus* there is the Demiurge, a craftsman deity that fashions the universe from preexistent material;[30] there is also the World Soul[31] and, most obscurely, the so-called Receptacle (48e–53a), which seems to function somewhat like space,[32] for it is something like a field in which items somehow derived from or related to the Forms come to be and thereby generate (or just are) spatial-temporal particulars.[33]

Here, then, we have in barest outline some (but only some) aspects of Plato's mature metaphysics. We might wonder how seriously to take Nietzsche's criticisms of Being given that he neglects to do the hard work required to engage with Plato's ideas on their own advanced level of development. This is a serious worry. On the other hand, no matter the sophistication of Plato's metaphysical system, if it is false, it is false. A fiction such as Being (if it is a fiction) does not become fact simply through complexity of elaboration. So perhaps it would be unfair to expect Nietzsche to shoulder the burden of demonstrating, point by point, Plato's mistakes. In any case, fiction or not, Platonic metaphysics has influenced the western philosophical and theological tradi-tions to an extent impossible to overestimate. The account of the Forms I laid out above (beginning with the early Christian interpretation and moving back through the Neoplatonic to the original Platonic understanding) is based on more than mere pedagogical utility. In composing it I adhered to the actual facts, though I reversed the historical sequence. But run through the presentation according to an accurate chronology (and insert Parmenides at the beginning and Thomas Aquinas at the end) and you have a rough sketch of the development of western metaphysics from around the beginning of the fifth century BCE to the high Middle Ages and beyond.

God

There is one element missing from the sketch of western metaphysics presented above, namely, the divine. Plato's influence on pagan and Christian conceptions of deity was as pervasive as his influence on other aspects of the metaphysical tradition, but it is much more complicated given the ambiguity of his theology. And quite apart from this ambiguity is the problem of Plato's radically indirect style of writing, which ultimately makes it impossible to state with certainty his personal beliefs about anything at all, the divine included. Yet the dialogues are replete with references to God, gods, and metaphysical beings and principles that to this day affect our thinking about religion, spirituality, and mysticism. Considering the enormity of Plato's influence, and bearing in mind Nietzsche's quip that "Christianity is Platonism for 'the people'" (*BGE* "Preface"), a brief survey of Plato's references and allusions to the divine will help to fill out our account of his metaphysics.

Whatever Plato's personal theological beliefs, he seems to have considered a proper orientation toward the divine imperative for the social, political, and ethical well-being of an individual or a people. In the *Laws* he suggests that atheism is a sort of illness (*nosos*) whose symptoms include a corrupt soul inclined toward unjust deeds (888b), and in the *Republic* he has Adeimantus round off his and Glaucon's (hypothetical) argument in support of the unjust life with the trilemma that either gods do not exist, or they exist but pay no heed to human affairs, or they exist and attend to our activities but may be persuaded through sacrifices and vows to overlook the crimes of wicked men (365d–366a). If this is so, and if one is clever enough to escape detection or punishment by men, then there would seem to be no reason to resist the lure of injustice. The *Republic* is Plato's attempt to demonstrate that even if a man could escape the notice of gods and men, he should nonetheless choose the life of justice; but the great "Myth of Er" at the end of the book is meant to show that the unjust man cannot in fact avoid divine detection and punishment. Similar "myths" appear at the conclusion of the *Gorgias* (523a–527c) and near the end of the *Phaedo* (107c–115a). Though they differ in detail, all three "myths" agree in general that souls at death are judged by divine beings, and that virtuous souls are rewarded and the vicious punished. In the *Gorgias* Socrates even insists that his description of the afterlife is not a "myth" (*muthos*) but is in fact a rational account, a *logos* (523a1–3; cf. *Lg.* 872d–e).

Reincarnation appears in the dialogues as well, and the fate of souls is determined by the merit they displayed in their previous embodiments as judged either directly by, or in connection with the activities of, divine beings.[34] Reincarnation is assumed also in the *Laws*, though with the stress on punishment for wickedness rather than on reward for virtue (870d–e, 872e–873a); and in Book 10 of this work (885b and 888c–d) Plato returns to the trilemma mentioned above. The main speaker of the dialogue presents these three unorthodox theological beliefs as motivating factors in the actions of impious and lawless men (885b). The whole of Book 10 revolves around this problem and is in substance a series of proofs, first, of the existence of gods, second, of their concern for men, and finally, of their indifference to the promises and gifts offered them by unjust men. These proofs are meant to prevent wicked men (*hoi kakoi*) from supposing they have the freedom or license to do whatever they wish (907c–d). But the Athenian does more than merely argue his case in order to eliminate the baneful influence these beliefs might have on the citizens of a city. After presenting his proofs, he formulates and proposes a law against impiety (declaring his proofs to have been only the proem to his legislation), the relevant parts of which state that anyone found guilty of acting unjustly as a result of these unorthodox beliefs must be put to death, and those who foolishly publicize such beliefs must be confined to a sort of rehabilitation facility for no less than five years, later to be put to death if convicted again of similar activities (908a–909a).

Given the ethical and social-political use to which these arguments, "myths," and laws are put in the dialogues, one might doubt whether they are sincere expressions or indications of Plato's beliefs and regard them instead as "noble lies."[35] But the characters in the dialogues regularly refer to the gods, even in contexts having no immediate ethical or social-political implications. Socrates speaks at length of Apollo (e.g. *Ap.* 20e–22e), employs the oath "by Zeus," prays to Pan (*Phdr.* 279b–c), and accepts Diotima's characterization of Eros as a great divinity (*daimôn megas, Smp.* 202d13); the interlocutors in the *Laws* speak of the gods throughout, and the Athenian advocates festivals in honor of the traditional twelve Olympian deities (828a–c); Timaeus and Critias, in their eponymous dialogues, not only mention the gods but attribute important phenomena to their activities;[36] and the Eleatic Stranger refers to traditional tales of the gods' gifts to humans in the *Statesman* (274c–d).

But the gods are called into question in the dialogues too, and many of the traditional accounts of their powers and activities are challenged quite explicitly. In the *Euthyphro* Socrates admits to being reluctant to accept[37] the traditional tales that report the gods' many enmities and conflicts, and he even speculates that this explains his being charged with impiety; in the second and third books of the *Republic* he criticizes popular Greek mythology at length, condemning Homer's and Hesiod's depictions of the gods as immoral and irrational beings; and in the *Phaedrus*, although he claims to accept the traditional tales, his main point is not that he believes them but that he is too busy obeying Apollo's decree that he know himself to waste time pursuing naturalist explanations of mythical events (229b–230a).

But more interesting than any direct and explicit questioning of traditional Greek religion are the many indirect or implied reformations of the concept of divinity that appear throughout the dialogues, reformations that at least seem to suggest a conception of the divine as one and impersonal. Plato, like the poets and philosophers who preceded him, refers through his characters interchangeably to "gods" and to "god," "the god," or "the divine," moving effortlessly from plural to singular and back again, with no overt philosophical implications.[38] Yet he writes in the wake of Xenophanes, an itinerant philosopher-poet who proclaimed that "God is one" and unlike mortals in body and mind (DK B23),[39] and Heraclitus, who proclaimed in his typically obscure style that that which men call Zeus is one (DK B32); and of course he is well aware of Parmenides' account of what-is as ungenerated, unchanging, and one. Each of these men also either referred or alluded to multiple gods, so we cannot assume an established monotheistic tradition among the early Greek philosophers. Still, when Plato has the Athenian in the *Laws* declare that God is the measure of all things (716c4–5) it is hard to believe that he had a plurality of deities like the twelve Olympians in mind.[40] As for the Greeks' anthropomorphic conceptions of the divine, Socrates in his great second speech in the *Phaedrus* insists that we humans have fabricated the idea that god has a body (246c–d).

So although it is true that Plato nowhere explicitly states that a unified eternal metaphysical being, force, power, or principle is the uncaused source of physical reality, he seems in many places to suggest that he believes something generally along these lines. I have mentioned the Demiurge, the craftsman god that in the *Timaeus* constructs the world (or "the All," *to pan*) and even the elements of which it is composed, though he does not create them. I have also noted disagreements among the ancients as to whether Plato intended his audience to take these details literally. Among those who took the Demiurge for an actually existing and active metaphysical principle (if not a personal being), some considered it the ultimate *archê*, or principle of reality,[41] but eventually it was standard within the tradition to identify the Demiurge with the *second* metaphysical principle, that is, with the Neoplatonic Mind (*nous*) or the Christian *logos*. First rank was accorded to the Form of the Good, which in Book 6 of the *Republic* Socrates characterizes not only as the source of the truth, existence, and essence of the other Forms (508d–509a), but also, famously (at 509b), as beyond *ousia* (essence). From this characterization many later Platonists and Neoplatonists concluded that the Form of the Good enjoys a status quite distinct from and superior to all other Forms; and since this Good came to be identified with a Platonic One of some variety,[42] it appeared very much like a divine *archê*, like the God above God, the Godhead itself, the source of everything other than its own source-less self, beyond which nothing is so much as even conceivable.

I began this section by stating that we cannot know Plato's personal theological beliefs. We simply have no access to them. Having said this, however, I will admit that I find it hard to imagine that Plato believed in the traditional Olympian deities as such. Considering his corpus as a whole, I am inclined to attribute to him a belief in a single ultimate metaphysical *archê* that one might reasonably designate divine (*theia*), and I can imagine that at times he may have been tempted to conceive of the divine as possessing something like personhood, if only in the form of an intentional intellect, and as a being whose intentionality is more broadly dispersed than Aristotle's god as thought thinking itself.[43] Regarding the gods of traditional Greek polytheism, I can at most envision his taking them for useful and sometimes perhaps even more or less reliable personifications of, or symbols for, powers or forces pervading nature whose source is divine. I would not, however, care to specify his theological beliefs any further than this.

At this point it may be useful to sum up the chapter so far by saying that the western metaphysical tradition as influenced by Plato includes in its account of reality as a whole two fundamentally different kinds of thing (using the word "thing" in the broadest possible sense), the metaphysical and the physical. The Forms are metaphysical, whether conceived as separate substances or as ideas in either the Neoplatonic Mind (*nous*) or the mind of the Christian God. Metaphysical as well are the ontological principles of the late dialogues, also souls, the existence and immortality of which Plato seems to affirm, there being no question but that Neoplatonists and Christians believe in them. And then there is the divine (God, gods, and minor divinities—*daimones*[44]—for Platonists and Neoplatonists alike, the one true God with many angels and demons for Christians). The physical includes all spatial, temporal, material objects—my body, this tree, that drop of water. The metaphysical is both more real and more valuable than the physical,[45] for the nature and perhaps even the very existence of the physical depends on the metaphysical, whereas at least in theory the metaphysical could exist and be what it is apart from the physical.

Finally, to return to the terms with which we began the two previous sections, we may take Being as shorthand for the metaphysical, or in other words for whatever is transcendent of the physical and that is, also, unified and indivisible, perfect, eternal, nonspatial, immutable, incorruptible, knowable, and of ultimate reality and value. Becoming we may take as shorthand for all that is physical, material, multiple and divisible, imperfect, ephemeral, spatial, changeable, corruptible, unknowable, and of limited (and derived) reality and value.[46] To understand the terms this way we shall have to overlook some of the nuances and complexities mentioned so far, and when considering Nietzsche's philosophy specifically we shall have to modify or eliminate some of the connotations of this terminology,[47] but none of this should present any serious problems, for in the dispute between Plato and Nietzsche the main issues can be put pretty clearly. We may, for example, sum up the disagreement by saying of Nietzsche what he once said of Heraclitus: "he altogether denied Being" (*PTG* 51).

God is dead

Among the general public Nietzsche is probably best known for his pronouncement that "God is dead." The phrase is so sharp, so provocative, that it is easily misunderstood; but taken correctly it provides a convenient entry into Nietzsche's philosophy. In one sense it sums up his rejection of Being, but the phrase is more nuanced than this reading is able to express. To capture the full force of Nietzsche's insight we must closely examine the short sentence in which he has encapsulated it, which we may do by considering what he intends to signify by the subject, "God," and the predicate, "is dead." Nietzsche himself offers at least the beginning of a clarification of the predicate immediately following one of his first deployments of the phrase. In aphorism 343 of *The Gay Science* he writes that "the belief in the Christian God has become unbelievable." His point is not that God once existed but has recently somehow perished. There never has been a God. People once believed there was, but now this belief is insupportable. We will want to know what to make of Nietzsche's expression "has become unbelievable" (my "is insupportable"), for it is evident that a great many people maintain their belief in God. If we take Nietzsche to be making a point about the belief itself, then we must wonder why the belief has not been unbelievable all along, throughout the course of history. The ancient world had its share of well-informed and thoughtful atheists who formulated counter-arguments to theism. Why was the belief not unbelievable then? Are we to think that recent advances in philosophy, religion, or science have somehow rendered the proposition of God's existence less credible? For this to be so, we must now be in possession of arguments or evidence against the belief more conclusive than any known to previous thinkers. But this is not the case. The logic of the arguments for and against God's existence remains what it has been since the standard arguments were formulated; only the details included in the premises have in some cases required modification. It is I think a more charitable reading to construe Nietzsche as making a point, not about belief, but rather about *believers*, as claiming that *we ourselves* have become less susceptible to believing in God as a result of recent trends in intellectual history and consequent sociological changes. The success of a purely naturalistic science does nothing to prove the truth of naturalism; but it does tend, as a matter of psychological fact, to cause those with a passionate interest in science or the practical and technological results of scientific advances to pay less heed to whatever there supposedly is of the non-natural, or super-natural. Biblical textual criticism as it flourished in the late eighteenth and early nineteenth centuries in no way disproves revelation, but it does tend to undermine the traditional understanding of revelation and so may shock those who learn of its conclusions out of their beliefs.

So despite Nietzsche's express formulation, the relevant matter is not the justification of belief, but rather human psychology. And this gives rise to another interpretive question, to wit, *for whom* has the belief in God become unbelievable—for European philosophers, for enlightened intellectuals more broadly, for citizens of the west, for every man, woman, and child on the planet? Nietzsche knew little to nothing of the intellectual and spiritual lives of the millions of his contemporaries resident in, say, India and China, and I do not believe that he had them in mind when writing. He thought and wrote in a European academic-literary milieu, though he had more than a mere passing interest in certain aspects of the intellectual atmosphere of western Russia and North America too. The charitable reading in this instance, then, would attribute to Nietzsche a concern primarily with western intellectuals. On this reading we may take his point to be that by observing modern artists, writers, philosophers, scientists, and scholars he has concluded that members of the western intellectual classes are gradually abandoning their belief in God.

Which God? In the passage I quoted from *The Gay Science*, Nietzsche refers to belief in the *Christian* God, and the "God" in "God is dead" doubtless includes in the scope of its reference the God of Christian faith. But its reference is broader than this, and we may arrive at some idea of its breadth by attending to Nietzsche's first declaration of the death of God, which appears in section 108 of *The Gay Science*. In this passage Nietzsche predicts—and laments—that the shadow of God will outlast God Himself. In the following section God's shadow has become a plurality,[48] and Nietzsche refers to "the God of the Eleatics" as one of these shadows (*GS* 109). The Eleatics are Parmenides and his followers,[49] and their God who is dead is just one among many such gods, including (to draw yet again from section 109 and then from the following section) a universal "astral order," "eternally enduring substances," "equal things," a good that is "good in itself." So the "God" at issue is shorthand for "gods" (or "all gods," as in *Zarathustra*[50]), and these expressions anticipate Nietzsche's later formulation "idols," under which term he includes not only God as traditionally conceived in Christian theology[51] but Platonic assumptions about Being as well.[52] In short, then, by "God" Nietzsche means all that we have included in the scope of the term Being, from Parmenides' *to eon* and Plato's Forms through Plotinus's first hypostasis of the One to the Christian God Himself.

We may, therefore, unpack Nietzsche's *Gott ist todt* as follows: "Modern western intellectuals have over the course of the past several generations become more and more inclined to deny, dismiss, or in some cases simply to ignore the metaphysics of Being as developed by the Platonic tradition (taking this tradition to embrace even Parmenides and Christianity)." There is doubtless a sense in which the expression means "I, Nietzsche, reject the Platonic metaphysics of Being," but the broad reading makes sense of the whole of Nietzsche's commentary on the subject and is, moreover, an accurate characterization of modern western intellectual history.

But though God is dead for many western intellectuals, it is not the case that they fully realize the meaning and consequences of this fact. This is part of what Nietzsche intends when, in a famous passage in *The Gay Science*, he depicts a "madman" announcing the death of God and then remarking that the "tremendous event is still on its way, still wandering; it has not yet reached the ears of men" (*GS* 125).[53] Our intellectuals have rejected Christianity, and the metaphysics of Being more broadly, in favor, typically, of the empirical sciences, yet they cling to social, political, and ethical notions that are supportable only by metaphysical assumptions. Take democracy, for example: at its core is the idea that humans are of equal dignity, in possession of equal rights, and deserve equal access to the mechanisms of political deliberation and action. But it is evident even to untutored observation that humans are not equal; any number of differences distinguish them one from another; and a few seem in some respects quite superior to their fellows. "I teach," to quote one of Nietzsche's starkest pronouncements on this matter, "that there are higher and lower men, and that a single individual can under certain circumstances justify the existence of whole millennia— that is, a full, rich, great, whole human being in relation to countless incomplete fragmentary men" (*WP* 997).[54] But if this is so, whence comes the idea of equality? Nietzsche insists that Christianity is the primary source in the west of the "poison of the doctrine of 'equal rights for all'" (*A* 43), which doctrine derives from the belief that each of us is a child of God, and "as a child of God everyone is equal to everyone" (*A* 29).[55] Thus it is a specific sort of metaphysics that prompts us to believe that all men are created equal, that they are endowed by their Creator with certain unalienable Rights, and so on. Natural science alone could never support these claims. We may if we like deny the Christian conceptions of soul and God, and admit that equality is no natural fact of human nature while nevertheless advocating *de jure* equal rights and privileges among citizens for the sake of social stability and the general welfare. We may, that is, adopt a pragmatic approach to the idea of equality without committing to any metaphysical doctrine. But this will require that we adopt and defend an account of a good social, political, and legal organization of men. For granting that we could demonstrate that a polity of *de jure* equals is the most stable, or that it provides "the greatest happiness for the greatest number," one might wonder whether stability or numerically maximized happiness is more to be desired than a frightfully severe but more "noble" arrangement. It is Nietzsche's contention that neither these nor related positions can stand without metaphysical support. In this, ironically, he sides with the metaphysician against the atheist. The death of God means the death of much that we hold dear, and to let go of God while clinging to all that depends on God is to act out of ignorance or a childish naiveté.

There is another sense in which God's death is real but unknown, or at least unassimilated, and this has to do not with intellectuals, but with the common man. A majority of westerners identify as Christians, and many others are religious or spiritual in some more or less specifiable way. True atheists and materialists are in the minority. But, as we have seen, this group is a minority only when measured against the general population; among the intellectual classes non-believers predominate. But members of these classes are primarily responsible for producing the culture in which the believing majority lives, thinks, and acts—the culture of science, literature, journalism, cinema, television, and music. And these cultural products more often than not transmit—explicitly or implicitly—the secular, anti-metaphysical worldview of the intellectuals who generate it. The result is a society of professed believers whose beliefs are adulterated by an admixture of the ideological commitments of the unbelieving minority. And this applies to more than just the believers' social and political ideas; it applies to their theology as well. Thus, today we have Christians whose beliefs about everything from sexual conduct to the nature and activity of the divine would be all but unrecognizable to Christians of previous eras. Nietzsche makes hay of Thomas Aquinas's depiction of the bliss enjoyed by the saints in Heaven as they witness the sufferings of the damned in Hell (*GM* 1.15), but few Christians today would countenance anything even remotely resembling Thomas's account. The point here is not to consider whether contemporary Christians' beliefs are harmful or wrong. The point is that they differ from the tradition, in some cases they differ quite radically, and they are different precisely because of the phenomenon that Nietzsche described as the death of God.

I have noted that Nietzsche was not particularly interested in arguments for or against the existence of God. The justification of theological belief seems to have absorbed him far less than did analysis of the psyches of believers. He wrote a good deal about the psychology of religious belief in general, to be sure; but his most original insights derive from his practice of excavating facts about believers by scrutinizing their specific theological commitments. His position, in short, is that the nature of the god a man believes in tells us something about the man himself. Philosophical and theological beliefs are symptoms of the believer's underlying condition of well-being or decadence. A people's conception of the divine is, in some sense and at least in part, an unconscious expression of its conception of the highest possible form of existence. Consider: a people whose god overflows with love probably values love among men more highly than does a people whose god is a fearsome expression of raw power. So, anyway, Nietzsche seems to believe; and he applies this hermeneutic to his study of Christian belief in particular. The Christian deity, represented by an emaciated man suffering the humiliation of a criminal execution by crucifixion, is a god of the downtrodden and weak, of the sickly lower orders of society who have no understanding of beauty, nobility, health, and strength. Their "god on the cross" is, for Nietzsche, "a curse on life" (*WP* 1052) because it is a symbolic celebration of traits that lead inevitably toward death. In the image of the crucified Christ the Christian projects his admiration for impotence, subjection, cowardice, and misery (though under such names as "goodness," "obedience," "patience," and "bliss"[56]), which is really an expression of his own inner nature; and this admiration is fundamentally an expression of his disdain for life. But the Christian is himself a living thing, and so his affirmation of the divine is simultaneously a denial of himself. But what sort of man, what sort of *life*, condemns itself? Only a "declining, weakened, weary, condemned life" (*TI* "Morality" 5).

Contrast this with the gods of the ancient Greeks. The Olympian deities are very much like the Greeks themselves, only taller and immortal. The lives they live are

Greek lives: they love, hate, play, and fight; eat, drink, deceive, and scheme; suffer, cheer, laugh, and cry just like the men and women who revere them. If a people's gods represent its conception of the highest possible life, then the Greeks conceived of *their own lives* as so great and so good as to be worthy of divinity. The Greek gods, then, are less realities in themselves than reflections in the mirror of the Greeks' self-regard; they are the awesome images through which the Greeks expressed their awe at themselves. This is theology as life-affirmation: a Greek affirming Zeus affirms the highest powers within himself. He celebrates himself through his celebration of his god. This is what Nietzsche referred to as one of the "*nobler* uses for the invention of gods" (*GM* 2.23), and how unlike it is to man's relation to the Christian God as the gruesome image of life-denial.[57]

Nihilism

Nietzsche's account of the nature and consequences of the death of God is closely related to his understanding of nihilism. The word "nihilism" comes from the Latin *nihil*, which means "nothing." Quite literally, then, the word means "nothingism." Odd as this sounds, the translation does capture something of the substance of the nihilist's position. It is often said that a nihilist believes in nothing, but it is not quite true that a nihilist has no beliefs at all—one need not decline to believe that one is alive or that the external world exists in order to be a nihilist; the main point is that the nihilist believes in nothing metaphysical, that he rejects belief in God, soul, postmortem immortality, objective moral value, Platonic Forms, the Neoplatonic One, and every other supposed metaphysical entity or truth. Nor does he believe that human life or the universe has any objective meaning, purpose, or goal, for the source of this meaning or purpose could only be metaphysical, which the nihilist's position rules out.

Nihilism has a history independent of and prior to Nietzsche, most prominently in nineteenth-century Russia.[58] Russian nihilism was less an anti-metaphysical philo-sophical movement than it was the expression of a social and political upheaval that manifested primarily as anarchistic revolt against established structures and systems of power. Opposed in particular to rigid class hierarchies, as represented on the top by the luxuriously wealthy ruling power of the Tsar and his family, on the bottom by the debased, impoverished serfs, Russian nihilists agitated for change, sometimes going so far as to resort to violent opposition to the existing order. These nihilists rejected more than mere secular authority; they rejected the moral authority of objective values as well. In this, many nihilists adhered to a philosophical outlook similar to what in twentieth-century Anglo-American philosophy was known as Logical Positivism, and what today is sometimes called Scientism. The nihilists were, in short, radical materi-alists who dismissed aesthetics and ethics as sweepingly as they rejected metaphysics.

Many Russian nihilists blazed into the public consciousness when arrested for participating in subversive plots or carrying out overt acts of terrorism, but the most famous of them all may have been a character in a novel. Yevgeny Bazarov, the protagonist of Turgenev's *Fathers and Children*, is a medical student who advocates a philosophy of nihilism, which for him involves, as he puts it, a denial or negation of "everything." In practice this amounts to opposition to traditional social structures, a stoic or cynical suppression of emotion, and the dismissal of beliefs not grounded on strict naturalist science. Bazarov believes exclusively in the body: he accepts as true all that he can learn from the probings of his fingers and eyes; he acts from a haughty sort of hedonism; and for broader ethical motivation he is guided by a form of utilitarianism, which measures human well-being according to the standard of pleasures and pains. Now Bazarov's commitment to this sort of anti-metaphysical scientific nihilism is a metaphysical commitment itself; it is a philosophical position whose validity no experiment can verify; but in this there is nothing surprising. Bazarov is neither the first nor the last man, real or imaginary, to believe he denies all gods while in fact he only substitutes a new deity for the old.

Dostoevsky's fictional nihilists were more consistent, and therefore more radical, than Turgenev's Bazarov. As his biographer Joseph Frank has written, "Dostoevsky portrayed Nihilist ideas not on the level at which they were originally advocated, but rather as they were refashioned by his eschatological imagination and taken to their most extreme consequence."[59] Raskolnikov, for example, the nihilist protagonist of *Crime and Punishment*, murders an old pawnbroker for her money, motivated by a bizarre form of what we might call utilitarian egoism. Raskolnikov believes that some men are superior to others, and that these superior men may violate customary mores to further their own ends, the expansion of their power and influence. He imagines, moreover, that by acting as such a superior individual he will benefit himself and society simultaneously, for he will rid the world of a vile old parasite while providing himself with resources to alleviate the sufferings of society's unfortunates. Whether or not he ever sincerely accepts this philosophy in its entirety, he is ultimately unable successfully to embody it in his actions. His rational principles conflict with his emotional inclinations, and the result is psychological turmoil.

Murder and disturbed psychologies motivate a good deal of the action in *The Brothers Karamazov*, and though from Dostoevsky's perspective the philosophical problem in the novel is atheism, we can recognize it as nihilism or at least as on the way thereto. The absence from the novel of overt political themes may have disinclined Dostoevsky himself from formulating the problem as nihilism, but the fear that without God everything is permitted can easily be elaborated to encompass more than the ethical, existential, and theological matters that occupy Dostoevsky in this work. In short, although we take Dostoevsky at his word, as expressed in a letter concerning *The Brothers Karamazov*, that in the book he had attempted a "refutation of blasphemy," we cannot overlook the bounty of material that provides access to still deeper problems, problems the author himself knew well and even hints at in this same letter when, after noting that arguments against the existence of God had become passé, he remarks that "God's creation, God's world, and its meaning are *negated* as strongly as possible. That's the only thing that contemporary civilization finds nonsensical."[60] In *The Brothers Karamazov* Dostoevsky strives for a realistic portrayal of his characters, their beliefs and problems. Still, we know he possessed the insight and talent to push his analysis of the implications of the rejection of meaning to the extreme had he wanted to, and had he done so he may very well have approached Nietzsche's own reflections on the dark possibilities inherent in the proposition that "Nothing is true; everything is permitted."[61]

Nietzsche knew Dostoevsky's work, having discovered the great novelist in French translations early in 1887.[62] He encountered *Notes from Underground* first,[63] and although Dostoevsky does not label the underground man a nihilist, the character's rebellion against everything, including even reason and logic, has its affinities to nihilism.[64] Nietzsche referred to nihilism in print prior to his discovery of Dostoevsky, even to "nihilism à la Petersburg" (*GS* 347), but his interest in the subject (especially as expressed in his notebooks) seems to have intensified in the year of this discovery. The underground man's disregard for politics and his obsession with the problem of the authority of reason parallels Nietzsche's own interest in nihilism. Nietzsche was concerned with the social, political, and existential consequences of nihilism, to be sure; but he knew that a proper understanding of these phenomena requires an analysis of epistemological and metaphysical nihilism. Dostoevsky chose not to explore the deeper philosophical implications of the denial of God in *The Brothers Karamazov*, but for Nietzsche the possibility that nothing is true, like the certainty that God is dead, called the philosopher to more than mere theological or ethical reflection.

When Nietzsche announced that God is dead in the first edition of *The Gay Science*, he drew no connections between the event and nihilism. But in the second edition he opened the freshly composed fifth and final book with the claim that this "greatest recent event" necessitates the collapse of "the whole of our European morality" (*GS* 343). We may take this as an allusion to nihilism, for just three sections later he explicitly mentions nihilism in the context of his questioning of the value of European morality, characterizing as nihilism the abolition of our reverence of a godly and moral world.[65] This is just one of a variety of brief but stark accounts of nihilism that appear in Nietzsche's publications of the late 1880s. In these works the term has numerous connotations: it may indicate a drive for metaphysical certainty regarding the "real world" (*BGE* 10[66]); a scientific objectivity that refuses either to affirm or deny, that only describes (*GM* 3.26); nausea at the sight of weak and sickly men (*GM* 2.24); a Schopenhauerian, Buddhist, or Christian renunciation of life (*GM* 2.21, *A* 7); an adherence to values other than or contrary to those that manifest the will to power (*A* 6), pity for example (*A* 7); a suicidal despair at the meaninglessness of suffering (*GM* 3.28, *GS* 346); the very realization of this meaninglessness (*GS* 346). These last two problems of human suffering and its meaninglessness seem to have consumed Nietzsche during the period when he composed Book 5 of *The Gay Science* and the Third Essay of *On the Genealogy of Morals* (1886–7).[67] In the latter of these two works Nietzsche promised his readers a composition of some sort on European Nihilism, but the piece never appeared. There is, however, a series of notes in *The Will to Power* that in his notebooks Nietzsche headed "*European Nihilism*. Lenzer Heide, June 10, 1887,"[68] which dates the notes to precisely this period and shows them in fact to have been written as Nietzsche was in transit to Sils-Maria, the town in which he produced his *Genealogy*. We may assume, therefore, that Nietzsche had these notes in mind when he wrote the announcement of his work on nihilism into this book.

In these notes Nietzsche develops his examination of the problem of suffering by reflecting on the "Christian moral hypothesis" that once gave suffering a meaning by situating it in the context of a perfect world and human freedom. The hypothesis explains the origin of human suffering by appealing, presumably, to the Fall and Original Sin (though in these notes Nietzsche is not explicit on this point), and if humans suffer due to a misuse of their free will, and so ultimately have only themselves to blame—well, even a gloomy explanation is better than no explanation at all. As Nietzsche would write in the *Genealogy* later that year, we humans can bear suffering so long as we imagine it to have meaning; any comprehensible explanation will prevent our decline into the "suicidal nihilism" that may result from despair at meaningless suffering (*GM* 3.28).

The Christian-moral hypothesis did more than account for human suffering. As Nietzsche points out in this same series of notes, Christianity "posited that man had a *knowledge* of absolute values and thus *adequate knowledge* precisely regarding what is most important." This enabled man not only to comprehend his suffering, but also to take comfort in knowing the good. Suffering may be our birthright given the events in the Garden, but we know the way out of it—in this life or in the next—and we know as well that beyond suffering there is redemption. Thus we may have hope; our knowledge of value and of the "moral order" of the world gives us reason to endure and perhaps even to strive.

Yet this "Christian hypothesis" was undermined by drives generated in part by Christian morality itself, in particular the will to truth. Our drive to know and to speak the truth led us eventually to uncover the origins of the Christian account in the all too human need to relieve our suffering by rendering it meaningful through explanation. We exposed the Christian-moral hypothesis as having developed in response to psychological pressures and so lost faith in its validity. And though to renounce the Christian explanation, including its postulation of objective morality and value, exposes one to existential and psychological danger, the truth drive is relentless. It is terrible to admit the truth in this instance, but to continue lying to ourselves is worse. And so we reject the Christian-moral interpretation, infer that our sufferings are meaningless and our lives valueless, and thereby add to our woe yet another burden of pain. The reasoning runs something like this: "I suffer evil—the evil of violence, pain, and death—for no reason and to no end or purpose. Of what is of highest value I know nothing. I do not even know whether anything at all is of value. Given my suffering and ignorance I infer at least that I myself am not of absolute value, that I am finite, ephemeral, insignificant, and small. As a creature conditioned thus—so much less than I once believed myself to be—I am miserable, as are all those like me. Therefore, I pass sentence on existence; I take sides against myself."

In many other notes collected in Book 1 of *The Will to Power* Nietzsche explores the origin, nature, and consequences of nihilism, but he does so under various formulations and from several angles, and almost always in the form of brief notes, some of which appear bare mnemonics indecipherable to others. Readers of these texts, therefore, must engage to some degree in a form of mind-reading, and this is as true with respect to many of the individual notes as to the interconnections among them. All this makes it impossible to summarize Nietzsche's understanding of nihilism in a simple formula, or even in one complex formula or series of formulae. Yet his most influential formulation of the phenomenon, which appears most consistently in his published works, involves the rejection of metaphysical explanations and interpretations of the world and our place in it, coupled with the despair we experience as a result of this rejection. "Radical nihilism," Nietzsche wrote around the time he composed the notes we have been considering, "is the conviction of an absolute untenability of existence when it comes to the highest values one recognizes; plus the realization that we lack the least right to posit a beyond or an in-itself of things that might be 'divine' or morality incarnate" (*WP* 3).

In his published and unpublished writings alike, Nietzsche sometimes associates his critical examination of metaphysical value and of a beyond in which Being or divinity might reside with the problem of human suffering. But some selections from his notebooks focus on the metaphysics of Being quite apart from any meaning it may bestow on human suffering. In a note written sometime between late autumn 1887 and early spring 1888, Nietzsche summed up this variety of nihilism as "the realization that the overall character of existence may not be interpreted by means of the concept of 'aim,' the concept of 'unity,' or the concept of 'truth'" (*WP* 12).

That existence has no "aim" means that neither human life nor cosmic history has any objective meaning or purpose. The Christian often assumes that God has a plan for his life, that God's hand is somehow guiding his progress through life, that God "opens doors" or "calls" one onto this or that path. The Christian assumes as well that the universe is progressing according to a sort of plot line—there was the beginning act of Creation and there will be the closing act of the Second Coming; along the way are various episodes like the Fall, the Incarnation, and the appearance of the Antichrist that move the plot along toward its denouement. Various sects disagree about whether the story was composed entire from the beginning or is being written moment by moment, but there is a general consensus that an Author is conceiving and executing the plot, and that this Author is God. According to this understanding, existence at every level—at the individual human as well as the total cosmic level—is infused with meaning, and that this meaning is at least to some degree intelligible to us mortals, for it is the product of the mind of our creator. All of this is rejected by the nihilist who denies that the concept "aim" may be applied to existence.

There being no "unity" means that the universe is not an organized whole of rationally interlocking parts, that the individual components that make up this world do not each have a place as designated by an overarching system or as situated in the context of some great and all-pervading Whole. If all things were modes of the deity; if the physical universe were the carapace or skin of God; if material reality were an emanation of the Neoplatonic One; if any one of these or some similar account were true of the universe, then each individual thing—ourselves included—would have its proper place in the whole, and we self-conscious beings could take some comfort from knowing ourselves to be situated safely in our assigned position. But we are not part of an encompassing All—or so says the nihilist who denies that the concept "unity" may be applied to existence.

There being no "truth" to the universe means that there is no "true world," no metaphysical reality "behind" or "beyond" the universe as we experience it through our senses. The man who finds no "aim" or "unity" in the surrounding physical universe may be tempted to postulate the existence of a *trans*-physical reality that does possess such properties and that is, moreover, our true home. If the material world disappoints us, fails to satisfy our desire—perhaps it is even a need—for existential comfort, we need not finally despair, for there is "another" world accessible to us—accessible now through meditation, prayer, or rational-dialectical investigation, or in the future as reward for right-living or correct belief. To this true world we truly belong, and though it may be hard to find our way through to it, it is not impossible for those who determine to dedicate their lives to the journey. This comfort is refused by the nihilist who declines to apply the concept "truth" to existence.

These rejections of "aim," "unity," and "truth" amount to nihilism as the rejection of metaphysics. Nietzsche describes this phenomenon in the context of discussing nihilism as "a psychological state." This is nihilism as the suffering or despair attending the rejection of metaphysics. There are those who need to understand themselves and their place in the universe in accordance with the concepts "aim," "unity," and "truth." Without this understanding their lives appear to them random, empty, and meaningless, for they imagine that they have value only as parts of a valuable whole. If such a person should somehow lose his faith in this whole, then he must draw the inference that his life, that he himself, is valueless. In a universe of no objective worth a human life appears to him not worth living. For such a man, to realize this is to suffer, and to suffer in this way is to despair. This despair—this suffering from the realization of the valuelessness of one's life—is a form of nihilism. To quote the conclusion of the first part of the note we have been considering: "the categories 'aim,' 'unity,' 'being'[69] which we used to project some value into the world—we *pull out* again; so the world looks *valueless*."

I have noted the great variety of Nietzsche's conceptualizations of nihilism. I have also attempted to highlight a few common themes, both as they appear in the published works and as we can piece them together from his notes. It will serve our purposes in this book if, drawing on these commonalities, we isolate two primary senses of nihilism. First, then, we may say that nihilism is the rejection of metaphysics, or as Nietzsche sometimes puts it himself, the denial of Being; second, nihilism is the despair one might experience as a result of this first sense of nihilism, which is to say the despair that attends the thought that since Being (as God, Platonic Form, etc.) is the only possible source of objective meaning and value, the lack of Being implies the meaninglessness and valuelessness of life.

Scholars have long debated whether Nietzsche was a nihilist himself.[70] The arguments on either side of the question turn on subtle points, and rightly so, for Nietzsche was at times a subtle thinker. But addressing the question with reference to our less than subtle, but broadly accurate, two-fold account of nihilism, I think it fair to regard Nietzsche as a nihilist in the first sense. He is the man who knows that God is dead, and this knowledge justifies his identifying himself as "the first perfect nihilist of Europe." But Nietzsche was not a nihilist in the second sense—or anyway he strove not to be. Immediately following his identification of himself as a nihilist, he insists that he "has even now lived through the whole of nihilism, to the end, leaving it behind, outside himself" (*WP* "Preface" 3). The nihilists who despair are those who have faith in, for example, the categories "aim," "unity," and "truth" (or "being") as discussed above. They *have* faith, in the present tense, for though they no longer believe that these categories apply to the world, they continue to believe in the *value* of these categories, which is to say that they believe that the world can have value only by embodying or manifesting these categories. And they apply this reasoning to themselves as well—the only value they can imagine for their lives (for any human life) is that which would derive from their existing as parts of a valuable whole. But since they have concluded that the world is neither purposeful, unified, nor true—and so are nihilists in the first sense as defined above—they infer that it is valueless as well, and then they infer that they themselves are valueless, their lives worthless, which leads to despair—and so are nihilists in the second sense too. But there is a way to embrace the first sense of nihilism while avoiding the second: we must "give up our faith in [these categories]," for "once we have devaluated [them], the demonstration that they cannot be applied to the universe is no longer any reason for devaluating the universe" (*WP* 12). This is the route Nietzsche chose to follow. It was not only God that died for him, but also his naive conception of God as the guarantor of meaning and value. This latter death removed any reason to despair at the former.

Nietzsche at times portrays the death of God as a cheerful, liberating event. If all along God was only *apparently* the source of meaning and value, but not *actually* so, then in the wake of his death we (some of us, anyway) may recognize in ourselves the freedom to forge our own, individual and particular, meaning and value. Those who are equal to this effort will affirm this new world—this new life—free of God. Hard as it may be, they will with Nietzsche strive to be "Yes-sayers." For such men the consequences of God's demise are "like a new and scarcely describable kind of light, happiness, relief, exhilaration, encouragement, dawn" (*GS* 343).

Nihilism, the rejection of metaphysics, the denial of Being, the death of God: we may use these expressions interchangeably, though always keeping in mind that nihilism may also mean the despair from which many suffer in the wake of God's uncanny withdrawal. The western world has been in thrall to "Platonism"—whether under the name of Parmenides, Pythagoras, Plato, Plotinus, Paul, or Augustine—for more than two-and-a-half millennia, an unnatural enslavement to Being so enduring that to this day many mistake it for man's natural condition. Some nihilists experience their liberation from the shackles of metaphysics as if they were set adrift upon a landless sea. Their freedom frightens and dismays them. Nietzsche was different. He celebrated our waking from Plato's dream of Being, which had, he thought, degenerated into the nightmare of Christianity. He celebrated our returning to our senses, which when properly attended to reveal to us no permanence, no stability, no Being, no cosmos, but rather a constantly changing chaos of Becoming.

Eternal return

Imagine cosmic history moving without aim, unity, or the truth of being; imagine your own life bound up with this history as utterly devoid of meaning and ultimate significance; now imagine all this without the respite of an end. There is death, to be sure; and for all we know the universe too may one day be consumed by fire or ice, or with no flourish fade into a pale oblivion. Yet even so according to Nietzsche there is no *final* end, for the play of Becoming is eternally active, and all that ever was or will be ceaselessly recurs.

According to Nietzsche's doctrine of the eternal return (or the "eternal recurrence of the same"), the history of the universe, overall and entire, and therefore also the history of every element of the universe, no matter how immense or minute, has played out already an infinite number of times in the past and will recur an infinite number of times in the future. By the universe and all its elements I mean to indicate everything from the grand sweep of world history to the smallest or most trivial fact or event, including for example the number and location of the motes of dust in the air around you as you read this sentence. And you yourself, too, reading this sentence: you have read these words an infinite number of times before, positioned precisely as you are positioned now, where you are and when you are right now—inside or outdoors, morning, noon, or night—breathing as you are, feeling the very heat or cold on your skin that you feel in this moment, with the same sounds (or silence) in the background as you presently hear (or don't), thinking exactly what you are thinking now, this very second, even including the new thought that has just come into your mind—all this has happened before and will happen again *ad infinitum*. You will die, true; and the world as we know it may come to an end. But eventually time and the sequence of events in time will begin anew and proceed as they have always done before, arriving one day at the very moment of your birth and, to say it again, at this very moment as well.[71]

In his note concerning European nihilism that I discussed above (pp. 71–2), Nietzsche writes that nihilism follows upon "the belief in the absolute immorality of nature, in aim- and meaninglessness," which themselves are consequent on the death of God. Aimlessness and meaninglessness in particular, which together amount to the "paralyzing idea" of "[d]uration 'in vain,' without end or aim," are expressions of nihilism. And this paralyzing idea of duration in vain "in its most terrible form," says Nietzsche, is the eternal return. More, the eternal return is "the most extreme form of nihilism" (*WP* 55); it is, in a way, nihilism infinitely compounded.

Compare the eternal return to the Christian view of cosmic time and history, according to which the story of the universe unfolds in conformity with something like an objective plot line. The universe began intentionally and is intentionally progressing toward an end-state. I refer to the intentionality of God: the universe itself does not act intentionally, and cannot do so, for it is not a conscious intentional agent. But God has, as it were, built his intentions into the universe by orienting it toward a *telos*. Therefore from the Christian perspective each stage of cosmic history is meaningful because it contributes to the attainment of this *telos*. The overall aim infuses each event with purpose. We might symbolize this idea with an arrow, which on one side has a definite beginning (God's creation of the world *ex nihilo*) and on the other points to a definite end (the Second Coming). The middle sections are as they are precisely because there inheres in them an objective directionality connecting the beginning to the end. The eternal return, on the other hand, we may symbolize with a circle: the series of recurring cycles has neither beginning nor end; neither this series nor the movements and events of universal history that occur within each cycle are actually going anywhere—they are not anyway heading toward any particular goal. Events are happening; this is undeniable. But why? To what end? Only because they do—always have and always will—but to no end whatever, without purpose and to that extent without meaning. Every section of the circle is as it is, not because it is "directed toward" any future state, but only because (redundantly, and therefore meaninglessly) it just is as it is. This is the "in vain" of nihilism.[72]

Nietzsche believed that the thought of a meaningless existence infinitely repeated would be unbearable for decadent men too weak and maladjusted to flourish, too burdened by suffering to want to relive their lives even once, much less countless times. Such men reconcile themselves to life through the idea that although they suffer, they do so for a reason, that as miserable as they are, they at least contribute to the attainment of an ultimate universal good. But deprive them of this belief and all that remains is their misery. Not only are their lives in vain, but their suffering too is devoid of meaning. Lacking the resources to provide themselves with a goal, and thereby to create their own meaning, they succumb to despair at the vanity of their situation, at the hopeless vanity of themselves as individuals, and this disorienting feeling of loss and deep existential despair is at the core of the nihilism that some men experience at the thought of eternal return.

Even the healthy among us must resist at least one nihilistic consequence of the eternal return, namely the recurrence of the small man, the sick man, the decadent. Zarathustra himself despaired of "the eternal recurrence of the smallest," crying "that was my disgust with all existence. Alas! Nausea! Nausea! Nausea!"[73] In the *Genealogy*, too, Nietzsche insists that nausea at the sight of the sickly weak failures of men, especially when united with pity, can drag one into the pit of nihilism (*GM* 3.14). But if this type recurs, then so must the nausea, or anyway the threat of nausea. And if even Zarathustra has to struggle against this variety of nihilism, the fact of the eternal return must be a heavy burden to bear.

The idea that the universe recurs in cycles goes back to the ancients, and Nietzsche was of course well aware of this. We know this from his allusion in an early essay to the Pythagorean teaching that events repeat in every detail, and from his speculation in *Ecce Homo* that "the unconditional and infinitely repeated circular course of all things" was taught by Heraclitus and the Stoics.[74] Plato's *Timaeus* refers to the complete or perfect year (*ho teleos eniautos*, 39d4), which is concluded when all the heavenly bodies simultaneously complete their circuits (i.e. when, after many thousands of solar years, they return to the positions relative to one another that they occupied at the beginning of the complete year). This has been taken by some to mark the beginning of a "return," a cycle of time whose events are identical to all previous and successive cycles of complete years, but Plato nowhere has any of his characters assert this. In any case, there is no indication in the sources that the ancients drew nihilistic inferences from the idea of recurrence, and it may be that the eternal return has the crushing effect that Nietzsche attributes to it only for those who have come of age in a Christian (or relevantly similar) context. Nietzsche regularly associates nihilism not only with a lack of objective meaning, but also with an anterior belief in meaning. Nihilism follows "when we have sought a 'meaning' in all events that is not there" (*WP* 12), or when an "interpretation has collapsed" that we previously mistook for "*the* interpretation" (*WP* 55). In short, only those who believe that God is alive and well will be disturbed by news of his death.

Although Nietzsche was acquainted with ancient accounts of recurrence, probably from as far back as his student days, the idea played no significant role in his thinking before 1881. But then one day in August of that year, while out for a walk along the banks of a lake near Sils-Maria, he stopped beside a large rock—a rock that has since become known as the "Zarathustra Stone"—and he was, it seems, overcome. To read his accounts of the event, or the accounts of those to whom he spoke about it, the thought of eternal return assailed him; he could not resist it, could not even try to resist it. In that moment he came to believe in recurrence, and not just to believe it but to regard it as the central thought of his philosophy, even of his life.[75]

Nietzsche first alludes in print to the eternal return in section 109 of *The Gay Science*, which section immediately follows the first formulation of the infamous announcement that "God is dead." He refers to the doctrine by name in section 285, but he develops the thought most famously in section 341, the penultimate passage of the first edition of the book.[76] Here Nietzsche invites his readers to consider how we would react if we came to believe that our lives will eternally recur. Would the thought crush us, or would we instead *"crave nothing more fervently"* than that it might be so? Nietzsche stresses the implications of the choice by positioning the passage specifically between two others. In the first of these (*GS* 340) he presents his reading of Socrates' last words as amounting to a denial of life, which reveals that Socrates suffered from life, which in turn implies that the old man was decadent. In the section immediately following the introduction of the eternal return (*GS* 342), there appears for the first time in Nietzsche's corpus the figure of Zarathustra, the great Yes-sayer and affirmer of life. Placed as it is between these representations of contrary existential attitudes, section 341 implicitly inquires whether the reader regards his life with a sickly Socratic eye or with an exuberant Zarathustran joy, and thereby whether he is decadent or healthy.

This manner of approaching the eternal return has led some scholars to conclude that Nietzsche intended the idea as nothing more than a thought experiment from which one may learn whether one affirms or denies one's life. He did not mean to imply that he accepted it as doctrine or took it seriously as a hypothesis.[77] By imagining one's reaction to coming to believe in eternal recurrence one acquires insight into oneself, for he who would affirm his life to such an extent that he could want to relive it eternally, even including its every pain and suffering, is an authentic Yes-sayer. He who suffers from the thought is decadent.

But on occasion Nietzsche appeals to the return for purposes other than mere existential-psychological evaluation. In *Beyond Good and Evil*, for example, he writes of "the most high-spirited, alive, and world-affirming human being" who "wants to have *what was and is* repeated into all eternity, shouting insatiably *da capo*—not only to himself but to the whole play and spectacle" (*BGE* 56). Although he does not name the doctrine here, it is evident that he has the eternal return in mind; and he suggests that the affirmation of recurrence is an ideal that the highest type of man might attain. By associating affirmation of the eternal return with the highest type of man in this way, Nietzsche suggests that he takes recurrence for something more than a thin theoretical possibility. Affirmation of a mere possibility might be only naive, or at best an indication of one's psychological condition. It may be, then, as Paul Loeb has suggested, that Nietzsche "actually believes that he has discovered the truth of eternal recurrence and indeed formulated his ideal of affirmation in *response* to this discovery."[78] To judge from Nietzsche's notebooks, this seems right, for at times he writes of the eternal return as a cosmological doctrine susceptible of confirmation.[79] And Loeb has argued further that in *Thus Spoke Zarathustra* Nietzsche actually published a proof of the doctrine grounded on the twin assumptions that time is eternal in the past and the future, and that all events are causally entangled (Z:III "The Convalescent" 2).[80] Given temporal eternity, all events that can happen must happen an infinite number of times; and if events are causally entangled, then these infinite repetitions must occur in precisely the same sequence.[81] Furthermore, if time has only a relative existence—relative, that is, to the events themselves—then the recurrence of events implies the recurrence of the moments of time in which they occur. Time itself repeats. The result is a numerically infinite repetition of qualitatively identical events (including even the events' temporal properties).[82]

Nietzsche rarely mentions the eternal return in his published works after *Zarathustra*, but in *Twilight of the Idols* he refers to himself as "the teacher of the eternal recurrence" (*TI* "Ancients" 5), and his notebooks are full of every sort of reflection on the idea, from speculations as to its consequences to attempted proofs based on contemporary physics. As we have seen, the doctrine serves a variety of Nietzsche's philosophical ends, functioning for him as an existential test, an ideal of affirmation, and a cosmological hypothesis. I have stressed its function as an expression or illustration of nihilism only because I have found that doing so is pedagogically efficacious. It may be that the cosmological or existential implications of the eternal return are more central to Nietzsche's philosophy, or were more relevant (or significant) in Nietzsche's own mind, than its bearing on nihilism. I am willing to concede this, but as I indicated in the Introduction, I am not here concerned to present *the reading* of Nietzsche but rather only one interesting and informative way into his thought.

There are those who insist that Nietzsche divinizes the absence of God and that nihilism is "his religion." This is objectionably facile, even admitting that he was a nihilist in the sense of one who rejects metaphysics and, with Heraclitus, declares Being an empty fiction.[83] Nor is there any justification for psychologizing his doctrine of the eternal repetition of Becoming as a deluded man's substitute for Being. It is true that Nietzsche once wrote that the thought that everything recurs "is the closest *approximation of a world of becoming to a world of being*" (*WP* 617), but this is no ontological assertion of a parallel between the universe conceived as recurring eternally and Being as a level or category of reality. Given that he introduces this note with the remark that "[t]o impose upon becoming the character of being" is "the supreme will to power," it is best to interpret him to mean that a recurring universe approximates Being in the metaphorical sense deriving from the fact of one's affirming all events, and thereby willing them to abide in accordance with Zarathustra's refrain that "all joy wants eternity."[84] Nietzsche once called his philosophy "inverted Platonism,"[85] and on this matter I am willing to take him at his word, at least with respect to the metaphysics of Being. If, then, Plato is *the* philosopher of Being (excepting, perhaps, Parmenides),

Nietzsche as his inversion is *the* philosopher of Becoming (probably even including Heraclitus). Having now examined Plato's account of reality, of reality as Being, and some aspects of Nietzsche's repudiation of this account, we may at last consider more closely what to Nietzsche's mind occupies the void of Being's absence, which is to say the endless, aimless, godless flux and play of Becoming.

Becoming

Heraclitus

In the third chapter of *Twilight of the Idols*, entitled "'Reason' in Philosophy," Nietzsche identifies the belief in Being as one of two fundamental idiosyncrasies of philosophers. For thousands of years philosophers have admired and sought to commune with that which is everlasting, perfect, and divine; they have pursued God under multiple guises—God as father, God as the Good, God as Being. These same philosophers have taken coming-to-be, change, and passing-away for objections, "even refutations" (*TI* "Reason" 1); they have assumed that that which comes to be *is not*, and that what is not has no claim to their attention. In other words, in their passionate quest for Being, western philosophers have turned their backs on Becoming.

But there was an exception, a single astounding exception by the name of Heraclitus. The eldest son of a noble Greek family resident in the Anatolian coastal town of Ephesus, Heraclitus spurned every family privilege and lived as something of a reclusive philosopher, artist, or sage. Diogenes Laertius informs us that he "flourished" just prior to 500 BCE and lived to 60 years of age, which dates him roughly to sometime between 540 and 480 BCE.[1] Heraclitus wrote only a single work, which was well known to ancient philosophers, but has come down to us as a disjointed series of well over one hundred fragments. As a writer Heraclitus is notoriously obscure, was so even to the ancients who had his text entire, and for us who possess only the scattered remains the difficulties of interpretation are compounded. Fortunately, it is not our business to present a thorough accounting of Heraclitus's philosophy. Our task is rather to relate those of his ideas that most interested Nietzsche. These ideas we may sum up by quoting Nietzsche himself, who admired Heraclitus for making bold to insist that Being is "an empty fiction" (*TI* "Reason" 2).

Nietzsche penned these words in his final active year as an author. But his admiration of Heraclitus stretches back to the beginning of his career, to a university course he offered on at least three occasions, whose lectures he attempted unsuccessfully to work into publishable material under the title *The Pre-Platonic Philosophers*,[2] and to a short manuscript, also unfinished, which today appears as *Philosophy in the Tragic Age of the Greeks*. In this latter work Nietzsche wrote that Heraclitus "altogether denied Being," and to stress the point he imaginatively attributed to him the declaration, "I see nothing other than Becoming" (*PTG* 51).

This ranking of Becoming over Being is just one among many themes Nietzsche found in Heraclitus that would later turn up in his own philosophy.[3] Among these themes is an anti-teleological interpretation of cosmic history, in other words the idea that "Becoming aims at *nothing* and achieves *nothing*," as Nietzsche expressed the thought in his notebooks (*WP* 12). There is also Heraclitus's amoralist interpretation of the universe and its history, according to which the world is "a beautiful innocent game" whose origin and development have nothing whatever to do with morality (*PTG* 6–14), which thought reappears in Nietzsche's conception of "the innocence of Becoming" (*TI* "Errors" 7–8). Related to this is Heraclitus's idea that "[m]an is necessity down to his last fibre, and totally 'unfree,' that is if one means by freedom the foolish demand to be able to change one's *essentia* arbitrarily" (*PTG* 63), which anticipates Nietzsche's insistence that the "fatality of [man's] essence is not to be disentangled from the fatality of all that has been and will be" and that "[o]ne is necessary, one is a piece of fatefulness" (*TI* "Errors" 8). Then there is the notion of "a periodically repeated end of the world, and … an ever renewed rise of another world out of the all-destroying cosmic fire" (*PTG* 60), with reference to which Nietzsche wrote in *Ecce Homo* that his own doctrine of the eternal return "*might* in the end have been taught already by Heraclitus" (*EH* "BT" 3). Finally there is Heraclitus's "extraordinary power to think intuitively," his hostility toward "the type [of thinking] that is accomplished in concepts and logical combinations, in other words toward reason" (*PTG* 52), which by no means characterizes Nietzsche in all of his moods, but does most definitely reflect his practice as both thinker and writer on more than a few occasions throughout the course of his career.

Historians of ancient philosophy are accustomed to set Heraclitus in opposition to Parmenides as the philosopher of the many against the philosopher of the One. The practice persists because there is something to it: Heraclitus stresses change and opposition in a way that Parmenides, with his mind's eye forever trained on a motionless and unified whole, could never countenance. Now it is true that Heraclitus is the philosopher of Becoming *par excellence*; he writes of a world whose multiple elements forever flow into and out of one another along a restless current of opposition, upon the streaming surface of which the ephemeral bubbles we mistake for beings arise and dissolve, come to be and pass away. Yet in back of this surging plurality Heraclitus too saw a unity, a One, as Nietzsche himself acknowledges: "Heraclitus … sees only the One, but in the sense opposite to Parmenides" (*PPP* 63). Heraclitus's difference with Parmenides involves, not his position regarding the existence of the One, but rather his conception of the One's *mode* of existence. In what sense, then, did Heraclitus see the One? Nietzsche attributes to Heraclitus the thought that "that which becomes is one thing in eternal transformation" (*PPP* 62), so it would seem that Heraclitus's One always changes in every way, to employ a Platonic expression. A One such as this would certainly differ from the One of Parmenides. But if the One exists in a state of "eternal transformation," if the One itself is "Becoming, the flowing" (*PPP* 62), in what sense is it actually a One? Nietzsche's explanation is not quite clear, or if it is clear it is underdeveloped. Be that as it may, we should at least attempt to make some sense of his explanation, for even if it fails to resolve the riddle of Heraclitus, it may provide a bridge to our main subject, namely, Nietzsche's own account of the world as Becoming.

The primary shortcoming of Nietzsche's explanation is the fact that he addresses the difference between Parmenides' and Heraclitus's visions of the One by discussing, not the One itself, but rather all that is other than the One. This other is "multiplicity," and for Parmenides multiplicity is "a deception of the sense" (*PPP* 63),[4] whereas for Heraclitus it is real; it is "the cloth, the form of appearance, of the One" (*PPP* 63). But what, exactly, does this tell us of the One itself? If there is a coherent message here, Nietzsche has scrambled it by employing incompatible metaphors. If multiplicity is "the cloth" of the One, then we can imagine the One's existing independently of multiplicity, behind and unaffected by the many, which shimmer before it while maintaining a discreet distance. If, on the other hand, multiplicity is the form of the One's appearance, then it may be that the One is ontologically distinct from the many but always *shows itself as* the many; but then again it may be that the many just are the mode of the One's existence, that the One *exists as* the many. Nietzsche's statement that "that which becomes is one thing in eternal transformation" would seem to imply this last account, and this reading is consistent with Nietzsche's attributing to Heraclitus, in *Philosophy in the Tragic Age of the Greeks*, the thought that "the one is the many," or again, that "the one is at the same time the many" (*PTG* 58). In this passage Nietzsche is attempting to distinguish Heraclitus from Parmenides and another early philosopher, Anaxagoras. For Heraclitus, he writes, the "many perceivable qualities"—which we may here regard as the elements of that which Nietzsche refers to in *The Pre-Platonic Philosophers* as "multiplicity"—these qualities are not illusory, as Parmenides taught, but neither are they ontologically distinct, fully and independently real in and of themselves, as Anaxagoras believed. Rather, multiplicity is the manifestation of the One. As he puts it in *The Pre-Platonic Philosophers*: "Heraclitus … places the entire world of differences around the One in the sense that it evidences itself in all of them." And lest we mistake the metaphor of "around" (like the metaphor of "cloth") to imply distinction between the One and the many, we note that in the following sentence Nietzsche contends that "Becoming and Passing Away constitute the primary property of the principle," which principle we know from earlier in the paragraph to be the One (*PPP* 63). We must, therefore, take Nietzsche's point to be that the fundamental mode of the One's existence (its "primary property") is "Becoming and Passing Away." The One *is* indeed, but it is *as* multiplicity.

But what are we to make of a One that exists *as*, and *only* as, a many? We expect there to be something to this One *as* a one; we expect for it, as itself, at least some degree of ontological independence. Otherwise there would be no reason to mention it, much less to stress it, apart from multiplicity. If the One just is multiplicity, why not discuss multiplicity and be done with it? Nietzsche does not have much to say that is clear about this in *Philosophy in the Tragic Age of the Greeks*, but in his lectures on the Pre-Platonic philosophers he claims that this One is "the law of [the] eternal trans-formation" of the world (*PPP* 62–3), and this law he identifies as the famous *logos* of Heraclitus. This *logos* is generally taken to have been for Heraclitus a principle of order internal to the world that by harmonizing the chaotic flux of Becoming generates the cosmos that appears before us. Nietzsche seems to have taken it this way himself, for in *Philosophy in the Tragic Age of the Greeks* he refers to a "cosmic principle" that is in some undefined way related to the "inviolable laws and standards that are immanent in the struggle" of the qualities that constitute our world (*PTG* 55). Although he does not here identify this principle with the *logos*, I think we can rely on the evidence of his lectures to make the identification ourselves. But as to his leaving undefined the relation between the principle and the laws (the former may be the source of the latter or the two may in fact be identical), as well as the relation between these and the multiplicity of Becoming itself: all this raises anew the question of the relation between the One and the many. Tempted as we might be to reply that the elements of multiplicity are the many and the logos is the One, Nietzsche insistently runs them together. Even greater than Heraclitus's insight into Becoming, he says, is his "no longer see[ing] the contesting pairs [the elements of multiplicity] and their referees [the laws and standards] as separate; the judges themselves seemed to be striving in the contest and the contestants seemed to be judging them" (*PTG* 57). He makes the same point more directly in *The Pre-Platonic Philosophers* when he writes (immediately following his identification of law, *logos*, and the One) that "the one overall Becoming is itself law; *that* it becomes and *how* it becomes is its work" (*PPP* 63). But these remarks suggest that the *logos* is simultaneously the law (or laws) and the multiplicity subject to law. Once again we arrive at the puzzling thought that the One exists as, and only as, multiplicity.

Nietzsche believes that Heraclitus arrived at his insight that the one is the many by way of an intuition independent of dialectical-logical analysis (*PTG* 57-8), and this might explain his own inability to relate the insight clearly and coherently. But there is also the contributing factor that Nietzsche's early studies of Heraclitus are contemporaneous with the period of his deepest immersion in Schopenhauer's philosophy. His interpretation of Heraclitus is explicitly influenced by his Schopenhauerian inclinations,[5] and I suspect that this accounts for the ambiguous wording we have been considering. Taking all the evidence together, it is clear to me that Nietzsche's decided opinion is that for Heraclitus the One has no existence whatever apart from its existence *as* the many. This is the reason for his formulating Heraclitus's "intuitive perception" as follows: "There is no thing of which we may say, 'it is'" (*PPP* 62). If the One endured as a unity "behind," "beneath," "within," or in any other way distinct from multiplicity, then we *could* say of it that "it is." What, then, are we to make of Nietzsche's images of multiplicity as the "cloth" of the One that as it were swirls "around" it, of the One's "evidenc[ing] itself" in multiplicity, and particularly of multiplicity as "the form of appearance" of the One? These metaphors, I believe, derive from Schopenhauer's description of the relation between will and representation. Schopenhauer's will is a being distinct from the representations in which, and *as* which, it appears; we could without question say of it that "it is." This is not so for the One of Nietzsche's Heraclitus, yet when it comes to expressing this fact Nietzsche cannot resist employing Schopenhauerian tropes that imply the opposite. Perhaps this is merely a verbal infelicity, but to make sure of this we shall have to track whether any such ambiguities resurface in his own descriptions of the world as Becoming.

Will to power

In *Ecce Homo* Nietzsche summarizes Heraclitus's philosophy, in words nearly identical to those we have already quoted, as the affirmation of "*becoming*, along with a radical repudiation of the very concept of *being*." This position he describes as "more closely related to me than anything else thought to date" (*EH* "BT" 3). So let's move away now from Heraclitus to concentrate on Nietzsche's own philosophy and attempt in this section to come to terms with his idiosyncratic understanding of Becoming.

Imagine wearing a pair of glasses that magnify your vision to such an extent that you can view the world at the subatomic level (ignoring for now the question whether particles actually exist as the tiny spheres depicted in science textbooks).[6] The world would appear much different than it does now. Where before you saw large-scale material objects distinct in themselves and individuated from other objects—this table and that chair separated by unoccupied space, or this body and this chair not at all separated by space (for I am sitting on the chair), but nevertheless distinct—now you would see only microscopic bits of matter swirling among vast tracts of empty space, some of these bits more closely associated with one another than with other collections of bits, these associated collections perhaps identifiable as vaguely particularized clumps separate from one another, but each collection itself a vibrating, lacunose, ill-defined ghost of a thing. In short, the sharp lines of demarcation between and among things on the macro-level would blur to such an extent that it would be difficult to specify, for example, where the surface of the back of my thigh ends and the surface of the seat cushion begins. We would still be able to distinguish the table from the chair across the room (not *as* a chair and a table, perhaps, but as *this* and *that* loosely organized collection of particles), though we might not readily distinguish the surface of either from the air that surrounds it, for the particles that constitute the chair and the particles of the surrounding air would swirl so in the dark expanse of space that they would intermingle and therefore blur, to at least some problematic degree, the boundary between chair and air.

Now imagine exchanging your glasses for a more powerful pair, brand $E = mc^2$. This new pair of glasses reveals the world at the level of pure energy, a level at which all particles are deprived of their distinct particularity precisely as macroscopic objects like tables and chairs are deprived of their particularity when viewed from a microscopic perspective. Now you see no tables or chairs, no clumps of associated particles, no particles even. Now you see no *things* at all, neither macroscopic nor microscopic things. Now there appears only an immense field of energy, undifferentiated but undulating, heaving, churning. At this level we encounter what might well seem a single thing, a One; but it would be a thing of an unusual sort, a thing that flows, not from here to there, for it fills all space, but that flows within itself, moving like a large sheet waving in a hectic wind, billowing and falling, vibrating, pulsating, swirling like water upon the surface of which an invisible finger traces arcs that generate ripples whose interpenetrations form a variety of ever-changing patterns as well as fields of movement of no identifiable design.

These are powerful glasses, and doubtless impossible to manufacture; but they reveal a world similar to that which appears through the lens of Nietzsche's philosophy.

Time and again Nietzsche stresses that "enduring things ..., equal things ..., things, substances, bodies" are errors of our intellect (*GS* 110), that in fact there are no "lines, planes, bodies" (*GS* 112), no unity, thinghood, or substance (*TI* "Reason" 2), that the world in which we live and move, about which we calculate and reason, is of our own making, a fabrication, a fiction (*WP* 516). In short, Nietzsche rejects our common-sense image of the world. But we must not be misled into thinking that he would replace this image with the scientific image, an image of the world as composed of molecules, atoms, and subatomic particles. Atoms exist no more than chairs, for both are (or are supposed to be) material objects, but Nietzsche does not believe in matter.[7] "Materialistic atomism," he writes in *Beyond Good and Evil*, "is one of the best refuted theories there are" (*BGE* 12). Precisely as the world as seen through our powerful glasses includes no microscopic entities, in the world as Nietzsche sees it there is no "particle-atom" (*BGE* 12). Nietzsche rejects "all the presuppositions of mechanistic theory—matter, atom, gravity, pressure and stress," insisting that these are not "facts-in-themselves," but merely the products of our own interpretations (*WP* 689). Nature's "conformity to law," too, is mere interpretation and "bad 'philology'" (*BGE* 22; see also *GS* 109 and *WP* 629–32). The commonsense and scientific images of the world are alike in one fundamental respect, and in this respect they are similar to Platonic metaphysics: they privilege Being over Becoming. To Nietzsche's mind subatomic particles, atoms, chairs, mountains, planets, suns—in short, anything and everything that we conceive as a *thing* falls under the category Being, for we imagine all such "things" to be enduring substances. Not permanently enduring, perhaps; not eternal like Plato's Forms; but beings nonetheless. It is one and the same impulse that drives the common man to say of his chair, the scientist to say of an electron, and Plato to say of a Form, that "it is." Each of these men is mistaken, for there is nothing of which we may accurately say "it is."

I do not mean to suggest that Nietzsche contends that nothing whatsoever exists, that the universe, that reality, is void, so abysmally vacuous that really there just is no reality. This position cannot be coherently expressed, and if Nietzsche on occasion is dismissive of coherence and consistency, he never goes so far as to insist that the world, including himself and his act of insisting, absolutely does not exist. What is there, then, at the bottom of things according to Nietzsche? What in his view corresponds to the pure energy we discovered in the world as viewed through our $E = mc^2$ glasses? Not energy, at least not by this name. Nietzsche is fond of the word "force," but to this he prefers the word "power" and the expression "will to power." So the world at bottom is will to power.[8] Here we have a concise statement of Nietzsche's position. But what, exactly, does it mean?

To answer this question it will help to recall Schopenhauer's view of the world as will and representation. Starting from the Kantian position that space, time, and causality are not features of the world as it is in itself, but are rather imposed on the world by the activities of the human nervous system, including of course the brain (Kant himself would have said "mind"), Schopenhauer concludes that the multiplicity of our daily experience, the world of things individuated by time and space acting causally on one another, is a phantasm of the human perceptual-cognitive apparatus. This world as it appears to us, as it is represented by us, he calls *representation*.

As to what this world as it appears to us is a representation *of*, this we can know by way of an insight arrived at by an altogether different route from that which proceeds along the pathways of our nervous systems. We know our bodies in precisely the same way we know all the other objects of our experience; we know them from the outside, as it were, through the operations of our senses. Yet we also have a special mode of access to our bodies, a mode impossible to apply to anything other than our bodies. This is so because we are related to our bodies in a way we are not related to anything else: we are identical to our bodies. As a result, we know our bodies not only indirectly by way of our senses, but also directly from the inside, without the mediation of our senses. From this perspective we discover ourselves to be, at our core as it were, quite different from what we usually imagine. From the inside we do not appear as physical objects among objects, but rather as that which is "known immediately to everyone, and is denoted by the word *will*" (*WWR* 1:18). And this will we know ourselves to be is not causally related to our bodies—one's willing to move one's arm does not cause the arm to move; the willing and the movement are one and the same act viewed from two different perspectives, from the inside and from the outside. The movement just *is* the willing; it is the willing objectified, which is to say it is the willing as experienced through the senses. In short, our knowledge of our bodies as physical objects in the world is mediated by our senses and the nervous system into which they are tied; but our internal knowledge of ourselves is immediate. And by this immediate knowledge we know ourselves to be *will*.

Schopenhauer insists that this word, "will," is the most appropriate term available to name what we are apart from being representation. To make his point he contrasts the word with "force," which has been viewed as the more fundamental of the two. But we have arrived at the concept of force indirectly—we have inferred from our observations of the activities of the world as representation to the presence of a something we know not what operating behind them, and this unknown something we name "force." Will, on the other hand, we know directly, for it is an object of our immediate experience. If, therefore, we would explain the less by means of the more known, rather than the other way around (which would be no explanation at all, but rather an obfuscation), then we must regard force as a specific instance of the more fundamental activity of will (*WWR* 1:22). Prior to Schopenhauer this procedure was reversed: we understood will as a species of force manifested in a certain sort of living organism; but Schopenhauer argues that "force" is what we call will when manifested in nature apart from intentionality. Just as our body from the inside is will, so *everything* internally is will. Our body is an object in no way different from any other object in the world, so we may infer from our insight into the nature of our bodies apart from representation to the inner nature of all bodies. As Schopenhauer says, "the force that shoots and vegetates in the plant, indeed the force by which the crystal is formed, the force that turns the magnet to the North Pole, the force whose shock [one] encounters from the contact of metals of different kinds, the force that appears in the elective affinities of matter as repulsion and attraction, separation and union, and finally even gravitation, which acts so powerfully in all matter, pulling the stone to the earth and the earth to the sun; all these [are] different only in the phenomenon, but the same according to their inner nature" (*WWR* 1:22). This "inner

nature" is will. In short, then, everything in the world, apart from being representation, is also will.

Having thus identified the fundamental reality of all things, it is vitally important
that we resist the temptation to include in our concept of will the consciousness
through which it usually expresses itself in human beings. As we are conscious,
rational, intentional creatures, so the will operates within us in association with our
rational intentionality. But though our own manifestations of will are directed, we
must understand that this directionality is a product of the human's highly developed
nervous system and is not an intrinsic property of the will itself. In itself will is as
independent of consciousness as it is of every other feature of the world as representation; in itself it is blind, aimless. The will strives—striving is of its essence—but it
does not strive *toward* this or that; any *telos* of its activity is extrinsic to the will itself
and is superadded by us, the many particular and ephemeral vehicles of this one
universal, eternal reality. Schopenhauer himself understands that his audience will
at first be inclined to confuse the will with its conscious manifestation in humans,
and he makes every effort to obviate misunderstanding on this point. Time and
again he reminds his readers that "the circumstance of [will's] being accompanied
by knowledge, and the determination by motives which is conditioned by this
knowledge … belongs not to the inner nature of the will, but merely to its most
distinct phenomenon as animal and human being" (*WWR* 1:19). The will, as I say, is
blind; and being blind its activity is devoid of meaning—and this insight evokes from
Schopenhauer the rather Nietzschean thought that the will is "[e]ternal becoming,
endless flux" (*WWR* 1:29).

For Schopenhauer, then, reality at its most fundamental level, the world as it is in
itself, is will. And will, existing independently of the human nervous system, has no
spatial, temporal, or causal features. And since multiplicity depends on spatial and/or
temporal divisions, the will must be one. It objectifies itself as a plurality, is represented
by the brain with its categories of space and time as a plurality; but in and of itself the
will is one. Thus Schopenhauer's world is a single but two-sided thing. The obverse
is a world of many particular objects that come to be and pass away and enter into a
variety of causal relations with one another; the reverse is an eternal, infinite unity to
which the principles of causality do not apply. This reverse side of the world is will, and
will is all there actually is; the obverse, the representation, has no distinct existence, for
it is nothing other than the will as it appears to certain experiencing beings.

Though a passionate Schopenhauerian early in his career, Nietzsche eventually
rejected Schopenhauer's metaphysics, as he rejected all metaphysics. This, anyway, is
the story he told of himself, to himself and to the world. But the fact is that throughout
his life Nietzsche's thought ran along lines laid down by his early engagement with
Schopenhauer, and this is so even when he resisted the natural trajectory of this way
of thinking. This is nowhere more evident than in his idea that the world at bottom
is will to power.

Recall our image of the mass of the universe converted into energy; recall the
roiling, swelling, surging flux and movement of this deepest stratum of reality.
Nietzsche has something like this in mind when he writes of the will to power, as we
can see from his portrait of the world as revealed "in [his] mirror." It is, he says:

a monster of energy, without beginning, without end; a firm, iron magnitude of force that does not grow bigger or smaller, that does not expend itself but only transforms itself; as a whole, of unalterable size, a household without expenses or losses, but likewise without increase or income; enclosed by "nothingness" as by a boundary; not something blurry or wasted, not something endlessly extended, but set in a definite space as a definite force, and not a space that might be "empty" here or there, but rather as a force throughout, as a play of forces and waves of forces, at the same time one and many, increasing here and at the same time decreasing there; a sea of forces flowing and rushing together, eternally changing, eternally flooding back, with tremendous years of recurrence, with an ebb and a flood of its forms ... (*WP* 1067).

The description is striking, not least for its manifold imagery. We note the appearance of "energy," "force," and "waves of forces," which expressions Nietzsche has borrowed from contemporary science. But when summing up his thought he reverts to the language of metaphysics, Schopenhauer's metaphysics in particular. "*This world is the will to power*," he writes, "*and nothing besides!*" (*WP* 1067). The idea, I take it, is that behind, beneath, or within the things of this world as we encounter them in our daily lives there is only the will to power. This will is the one and only fundamental reality, and in some way it gives rise to the multiplicity around us. In a sense it just *is* this multiplicity. The will to power is the "*one* basic form of the will" (*BGE* 36) manifesting as distinct centers, or quanta, of force, "will force" (*BGE* 36), or power.[9]

At times Nietzsche seems almost to imply that the will to power is an ontological unity, a One, much like Schopenhauer's will. But I would not insist that Nietzsche conceived of the will to power as a single continuous field of force that somehow acts as (and perhaps *only* as) a multiplicity, despite his remark in the passage above that the world (which just is the will to power) is "at the same time one and many," and despite the echo here of his early interpretation of Heraclitus as affirming that "the one is at the same time the many" (*PTG* 58). His standard practice is to stress the plurality, for when he writes of the will to power he regularly does so in terms of quanta of power acting on and against one another. In a late note he comments that "whatever is real, whatever is true, is neither one nor even reducible to one" (*WP* 536), but it is impossible to say what he had in mind when he wrote this. In truth there is little material to draw on for an accurate account of the ontological status of the will to power with respect to its being a one or a many (or both), and what little there is is often puzzling.

Having called attention to this problem of ontology I set it aside to say what I can say with confidence, namely, that for Nietzsche there is nothing that is not will to power.[10] If the world at large could be explained by way of his own hypothesis, then "the world viewed from inside, the world defined and determined according to its 'intelligible character' ... would be 'will to power' and nothing else" (*BGE* 36). Nietzsche evidently intends his readers to think of Schopenhauer here, for the idea of viewing the world from the inside is his, and in this context the expression "intelligible character" alludes to Schopenhauer as well. Whatever he intended by summoning the shade of his great predecessor at this point in his work, his doing so demonstrates his ongoing indebtedness to the man's metaphysics.[11]

In the previous chapter I explained the contrast between Being and Becoming as amounting to a contrast between the metaphysical and the physical. I also noted that when dealing with Nietzsche we would have to modify or eliminate some of the connotations of our standard vocabulary. Nietzsche often writes in such a way as to suggest that the physical, material world around us is Becoming, but when he penetrates more deeply he exposes this for a mere surface level of analysis. When he suggests, as he does in *Twilight of the Idols*, that the world as revealed to our senses is Becoming (*TI* "Reason" 2), we might take him to refer to all those things to which we have access through our senses, namely, physical, material objects. To read him this way, however, we must overlook reason's role in the construction of experience. According to Nietzsche, things—things as unified, stable, and enduring substances— are not revealed by our senses; they are constructs of reason; they enter into our experience only because reason as it were slips metaphysical postulates behind the chaotic flux of our sensations (*TI* "Reason" 2, 5). In short, by the activity of our minds we impose stability on an inherently unstable tide of change. It is true that physical, material things come to be, change, and pass away; but we humans instinctively conceptualize these things as enduring throughout the period between their gener- ation and annihilation, during which time they serve as the unalterable substratum of motion and change. Consider our commonsense conception of a thing: when we say of something that it has changed, we mean that one or more of its properties has changed, while the thing itself, *as* itself, has remained the same. When, for example, my weight, skin tone, or thoughts change, I myself endure, otherwise it would make no sense to attribute the properties before and after the change to one and the same *me*; and if this made no sense, it would be no more sensible to speak of *my* having changed than to speak of two different but similar individuals.

To see Nietzsche's point about the metaphysical nature of physical, material things (of our *conception* of them) it may help initially to think of obviously metaphysical entities like Plato's Forms as straightforwardly "permanent" and as "Being," while thinking of less obviously metaphysical entities like the physical objects of our daily experience as "temporarily permanent" and as "Being within Becoming." A physical, material thing like a tree is temporary in that it came to be at some definite point in the past and will cease to exist at some point in the future, but relative to its changeable and changing properties the tree itself is permanent—it remains the same tree even as its height, age, number of leaves, etc. change. Similarly, a tree is "within" Becoming in so far as it is located here and now before our eyes (and other senses) as opposed to occupying an inaccessible sphere of metaphysical reality, but it qualifies as Being to the extent that we take it to be the enduring and stable substratum of change described in the previous sentence. Any imagined cessation of the flow of Becoming is a metaphysical delusion, and this is as true for temporary as for eternal stoppages. These contrasts between the permanent and the temporarily permanent, between Being and Being within Becoming, are heuristic expedients only; they highlight the evident differences between physical, material things and Platonic Forms, but these differences are superficial. Beneath the surface, the one no less than the other type of entity falls entirely under the category Being.

In *Philosophy in the Tragic Age of the Greeks* Nietzsche attributes to Heraclitus the idea that "everything which coexists in space and time has but a relative existence, [and] each thing exists through and for another like it, which is to say through and for an equally relative one." From this insight, Nietzsche continues, comes "the Heraclitan conclusion" that "the whole nature of reality lies simply in its acts" (*PTG* 53). The assumption that things have any other than a relative existence is yet another result of reason's constructive activity, and in his late notes Nietzsche insists that "one must break absolutely" with this idea (*WP* 559). In reality a thing is constituted by its properties, and its properties are nothing in themselves but exist only as "effects on other 'things'" (*WP* 557). So not only is our idea of a substratum an illegitimate metaphysical postulate, but the properties we suppose to inhere in the substratum are postulates, or constructs, as well. To attain to this insight is to dissolve all islands of Being into the ever-flowing river of Becoming.

So what are we to make of Nietzsche's Becoming? Becoming is the world regarded as the flux that it is independent of the creative-interpretive activity of our reason, and when we penetrate beneath all those aspects of reality fabricated by reason we arrive at will to power. As for how exactly we should conceptualize the claim that the world is will to power, how to hold it before our mind's eye to examine and work with it—unfortunately, there is little we can do but consult Nietzsche's relatively few, and frequently obscure, remarks on the subject and rely on the thoughts and figures they generate, and perhaps it will help to conjure an image of the world as revealed through glasses that transform mass into energy. Nietzsche himself employed the terms "force" and "energy" to describe the will to power to himself. This may do for us too, for we are familiar with these terms, having encountered them from early in our education. So long as we keep in mind Schopenhauer's points that force is a manifestation of will (not vice versa), and that the will in itself is in no way conscious, we can rely on these terms at least to bring us near to Nietzsche's intended meaning.

There are those who make much of the "doctrine" of will to power, but to my mind Nietzsche is not at his best when writing about this subject, for he writes in this context as a typical natural philosopher (with notes of the typical metaphysician). His ideas may be unusual, perhaps even radical, but they are well within traditional philosophical paradigms. Nietzsche is more challenging, and therefore more inspiring, when at his business of unsettling paradigms. This he does with his controversial idea that the physical, material world of our daily experience is so thoroughly the work of the creative-interpretive activity of our minds that we would do well to regard it as a fiction.

Historical background

The idea that the world of our experience is a fiction is, to say the least, a challenge to our normal way of thinking about reality and truth. To understand Nietzsche's views on these matters it will help to have in mind the historical developments that provide the context in which he thought. It is a history of more than two thousand years, but I shall strive for brevity by covering only the essentials.

Socrates' near contemporary Democritus, and a more obscure figure called Leucippus, formulated the original version of atomic theory. Reasoning that matter cannot be infinitely divisible, they concluded that there must exist indivisible particles of matter so small that they cannot be detected by the senses.[12] Every such particle they designated an *atomon*, which word means, literally, "that which cannot be cut." The infinite universe is filled with an infinite number of atoms of every possible shape, which, moving through the void, collide with one another and sometimes bond together, thereby forming larger compound items, from grains of sand to human beings, the heavenly bodies of our solar system, and infinite other worlds besides. Each atom resembles Parmenides' *eon* in that it neither comes to be nor passes away, but the aggregations and disaggregations of these atoms account for the coming-to-be and passing-away of the objects of our experience.

The aspect of atomism that concerns us here is the implied difference between the world as it appears to us and the world as it actually is in itself. According to Democritus's theory of perception, sensation arises from interactions between "images" given off by physical objects, the nature and condition of the relevant sense organ, and the intervening medium (the water or air, for example, through which the images pass before contacting our sense organs). One consequence of this idea is that we do not know the world directly, but only by way of images, which themselves may be distorted by both the intervening medium and our sense organs. But this implies that we have no knowledge of the world as it is in itself (beyond the general theoretical knowledge that the world is composed of atoms and void). We know only the appearances. Democritus himself was aware of the epistemological implications of his theory, as is clear from the following fragment: " ... in reality we understand nothing as it actually is, but only as it changes according to the disposition of the body and the things that enter it and that offer resistance to it" (DK B9). Then there is this famous fragment, more specific than the first: "By convention sweet, by convention bitter, by convention hot, by convention cold, by convention color, but in reality atoms and void" (DK B125).[13]

Atomic theory was taken up by Epicurus (341–270 BCE), who in his famous Athenian garden taught a doctrine of materialistic hedonism. Unlike Democritus, Epicurus was not a skeptic regarding sensible properties; colors, for example, are real properties of macroscopic physical objects. Yet they are relational properties, which is to say dispositions in bodies to produce color sensations in perceiving subjects; they are not properties of the microscopic atoms themselves, which are characterized only by shape, size, and weight. Three letters and several sayings attributed to Epicurus survive, and his teachings were expressed at length by his Roman disciple Lucretius (first half of the first century BCE), whose *De rerum natura* articulates and expands Epicurus's teachings in six books of eloquent dactylic hexameter verse.

Atomism is a materialist doctrine. It admits of souls and gods, but even these are composed of atoms; and the gods, according to Epicurus, pay no heed at all to human beings.[14] It will come as no surprise that this philosophy fell out of favor with the ascent of Christianity. It did not return to prominence in the west until atomism was reintroduced in the early modern period by Pierre Gassendi (1592–1655).

But to return to the ancient period, and to more explicitly skeptical traditions: sometime just after the year 270 BCE, and so not long after the death of Epicurus,

Arcesilaus assumed the position of scholarch of Plato's Academy. Under his leadership the school took a turn toward skepticism that lasted, in one form or another, until the Academy itself as a physical institution came to an end through the aggression of the Roman general Sulla, who sacked Athens in 86 BCE (having entered the city through a breach in the wall very near the grounds of Plato's school). The Academic skeptics—the most prominent among them besides Arcesilaus were Carneades (scholarch c. 155 BCE), and Philo (scholarch c. 110 BCE)—were motivated in their skepticism by an ongoing dispute with the Stoics, who claimed that a certain sort of cognitive impression, which they called a cataleptic impression, is both an accurate representation of its object and also, crucially, self-certifying. Whoever experiences a cataleptic impression *knows* something, and he knows that he knows it. The skeptics argued that there are no cataleptic impressions and therefore there is no knowledge. The logic here suggests that the Academic skeptics believed they could demonstrate, and therefore know, that knowledge is impossible. But this seems paradoxical. Can one know that knowledge is impossible? Since the ancient period it has occasionally been suggested that the Academics were in fact traditionally dogmatic Platonists who insisted only that knowledge is impossible *if* one adopts the Stoic criterion of the cataleptic impression, but that they themselves did not accept this criterion and so were not skeptics. According to this interpretation, then, the Academics' skepticism was not absolute but merely dialectical, a position they adopted against the Stoics while maintaining their own Platonic commitment to seeking knowledge of metaphysical truth as manifested in the Forms.[15]

The evidence is too scant to determine with confidence whether the Academics were dogmatic skeptics or dogmatic Platonists, but they were not the only skeptics among the ancients; there were also so-called Pyrrhonian skeptics, about whom we are much better informed. I mention the Pyrrhonists after the Academics, despite the fact that Pyrrho himself flourished well before Arcesilaus took charge of the Academy (in fact he died right around this time), because the movement that took his name is a later development. There is some dispute whether Pyrrho was a skeptic at all, for he may have argued, not that we cannot know the world around us (an epistemological claim), but that the world in itself has no determinate nature to be known (an ontological claim). This would be a dogmatic metaphysical position, which would make Pyrrho precisely the opposite of a skeptic. But, as I say, this is disputed. The question turns on the interpretation of the ideas attributed to Pyrrho by his associate Timon of Phlius, as reported much later by the Aristotelian philosopher Aristocles. Fortunately, we need not tarry over this matter, for Pyrrhonism exercised its greatest influence on the tradition of later western philosophy through the works of Sextus Empiricus (c. 160–210 CE), and these works are extant.

From Sextus's comprehensive *Outlines of Pyrrhonism* we learn that Pyrrhonian skeptics employ a series of arguments (or "modes") that tend to lead those who encounter them into a state of *epochê*, or suspension of judgment. One of these modes, for example, argues that since non-human animals possess acute powers of sensation that enable them to survive and even to flourish, we cannot be sure that those of our impressions that differ from theirs are accurate representations of the world, for it may be the animals' representations that are accurate; another argues that since we experience different impressions in different conditions, for example depending on whether we are awake or asleep and dreaming, it is impossible to determine in which condition we experience the world aright; and a more broadly applicable mode argues that since everything that appears, appears in relation to something—particularly in relation to the person to whom it is appearing—we cannot know the object of our experience as it is in itself. For the Pyrrhonists these arguments are as arrows in a quiver to fire at and puncture every claim to knowledge; so effective are their weapons that the Pyrrhonists suspend judgment about all matters. They claim to be seeking the truth, and it does no harm to take them at their word. But in practice they adopt, at all times and everywhere, an attitude of *epochê*.[16]

The sixteenth-century reintroduction of Sextus's works into the European philo-sophical mainstream was one of the major events of western intellectual history. The eruption into early modern Europe of Pyrrhonian skepticism shook the confidence of philosophers and theologians that they could, and in some cases did, know the truth about nature, man, and God. Moreover, the reemergence of Pyrrhonism was not an isolated intellectual event; it occurred in conjunction with the Protestant Reformation and the early phases of the Scientific Revolution.[17] Together these three episodes undermined the ancient and medieval foundations of western philosophy. The history of philosophical skepticism that followed, and the many unsuccessful attempts to refute it, were among the proximate intellectual progenitors of Nietzsche's radical mind.

In the fall of 1517 (October 31, to be exact: All Saints' Day) Martin Luther nailed to the door of All Saints' Church in Wittenberg, Germany, his famous Ninety-Five Theses against indulgences and other of the pope's abuses of power. In doing so he initiated what has come to be known as the Reformation, which had among its many consequences the effect of undermining the authority of the Catholic Church as the sole earthly caretaker of divine truth. It was the sort of event that causes men to fear the collapse of their world's foundations,[18] for after a millennium of knowing exactly where to turn for theological truth there soon resounded a cacophony of voices, each one singing of its own special knowledge. Thus a great impulse was given to theological skepticism that would eventuate, for example, in the sire of a family of Lutheran ministers publically proclaiming the death of God.

A similar unmooring of the world was effected by the work of Copernicus and Galileo, who taught quite literally that the earth moves, and that hurtling as it does through the heavens it cannot be regarded as occupying the center of the universe. Under the influence of Aristotle, the Church had adopted a geocentric cosmology, so the new astronomy had theological ramifications every bit as profound, in their way, as the changes wrought by Luther. The fresh ideas that flooded Europe during the Scientific Revolution gradually eroded Aristotle's authority, not just as a scientist but as a philosopher more generally. And since Aristotle's ideas had provided the foundations for the greatest of the medieval philosophical and theological edifices, the weakening of the structure of his system prompted many to reject traditional conceptions and to conceive new methods for understanding the world. When Francis Bacon in 1620 entitled his book on logic and scientific method the *New Organon* he announced quite explicitly his intention to replace Aristotle (whose own works on these subjects had long been collectively known as the *Organon*), but the majority of Bacon's intellectual peers were involved in the same endeavor. Indeed, the greatest of philosophers and scientists of this period were consciously and resolutely engaged in developing a New Philosophy (including in this term the discipline of natural philosophy, which we would call science).

This new philosophy had many branches, but we shall explore only those along which skeptical trends developed, for this is the way that leads to Nietzsche. This is not to say that Nietzsche himself was a skeptic, but whatever label or labels we affix to him, it is fair to say that his thought developed as it did in part because of the generations of skeptics that preceded him. Consider, for example, Michel de Montaigne (1533–92), who wrote his famous *Essays* under the influence of his encounter with Sextus Empiricus. Four years prior to the publication of the first edition of his book Montaigne commissioned a medal to be fashioned and engraved with the word ΕΠΕΧΩ (*epechô*), the first person singular verb–form of the noun *epochê*, which, as we have seen, expresses the Pyrrhonist's state of suspension of judgment.[19] Thus Montaigne had always around him a reminder that "I suspend judgment."

Montaigne's influence on modern philosophers as diverse as Descartes and David Hume has long been acknowledged, and his influence on Nietzsche has more recently been examined in detail.[20] Skepticism appears in Descartes' work most famously in the first of his six *Meditations on First Philosophy*, which book, however, is not a skeptical treatise, but is rather Descartes' effort to overcome skepticism. This feat he attempts to accomplish by presenting the most powerful arguments in favor of skepticism and then refuting them. So, for example, he raises doubts about the reliability of our senses and reason with considerations ranging from the observation that our senses sometimes deceive us to the twin possibilities that what we take for knowledge is no knowledge at all but rather the fantasies of a dream or, worse, falsehoods deliberately implanted in our minds by an omnipotent malicious deity. He then attempts to resolve these doubts by appealing to the "cogito ergo sum" to demonstrate that he does know one thing, namely, that he exists. And on the basis of this knowledge he formulates an argument for the existence of a God whose goodness secures the reliability of human judgments arrived at according to a proper methodology. The upshot of all this is that despite skeptical challenges, we do in fact know all that we perceive clearly and distinctly. Unfortunately for Descartes, his refutation of skepticism never has been widely accepted; ironically, his presentation of the skeptical challenges has been of more lasting influence than his specific solution.[21]

Descartes is a dualist, which is to say he believes that the world is composed of two fundamentally different kinds of substance, namely, mind, the essence of which is to think, and matter, the essence of which is extension in space. He draws this distinction in the second of his *Meditations*. In his treatises on science and scientific method Descartes elaborates his conception of matter, and we would do well to note this conception because it is one among many modern views of the world that picture it as quite different than we normally imagine it to be, and these revisions of our understanding of nature set the stage for Nietzsche's more radical revisions. When I write that for Descartes the essence of matter is extension in space I mean that this is the one and only property inherent in any particular bit of matter. Color, odor, sound, and other such properties accessible to our senses are not in the world itself but rather in our minds. Versions of this view proliferated in the modern period, and it has since become standard. The idea is perhaps most closely associated with John Locke (1632–1704), the first of the three great British empiricists, the other two being George Berkeley (1685–1753), and David Hume (1711–76). These men developed empiricism in different and surprising directions, each in its way unsettling our commonsense image of the world.

Locke expresses the division of the world into its objective and subjective features in terms of primary and secondary qualities. The commonsense view of the world, shared even by the philosophers of antiquity and the middle ages (though not, as we have seen, by the ancient atomists), assumes that the world in itself contains colors, sounds, odors, tastes, and textures—in short, all those properties we experience by way of our senses. This idea was questioned and eventually rejected in the modern period, largely due to the fact that modern conceptions of physics take no account of these properties. One need not speculate about the color of particles of matter in order to formulate laws to explain their various interactions. The size of these particles, their mass, their positions in space, their inherent tendencies toward motion or rest—these are examples of the properties of matter the scientist must sort out and either assume or reject in order to develop a workable physics. In short, then, since science makes no use of the ordinary sensible properties of matter, scientists (and, today, every layman with a minimal degree of scientific education) subtract them from their view of the way the world is in itself. Consider the examples of color and sound. When you look at what we call a colored object, the color is not actually in the object itself; the color exists only in your mind. There *is* something in the object that causes you to experience it as colored, but this something is not its color. Rather, the surface of the object reflects light waves at certain frequencies, and when light waves of this or that particular frequency contact a human eye, assuming the eye and the related visual system are functioning properly, the light waves are transmuted into electrical impulses that travel along the optic nerve into the visual cortex, at which point they are somehow (we have no idea how) transmuted again into the subjective experience of this or that color. So the object actually is "out there" in the world, as are the light waves and the fact of their having some specific frequency; but the color we experience as a result of the waves interacting with our visual-cognitive system, this is not in the world but only in the mind of the perceiver. Similarly, when a friend is speaking to you, no sounds are coming out of his mouth. Your friend is emitting nothing but air, but he is moving his throat and mouth in such a way that this air is causing the surrounding air to move in specific ways, producing sound waves. When this moving air enters a human ear it sends impulses through the auditory system that eventuate in your experiencing a sound. The air and the fact of its moving in a specific way are "out there" in the world, but the sound you experience as a result of these objective facts is a subjective phenomenon of, or in, your mind.

You may extend this line of reasoning, with the appropriate modifications, to all that we experience by way of taste, touch, and smell. Such sensible qualities are not features of the world as it is in itself; they are, rather, the subjective phenomena we experience as a result of our interactions with those properties of the world that do exist independently of our minds, light wave frequencies for example. There is some degree of scholarly dispute concerning Locke's own distinctions between primary and secondary qualities, for he did not express himself on the subject with absolute consistency. But I have here stated the distinction broadly enough to capture the contemporary view without ambiguity.

Berkeley, an empiricist but also an idealist (which is to say that he thought all of reality, including what we call matter, to be mental), radicalized Locke's position by arguing that all the so-called primary qualities, which are supposedly features of the world as it is in itself independent of any mind, are in fact secondary qualities, which is to say that they are all mind-dependent. In brief, the spatial extension, figure (or shape), and motion of bodies that Locke regarded as objective features of the world Berkeley assigns to subjective experience. Ultimately they depend on the mind of God rather than the minds of humans, but even so they are subjective through and through. The world, quite literally, is a world of *ideas*, and ideas by definition are mental. This conception of reality, typically summarized in the expression "to be is to be perceived," is no doubt unfamiliar and more than a little surprising, but it is not our business here to evaluate Berkeley's arguments, but only to point out the many ways in which philosophical and scientific conceptions of reality in the period leading up to Nietzsche diverged from common sense.

Locke and Berkeley were not skeptics; they regarded their accounts of reality, however unusual, as expressions of the truth. Hume, on the other hand, the last of the three great British empiricists, was the most forceful advocate of skepticism since the ancient Academic and Pyrrhonian philosophers. This is not the place to examine every aspect of Hume's skepticism; we shall instead concentrate only on those of his positions that lead to Nietzsche through Kant (by way of Schopenhauer). Hume's presentation of the problem of induction (as we call it today) and his related skeptical reflections on causation were troubling to those of his contemporaries who read his work, and they continue to exercise philosophers today. Induction in this context means the ability to predict future events based solely on past experience. I write "solely" because Hume, being an empiricist, held that knowledge of the world comes from, and *only* from, experience. If, then, I am to have confidence that gravity will operate tomorrow as it has operated to date, I must base my confidence on nothing other than my past observations of its functioning. But what reason do I have to believe that gravity will operate in this or that particular manner (or at all) tomorrow (or later today, or one second from now) just because it has done so in the past? Hume argues that we can justify this inference only if we have reason to believe that the future will resemble the past. But what reason might we have to believe this? We are limited to experience in this case too, so we can say only that the future will resemble the past because it has always done so to date. But this is precisely the form of reasoning we were trying to establish as legitimate to begin with. If the question at issue is whether the future will resemble the past, we cannot answer it by noting that in the past the future has regularly resembled the past. This may well be so, but the problem is to establish that in the future the future will *continue* to resemble the past, and this line of reasoning only begs this question.

The problem of causation is related to this in so far as we believe, for example, that the force of gravity *causes* two bodies of a specific combined mass at a specific distance from one another to generate some specific and calculable degree of mutual attraction. This is so because our use of the word *cause* in this instance implies that the law of gravity holds in all parts of the universe at all times (with certain unproblematic exceptions), including those parts of the universe and those times in its past and future history that we have not experienced or, in some cases, cannot experience. But this belief is obviously problematic if we cannot appeal to past experiences in order to reason about events beyond these experiences; and this is precisely what the problem of induction suggests that we cannot do. The problem of induction, then, is simultaneously a problem of causation. Is there any way to solve this latter problem without begging the question in favor of the former? We could perhaps solve the problem if our experience of what we call causal relationships were an experience of something more than just one event regularly following another, if, for example, we experienced that the latter event *must* follow the former. This *must* is the conceptual point that distinguishes causal relationships from mere accidental connections between two events. If one billiard ball smacks into another one and then someone coughs, we take this for an accidental connection; but the second ball's moving we take to be *necessarily* connected to the first one's hitting it. We can express this in Hume's terminology by saying that our idea of a cause includes the idea of a *necessary connection*. A cause does not just happen to precede an effect; a cause necessarily produces an effect. With this in mind, then, consider: if our experiences of gravitational attraction or billiard-ball impact included not just two massive bodies and such and such a degree of attraction, or one ball hitting another and the second one moving, but if our experiences also included between the two events another event or phenomenon that we could legitimately represent in language with a "must," a "necessarily," or an "at all times and everywhere" clause, then we would not have to rely solely on past experiences. The expressions "necessarily" and "at all times and everywhere" imply the expression "in the future," so the experience of a necessary connection between two events would secure the causal relation between them and thereby warrant reasoning beyond the bounds of our experience. Unfortunately, however, examine our experiences as we will, we do not find any such necessary connection. Regular connections we find in abundance, but these will not do to secure causality and overcome the problem of induction.

Hume's skepticism with respect to induction and causality is especially troubling to anyone interested in science as a source of knowledge. The formulation of laws is essential to the practice of science, for laws enable prediction and retrodiction, which is to say that laws justify a scientist's claims about past, future, or present but spatially distant states of the world. This justification depends on the universality of scientific laws, on their applying at all times and everywhere under relevantly similar conditions. But if we cannot justify induction, and if we cannot be sure that those relationships we think of as causal are not instead highly regular but non-causal connections, then we cannot formulate *universal* laws, in which case the pronouncements of scientists that stray beyond the bounds of past experience are unjustified. And it is important in this connection to note that Hume's arguments as outlined above demonstrate not only that past experience does not suffice to generate certain knowledge of future experience, but also that it does not suffice to generate any degree of probability whatever. You may experience one event following another one time, one thousand times, or one trillion times—the probability that the one event will follow the other the *next* time is in every case *precisely zero*. If we limit our considerations to the purely practical, then it may well make sense to expect the one event to follow the other (and given the nature of human psychology it is understandable that we do expect this), and this expectation has led to every theoretical and technological success of which scientists may boast. But as to the question whether science is a source not just of practical service, but of knowledge, until someone solves Hume's skeptical problems the most we can say is that we do not know (and to reiterate the point about probability, we cannot even say that it is more rather than less likely).

The idea that the foundations of science might be so insecure was particularly distressing to Immanuel Kant (1724–1804). Though we think of Kant primarily as a philosopher, he made at least one noteworthy contribution to science, the Nebular Hypothesis, according to which our solar system formed when a rotating cloud of gas and dust cooled and collapsed under the force of gravity. This hypothesis clearly applies the law of gravitational attraction well beyond the bounds of past experience and assumes causal activities of a sort no human has ever directly experienced. We can, therefore, imagine that Kant would be eager to reply to Hume's arguments. His reply, laid out in the *Critique of Pure Reason* (1781) and condensed (though with more explicit attention to the problem of causation) in the *Prolegomena to any Future Metaphysics* (1783), revolutionized philosophy. Kant agrees with Hume that we cannot acquire the concept of causality from experience, for, as Hume says, we never experience a necessary connection between the supposed cause and what we take to be its effect. If, then, experience were our sole mode of access to the world, Hume's skeptical problems would be unresolvable. So to resolve them Kant argues that we possess some knowledge of the world apart from and prior to experience, which he refers to as *a priori* knowledge. We do not extract this knowledge from the world, but rather (to express the idea somewhat loosely) we impose it on the world. The idea is that the human mind comes equipped with certain concepts to which the totality of our experience must conform, and among these is the concept of causality. Our minds simply organize the input they receive from the world in such a way as to place all events into a vast web of causal relations. Experience alone can distinguish causal (and therefore necessary) from accidental connections, but even quite apart from experience we can be sure that causal connections do in fact exist.

I have said that Kant's resolution of Hume's skeptical problems revolutionized philosophy. The point is worth elaborating, for it is only in the wake of Kant's revolution that Nietzsche's most radical ideas about knowledge, truth, and the nature of reality are possible. But since Nietzsche first encountered the Kantian philosophy by way of Schopenhauer, and since more often than not throughout his career he expresses himself on these matters in a vocabulary derived more directly from Schopenhauer than from Kant, I shall for the most part present Schopenhauer's version of Kant's ideas.[22] We have seen that ancient and medieval philosophers (excluding the skeptics) believed that the world exists independently of the human mind with features identical to, or at least quite similar to, the features we perceive it to have when our perceptual and cognitive systems are functioning properly. Early modern philosophers revised this picture by removing colors, odors, heat and cold, etc. from the world as it is in itself to relocate them in the human mind; but they did not doubt that spatial extension, for example, was a genuine feature of the world as it is independent of human experience. Berkeley removed even space from the world independent of mind, but he did not suggest that it depends on the human mind, at least not ultimately; for Berkeley the world exists independently of us in the mind of God. In this sense, then, the world is what it is apart from the human perceptual and cognitive systems, even though it does not exist independently of the divine mind. Kant reversed the traditional conception of the relation between the world and the human mind—the most fundamental features of the world as we know it are not in fact features of the world as it is in itself, but are imposed on the world by the human perceptual-cognitive apparatus. Among these—and here I employ Schopenhauer's terminology—are space, time, and causality. In and of itself, apart from human experience, reality has neither spatial nor temporal features, nor are there causal relations between or among events. The world as we experience it, then, the world as a plurality of objects, each one identical with itself and distinct (spatially and temporally) from every other object, each acting causally on others and being in turn effected by others—this world is a phantasm of the human mind, or as Schopenhauer puts it, this world is our representation.

In *Twilight of the Idols* there is a chapter entitled "How the 'True World' Finally Became a Fable." Consisting of but a single page of fewer than 250 words, the chapter is Nietzsche's concise history of western philosophers' rejection of Being, whether of the Platonic, Christian, or modern materialist variety. The philosophical history I have just related is not at all intended to correspond to the specifics of Nietzsche's account. In general terms, however, it reveals in its own way the many transformations of western philosophers' thoughts about the nature of the world as it is in itself. The dominant trends of this history are skeptical doubts about our ability to know the world and realist transferals of properties that once were thought to belong to the world in itself to the human way of experiencing and cognizing the world. The lesson is that the world of Being ostensibly "out there" is either unknown, unknowable, or a projection of our own minds, and thus no Being at all. These ideas provide the context for Nietzsche's own philosophizing, and their divergences from traditional ways of conceiving reality, divergences that become more pronounced over time, prepare the ground for Nietzsche's own doubts about there being a way the world is in itself and his consequent inclination to dismiss the idea that humans have access to anything plausibly conceived of as "the truth."

Reality and truth

Nietzsche's most famous early discussion of truth and knowledge appears in his abandoned and fragmentary essay "On Truth and Lies in a Nonmoral Sense." Writing in 1873, one year after the publication of *The Birth of Tragedy*, Nietzsche expressed in this work an early version of his epistemological pessimism.[23] I almost wrote that he expressed himself *eloquently*, but though there is an appealing youthful vigor about his prose, no one can accuse Nietzsche of having formulated his ideas with pedantic precision, for throughout the piece he obscures the distinctions between knowledge and truth. He begins by writing of the human "invention" of knowledge, but soon slides into discussing our "possession of truth," and finally he winds up issuing declarations concerning "truth," period (or anyway concerning traditional conceptions of truth). The lessons he takes from his account of our way of knowing he transfers to the idea of truth without pausing to consider whether the move is legitimate. It may or may not be legitimate; my point is that Nietzsche seems unaware that he should defend his inferential leaps, or that he is unconcerned to do so. In any case, he argues that the number and the nature of the intermediaries that stand between our supposed knowledge of the world and the world itself are such as to undermine our claims to know the truth about the world. Consider, for example, our knowledge (or what we take to be our knowledge) of a leaf. The process begins with a nerve stimulus in the eye.[24] That there is this nerve stimulus is all that we know directly. That it has been caused by an external object is an assumption resulting from "a false and unjustifiable application of the principle of sufficient reason" (*TL* 81). Nietzsche is following Schopenhauer here,[25] and he means that since we cannot help but experience the world in causal terms, we take nerve stimuli for the effects of causes. The faculty of the understanding then applies its categories of space and time to project these causes into the external world as spatial-temporal objects acting on our senses. The objects themselves as well as their causal activities are in fact products of the constructive operations of our intellect; they do not actually exist in the world as it is in itself. Yet we take them for real external objects, and we cannot help but to take them this way. Nevertheless, according to Nietzsche our inferences in this case are "unjustifiable." And even if we grant for the sake of argument that something "out there" causes the nerve stimulus, our access to the thing is mediated so radically that we can know nothing of it. The object itself does not enter into our perceptual system, in which there are only electrical neural impulses. Of the thing we take to cause this activity we can say only that it is "the mysterious X of the thing in itself" (*TL* 83).

Now consider for a moment the neural activity itself: it too is transformed in the processes of perception and cognition. The external object as perceived and known does not manifest to the mind as a collection of neural impulses but as, for example, a mental image. But how is it that electrical signals travelling through our nervous systems appear in our minds as images? A mental image is as different from a series of electrical impulses as such impulses differ from a physical object. And then there is our method (one of our methods) of communicating our experiences of the external world, to ourselves and to others, namely, sounds. Sounds result from yet another transformation in the process, the transformation of our mental images into verbalizations. But can a sound capture the information contained in an image? Nietzsche intends to imply that it cannot. He intends to imply, in fact, that no stage of the process captures the information contained in the previous stages, and though he does not address the matter directly, we may assume he would deny that any one of these stages contains *information* to begin with, much less *reliable* information.

Each of these transformations—from object to nerve stimulus; from nerve stimulus to electrical neural impulses; from electrical impulses to mental image; from mental image to sound—each of these Nietzsche refers to as a "metaphor." The word is appropriate here, for the Greek *metaphora* means, literally, the act of carrying a thing from one place to another. With this word Nietzsche directs our attention to the fact that perception is a process by which an object in the external world (assuming that an external object begins the process) is transferred from one state (physical object) to another (neural impulse, image, etc.), and we are meant to worry that nothing of the original is maintained through so many and so radical a series of transitions of state (with the stress on transition of *state*, for we are not here dealing with the mere transference of a single object from one place to another, but rather with the transition of an ostensibly external object from one mode of being [mind-independent spatial-temporal substance] into another mode of being [collection of nerve stimuli], and then into another [mental image] and yet another mode [meaningful sound]).

The metaphors are piling up, and each one stands between us and the world we would like to know. All this, and still the process under consideration is not yet complete. So far we have considered only the perception of a single object, an individual leaf for example; but our primary concern is to understand human knowledge, which involves the formation of concepts. Concepts are abstractions we construct by extracting from numerous different objects a selection of similar properties that we then treat as a unity. So, to continue with our example, we formulate the concept "leaf" by ignoring the many different colors, sizes, shapes, and so on of the multitudinous variety of plant foliage to concentrate only on their similarities. We then gather these different but similar things under a unified category and refer to them by a single name, "leaf." This process involves our discounting what we otherwise believe to be real features of the world (the leaves' various sizes, shapes, etc.), so one might be forgiven for doubting that it could ever generate knowledge. It seems more appropriate for the production of fictions by way of reduction and simplification, and Nietzsche regards it as precisely this sort of illegitimate procedure. "Every concept," he writes, "arises from the equation of unequal things" (*TL* 83). But to take the unequal for the equal is to *mistake* things, which seems an odd route to take in search of knowledge.

But there is more. Having constructed our abstract concept "leaf," we imagine that it must correspond to something real, and we reason that since there is nothing in nature so general as to correspond to the abstraction "leaf" (but rather only specific and particular leaves) there must be some non-physical or trans-physical reality that is the leaf-in-general. Thus we arrive at the Platonic Form of *leaf*. It is a stupendous abstraction—and, according to Nietzsche, it is utterly insupportable. Plato would have us believe that this Form is ultimately real, more real than any particular leaf, also that this Form is the one and only object of knowledge, individual physical leaves being objects only of perception. But this is all just verbiage; there are no such realities, and therefore no knowledge of them. The Platonic account of truth, and the various accounts that descend from it, are intellectual fantasies. Nietzsche sums up the matter as follows: "Truths are illusions which we have forgotten are illusions" (*TL* 84).

In this essay Nietzsche is interested in more than just the nature and possibility of truth and knowledge. He inquires as well into the origin of "the drive for truth" (*TL* 84), and he traces this drive back to pressures attending individual and social preservation. Our construction by metaphor of what we call truth is valuable only to the extent that through the process we come to share concepts and so can communicate and "exist socially and with the herd" (*TL* 81). Thus it is irrelevant whether our shared concepts capture reality as it is in itself; all that matters is that they suffice for social interaction and survival. Nietzsche writes about truth throughout his career— what we take it to be, whether we can acquire it, why we believe it exists—but more than this he speculates about the *value* of truth, or, better, about *why* we value it, which amounts to reflecting on our "drive for truth," which in his later writings he refers to as our *will* to truth. The idea of truth itself presents many problems, but for Nietzsche the most interesting problems are those that lead into the labyrinth of human psychology. Therefore, of more interest than the question "What is this truth that we want?" is the question "Why do we want truth to begin with?"

If, then, when considering Nietzsche's "On Truth and Lies in a Nonmoral Sense" we set aside his specific proposals and conclusions to concentrate instead on his more general themes—his doubts whether the truth about the world is anything like we imagine it to be and his critical inquiry into the origin of the will to truth—we can say that in this early essay Nietzsche sets the agenda for his thinking about our relation to truth for the rest of his career. He consistently maintains that our so-called "truths"— be they the truths of the common man, the scientist, or the philosopher—are lies, fictions, falsehoods, errors, that they are, in short, *untruths*, and at times he even plays with the idea that there is no truth at all.[26] He maintains as well that we place far too high a value on the truth, that our will to truth is vain, misguided, or at a minimum inappropriately ranked above superior drives. Through all his many intellectual advances, alterations, and reversals, some version of these ideas is always with him.

It used to be that discussion of Nietzsche's views on truth and knowledge centered on his so-called "perspectivism."[27] Today, however, scholars are as interested in his "falsification thesis."[28] Perspectivism is the idea that whatever there is that we may usefully refer to as truth is dependent on the perspective of the person who possesses it (or the drives that dominate in that person), that there is no truth in itself but only truth-as-conditioned-by-a-perspective. Falsification is the idea that the world around us, and thus the things, events, thoughts, and propositions that we take to be true, are fabrications of the human intellect, are fictions. When Nietzsche denies the existence of facts or of facts-in-themselves (as at *WP* 481, 556, and 604) he may have one or the other, or both, of these ideas in mind. If there are no "facts" until we impose some interpretation on the world of Becoming, a world that apart from interpretation is forever "in flux, incomprehensible, elusive" (*WP* 604), then we may conclude that our world of relatively stable and abiding objects is the product of the creatively constructive activity of one or more subjective points of view. It will be useful to unravel these ideas and to discuss each in turn.

Regarding falsification, recall the image of the world as presented in the section above entitled "Will to power." This is a world without things, without the elements of things, without even matter, a world as a flux of Becoming through and through and all the way down, with no foundation of Being. We have seen that it is unclear whether Nietzsche conceives this world as a single undifferentiated sea of force or power, a unified field of force that manifests as distinct quanta of power, or a fundamentally non-unified multiplicity of such quanta, but we know that he believes that the unities (individual substances, self-identical and enduring things) and pluralities (many such objects spatially and temporally distinct from one another) familiar to us from experience do not exist independently of the activities of our perceptual and cognitive systems. Think of a substance in the most commonplace, mundane sense, in the sense that Aristotle gives to the word in his *Categories*, namely, as this man or this horse, as, in short, a thing or object according to our everyday use of these words: things of this kind, Nietzsche insists, do not exist in the world as it is in itself; they are constructs generated by our manner of imposing order on the flux of Becoming (or on the chaos of our sensations). The world as it is in itself is quite different from all this; it is will to power, as described above, or it may be that this description too is incorrect and *there just is no way the world is in itself*. Be that as it may, the world is *not* as we experience it to be; our experience alone is this way. This is precisely the point Nietzsche has in mind when in *The Gay Science* he mocks as crude and naive, possibly even deranged and idiotic, the expectation of discovering anything beneath the pale surface of the world by founding one's interpretation exclusively upon those objects of our experience that can be counted, calculated, weighed, seen, and touched (*GS* 373); when in *Beyond Good and Evil* he dismisses as refuted the postulates of substance, matter, and the "particle-atom" (*BGE* 12); and when in *Twilight of the Idols* he characterizes the ideas of unity, thinghood, substance, and permanence as "lies" (*TI* "Reason" 2) and declares that our reason forces us into the "error" of unity, identity, permanence, substance, cause, thinghood, and being (*TI* "Reason" 5). All this is to say that the world we think we know—the world as imagined by theology or metaphysics, obviously, but also the world as described by physics or experienced by common sense—this world is a fabrication, and we ourselves are its unwitting draftsmen and architects.

Nietzsche famously rejects the traditional distinction between reality and appearance, the "real" and "apparent" worlds (*TI* "Reason" 6 and "Fable"; *EH* "Preface" 2). The traditional distinction I have in mind is a metaphysical distinction, particularly as deriving from Plato. Nietzsche sees a similar illegitimate sundering of reality in Kant's distinction between noumena and phenomena and Schopenhauer's between the world as will and as representation, also in the scientists' belief in truth (*GM* 3.24). Yet Nietzsche himself makes use of a parallel distinction, labelling it a distinction between "text" and "interpretation" (*BGE* 22) or between "the testimony of the senses" and "[w]hat we *make* of their testimony" under the influence of the falsifications of reason (*TI* "Reason" 2, 5). It is evident that Nietzsche judged his own distinction to be legitimate, presumably because he regarded it as somehow non-metaphysical; but what substantive difference there is behind this linguistic variation is hard to determine. In any case, when I employ the expression "the world as it is in itself" while discussing Nietzsche's own views, please read this as a non-metaphysical reference to the world independent of the falsifications of reason. And since there may not even be a way the world is in itself, the stress in any such distinction with reference to Nietzsche is not on the truth of the world in itself but rather on the falsity of our experience (as generated in part by reason). The fundamental idea is that there is no world of stable, enduring substances, and this is another way of denying the reality of Being. There is only Becoming, which is to say there is nothing over and above, nor anything behind or beneath, the unceasing activity of motion and change, the eternal flux.

Think of our normal way of conceiving the world as populated by substances that remain the same despite the many alterations of their attributes; think of these substances as the substrata upon which the attributes are grounded, or in which they adhere: now imagine a substance as analogous to a lump of clay that may be molded into a figure with a variety of specific attributes. Consider this clay cast in the form of a man with the attributes "lean," "clean-shaven," and "holding a book by Nietzsche." We can crush this figure, ball it up, smooth it over, and recast it in the form of a man with the attributes "thickset," "bearded," and "holding a book by Plato" without affecting the identity of the lump of clay. In the same way, we think of a man as remaining identically the same despite his changing weight, appearance, and philosophical interests. This is just our commonsense way of conceiving the world, though we may never consciously notice the fact until someone (Aristotle, for example, or Nietzsche) calls our attention to it.

Nietzsche sometimes puts this conception of the world in terms of doers (substances) and deeds (attributes and actions). We are accustomed to thinking that behind every action there is an agent, whether the action be the manifestation of an attribute or the occurrence of some event. So, for example, we think that a bolt of lightning is the substratum that supports a particular appearance of the color yellow, also that the bolt is a thing that flashes forth as lightning. We think, in other words, that the bolt, existing independently of its color and its flashing, somehow produces them; it is the doer and its appearing as yellow as well as its flashing are its deeds. Thus we say "the bolt is yellow" and "the lightning flashes," distinguishing the doer as agent from the deed as act. But these formulations are misleading, and they reinforce a conception of the world as populated by entities to which we have no cognitive access and that, on a Heraclitean view, are superfluous. The unchanging substratum is no object of our raw experience; it is a postulate our intellects introduce when processing our raw experiences into perception or understanding. Nietzsche would have us do away with this postulate, at least in our theoretical accounts of the nature of things. To his way of thinking, there is no bolt behind and distinct from the color and the actions; there is a yellow flashing and nothing more. The world, in a phrase, is all deed and no doer.

If Nietzsche is right about this, why do we conceive the world as we do? Nietzsche assigns the blame to the "prejudice" and "basic presuppositions" of reason, which expressions we may take to designate our perceptual and cognitive systems as discussed above. Reason in this sense "forces" us into the "error" of understanding the world in terms of substances and their attributes. The original mistake seems to be our misunderstanding of ourselves. When we introspect we find, or believe that we find, an enduring nature at the center of all our activities, and we take this for the source around which our mind and body are organized and from which flow our thoughts and actions. This nature we call "self," "soul," "I," or "ego." By whatever name we call it, we take it for a self-identical enduring nature, the substratum of all our attributes and actions, in a word, our substance. And this substance seems to us to act causally on the world through the activity of will. So we understand ourselves as substances that will, or in other words, as enduring entities that act causally on their surroundings.

And from this conception of the ego as the causal agent within, as the subject of all our actions—the doer of all our deeds—and as the "I" that persists through every change, we derive the concept of *being* as the enduring substratum of action and change. This concept we then project into the world; we insert this "being" behind and beneath the actions and attributes around us, referring every change to the agency of a stable subject, and the compound of this subject and its attributes, taken as a causal agent, provides the content of the concept *thing*. Nietzsche puts the matter concisely when he writes that man "took the concept of being from the concept of ego; he posited 'things' as 'being,' in his image, in accordance with his concept of ego as a cause" (*TI* "Errors" 3).[29] A world of things of this sort is a world of Being. But this is to say that the world we fancy ourselves to inhabit is a metaphysical illusion. Or if "illusion" is too extreme, the best we can say for this world of Being is that it is an artifact of the errors of reason, a fabrication in both senses of the word.

So deeply embedded are the errors of reason that they affect the fundamental structure of our language, which encodes an entire metaphysics in its system of nouns, which represent substances (doers), and verbs, which represent actions (deeds). So, for example, although we experience only a flash, we say "the lightning flashes," and this noun-verb arrangement implies a world of subjects and their actions. Nietzsche writes of "the metaphysics of language" that "it believes in the ego, in the ego as being, in the ego as substance, and it projects this faith in the ego-substance upon all things—only thereby does it first *create* the concept of 'thing.' Everywhere 'being' is projected by thought, pushed underneath, as the cause; the concept of being follows, and is a derivative of, the concept of ego" (*TI* "Reason" 5). The simple sentence "I think," for example, implies the existence of Descartes' "thinking thing," which is to say it assumes an ego, an "I," as the cause of thought, and from this we derive the concept of substance as being: enticed by "the seduction of words" we posit a mind or soul as the unified enduring subject of the individual's many changing thoughts, moods, and experiences, and so we uncritically accept an assortment of questionable metaphysical hypotheses (*BGE* 16). The sentence "I am" is similarly misleading. Here again we have a noun and a verb, the former apparently signifying a doer and the latter its deed. And if we conceive of the world in these terms, it seems reasonable to take "living in this physical world" to be the act of a soul-agent, and to conclude that this soul can exist independently of this particular deed. But down the road of this way of thinking one eventually encounters eternally enduring Platonic or Christian souls that after living in this physical world may perform a new deed, namely, "living in the transcendent heavenly sphere." Precisely this same sort of error leads, at least in part, to the concept God. God is the ultimate doer whose deed is everything that is: "God" is the noun associated with the verbs "creates" and "sustains," whose object is "the universe," "the All." So when Nietzsche writes that he is "afraid we are not rid of God because we still have faith in grammar" (*TI* "Reason" 5), he means to allude to our habit of taking nouns to refer to substances, and the related pattern of reasoning that infers from the cosmic collection of acts that is this universe to a substance as the agent-cause of these acts, which substance we call "God." Nor, by the way, are those scientists any more reasonable who posit atoms or subatomic particles as the material elements of things. These are no less substances than the theologians' God, and the materialist scientist is as duped by the metaphysics of Being as is his religious counterpart (*TI* "Reason" 5 and "Errors" 3; see also *GS* 109).

In *The Gay Science* Nietzsche remarks that the world has "become 'infinite' for us" because, for all we know, the world may be infinitely interpretable. In other words, the world may have no "in itself," no nature independent of the perspective from which it is interpreted (*GS* 374). I said above that for Nietzsche the world is flux through and through and all the way down, and if this is so then in this world there are no substances with determinate, fixed natures to which our interpretations must conform to capture the truth. There are no facts, only interpretations; and interpretations are necessarily subjective. It goes without saying that there is "*only* a perspective seeing, *only* a perspective 'knowing'" (*GM* 3.12), but (and this is a more radical claim) we cannot even believe that "a world would still remain over after one deducted the perspective," for "there is no 'other,' no 'true,' no essential being" (*WP* 567; see also *WP* 568). So the falsification of the world as described above is inherently perspectival. It is true that human beings have similar perceptual and cognitive systems, so our subjectively constructed worlds are generally similar. But this does nothing to alter the fact of their subjectivity: a perspectival falsification is a perspectival falsification even if numerous individuals share one and the same perspective. And in any case, we are here considering only one general aspect of the world, namely, its division into substances and attributes. Human perception and cognition may be uniform here while differing among individuals in many other more subtle respects. Besides, humans are not the only perceiving and cognizing beings around. There are, for example, amoebae, gnats, jellyfish, and moles, whose various and presumably radically divergent perspectives we have no way to inspect; and even if we could inspect them, we have no access to an objective standard against which to compare their perspectives with our own.[30] Then there is the possibility that evolution one day will generate hominid-like animals with nervous systems very different from our own; and even now there may be in other regions of the universe creatures as unlike ourselves as we are unlike plants or minerals. In short, then, we experience the world only as *we* experience it, and there is no way either to transcend our perspective or to verify its reliability. Nietzsche, as usual, sums up our predicament concisely: "we cannot look around our own corner" (*GS* 374).

So far I have written of perspectives at the level of species and individuals. But since Nietzsche regards individuals as harboring within an assortment of drives,[31] he does at times identify a perspective with the tendencies of some particular drive. The drive for disinterested knowledge that dominates the other drives resident in the pure scholar, for example, constitutes a perspective altogether different from that of the drive for power that dominates in the warrior. Often it may be difficult to determine which drive is really at work, as when the drive for power employs the intellect to achieve its ends, in which case an observer may mistakenly conclude that the drive for knowledge is dominant. But despite every difficulty of analysis and identification, we may be sure that in each individual some drive or coalition of drives is struggling to force its own distinct perspective on the whole. In this connection Nietzsche writes, taking the philosopher as his example, that "every single [basic drive of man] would like only too well to represent just *itself* as the ultimate purpose of existence and the legitimate *master* of all the other drives. For every drive wants to be master—and it attempts to philosophize in *that spirit*" (*BGE* 6). In this passage Nietzsche is making an epistemological claim, namely, that the philosopher's drive for knowledge is often influenced by or subservient to other more fundamental drives, particularly those bound up with his moral presuppositions. But we must keep in mind that Nietzsche's perspectivism is also an ontological thesis, and as such it is related to his falsification thesis. Thus he writes, regarding perspective, that "questions, what things 'in-themselves' may be like, apart from our sense receptivity and the activity of our understanding, must be rebutted with the question: how could we know that things exist? 'Thingness' was first created by us. The question is whether there could not be many other ways of creating such an apparent world—and whether this creating, logicizing, adapting, falsifying is not itself the best-guaranteed reality" (*WP* 569). Note that in this single passage Nietzsche associates two varieties of perspectivism, epistemological ("how could we know … ?") and ontological ("many other ways of creating … "). The two phenomena are not necessarily related, for one could admit cognitive perspectivism while insisting that the nature of reality is objectively fixed. But in Nietzsche's account they are intertwined: the falsification/creation of the world always occurs from some particular perspective, and because the world apart from this fiction lacks "essential being" (*WP* 567) our knowledge of the world is inescapably perspectival as well.

I began this chapter by stressing Nietzsche's admiration of Heraclitus as the one and only western philosopher to see through the illusion of Being and to affirm in its stead the world as Becoming. I then proceeded to present in some detail Nietzsche's own account of just such a world, interspersed with arguments, contextualizations, and historical genealogies. Since among all this peripheral matter one may easily lose sight of the central idea, sufficiently obscure in itself to begin with, it may be useful at this point to gather the details into a brief, general description of the world as Becoming. In *The Gay Science* Nietzsche writes, regarding cause and effect, that "such a duality probably never exists; in truth we are confronted by a continuum out of which we isolate a couple of pieces … " (*GS* 112). The context in which this passage appears justifies our extending its thesis beyond cause and effect to apply to reality as a whole,[32] which we may therefore regard as a construct dependent entirely on our manner of dividing into separate and discrete units what in actuality is an undivided continuum. The image of a continuum suggests that the world in itself is nothing like the multiplicity of self-contained, self-identical, independent things of our experience. This world of our experience is the result of "an arbitrary division and dismemberment" of the continuum and flux (*GS* 112); what Plato might describe as our carving reality at its natural joints (*Phdr.* 265e1–3) Nietzsche regards as our hacking away at what in itself is a homogenous slab of meat. To acquire some idea of what the world might be apart from the arbitrary sorting activity of reason, call to mind our commonsense conception of the world as composed of substances and their attributes and then subtract the substances; there remains only a floating field of constantly shifting qualities unattached to enduring substrata. Now look more closely at these qualities themselves: they are flashings in the light of a ceaselessly shifting field of power whose contending forces here and there concentrate to emerge, ever so briefly, from the depths. But at bottom there is only the deep—the indistinguishable, because indistinct, abyss of depth.

We are now far away from the world we normally experience ourselves inhabiting, and the new world Nietzsche would have us envision is unfamiliar and uncanny, a world beyond accurate description, if not wholly beyond the reach of metaphor. We may think of this world as a restlessly flowing river of process and power, a Heraclitean world indeed, thing-less, substance-less, Being-less. The thought does not communicate the truth entire, but it may affect a change in our minds and thereby direct us toward this world's orbit—and perhaps this is as close as one may hope to approach to a world of Becoming. This much is certain: neither pure reason nor experience will provide us the access we seek.[33] Insight into Becoming arrives only by way of the inspiration of insight itself. We may later elaborate some conception of the preconditions and consequences of that which is only Becoming and nothing besides; but neither common sense nor science, neither religion nor traditional philosophy can disclose the fundamental reality of radical Becoming. Perhaps in this context it is fitting to apply to Nietzsche the words he once wrote concerning Heraclitus, namely, that he took "pride not in logical knowledge but rather in the intuitive grasping of the truth: we must recognize the enthusiastic and inspirational in his nature" (*PPP* 55).

Nietzsche and science

Nietzsche has been a subject of curiosity and controversy in the English-speaking world since early in the twentieth century, and no strand of his thought has inspired more scholarly activity than his ideas about the nature and accessibility of reality and the value and even the very existence of truth. On these topics, as on others, his work has been for many a screen on which to project images of their own ideals and aspirations. The only other philosopher who has been made so often to serve a similar function is Plato, from the intricately woven dramatic context of whose works scholars have long been in the habit of wrenching arguments, which they then interpret and analyze according to their own preferred terminology and intellectual concerns. Thus Plato has been in turns an optimist and a pessimist, an advocate of tyranny and a proponent of democracy, a dreamy metaphysician and a sober linguistic analyst.[34] This tendency has begun to decline in recent years as subtle readers have demonstrated the integrity of the dialogues as artistic-literary-philosophical *wholes* whose individual components cannot be detached without distortion. As for Nietzsche, there is undeniably a degree of unity and consistency among his ideas—and even when he changes his mind we can, generally, track the transformations and discern the rationale behind them—but he organized the contents of his books at times according to so mystifying a plan, and he adopted such a diversity of rhetorical postures, that it never is a simple matter to find the thread through the labyrinth of his argument. This is not to everyone's taste; but a certain type of reader is drawn to Nietzsche, as he is drawn to Plato, precisely because of the richness, complexity, and occasional ambiguity of his ideas. These same qualities, however, are problematic to the extent that they provide opportunities for the sort of projections I described in connection with Plato.

In 1908, H. L. Mencken published the first book-length treatment of Nietzsche's ideas in the English language. In the course of the following two decades Mencken became an intellectual force with a national influence unparalleled by any but the rarest of public intellectuals today, and throughout the period of his greatest power he wrote constantly about Nietzsche. Mencken was a social-Darwinist, a rebel against authority (especially as exercised by the masses via democratic and religious institutions), and a passionate advocate of fallibilist science. His Nietzsche is all these things as well. Most relevant to our present concerns, Mencken's Nietzsche is a truth-seeker who charts his course by the guiding star of science. "It is evident," Mencken writes in his early study of Nietzsche, "that science ... will eventually accomplish with certainty what philosophy ... is now trying to do in a manner that is not only crude and unreasonable, but also necessarily unsuccessful."[35] The critique of philosophy may remind one of Nietzsche, but the naive faith in science does not. Mencken acknowledges that Nietzsche's views on truth are "so abstruse" that he cannot provide "an understandable summary" of them in his book.[36] Nonetheless, he is confident that Nietzsche believed that through the gradual refinement of scientific thought as guided by the will to power "man [has] constantly increased his store of knowledge,"[37] and that "the will to power might be relied upon to lead man to the truth."[38] In short, Mencken was either unwilling or unable to understand a point that Nietzsche insists on more than once, and particularly in connection with his radical position with respect to reality and truth (the *value* of truth), namely, that power over the environment does not imply veridical cognitive access to the world (*GS* 110; *BGE* 4 and 11; *WP* 535 and 568).

I have introduced Mencken at this point in my account because after a period of Nietzsche's being associated with a postmodern deconstruction of the very idea of truth (a period lasting, roughly, from the late 1960s to near the turn of the twenty-first century), there are active today any number of scholars who, like Mencken before them, are eager to recruit him for a friend of science. These scholars readily admit that for a time Nietzsche indulged a rococo taste for a radically Heraclitean philosophy of Becoming and as a consequence developed his falsification thesis, according to which the world of enduring things we think we inhabit is a fiction generated by the "categories of reason." But these same scholars argue that in his mature works (beginning with *Beyond Good and Evil*) he rejected the assumptions on which the falsification thesis depends and eventually abandoned the thesis itself to embrace a form of scientific naturalism. The idea, in short, is that in the end Nietzsche decided that truths about the world do exist, and that we can know these truths by conscientiously minding the scientific method.[39] Although I do not here intend to argue against this position, I will say that I find it unconvincing, which is why I have taken no account of it in my presentation so far. It is undeniably the case that Nietzsche is a naturalist in the sense that he regards man as an animal produced in history by the blind motions of a godless world. He himself declared his intention to "translate man back into nature" (*BGE* 230), by which he meant to deny man any supernatural origin, metaphysical meaning, or special relation to the divine. But that anyone ever felt the need specifically to stress and defend this says more about the influence of certain ecstatic and, let's say, less than meticulously faithful appropriations of his work than it says about the work itself. Only those who read more *about* Nietzsche in certain twentieth-century literary and philosophical theorists than read Nietzsche himself could be so mistaken about these matters.[40] I suppose it serves a purpose to set the record straight, but the record was always clear enough had one only bothered to read it. The problem today is that some of the scholars who have taken it on themselves to set the record straight have bent it too far from center in the other direction. Their idea that Nietzsche in his maturity concluded that science (and science alone) reveals the truth about the nature of things is, to my mind, as mistaken as any "postmodern" interpretation.[41]

It is true that in his last works Nietzsche sometimes appeals to truth and science when arguing against Platonic or Christian metaphysics. Yet the question remains whether we should take these appeals to indicate that Nietzsche has changed his mind about fundamental matters, for there may well be other explanations. It may be, for example, that in these passages Nietzsche temporarily abandons a global perspective to speak from within the context of the falsified/fictional world in which we live and act, which of course he does more often than not even in those works in which the falsification thesis is agreed by everyone to be in place. Whenever Nietzsche writes anything at all about history, tragedy, morality, values, society, scholarship, philosophy, religion, or science (the list could be extended) he assumes a world not only of things, but of things of a very specific kind with identifiable attributes, histories, and, in some cases, psychologies. I have said already that Nietzsche does not deny that the world exists, which would be an outrageous, and perhaps an impossible denial. His position is rather that the world is a construct of reason, a construct in which we live and to which we can and must refer if we would speak about matters relevant to our lives. In short, Nietzsche's falsification thesis is entirely compatible with shifts of perspective between a view from the heights that reveals the ultimate insubstantiality of the world of our experience to a view from within this world that includes things that we can describe and activities we can evaluate. Thinking and writing according to the postulates of this latter perspective, one may argue that this proposition is true while that one is false, that this code of values is superior to that, or that by employing one rather than another methodology we may more readily identify and account for the facts of human psychology, the movements of history, or the causal properties of natural objects. Considering that Nietzsche's appeals to science appear in works that also include his rejections of matter, substance, beings, and things, we must either assume some such "dual perspective" approach[42] or convict Nietzsche of blatant inconsistencies or a really quite surprising tardiness in understanding the implications of his own views.[43]

There is also the possibility that Nietzsche's appeals to truth and science are rhetorical. They occur almost exclusively in the context of his criticisms of metaphysics and religion, and they are most prominent in his assault on Christianity in *The Antichrist*. This latter is a polemical work through and through, and it is so in large part because of the stridency of the rhetoric. Nietzsche hurls at Christianity most every weapon in his arsenal, and there is nothing in his past as an author to suggest that he would spurn any potentially effective tactic—and even those tactics that would prove futile against Nietzsche's own position as presented in this chapter (appeals to the authority of science, for example) might succeed against an enemy as exhausted and impotent as modern Christianity. Everyone knows, and in most cases will insist, that we must always be aware of Nietzsche's masterful variations of style and approach. Yet the moment he writes apparently as an ally of science those who are its allies themselves are eager to take him literally. To do so they must produce rather strained interpretations, for Nietzsche never really ceases to insist on some version or other of falsificationism.[44]

More plausible than any attempt to portray Nietzsche as an adherent of scientific realism is the reading of Nietzsche as a Pyrrhonian skeptic (or at least as decisively influenced by the tradition of Pyrrhonism).[45] On this reading Nietzsche adopts no dogmatic positions whatever with respect to metaphysics and ontology, neither positive nor negative positions. Although I regard this approach as more promising than those that would attribute to Nietzsche a positive commitment to any form of scientifically inspired metaphysical naturalism, I do not think it is unqualifiedly accurate. Nietzsche was always ambivalent about skepticism, regarding it sometimes as a sign of health and strength, at other times as an indication of exhaustion, nihilism, and decadence.[46] Besides, even if we admit (*arguendo*) that Nietzsche's approach to metaphysics is exclusively skeptical or suspicious, we must also admit that he directs his skepticism at philosophies of Being, that he often does so from the perspective of a radical philosophy of Becoming, and that he never subjects this latter philosophy to rigorous skeptical scrutiny. So if Nietzsche did in fact adopt a skeptical approach, he would appear to have done so in order to lead his readers away from Being while directing them toward Becoming by subtle implication, which is to say that he sought a way to deny Being and affirm Becoming without exposing himself to the charge of dogmatism. But this suggests, to me at least, that Nietzsche was no skeptic at heart.

More plausible still than the Pyrrhonian reading, then, are those that argue that Nietzsche really did accept the falsification thesis, and that he maintained his commitment to the end. These readings are particularly noteworthy for taking account, in great detail, of Nietzsche's engagement with the work of various contemporary or near-contemporary scientists, scientific theorists, and Neo-Kantian philosophers. Maudemarie Clark, who initiated the recent discussion of the place of the falsification thesis in Nietzsche's development, deserves credit for taking more seriously than many had done before her the influence of Schopenhauer, and Nietzsche's working through this influence, on Nietzsche's philosophy. But more recent studies have expanded our knowledge of the influences operative on Nietzsche's thinking, specifically with respect to all that surrounds the subject of his falsification thesis, and they suggest that he never abandoned it.[47] These studies are all the more convincing for being consistent with the most straightforward reading of Nietzsche's texts. Those commentators who reject this reading (and who therefore argue that it is not in fact the most obvious reading of his texts) are put off by the apparently irrational consequences of the thesis. If there is only Becoming, then knowledge and meaningful thought and language would seem to be impossible, for there would be no stable things to know, to intend, or to think of. Every sentence, every word, that the falsificationist philosopher thinks, speaks, or writes must contradict the thesis itself. Hence, the very act of believing the thesis renders the thesis and the belief itself radically meaningless.

Nietzsche seems to have been aware of this problem, but he rarely addresses it directly. He is on occasion willing to acknowledge that his own interpretations of reality may themselves be no facts but only interpretations,[48] and his indirect, ironic, and sometimes ardently poetic style may serve to avoid or finesse the hazards of self-contradiction. But he does not often investigate or emphasize the apparent inconsistencies of his position as we might imagine, say, a Zen master indirectly acknowledging the absurdity of his very act of speaking by, for example, buffeting the ears of a disciple who asks about the matter, or by posing to him an obscure but pregnant riddle. The apparently contradictory, and therefore irrational, character of the position Nietzsche seems to have adopted has motivated much of the recent interest in reading him as having abandoned his falsification thesis for some version of scientific naturalism/realism. I have noted my disagreement with this interpretation, which seems to me to require our ignoring or misconstruing significant elements of his work. If in the end Nietzsche's considered opinions violate contemporary philosophical pieties—well, this strikes me as appropriate and entirely consistent with his intellectual character.

However we understand the details of Nietzsche's position, there is no way around the fact that he drew a line across the history of philosophy and stood with Heraclitus on the side opposite that which Plato occupied—or anyway there is no avoiding the fact that this is how he liked to present himself. Nonetheless, and most ironically, it may be that Nietzsche was closer to Plato than he realized or wanted to admit.

Plato on becoming

It has not escaped the attention of scholars that the radical philosophy of Becoming that Nietzsche associates with Heraclitus does not obviously appear in Heraclitus's extant fragments.[49] This does not prove that he did not affirm such a philosophy. Ancient philosophers familiar with Heraclitus's book attribute to him, at least in general terms, something like the radical ontology that we have examined in this chapter, and the surviving fragments provide at least some support for their testimony. Yet the most explicit presentation of a Heraclitean philosophy of Becoming is to be found, not in the fragments of Heraclitus, but, remarkably, in Plato's dialogues. Consider the following propositions: (a) there is no way the world is in itself, for (b) a thing's being *what* it is and *as* it is, is conditioned by its appearance to each individual, and this is so because (c) there is no Being but only Becoming. Serviceable as these three propositions may be for a summation of Nietzsche's variations on Heraclitean themes, they are in fact Plato's own account of the ideas of Heraclitus himself and those of his latter-day disciples with whom he was familiar. This, anyway, is how Plato presents the matter in his *Theaetetus*. Yet it may well be that this radicalized philosophy of Becoming is the product of Plato's own mind, or at least of his extending and deepening of Heraclitus's ideas according to a pattern that never occurred in quite this form to either Heraclitus or his disciples.[50] It does seem that Plato was for a time a student of the Heraclitean philosophy. Diogenes Laertius reports this regarding Plato's activities prior to his association with Socrates, and he adds that after Socrates' death Plato "attached himself" to Cratylus the Heraclitean.[51] The Plato we know is in no way a mere disciple of Heraclitus, and it may be that even before meeting Socrates he was interested in more than the doctrine of flux. Nevertheless, scholars generally agree with Diogenes' assertion that Plato's knowledge of Heraclitus's philosophy influenced his account of sensible things as never enduring with respect to either quality or quantity, but rather as always only becoming.[52] The Heraclitean provenance of this point is obvious, even if we admit—and many scholars would insist that we must admit—that this influence was augmented tremendously by Plato's own philosophical-artistic genius.

Plato's *Theaetetus* is, at least on the surface, an epistemological work.[53] It addresses most directly the problem of defining and accounting for knowledge and related cognitive phenomena. The dialogue tracks the dialectical progress of Socrates and a young man, Theaetetus, as together they consider and reject three popular accounts of knowledge while simultaneously investigating a variety of related topics. As often happens when reading Plato, one has the impression when engaged with this work that Plato's primary interest lies less in the question explicitly at issue (in this case, "What is knowledge?") than in the related and ostensibly subordinate topics. For example, Socrates introduces the doctrines of Heraclitus as if they are necessary to a thorough explication of Theaetetus's first definition of knowledge ("knowledge is perception"), but it seems his actual motivation is to expound his own (or rather Plato's) radical ontology of Becoming (at least as applied to sensible objects). I do not insist that Plato composed the dialogue for no other reason than this; there is too much else of interest in the work for this to be so. Still, it can be no accident that a close study of the philosophy of Becoming consumes most of the entire first half of the work.

I have noted that the radical account of Becoming as presented in the *Theaetetus* may be fundamentally of Plato's own invention or elaboration. Please do keep this in mind, for I intend to follow Plato in referring to this philosophy simply as Heraclitus's doctrine, if for no other reason than ease of expression.[54] Having disposed of these preliminary matters, then, let's now recall the three features of Heraclitus's philosophy as presented in the first paragraph of this section, taking them one by one. First is the idea that there is no way the world is in itself. Plato puts this point in many ways, and several of his expressions are striking anticipations of Nietzsche. In the first place, Socrates attributes to Heraclitus the doctrine that "there is nothing that is one thing in and of itself, nor anything that you could correctly call either something or some type of thing" (152d2–4).[55] Then, after spurning materialism by admitting into his ontology "actions and instances of becoming" (155e), he extends his point by binding to these actions and instances of becoming the very existence of sensible, physical, material objects. His idea, in short, is that the world at bottom is devoid of things. Neither substances nor their attributes exist in and of themselves: in reality there are only various "motions" that when suitably related give rise to transient versions of what we normally take to be things (things as compounds of substances and attributes). In Socrates' words, "nothing exists in and of itself ... but all things of every sort come to be in association with one another through motion, for one cannot think ... that either the active or the passive among things is something taken by itself. For the active is not something until it comes together with the passive, nor is the passive anything until it comes together with the active" (156e9–157a5).[56] This is all very unusual talk, and we might expect an advocate of so strange an ontology to propose modifications to our language, and, indeed, Socrates remarks that the wise men who teach these doctrines prohibit the use of the words "something," "this," and "that," whether in reference to individuals or to classes (157b–c). The connection between ontology and language is made even more explicit, and more explicitly radical, when after reiterating the point that "nothing is one in and of itself, but (everything) always comes to be in relation to something (else)," Socrates insists that "we must altogether remove the verb 'to be'" from our philosophical vocabulary (157a8–b1).

Socrates' claim that a thing's being *what* it is and *as* it is is conditioned by its appearance to each individual (the second feature of Plato's account of the Heraclitean philosophy as presented above), has both epistemological and ontological implications, the latter being most relevant here. Since, as we have just seen, there is no way the world is in itself, the world must become what and as it is by way of some process. This process is the intercourse of the active and passive motions mentioned in the previous paragraph. An eye that sees a white stone and the white stone itself come to be in association with one another, neither of them having existed prior to the intercourse of their motions (or, to state the matter more accurately, neither exists prior to the intercourse of themselves *as* motions, which anteriorly is their sole mode of existence).[57] This explains Socrates' remark that "if someone employs of something the term 'being' or 'becoming,' he must say that it is 'for,' 'of,' or 'with respect to' someone or something" (160b8–10). In short, the world is constantly becoming through the intercourse of active and passive motions. Moreover, every state of the world that comes to be, comes to be different from every other state. The differences are due to the fact that the intercourse of different active and passive motions engenders different things. And since any difference of properties implies different individuals—as, for example, Socrates healthy and Socrates ill are different individuals (159a–c)—every instance of intercourse between active and passive motions—each instance differing from every other instance, if in no other way then at least in being a different instance—will produce different things. Thus the world is a collection of infinitely many different states, ceaselessly coming to be and passing away, each state relative to the individuals that (as active and passive motions) engender it. And since neither member of an active and passive pair ever recurs, but every member of every pair is different from everything else without exception (159e–160a), the passive member of each of these pairs, Socrates perceiving sweet wine, for example, occupies his own distinct reality (*tês gar emês ousias aei estin*, 160c7–8). The epistemological implication of all this is that perception is knowledge. One knows whatever one perceives, for one's act of perception brings the thing or the state perceived into being precisely *as* the very sort of thing or state one perceives. In the latter half of this sentence we may read the ontological implications of this position. Perception is knowledge because the act of perception produces the object of knowledge in conformity with the act. In short, appearance captures reality because appearance *generates* reality.

As for Socrates' claim that there is no Being but only Becoming (the third feature of Plato's account of the Heraclitean philosophy as presented above), this is perhaps the most directly Heraclitean of them all. "All things move like streams," he says (*Tht.* 160d7–8). But this claim too he develops in as radical a direction as possible. All things always move in every motion, they move completely (this from Theodorus at 182c8), and they move in all ways (182e5–6). Socrates stresses the universality of motion in order to bring out the fact that things move not only with respect to place, but also with respect to state or condition. In other words, all things *alter* or *change*, and they are continually changing in every possible way. Our standard ontology of substance can make sense of one and the same thing changing position in space (i.e. moving), even of a thing changing properties (i.e. altering) while fundamentally remaining the same. We can say that "the stone rolls from here to there" or that "the stone has turned from grey to white." In each instance, the expression "the stone" names a fundamentally unchanging substratum. But if all things are continually changing in every possible way, then there can be no underlying stable subject of change. This radically fluid ontology was prefigured in Socrates' earlier remark that "from movement and motion and mixing with one another all those things *become* that we say 'are,' speaking incorrectly: for nothing ever is, but it always becomes" (152d7–e1).

We have seen that Nietzsche characterized Heraclitus as having "altogether denied Being," as having arisen in the market place, as it were, to declare "I see nothing other than Becoming" (*PTG* 51). We have seen as well that with reference precisely to the denial of Being and the affirmation of Becoming Nietzsche declared that Heraclitus's philosophy is "more closely related to me than anything else thought to date" (*EH* "BT" 3). This self-assessment strikes me as accurate, especially considering Nietzsche's own insistent and repeated critiques of thinghood, substance, and Being. Yet it must be said that with respect to explicit statements of the specific implications of a radical philosophy of Becoming, Nietzsche's view is closer to Plato's elaboration of the Heraclitean philosophy than to the contents of Heraclitus's book that have come down to us.[58] There is no reason to believe that Nietzsche derived his account of the world as composed of no things but only of the will to power directly from Plato's *Theaetetus*, but the similarities are remarkable. Likewise, Socrates' claim that a thing's being *what* it is and *as* it is is conditioned by its appearance to each individual is neither identical to, nor the proximate cause of, Nietzsche perspectivism. But, again, it is hard not to notice the similarities. As for the denial of Being and the affirmation of Becoming, in this regard their versions of Heracliteanism are nearly identical. The most relevant difference between them has less to do with the philosophy itself than with their own relations to it, with the matter of their accepting or rejecting it as a comprehensive account of reality. Nietzsche does accept it: like his Heraclitus, he sees nothing other than Becoming. Plato, on the other hand, sees Becoming but also something else. This something else is Being, which Plato believes to be a precondition of knowledge and intelligible discourse. If there is only Becoming, then since everything always changes in every way, every potential object of knowledge is inherently unstable as an object. Nothing is any more this than that, and whatever we try to know or name continually withdraws or slips away from us (182d). On these assumptions there can be no knowledge. Moreover, a radical philosophy of Becoming makes meaningful speech impossible. We cannot say, for example, "x is thus" because, as we have seen, there is no x in itself, the verb "to be" is illegitimate, and nothing is any more *thus* than it is *not thus*. But this latter point implies that we cannot even articulate the philosophy of Becoming itself; any expression of the philosophy is necessarily inconsistent with the philosophy's own implications. The propositions "the philosophy of Becoming denies Being" and "the philosophy of Becoming is true" are no more accurate reflections of the state of things than the propositions "the philosophy of Becoming affirms Being" and "the philosophy of Becoming is false." According to this philosophy, none of these propositions is more accurate than any other, nor are they more meaningful than a random arrangement of words (182c–183c).

Plato took these implications of the philosophy of Becoming as decisive reasons either to reject it outright or to modify it and limit its application to sensible objects, and in either case to introduce his own metaphysics of Being. He could not imagine an unintelligible world, in part because he understood that radical unintelligibility undermines all cognitive acts, imagination included; and since he clearly could and did engage in every kind of cognitive activity, he concluded that any philosophy that implies such unintelligibility must be false. To affirm radical Heracliteanism and to go on thinking, talking, or writing is to entangle oneself in self-contradiction. Plato's old teacher, Cratylus the Heraclitean, understood this and so stopped speaking altogether; they say he would only wiggle his finger. But this would not do for Plato, a man so full of ideas, images, and words that he seems never to have stopped thinking and writing. His intellectual and artistic gifts were titanic, and he employed them in part to justify his own peculiar mode of philosophical-artistry. He set no dam against the always flowing river of flux, but raised over it a bridge, so as Becoming rushes past below, the philosopher may linger serenely above and gaze on the stillness of Being.

Noble and Good

Kalokagathia

The word at the head of this section is a noun derived from the adjective *kalos kagathos*, which is itself a compound of two adjectives and a conjunction. On either side of the conjunction *kai* are the adjectives *kalos*, which may mean "beautiful," "fine," or "noble," and *agathos*, the basic meaning of which is "good." These two adjectives play key roles in two important Platonic dialogues, each of them in context designating a fundamental, or ultimate, metaphysical principle. In the *Symposium*, the neuter form of *kalos*, *to kalon*, designates the Form of *beauty*, Beauty itself, the final and highest goal of philosophical ascent (210a–212a). In the *Republic*, the neuter form of *agathos*, *to agathon*, designates the Form of *good*, Good itself, which is the Form on which all other Forms depend for their intelligibility, existence, and essence (505a–509b). It may be that these two terms designate one and the same entity, that the Beautiful just is the Good, and vice versa, under a different name; Plato appears at times at least to hint at their unity. In any case, *kalos* and *agathos* are most definitely deeply embedded and centrally located in Plato's metaphysical system. The fact maddens Nietzsche to no end, particularly with respect to the Good, for he objects to anyone's infecting what ought to be a social, political, or ethical concept with a poison that transforms it into a *moral* idea.[1]

I shall have more to say about the role of the Good in Platonic ethics (or morality) below. For now I note that Plato's notion of *kalokagathia* is not obviously moral in the sense to which Nietzsche objects. The term (in the adjectival form *kalos kagathos*) appears in both the *Symposium* and the *Republic* in a context that has nothing to do with morality, but that rather stresses an (amoral) association between philosophical and martial excellence. In the former dialogue Alcibiades (*kalos kagathos* himself) praises Socrates' courage on the battlefields of Potidaea and Delium, then associates him (at least indirectly) with the warriors Achilles and Brasidas (against whose forces Socrates fought at Amphipolis), and finally, by way of reference to accomplished speakers like Pericles and Nestor, he transitions to an estimation of Socrates' incomparable philosophical qualities. Although, he says, Socrates' *logoi* appear outrageous on the surface, one realizes upon opening them up and peering inside how needful they are to the man who would become *kalos kagathos* (222a6). In the *Republic*, Socrates himself argues that the guardians of the ideal city must possess the traits of a warrior and a philosopher simultaneously, for they must be gentle with their fellow citizens but harsh to their enemies, and they must distinguish the two by understanding acquired through love of learning.[2] Only he who combines both the spirited and philosophical natures, Socrates says, will be *kalos kagathos* as a guardian of the city (376c5).

In ancient Athens the *kalos kagathos* was "the noble and good man," in a sense having little to do with what we might think of as morality. *Kalokagathia* was an aristocratic ideal, aspired to by men who were by station hoplite warriors or caval-rymen. By station, I say, because these military classifications were tied to wealth; one had to possess the resources to purchase and maintain one's own hoplite equipment, and to serve with the cavalry one required sufficient land to pasture horses. These positions were in sharp contrast to naval service, which was harsh, dirty, dangerous, and ignominious. It was for the poor and the slaves of Athens to sit in the cramped and clammy bowels of the city's triremes and row, quite literally, for their lives.

But military service and wealth, as significant as they were in themselves, were components of a broader social-political complex that was itself the primary object of value. To be and to live as an aristocrat, this was the thing: to descend from old and propertied stock; to own farmland or pasturage oneself; to be admired by friends and feared by enemies; to be handsome and strong; to attend symposia; to know by heart the rousing poems and drinking songs popular among the elite; to participate in the momentous political and military events of one's day; to be, in short, an Achilles returned above ground—he who was "cultured" in these ways was *kalos kagathos*.

The aristocratic ideal was not foreign to Plato, who not only thought and wrote about it, but who embodied it himself in many ways. He may well have attempted through his work to modify the ideal by supplementing its predominantly military ethos with the more thoughtful traits of the philosopher, but he did not attempt to overthrow it (as Nietzsche sometimes suggests). Socrates, too, seems to have aspired to this ideal, though in his case the fact is most unusual. Plato was born to an old and noble family, but Socrates sprang from the lower orders. By all rights he should have passed his time among the city's poor, his fellow laborers. He should have rowed with the fleet. Yet Socrates cultivated friendships among the *kaloi kagathoi*; he adopted their manners and traditions, associated with them and their children, attended their symposia, and he fought beside them on the field as a heavily armored hoplite soldier.[3]

Given these facts, and others to be related in this chapter, we must regard Nietzsche's assertion that Socrates and Plato were "tools of the Greek dissolution, pseudo-Greek, anti-Greek" (*TI* "Socrates" 2) as an eruption of hyperbolic rhetoric. Either this, or he was blinded intellectually by an intoxicating brew of one part determined opposition to Socrates, one part hostility to Christianity, and one part inclination to regard Plato as "pre-existently Christian" (*TI* "Ancients" 2). The fact is that Socrates and Plato were more thoroughly Greek than Nietzsche was ever able to admit, and that Plato as a thinker and artist was closer to him than he cared to acknowledge, even to himself. But before we examine these matters in greater detail, I should clarify the content of a few terms that will be in the back of much of the substance of this chapter.

Objectivism and relativism

The object of knowledge, according to Plato, is that which is, whereas the object of belief is that which both is and is not. By this Plato means that the objects of knowledge are the Forms, which possess, or which just are, Being, whereas the objects of belief are the many particulars caught up in the ceaseless flux of Becoming.[4] For our present purposes, however, we need not concentrate on the ontological implications of the difference between knowledge and belief; our concerns for the moment are more narrowly epistemological. Let's say, then, that knowledge is true—that it *must* be true if it is to count as knowledge—whereas beliefs may be either true or false. This distinction will be evident to some, at least as a sort of baseline account, but others may be dubious. These latter will retort that everyone once knew that the earth is flat, but they were wrong, and they will add that it is entirely possible to have beliefs that are simply true. But this misses the point. Even admitting that there was a time when everyone thought the earth to be flat, we need not concede that they "knew" this. *They* may have said that they knew this; they may if pressed have *insisted* that they knew this; and they may well have flamed with indignation if seriously challenged. But none of this means that they did in fact know it. Consider the matter this way: the "it" they ostensibly knew is *the flatness of the earth*, but this does not exist, never did exist, so there just was no "it" for them to know. Their supposed knowledge lacked an object, for no fact has ever corresponded to the proposition "the earth is flat." The flatness of the earth *is not*, and no one can know what is not. We can know *that* something is not: we can know, for example, that the earth is not flat. This fact, though expressed negatively, is positively true, and so we may say that it, the fact itself, is. But the "fact" of the earth's being flat, or (expressed differently) of its not being a sphere, this fact *is not*. This is the sense in which I say that no one can know what is not; but this is just another way of saying that we cannot know a falsehood to be true, which I assume is unobjectionable.

So our imaginary flat-earthers only *thought* that they knew that the earth is flat, which is to say they *believed* it. There is nothing at all unusual in believing that which is not (that which is false), for beliefs, as I have mentioned, may be either true or false.[5] And as for the objection that some beliefs may be true, period—well, this is no objection, but rather the expression of a misunderstanding. When I say that beliefs may be either true or false, I mean that any particular belief either is true, period, or is false, period. The point is that whether it is simply true or simply false, in either case it qualifies as a belief, whereas no proposition can count as knowledge if it is simply false.[6]

Having clarified the various relations among knowledge, belief, and truth, I would like now to attend to the notion of truth itself. It is redundant to say that the truth is true, and to say that the truth is false is contradictory. We should, therefore, avoid both locutions. Let's say instead that the truth just *is*. Now we need not read any element of Platonic metaphysics into this "is." We have only to admit that the truth, as one says, is "out there," and by this to mean that the truth is what it is independently of what anyone believes, knows, says, or imagines about it. And for our present purposes it makes no difference whether we have in mind unchanging permanent truths (that triangles have three sides, for example) or alterable temporary truths (that

I am now writing this sentence). We are not at the moment concerned with Platonic metaphysics. I intend only to articulate what I have identified as the "baseline view," which we may regard as the view of educated common sense.

The idea that the truth is "out there," that it is what it is independently of what anyone thinks or says about it, is known as *objectivism*. To qualify as an objectivist, therefore, one need only believe, about some particular subject, that there is a truth or fact of the matter unaffected by human opinion. In short, the objectivist believes that man is *not* the measure of all things. The objectivist may have further opinions regarding the source of the truth (how it came to be, and how it came to be what or as it is) and whether humans can know it, but these details are, strictly speaking, peripheral to objectivism itself. The central point, really the *only* point of objectivism is *that* there is an independent truth. He is an objectivist who says, for example, that "there is a truth about *x* independent of what I or you or anyone else has ever thought, presently thinks, or will at any time in the future think about the matter," no matter what he goes on to opine regarding the source of the truth and the possibility (or impossibility) of our knowing it with certainty. A Christian may insist that God created some particular fact, and that we can know the truth because He has communicated it to us in scripture; an atheist may claim it is a fact that there is no God, and that we can know this through scientific observation and logical argumentation; a certain variety of skeptic may believe that there is a truth as to whether there is or is not a God, but suspect that the human intellect is insufficient to the task of determining the fact of the matter—all three are objectivists with respect to the question of God's existence, regardless of their differences as to *whether* God exists and how, if at all, we may know this.

The idea that the truth does *not* exist independently of the human mind, but that humans really are the measure of at least some things, is *relativism*. The relativist does *not* claim that there is no truth, nor merely that although there is a truth we humans must discover and evaluate it for ourselves. The relativist believes in truth; it is just that he ties the existence and nature of the truth in some way to the human intellect, which is to say that by "measure" the relativist intends something more than mere discovery or evaluation. For the relativist, humans are the "measure" of truth in the sense that the truth is conditioned by, quite literally *generated* by, human subjectivity. We, somehow, make the truth. The relativist, then, is one who says both that "*x* is true" and that "*x* is true *because* I believe it to be true."

Strictly speaking, the idea that the truth is what "I" make it is *individual relativism*, also known as *subjectivism*. According to this account, truth is relative to—which is to say, *generated by*—each and every individual. This contrasts with *cultural relativism*, according to which truth is relative to—or generated by—each and every individual culture. Please note that in either version it is *truth* that is relative, not our *beliefs about* the truth. It is not in the least philosophically interesting to assert that our beliefs about the truth are generated by ourselves or our culture; this is just an obvious fact about the origin of our beliefs. So the observation that, for example, different cultures have different beliefs and practices, even *radically* different beliefs and practices, is not an expression of relativism. Nor is it relativism if we add that we have no way to determine which culture is right. All this is compatible with objectivism, which can acknowledge disagreement, even unresolvable disagreement. To qualify as an objectivist one has only to maintain that there is a truth independent of human subjectivity, whether or not people disagree as to its nature or can reasonably hope ever to know it. The relativist must insist on more than disagreement and the difficulty, even the impossibility, of adjudication between contending beliefs—or rather he must insist on something *other* than this, for neither disagreement nor problems of adjudication are necessary to relativism, which is compatible with permanent and harmonious agreement among all relevant parties. The relativist must insist that regardless of agreement or disagreement, there is no truth independent of the beliefs themselves by which to judge the truth claims of any individual or culture.

But if for the relativist truth itself is relative to human subjectivity, then he must revise the conditions of belief and knowledge as presented above. Subjectivism, to take the most radical example, completely abolishes the line between the two. If x is true solely because I believe it to be true, then if I believe x (assuming that I know that I believe it) I also *know* it. There is no possibility of error, for anyone. If I believe x and you believe not-x, then x is true for me and not-x is true for you; we are both correct— and that is all there is to it, for there is no truth or fact of the matter independent of our beliefs according to which one of us might be right and the other wrong. And this is true also if we both believe x: we are both correct, not because x is true independent of our beliefs and our beliefs correspond to the truth. Rather, x is true because we believe it: I believe x, and therefore x is true for me; and you believe x, and therefore x is true for you. The truth is generated by our beliefs; it just happens that in this case our beliefs coincide.

I mentioned above that the objectivist believes "about some particular matter" that the truth is independent of human subjectivity. This suggests that objectivism is not necessarily a universal thesis. One *might* be an objectivist regarding all substantive truth claims, but one need not be. Relativism, too, may be limited in scope. The question, then, is with respect to what sort of truth claims one is an objectivist or a relativist. Most people are objectivists regarding mathematical truths and truths having to do with physical reality. These matters, they believe, are subject to proof and/ or evidence. Metaphysical matters, on the other hand—religion, for example—people tend to regard as relative. This is so even for many religious believers. In this case, however, the relativism usually is due to confusion. Expressions of the form "true for you," "true for me," "his truth," "her truth," "their truth" are common in our society, and if employed literally they may serve as expressions of relativism. Yet despite their literal meaning, many people use them merely to indicate personal belief, without intending any philosophical implications. Thus, expressions such as "x is true for me" or "y is true in their reality," which might seem to imply the existence of relative truths and different realities, often in use mean nothing more radical than "I believe that x is true" and "given their perception of reality, they believe that y is true." But as I mentioned above, neither objectivism nor relativism has anything to do with beliefs about the truth of x or y (unless, of course, x or y is a statement of the thesis of objectivism or relativism); nor do they have to do with anyone's perception of reality. Rather, they have to do with the truth itself, or with reality itself. But the fact is that many objectivists grow up speaking the popular language of relativism, and these same people learn (along with most everyone else) that those who believe in objective, "absolute" truths are narrow minded and quite possibly dangerous, whereas the open minded and tolerant recognize that we all have our own truths and "who's to say?" that another person's truth is false. Having learned to speak and to think this way, these people, despite their objectivism, genuinely mistake themselves for relativists.[7] Now all this is based on misunderstanding, for surely something has gone awry in the mind of, say, a traditional religious believer who thinks that the best way to express (what he would take upon reflection to be) an objectively true belief is to imply that his belief is only relatively "true," or who fails to recognize the disagreement between his (object-ivist) beliefs and his (relativist) words. And as for the lesson he has learned regarding the intolerance of objectivists: this idea carelessly confuses psychological with logical associations. It may be that some objectivists are intolerant of dissent and eager to force their beliefs on others, but this is a psychological condition not caused by their objectivism. An objectivist may, with perfect consistency, believe that he knows the truth and yet be tolerant and even lovingly supportive of those who entertain beliefs he takes to be false; and a relativist may hold that there is no objective truth regarding *x* but, as a matter of contingent psychological fact, he may also be the sort of person who cannot brook disagreement and who must, therefore, induce others to agree with him, whether by rational persuasion, sophistry, or force.

But to return to the matter of the scope of one's objectivism or relativism: one may be an objectivist regarding one domain—the physical world, for example—and a relativist regarding another—the metaphysical. These are epistemological (or epistemological-ontological) theses, and we are free citizens of a free country and so at liberty to adopt any philosophical thesis we like. Still, the relevant question is whether we can justify our decision to draw the line here rather than there. It is popular to distinguish the physical from the metaphysical by claiming that the former can be proven with evidence while the latter depends entirely on faith or belief. But this idea is problematic in itself, for it is not easy to defend the standard accounts of proof and evidence without begging the question against metaphysics. But more to the point, neither Plato nor Nietzsche embraces our popular idea. Plato generally comes across as confident that objective and cognizable metaphysical truths exist (regarding Forms, the soul, the divine); he certainly develops and defends arguments apparently intended to prove at least some of his metaphysical positions (see Book 10 of the *Laws*, for example); and Nietzsche at times (*most* of the time, I would say) insists that even our most successful scientific accounts of the physical world are at every level mere tissues of falsehood and fantasy. We have seen, moreover, that in the *Theaetetus* Plato experiments with applying relativism to physical reality, and Nietzsche's perspectivism may be closer to this than to a naive scientific realism. In any case, we are not now concerned with either metaphysics or physics, at least not directly. We are instead treating of Plato and Nietzsche on the noble and the good, so let's turn now to consider objectivism and relativism with respect to what we might designate broadly as ethics.

Eudaimonia

Aristotle begins his *Nicomachean Ethics* with the claim that the highest of all goods attainable by action is "happiness." He reports as well that this was the standard opinion of the time.[8] Plato occasionally suggests that there is a higher condition to which humans should aspire (on which, see p. 132 below), but usually his dialogues are consistent with Aristotle's idea that happiness is our highest good. It goes without saying that neither Plato nor Aristotle ever uses the word "happiness." Rather, this is the common English translation of the Greek word *eudaimonia*. It is worth dwelling on the fact because the translation is misleading, for in at least one important respect our word carries a sense diametrically opposed to Plato's Greek.

The problem, in brief, is that whereas our idea of happiness is of a *relative* state of *mind*, Plato understands *eudaimonia* to be an *objective* state of *being*. Happiness according to contemporary popular usage has to do with how one *feels*, and thus it may differ from person to person. I have my happiness, you have yours, and everyone else has his or her own. This is so precisely because happiness is a subjective phenomenon; its very mode of existence is bound up with an individual's psychic state. We use the word in such a way that introspection alone suffices to inform us whether or not we are "happy," and if we find that we are, no one else may legitimately dispute this. Another person may remark that I do not appear to be happy, that in his opinion I ought not to be happy given, for example, what I have recently done, or that he would not be happy should he suffer what I have suffered; but it is not for him to pronounce me happy or unhappy. He may guess my state by closely observing my words and deeds, which in normal circumstances are reliable indicators. Still, in the end this is only a guess. I alone can confidently declare myself happy—and, as I say, once I have done so the matter is settled. Perhaps we should allow for the possibility of self-deception and other forms of error, but this does nothing to alter the fact that my happiness is my own, with a source, intensity, duration, and significance independent of everything other than my personal, private psychic condition. Happiness, in short, is a feeling, a sentiment, a mood, and as such it is by nature relative to individual subjectivities.

Eudaimonia, on the other hand, does not differ among individuals. What counts for one as *eudaimonia* counts for all. This is so because *eudaimonia* has to do primarily with the course of one's life. In the end it comes down to whether one lives a life of virtue, and by virtue I mean those habits that enable one to live well as a human. Plato—and it is Plato's position I am relating here—Plato believes in human nature, which is to say that he believes there is an essence that serves as a paradigm for a proper human life. Whoever lives in accord with this paradigm lives well; those who deviate from it do not.[9] The virtues are, let's say, ways of being and acting in the world in accord with human nature. Therefore, a man or a woman who actualizes the human essence through virtuous activity is *eudaimôn* (to use the adjectival form of the word); all others fall short of this goal and are, in a sense, living lives less than properly human. Those who habitually indulge their taste for vice may very well be happy, for they may have been reared to associate criminality or self-abuse with feelings of pleasure and contentment. Yet no such person is *eudaimôn*, whether or not he is willing to acknowledge the fact.

I have remarked that what counts for one as *eudaimonia* counts for all, and this is so because the virtues do not differ among individuals. Courage, for example, is a virtue for everyone. It is worth noting, however, that different individuals, or the same individual in different circumstances, manifest the virtues differently. One manifestation of the virtue of courage involves experiencing degrees of fear and resolve appropriate to the relevant situation. A well-trained hoplite standing with his phalanx across the plain from a roughly equivalent enemy host will, no doubt, be afraid; but if he is courageous, his fear will be outmatched by his resolve. He will stand and fight with his fellows. If the same soldier in this situation is so dominated by fear that he lacks the resolve to fight, and so turns and runs from the field, then he is a coward. And if he leaps from his ranks to charge the massed enemy on his own with no thought for the danger, then he is rash. This same soldier confronted by a different enemy should experience different degrees of fear and resolve, less fear and greater resolve if the opposing force is inferior to the enemy in our original example, more fear and less resolve if it is superior. Similarly, a different man standing on our original field of battle should experience degrees of fear and resolve different from those experienced by the soldier we have considered so far, less fear and more resolve if his conditioning and training are superior, more fear and less resolve if they are inferior.

Virtue, then, amounts to feeling and acting appropriately in any particular situation; and what counts as appropriate varies with circumstances. Yet this is not relativism. Given the relevant details of the situation, only those feelings and actions that fall within a certain range are appropriate; those that exceed or fall short of this range are inappropriate. And the measure of appropriateness here is no man's subjective opinion; the sole determining factors are the facts of the situation—what is happening and who is involved—in conjunction with human nature (i.e. the essence of human being). Only an individual human can say that "this (or that) is appropriate here." But by "say" in this case I mean simply that it takes a particular human literally to formulate the thought or to speak the words. But as to whether or not the judgment is correct—this is up to no individual. The one and only relevant standard is reality. This is objectivism through and through.

If the virtues are habits that enable one to live well as a human, and if to live well as a human is to be *eudaimōn*, then we may substitute for "happiness" as a translation of *eudaimonia* the phrase "a good life." The phrase is not only more appropriate; it is also more literally accurate. The "*eu*" in *eudaimonia*, taken by itself, is an adverb meaning "well." The "*daimon*" taken by itself (in which case it appears, with an omega for the omicron, as *daimōn*) is a noun that may apply to a divinity, including the sort of divinity that oversees the course of one's life, from which use it comes to apply as well to one's life course itself. We might, therefore, translate *eudaimonia* as "a life well overseen by the divine," or as "a well-conducted life." But these are clumsy translations, and the phrase "a good life" combines accuracy with concision and elegance of expression.

As a concluding remark on this subject I will add that the psychic state we know as happiness, in normal circumstances, naturally attends the good life.[10] He who truly lives well, who lives virtuously and does so intentionally, experiences peace of mind, pleasure, and contentment as a result. But the influence does not run in the other direction. We have seen that a vicious man may be happy, and this fact alone suffices to demonstrate that the good life neither depends on nor, more loosely, follows from happiness. The two often appear in conjunction, but whenever they do it is *eudaimonia* that produces the happiness, never the reverse. We may express this insight in brief as follows: where there is *eudaimonia* there is happiness as well; but where there is happiness *eudaimonia* may or may not be present.

Soul over body

One way of putting the central question of Plato's masterpiece, the *Republic*, is whether justice or injustice produces *eudaimonia*.[11] Some version of this question is at the core of Platonic ethics. Entire books, scores of books, have been written on Plato's ethics. This is so at least in part because the Platonic corpus is vast, and every dialogue without exception touches more or less on some aspect of human life and action. It is fortunate, then, that our business here is not to attempt a comprehensive survey of Platonic ethics, but rather to cover only so much as is required to set forth the substantive differences between Plato and Nietzsche on the noble and the good. Since we cannot cover all of the relevant material, I will limit myself to the most enduring and influential of Plato's ethical ideas, namely, those he developed at length in the *Republic*, with reference as well to the *Gorgias* and *Phaedo*.

In his magnificent preface to *Beyond Good and Evil*, Nietzsche declares that "Plato's invention of the pure spirit and the good as such" is "the worst, most durable, and most dangerous of all errors so far." Of course he knew better than to believe that Plato was the originator of either of these ideas, but he also knew that their hold over the west (especially as embodied in Christian theology) is due in large part to the pervasive influence of Plato's philosophical-artistic genius. Plato's account of the Good in Book 6 of the *Republic* is more properly his "invention" than is his account of spirit, or soul (*psychê* in Greek, which word serves wherever we might use either "soul" or "mind"). But it is true that a conception of the soul as independent of and superior to the body is central to the argument of the *Republic*, and that an even more radical distinction between soul and body (according to which the soul alone is of value, the body being its prison or tomb) informs the whole of the *Phaedo*. And these two ideas in Plato are not independent of one another, for the primary activity of the soul is to seek knowledge of the good as such.

In Book 4 of the *Republic* Plato divides the human soul into three parts or aspects.[12] There is the appetitive part of the soul, which is the source of desire. From here arise our desires for food, drink, sex, and all those other bodily pleasures that in themselves tend toward infinite expansion and insatiability. Some of these desires are necessary to the maintenance of human life, but left to themselves without regulation they may be harmful to the organism as a whole. Their regulation is the responsibility of the appetitive soul's immediate superior, namely, the spirited part of the soul. This word "spirited" is the standard translation of the Greek *thumoeidês*, which in common Greek usage may mean "courageous," "high spirited," or "hot-tempered." The idea is that this is the seat in humans of passions and emotions, anger, courage, and the love of honor. This part of the soul, when functioning properly, keeps the desires in check; it grows angry whenever they overstep their bounds and maintains discipline by force or the threat of force. The boundary lines thus enforced are staked out by the rational part of the soul. Reason's business is to know what is good for the whole of the soul (without favor to itself or to any other individual part) and to translate this knowledge into principles of conduct conducive to a life of virtue. Having acquired knowledge of the good through philosophical investigation, reason declares its principles to the soul as a legislator proclaims his law before the assembly of citizens. The spirited part of the soul then acts as something of a joint military and police force whose duty is to preserve the laws from external assault and internal subversion. The appetites and desires function in a manner similar to a city's unthinking laborers and money-makers in that they may attain satisfaction and peaceful contentment by minding the authority and power of their superiors.

Here we have an image of the soul as a tripartite hierarchy of parts, aspects, or seats of specific functions. Each part has a clearly defined place in the overall structure, which place corresponds to its relative degree of authority. The appetitive part of the soul is inferior, for it has no share in reason. It is neither rational itself nor does it comprehend the dictates of reason. It is, therefore, utterly subordinate to the other two parts. The spirited part of the soul, though not rational in itself, is able to comprehend and heed reason's decrees. Thus it occupies a middle position, being superior to arational appetite but inferior to the rational soul. Reason itself is the ultimate authority, for it knows the truth on which the soul in its entirety depends for its sound condition. If the soul is good, it is so only because reason knows the good—the Form of *good*—and molds the soul in its likeness. We may imagine a properly ordered soul as resembling a well-run city, a city in which the members of the various classes fulfill their functions as directed by a wise and benevolent monarch. Indeed, the argument of the *Republic* proceeds quite explicitly by comparing a human soul to a city. A soul is good if it is virtuous: it is just when each of its parts—which, as I have already suggested, correspond to a city's three classes: the laborers, the warriors, and the ruler or rulers—performs its proper function without interfering with the operations of the other parts; it is temperate when each part harmonizes in agreeing that this condition is best; it is courageous when the spirited element preserves and enforces the decrees of the ruling authority, even when confronted with temptation or fear; and it is wise when reason knows what is good for the whole (427d–444a).

Plato's other images of the soul, though less elaborate, serve to make the same point. Consider, also from the *Republic*, the soul imagined as a chimeric amalgamation of a hydra, a lion, and a human (588c–589b). The many-headed hydra represents the appetitive part of the soul, the powerful lion the spirited element, and the human the soul's rationality. The hydra is large and unruly, and the human in alliance with the lion must discipline its tamable heads and cut off the intractably wild ones. Yet another image, this one from the *Phaedrus*, likens the soul to a charioteer and his two horses, one of them noble and good (*kalos te kai agathos*), the other one base (*kakos*) and unruly. The noble horse is naturally obedient and constrained by an innate sense of shame; its ignoble partner is shameless and must be disciplined and restrained by force. The charioteer himself oversees the team with knowledge acquired by way of the Forms (246a–256e). Different as these images are, they have in common a tripartite analysis of soul arranged hierarchically with reason, conceived as the seat of wisdom attained through knowledge of the Forms, securely enthroned at the top.

In the *Republic* Plato famously stresses reason's authority over souls and cities alike by introducing the idea of the Philosopher-King (473cff.). As Socrates puts it, unless philosophers exercise kingly rule, "there will be no rest from ills ... for cities or ... for the human race" (473c11–d6). He distinguishes the philosopher, who possesses knowledge of that which is (Being), from the non-philosopher, who entertains beliefs concerning that which both is and is not (Becoming) (474b–480a). Returning then to his contention that philosophers must rule, Socrates claims that by consorting with the divine and orderly, philosophers become divine and orderly themselves, so far as this is possible for humans (500d1–2). Much later in the work, just prior in fact to the conclusion of the argument, he extends this idea by remarking that the pure soul that loves wisdom and consorts with the divine, the immortal, and that which always is (Being) "likens itself to god" (*homoiousthai theôi*), so far as is possible for a human, by practicing virtue (611b–613b). All this recalls Socrates' famous assertion in the *Theaetetus* that men must strive as far as possible for "likeness to god" (*homoiôsis theôi*), which amounts to their being just and pious with wisdom (176a–b). Those who do so, Socrates continues, live according to a divine and most happy paradigm, which paradigm they come to resemble themselves (176e–177a).

We shall have to return to Plato's idea of "likeness to god," for there are those who consider it his central ethical teaching. But for now we should investigate further his understanding of *eudaimonia*, with particular attention to the problem of how we humans may acquire or attain it. The *Gorgias* will be helpful here, for in this work Plato pursues quite explicitly the question whether the life of justice and knowledge, represented by the philosopher, or the life of power and pleasure, represented by the sophist, leads to *eudaimonia*.[13] The dialogue portrays Socrates in conversation, first with Gorgias himself, a famous sophist from the Greek town of Leontini on the island of Sicily, and then in turn with two of Gorgias's students, Polus and Callicles. Proceeding as it does as an increasingly heated verbal competition between different ways of life, the dialogue is an *agon*, a competition, contest, or struggle. The first three words of the dialogue, "*polemou kai machês*," translate literally as "of war and of battle," and this image sets the tone for the work as a whole, particularly the titanic confrontation between Socrates and the inflexible Callicles. But this confrontation concludes the work. We begin at the beginning.

Early in the dialogue Gorgias boasts of the awesome power the skills of the sophist can bring, explaining that practiced rhetoricians can easily dominate experts in fields of which they know nothing whatever (452e and 456a–457b). In the course of his encomium, however, he mentions the possibility of a sophist deploying his skills unjustly, and he contends that in such a case the sophist's teacher should not be held responsible (456c–457c). But Socrates latches on to this point and drives Gorgias to concede that he will teach justice to students who are ignorant of it (459d–460a). He then argues that since anyone who has learned justice is just, and so will never act unjustly, Gorgias has contradicted himself by both claiming to teach justice to his students (who will then necessarily be just) and preemptively defending himself from the unjust deeds his students might commit (460a–461b).

I do not for a moment believe that Plato considered Socrates' argument invulnerable to objection. No doubt he thought he could develop it along such lines as to complete it, but in the *Gorgias* this is not his task. He is rather concerned to demonstrate Gorgias's own vulnerability to conflicts between his desire for power and his desire for honor. As Polus points out, Gorgias stumbled only because he was ashamed not to agree that he would teach justice to students who knew nothing of it (461b–c). To disagree would be to confess to a disrespect for justice, which would harm Gorgias's public reputation. The situation reveals that Gorgias's desire to acquire power by recruiting the several potential students present for the conversation (455c–d)—the power that accompanies financial gain and an enhanced reputation as a teacher in demand—this desire for power is in conflict with his desire to be honored by these young men, which desire he fears will not be satisfied if he admits in public to disdaining justice.[14] There is also the implication that the students' own desire to acquire power by studying with Gorgias is in conflict with their desire for honor, which also would be threatened were they to admit that they cared nothing for justice.

Taking over the conversation from Gorgias, Polus does not shrink from approving of injustice. Power and the freedom to do whatever one wants are all that matter to him, and sophistry bestows such power on its diligent practitioners, who dominate their surroundings as a tyrant dominates his city. Polus will not be so easily caught out as his teacher, for he is not ashamed of his ambition for ruthless supremacy. Eventually, however, young Polus is tripped up by his admiration—or anyway his professed admiration—of the good (*agathos*), for he admits that power is good and that men want the good, but then also admits that those who are ignorant are more likely to harm than to benefit themselves (466b–467a and 467b–468e). And since no one disputes the fact that the sophists are ignorant—in fact they themselves readily admit it, beginning with Gorgias at 454c–455a—Polus must concede that sophists neither have power nor do what they want, despite acting unjustly with impunity. Flustered perhaps by this surprising reversal, Polus agrees that doing injustice is more shameful than suffering it (474c). Socrates then exploits this admission to argue that acting unjustly is shameful because it is harmful and bad (*kakos*) for one's soul (474c–475e), from which he concludes that whoever commits injustice should be punished, for punishment in this case is just, and, if just, it is noble (*kalos*), and if noble it is good (*agathos*), and if it is good it is beneficial (476a–477a). In short, just punishment is beneficial because it heals the corrupt soul by cleansing it of its badness. The upshot of all this is that the life of the unjust man is base (*kakos*) and miserable, whereas the just man is noble (*kalos*), good (*agathos*), and most happy (*eudaimonestatos*).

When at this point an exasperated Callicles bounds into the conversation, he accuses Socrates of playing the demagogue by exploiting the shame that restrains Gorgias and Polus from publically expressing their sincere opinions. He himself will concede nothing to Socrates; he refuses in particular to admit that injustice is either bad or shameful. In fact, he claims that what men call injustice is actually justice, so although he agrees, verbally, with Socrates' position that the just life is superior to the unjust life, the substance of the words as he understands them is precisely the opposite of what Socrates has in mind. Here Callicles distinguishes between natural and conventional justice, and he insists that by nature it is just that the powerful subjugate the weak, dominate them and have a greater share of goods than them. But the weak have managed to avoid being dominated by convincing everyone that men should be treated equally and goods distributed fairly, and this idea has been adopted by custom and enshrined in law. In short, what the weak could not win by force they have claimed through cunning; they have contrived a free life for themselves by manipulating the ideas of those who ought by right to be their masters (482c–484c).

Callicles' position is so thoroughly radical, and also so consistent, that Socrates cannot defeat him by drawing out contradictions in his conception of justice. Therefore he changes tactics, shifting ground to attack Callicles' desire for pleasure. If the best life is a life of domination and rule, he asks, should the good man also rule himself? Should he, that is, practice self-control with respect to his appetites and desires for pleasure? Callicles scoffs at the suggestion, insisting to the contrary that all pleasures are good and that the best men are those with the most extensive appetites and the power to satisfy them at will. He declares, in sum, that *eudaimonia* attends the life of debauchery, self-indulgence, and freedom (491d–492e). He is not at all pleased when Socrates points out that this position implies that the best life might be that of a man who does nothing but scratch his itches, or of a passive homosexual, but still he refuses to admit a distinction between pleasure and the good. But after Socrates stumps him with two technical arguments, Callicles finally admits that some pleasures are good and some bad (495c–499b). Now Socrates has him where he wants him, for if good pleasures are beneficial and bad ones harmful (499c–d), then he who would live well must be competent to distinguish them. But this requires knowledge, which (as we have seen) the sophists lack (500a–501c). And having established these points to Callicles' dismay, Socrates concludes that since with respect to pleasure our aim is the good, and since the good for a human results from—or just amounts to—the presence of virtue in the soul, and since a soul is virtuous only when properly ordered, which is to say when organized in accord with human nature—since all this is so we may affirm with confidence that *eudaimonia* depends on a soul whose various aspects or elements are hierarchically harmonized, which is the condition of no other than the just soul.

The *Gorgias* concludes with Socrates insisting to Callicles that souls at death separate from their bodies (524b), and that just souls abide on the Isles of the Blessed in a state of complete *eudaimonia* (523a–b). This is consistent with the so-called "Myth of Er" that closes the *Republic*, which is Socrates' report of the narrative of a man named Er who died, visited the afterlife, and returned to recount what he witnessed there. He saw disembodied souls suffering punishment or being rewarded according to their deeds in life. Those who had been just and pious fared well in the afterlife (615b–c), particularly those who had practiced philosophy properly, for these latter when reborn on earth enjoy *eudaimonia* (619d–e). In the *Phaedo*, too, Socrates defines death as the separation of the soul from the body (64c) and claims to believe that souls in the afterlife are judged with respect to whether they have lived nobly and piously (113d). Those who have lived well are transferred to the true surface of the earth (we ourselves actually inhabit the hollows of the earth), which is beautiful, pure, populated by the gods, and blessed with *eudaimonia* (110b–111c). As fine a condition as this surely is, there is a yet higher state, for "those who have sufficiently purified themselves by philosophy" go on to live "altogether without a body" in dwellings so exceedingly beautiful they are difficult to describe (114c).

Earlier I called attention to Socrates' claim in the *Theaetetus* that whoever attains to likeness to god lives a divine life of "the greatest happiness." Plato employs here the superlative form of the adjective *eudaimôn*, so to the extent that he associates the term with the virtues of justice, piety, and wisdom, his point is consistent with the account of *eudaimonia* I presented in the previous section and have expanded on in this. Yet in the *Theaetetus* Socrates goes well beyond this account, which is why the passage is remarkable. I have noted that later philosophers active in the Platonic tradition regarded the idea of "likeness to god" as Plato's central ethical teaching, and the doctrine exercised a profound influence on Neoplatonism and through this channel on western mysticism.[15] Even Schopenhauer insisted that with this teaching Plato transcended all other ancient systems of ethics, which were merely "eudaimonistic."[16] He, too, regarded as "mystical" the thought that the life of reason, which mimics the gods by loving wisdom, practicing virtue, and consequently attaining supreme happiness, is divine.

Of all Plato's dialogues, the most thoroughly and consistently mystical is the *Phaedo*. Although no character in the work makes mention of "likeness to god," the idea of the philosopher as truly at home in a world transcendent of nature permeates the dialogue. With its emphasis on the soul as imprisoned in the body and the philosopher as striving for separation and release through purification, the dialogue is overtly Orphic and Pythagorean.[17] We should note, however, that no other Platonic dialogue devalues the body so insistently, and that in this case the excess may be due to the work's being set on the day of Socrates' death. Socrates' immediate concern is to relieve the despair overwhelming his friends at the thought of his passing, and he chooses to do so by insisting that he is not his body, which will die, decompose, and blow away, but rather he is a soul, which is immortal. Yet he deceives neither himself nor the others regarding his ability to prove his bold metaphysical assertions. He acknowledges more than once that his arguments are incomplete (84c, 107b), and following his great "myth" of the underworld and postmortem judgment he remarks that "it is not fitting for a man of sense confidently to affirm that these things are as I have related them" (114d1–2; cf. 108d–e).[18] He does, however, maintain that it is worth daring the belief that some such things are true regarding our souls, for the risk, he says, is noble (*kalos*), and he advises his friends to sing these things to themselves as charms (114d). The dialogue is full of such bizarrely arational and irrational elements, full of references and allusions to poetry, prophecies, dreams, mystery rites, initiations, riddling speech, and Dionysian frenzies. It would be rash to read the *Phaedo* without attention to all that is strange in the work, for this content might imply that the dialogue is something other than a straightforward document of Platonic doctrine. Still, since Nietzsche himself made much of the anti-natural elements of Plato's philosophy, I shall briefly relate those that appear in the most otherworldly *Phaedo*.

It is widely believed that the *Phaedo* is the dialogue in which Plato introduces his theory of Forms. This may or may not be so, but in any case the Forms are not the central theme of the work. They are introduced only in connection with Socrates' attempts to persuade his friends that the soul is immortal. The problem arises from Socrates' appearing uncannily calm and relaxed on the day he is to die: his friends cannot understand his attitude. Socrates accounts for his cheerfulness by claiming that as a philosopher he has for years prepared to die. Philosophy, he explains, just is a way of practicing and training for death and dying (64a, 67e). Death is separation of the soul from the body, and the philosopher regularly strives to effect such separation to the extent this is possible while living. This is particularly true with respect to the philosopher's search for knowledge, for the body is a hindrance to this pursuit because Being (the Forms) cannot be grasped by the senses but is accessible to the soul alone. The philosopher, therefore, must endeavor to adjust his intellectual center of gravity in such a way that his soul is unaffected by his body and its distracting desires and unceasing influx of sensory information. This is philosophical separation, and this variety of the soul's "release from the bonds of the body" is known as purification (*katharsis, katharmos*).[19]

Purification is central to the *Phaedo*, and its metaphysical orientation is explicitly opposed to the sort of physically oriented philosophical perspectives that we might identify with contemporary scientism or naturalism. Plato associates the idea of the pure soul with Socrates' rejection of a position that combines empiricism and materialism, or the belief that corporeal things that affect the body are manifest and true (81b, 83b–e), and this rejection he associates in turn with Socrates' warning against "misology," the hatred or mistrust of reason (89c–91a). His idea seems to be that since through reason we may acquire knowledge of metaphysical realities, only one who despises reason could believe that knowledge comes only through the senses and that physical objects alone are real. Socrates even declares that empiricism-materialism and misology are together the basest condition from which a man can suffer,[20] and he explains that in both cases the condition results from a disorder of the soul: it is not pure (*katharos*) or healthy.[21] The disorder of impurity is a terrible calamity indeed, for, you will recall, only "those who have sufficiently purified themselves by philosophy live in the future altogether without a body."

The *Phaedo*, then, is "mystical" in the sense that its ontology is metaphysical and its ethics ascetic. The body is devalued throughout. Nietzsche seems often to have had the radical asceticism of this dialogue in mind when he condemned the Socratic-Platonic worldview. He was particularly interested in the dialogue's depiction of Socrates' death, which he wrote about on several occasions. The *Phaedo* concludes with Socrates' death scene, at the climax of which the philosopher speaks his last words: "O Crito, we owe a rooster to Asclepius. So offer it (to him) and don't neglect it" (118a). It has become something of an academic parlor game to guess at the hidden significance of these words.[22] I will not here contribute my own proposal, not directly anyway; but I would like to remark on a feature of Socrates' death scene that, as I hope to show, anyone who would offer a plausible interpretation of Socrates' last words must reckon with. Scholars have from time to time noticed this feature, but to date no one has paid it the attention it merits.[23]

Socrates' final utterance is not all that is strange at the end of the *Phaedo*, for in order to speak his riddling words he must perform a most unusual act. Recall the scene: Socrates calmly downs the poison (*pharmakon*), which causes those present to cry and wail. He insists that his friends keep quiet, for he has heard it is best to die in silence. He then walks around until his legs are numb, at which point he lies down. At this moment, or soon thereafter, he covers himself with a cloak, blanket, or veil. The guard then touches (*ephaptomenos*, 117e6) Socrates to determine the poison's progress through his body, and just after the man touches him again (*hêpteto*, 118a3) Socrates uncovers himself and speaks.[24]

Socrates uncovers himself? Imagine the effect this must have had on everyone present. Imagine *yourself* at the deathbed of a loved one or friend: his apparently lifeless body is fully enshrouded with a sheet from the bed on which just moments before he exhaled his last breath. You have watched him die, and now this man once so full of vigor and fire is a silent and motionless shape covered with a makeshift burial shroud. Once he was a man, your companion and friend; now he is only a corpse.

Like everyone else in the room you are weeping, hiding your face in your hands or exchanging with others looks of wounded dismay. There is nothing to say, nothing to be done; perhaps there never will be. An uneasy muffled silence descends...

But then, quite suddenly and most unexpectedly, the corpse stirs. A hand reaches out from beneath the shroud and lifts the veil from its face. Perhaps the man even sits up. How remarkably surprising this would be. Shocking; perhaps even terrifying.

Now ask yourself: what must Socrates' friends have thought when the philosopher uncovered himself? Had Socrates somehow cheated death? Had he survived? Or had he died but come back to life, returned? As enigmatic as Socrates' last words undeniably are, his last act is no less curious. Among the Greeks a dying man might well cover himself or be covered by others before finally expiring, but as among us the standard practice was to cover the corpse after death.[25] It would be most unusual for a man lying covered on his deathbed suddenly to *un*cover himself. When Xenophon's Cyrus covers himself while on his deathbed at the end of the *Cyropaedia*,[26] it is clear that he does so immediately before passing away. So sure is he that death is imminent he implores those present not to look at him once he has covered himself. Had he covered himself and then *un*covered himself, his deed would have been, at least for a moment, unfathomable and frightening.

We do have accounts of men near death covering and then uncovering themselves, yet these men are not so near to death that their uncoverings would stand out as particularly extraordinary. Plutarch in his biography of Pericles relates an episode involving the statesman and his old associate Anaxagoras, which considering the details seems intentionally to recall the conclusion of Plato's *Phaedo*. Anaxagoras, whose ideas Socrates analyzes at *Phaedo* 97b–99d, and who will later be exiled from Athens on a charge of impiety, a charge not unlike that brought against Socrates himself, feels slighted or neglected by Pericles in some unspecified way. When Pericles learns that Anaxagoras is at home isolated and desperate, and that moreover he is starving himself to death, he hurries to the philosopher's side. He finds the man covered (*sugkekalummenon*) and waiting to die. Upon seeing his old friend in this state Pericles laments, not for Anaxagoras but for himself, which expression in the Greek recalls Phaedo's report of his own emotions as he watched Socrates drink the poison.[27] Then Anaxagoras uncovers himself (*ekkalupsamenon*, the same word in the same form that Plato applies to Socrates before he utters his last words) and issues to

Pericles the enigmatic remark, "O Pericles, even those who have need of a lamp pour oil in it."[28]

Similarly, in Plutarch's biography of Demosthenes, the orator takes his own life by sucking poison (*pharmakon*) from a pen. After draining the liquid he covers himself (*sugkalupsamenos*) and soon thereafter uncovers himself (*exekalupsato*), speaks directly to his persecutor Archias (his last words are allusive, but not as obscure as Socrates'), leaves the temple in which he had taken sanctuary, and dies.[29]

As similar as these two scenes are to Plato's depiction of Socrates' death, there are important differences. First, although Anaxagoras and Demosthenes cover themselves, they are manifestly alive and by no means lying already on the very precipice of death. No one seeing them would have mistaken them for dead.[30] Therefore, their uncovering themselves would not have shocked those present as Socrates' doing so must have shocked his friends. And quite apart from the behavior of Socrates as a character in the dialogue, we must consider the significance of Plato's authorial decision to depict the scene as he has done, which brings us to a second relevant difference between Plutarch's and Plato's presentations. In Plato there is more to Socrates' covering and uncovering himself than the act itself, for this act is only one member of a more extensive sequence of covering-uncovering oppositions.

Less than half a Stephanus page before Socrates uncovers himself to speak, Phaedo reports that he, Phaedo, covered himself (*egkalupsamenos*, 117c8) when he cried upon seeing Socrates drink the *pharmakon*. Then we learn of Socrates' uncovering himself (*ekkalupsamenos*, 118a6), having previously covered himself (*enekekalupto*, 118a6[31]). Finally, just six lines later, the guard uncovers Socrates (*exekalupsen*, 118a12–13) to verify that he is dead. Attending to the sequence of the relevant Greek words, then, we have a progression of covering, uncovering, covering, and uncovering. Now it seems to me that Plato must have intended this, and even that he went out of his way to present the series in precisely this oppositional order. His account throughout the dialogue of Socrates' movements is unusually specific, as illustrated by his curious remark near the beginning of the work that Socrates placed his feet on the ground and remained in this position throughout the conversation (61c–d). Yet when relating Socrates' final movements, including his lying down, Plato makes no mention of his covering himself. He defers referring to the covering until *after* noting the *un*covering. His narrative, then, does not follow the actual order of events. Yet this arrangement is necessary to produce an oppositional sequence following the mention of Phaedo's covering: Phaedo covers himself and then Socrates *un*covers *him*self. Plato could have achieved the same effect by explicitly depicting *all* the acts of covering-uncovering in their actual sequence, in which case he would have noted that Phaedo covered his eyes and then uncovered them, and after this that Socrates covered and uncovered himself. But this more exact approach would lack all literary charm, for if in this context one writes that a weeping man has covered his eyes, it goes without saying that he soon uncovers them. To state the fact explicitly would be to strive for the mechanical thoroughness of a recording device rather than for the subtly suggestive touch of an artist. Having said this, however, it is worth attending to the actual sequence of coverings and uncoverings, for it is itself an ordered series of oppositions.[32] We know, then, that the words on the page depict an oppositional series of covering, uncovering, covering, and uncovering, but the acts themselves (that is, including those not explicitly mentioned but implied in the text) form a series of covering, uncovering (Phaedo), covering, uncovering, covering (Socrates), uncovering, covering (the guard). I have remarked that I believe this to be intentional. But what can it mean?

We return to the scene: Having uncovered himself and delivered his enigmatic lines, Socrates lies back down and covers himself over once again. When Crito inquires whether he has any other request, Socrates does not respond. He is dead, really dead this time.

Or anyway his *body* is dead.

Since Socrates uncovers himself specifically in order to speak of Asclepius, we would like to have evidence that covering and uncovering played a role in ritual practices associated with this god. Unfortunately, there is virtually no such evidence; but there is something, and what there is is at least suggestive. A fragmentary "miracle inscription" from Epidaurus recounts an episode involving a woman's seeking a cure for infertility by incubating in the god's temple. The woman must have been covered, for we are told that she dreamt of someone uncovering her (*agkalupsai*) and of the god, then, touching her (*hapsasthai*).[33] Although the fragment contains no further information, it recalls a scene in Aristophanes' *Ploutos* in which the characters, seeking a cure for the blind Ploutos, lie down in silence in an Asclepeion and cover themselves. They have brought with them *ta strômata* (624), which the Greeks used for bedclothes as well as for burial shrouds,[34] though the characters in the *Ploutos* may have used theirs only for their beds of straw (*stribada*, 663) in the temple.[35] In any case, the slave narrating the story was certainly covered (*enekalupsamên*, 707; *egkekaluphthai*, 714) during the events he relates, as was an old woman lying near him (*hautên entulixas'*, 692). When Asclepius appears he prepares and applies a *pharmakon* (716) to one of those present, then he sits beside Ploutos, touches (*ephêpsato*, 728) his head, and wipes his eyelids with a pure (*katharon*, 729) cloth. The goddess Panacaea then covers (a different word this time) his head and face with a purple cloth, beneath which two snakes creep to lick his eyes, at which point Ploutos is healed. He has transitioned from blindness to the opposite state of sighted.[36]

The cloth with which Asclepius covers Ploutos's face is *katharon*, or pure, and this recalls the theme of purification so prominent in the *Phaedo*. Purification is associated with covering and uncovering in the *Phaedrus* as well, and in relation to the restoration of a blind man's sight. Having delivered a speech of which he was ashamed and so covered himself (*egkalupsamenos*, 237a4) while speaking,[37] Socrates, in order to forestall the affliction of blindness that befell the poet Stesichorus, purifies himself (*kathêrasthai*, 243a3; *katharmos*, 243a4) by offering[38] a palinode with his head uncovered (*ouk … egkekalummenos*, 243b6–7). The palinode deals specifically with the immortality of the soul and the nature of life after death.[39]

There is evidence of covering (veiling) in Greek purification and initiation rituals, some of them having to do with life after death.[40] In the *Homeric Hymn to Demeter*, for example, the goddess in mourning is depicted as covered (*kekalummenê*, 182) and as holding before herself a veil (*kaluptrên*, 197), holding it presumably in front of her face, before being reunited with her daughter and founding the mystery rites at Eleusis.[41] In Parmenides' poem the daughters of the sun, "having thrust from their heads with their hands their veils (*kaluptras*)," carry the philosopher to the realm of the goddess (DK B1.10).

It has been argued that *kaluptô* is "a religious verb, closely bound to contexts of the gods, death, sleep and sorrow."[42] Homer employed the word as a metaphor for death, and the formulation never fell out of use. To be covered by the earth is to be dead.[43] By extension, then, uncovering may serve as an image of rebirth or of life after death. The metaphor is by no means standard, but it does appear in the Platonic tradition, particularly in connection with purification. The narrator of Plutarch's *Septem sapientium convivium* (a work reminiscent of Plato's *Symposium*, particularly in the prologue) is known for his skill at purification (149d). In the course of a dinner party at which this man was present, Solon remarks in connection with purity (*katharmos*), death, and the discernment of truth that the soul is "covered" by the body (*tôi sômati tên psuchên egkekalummenên*, 159d). And in his *De defectu oraculorum*, Plutarch characterizes the separation of the soul from the body as the purification of the soul from that which covers it (*katharsin tou kaluptontos*, 431f).

So the body covers the soul as a cloak covers a body, and the narrator of *De defectu oraculorum* describes the soul quite explicitly as clothed by the body (*psuchên eneskeuasmenên sôma*, 431c). In the *Phaedo* Cebes employs this image when objecting to Socrates' arguments that the soul exists after death. In one of these arguments Socrates reasons that all things that have opposites come to be from their opposites, and so just as being dead comes from being alive, being alive must come from being dead, and therefore souls exist in a disembodied but living state (which we call "death") prior to entering human bodies at birth (70c–72e). The paired opposites as they appear in this argument are mirrored by the opposition of covering and uncovering at the end of the dialogue. Perhaps we are meant to recall this argument and infer that although Socrates' body is dying, his soul one day will be reborn from out of this temporary condition of "death" or, better, having been purified of that which covers it, will live on "altogether without a body."

This sort of transition from life to death and death to life is a theme in the ancient "Orphic" gold tablets, thin gold plates inscribed with initiatory formulae and instructions regarding the afterlife for those with whom they were buried.[44] On more than one tablet it is stated that to die is simultaneously to be born.[45] Purification and release (*lusis*) are themes on the tablets as well,[46] as they are also in the *Phaedo*,[47] which dialogue seems at least in part to be Plato's attempt to substitute a program of philosophical purification-initiation for the bogus initiatory practices condemned in the *Republic* (364b–365a).[48] In this connection the play of covering and uncovering at the dialogue's end, centered as it is on Socrates' death, gathers together and concentrates the symbolic power of the oppositions of darkness and light, impurity and purity, death and rebirth that were traditionally associated with the mystic rites of purificatory initiation ceremonies.

Scholars have for generations overlooked these unusual details of Socrates' final moments. So preoccupied have they been with the man's last words they have neglected his last act, which may have been the performance of a purificatory ritual intended to secure a good life after death. I say that scholars have overlooked this, but there is one who just might have noticed. When Nietzsche writes of "the *dying*

Socrates" in *The Birth of Tragedy*, he contrasts the theoretical man with the artist by setting the former's pleasure in the act of uncovering (*Enthüllung*) against the latter's admiration of that which covers (*Hülle*). In the course of a single sentence he writes of uncovering, uncovering, the cover, the cover, and uncovering. Socrates is the paradigmatic theoretical man dedicated to the act of uncovering, but since the scientific-logical inquiries initiated by Socratic optimism must inevitably fail, resulting in a renewed need for art as represented by "the *Socrates who practices music*" (an allusion to Socrates' dream as reported at *Phd.* 60e), culture must turn once again toward that which covers (*BT* 15).

Like Plato before him, Nietzsche is playing with these pregnant oppositions. Nor is this the only instance of his doing so. Some ten years after *The Birth of Tragedy*, when writing of Socrates' last words in the antepenultimate section of *The Gay Science*, entitled "*The dying Socrates*," Nietzsche characterizes the philosopher's "letzte Wort" as "veiled," or "covered" (the word is *verhüllten*), and laments that the man did not manage to keep silent (*GS* 340)—this, even though in an earlier section headed "*Letzte Worte*" he contrasts Socrates' power of silence with the deathbed garrulity of two Roman emperors, whom he describes as the opposite of "the dying Socrates" (*GS* 36). Socrates, then, is the silent one who speaks in the end; and even though his meaning is obscure, he reveals too much. What does he reveal? That he regarded life as a disease from which he suffered (*GS* 340). Asclepius is the Greek god of healing, so Nietzsche takes Socrates' last words to imply that death is a cure from the illness that is his life. Since upon his death—and *through* his death—he will at last be healed, Socrates asks his friend to present an offering to the god in gratitude.

In the section immediately preceding "*The dying Socrates*," Nietzsche remarks that "the highest peaks of everything good, whether it be a work, a deed, humanity, or nature, have so far remained concealed and veiled (*Verhülltes*) from the great majority and even from the best human beings. But what does unveil (*enthüllt*) itself for us, *unveils* (*enthüllt*) *itself for us once only*." The world, he continues, is poor when it comes to such unveilings (*Enthüllungen*), but this after all may be its magic. Socrates' last words, like his final act, are one such rare unveiling; and if I am right to associate covering and uncovering with rituals of purification through death, then Plato's presentation of Socrates' final act may lend support to Nietzsche's reading of his last words.[49] It will not, however, either confirm or disconfirm the validity of his inference from this reading to his conclusion that Socrates was decadent.[50]

Decadence

In *Twilight of the Idols* Nietzsche reveals the hidden significance of Socrates' last words in the following paraphrase: "Socrates is no physician … here death alone is the physician. Socrates himself has merely been sick a long time" (*TI* "Socrates" 12). But what, exactly, was Socrates' illness? And why would anyone have mistaken him for a physician? We may approach these questions through an examination of the formula Nietzsche employs to summarize a core component of Socrates' worldview: "reason = virtue = happiness." Nietzsche rates this the "most bizarre of all equations," and he condemns it for having been "opposed to all the instincts of the earlier Greeks" (*TI* "Socrates" 4). He attributes the equation to Socrates rather than to Plato, but it is evident that to his mind it suffices to express Plato's "moralism" as well (*TI* "Socrates" 10). Nietzsche's complaint, broadly expressed, is that the Greek philosophers' lust for knowledge and "esteem of dialectics" (*TI* "Socrates" 10), especially in relation to what we might term existential matters, indicate the declining condition of the Greeks themselves. The decline he has in mind is neither political nor cultural, not primarily; it is, rather, *physiological*. Socrates and Plato were driven to *reason* their way to the best course of life because their instincts failed to generate a natural state of health and power. As men—or more basically as animals, as organisms—they were fundamentally unsound. Nietzsche has a word for their condition: decadence.

Like so much else in the world today, the meaning of this word, "decadence," has been turned on its head since Nietzsche's time. The word traditionally indicates the most pernicious sort of degeneracy, but in contemporary usage it generally applies to something good, or at worst to something tempting with only the slightest intimation of a problem. It recurs quite often in advertisements for dessert foods, in company with, for example, an image of a thick, milky stream of chocolate poured over generous scoops of ice cream and a layer of sugared strawberries. The only vice in the offing here is a minor overindulgence in calories. For Nietzsche, decadence is a much more serious matter; it has to do with nothing less than the root-corruption of an organism. A decadent animal—a human, for example—is one whose physiology tends toward either the death of the organism or its survival at the lowest possible level of functionality. Nietzsche expresses the idea concisely, having identified decadence and corruption, as follows: "I call an animal, a species, or an individual corrupt when it loses its instincts, when it chooses, when it prefers, what is disadvantageous for it" (*A* 6). Although he sometimes calls an animal in this condition *sick*, he has in mind no temporary illness but rather, let's say, a permanent condition of sickliness. A fundamentally healthy animal falls ill from time to time; this is perfectly normal. On these occasions the animal's underlying health eventually fights off the sickness and returns the organism to a balanced state of wellbeing. A decadent animal, however, has no underlying condition of health; it is corrupt at its core. Sickness in such an animal is not a mere temporary abnormality of an otherwise sound organism; it is rather a symptom of the organism's unsoundness. Its decadence manifests as a tendency to self-harm.

I have quoted Nietzsche as referring to an animal losing its instincts; but in fact what has been lost, or rather was missing from the start, is not the instincts themselves but their arrangement according to a hierarchy of value that could, were it in place, raise the overall system (the animal itself) to a state of peak fitness. Socrates' decadence, for example, involved the "anarchy of his instincts" (*TI* "Socrates" 4), and his contemporaries were decadents inasmuch as their "instincts turned *against* each other" (*TI* "Socrates" 9). Decadence, then, is not so much an absence of instincts as a condition in which an animal's instincts are at odds with each other and therefore work against the interests of the animal itself. "To *have* to fight the instincts," Nietzsche writes, "that is the formula of decadence" (*TI* "Socrates" 11).

Socrates and Plato, then, were at war with themselves, or rather they were at war *within* themselves. Their philosophical innovations consisted in part in recognizing their anarchic internal condition and attempting to devise a solution. Their emphasis on self-control—*enkrateia*: literally, "internal mastery"—was a reaction to the chaos within. Like desperate animals struggling to escape an imminent doom, they were reduced to having to pause, concentrate, and formulate a plan on the model of which they might organize their impulses and desires, which left to themselves only raged, pushing and pulling in a confusion of contrary directions. The animal whose instincts are properly ordered knows no such desperation; beneath the level of consciousness the organism flawlessly functions, moving by natural predisposition ever toward the highest goal by way of the straightest path. Like a dancer whose muscles are so thoroughly conditioned they act without intentional direction, sweeping the dancer along in the flow of their beauty and grace—so moves every animal in the fullness of its natural strength. But the human animal of Classical Athens was in decline. Nearly a century of ever-expanding democracy and the long and unusually nasty struggle of the Peloponnesian War were no help; but the problem was not caused by cultural or political events. The condition at bottom was physiological, organic, and most every Greek was ill. According to Nietzsche's diagnosis, Socrates' decadence was "merely the extreme case, only the most striking instance of what was then beginning to be a universal distress" (*TI* "Socrates" 9). This is how Socrates came to fascinate his fellow citizens, and ultimately how Plato attained such extraordinary influence: their rational inquiries into virtue, from which they derived their suggestions for the ordering and discipline of desire, seemed a method for mastering the unruly instincts, seemed a cure. But to Nietzsche's mind the apparent cure was just one more symptom of the disease.

There are those who take Callicles in the *Gorgias* for an ancient proto-Nietzschean, and their idea is by no means outlandish;[51] but if decadence is anarchy of the instincts, then by insisting that wellbeing requires that one's desires and drives be properly ordered, Plato rather than Callicles is the authentic opponent of decadence and thereby at bottom in harmony with Nietzsche. Consider the method Plato's Socrates employs to lead his interlocutors into self-contradictions: he plays on their conflicting drives, exposing the anarchy of their instincts. Recall that Gorgias's drive for power, which depends in part on his reputation as a teacher, is in tension with his drive to be honored by prospective students, which tension provides Socrates the opportunity to make Gorgias contradict his earlier reference to unjust students by denying that he would share his potent skills with unjust men.[52] Similarly, Callicles' drive for power is in tension with his lust for pleasure, for bad and harmful pleasures are debilitating, and Socrates exploits this tension to make Callicles contradict his assertion that all pleasures are good, which sets up Socrates' victory in the debate. And consider the image of the tripartite soul in the *Republic*: preservation of the soul's proper order is crucial to an individual's wellbeing, for any disruption of the hierarchy is as damaging to the soul as civil unrest is to a city.

Plato's consistent message seems to be that any attempt to substitute power or pleasure for justice as one's regulative drive must result in an "anarchy of instincts," and by resisting this substitution he works against the spread of decadence. Nietzsche would likely dispute this suggestion, and the tack he would probably take would be to argue that at best Socrates and Plato were decadents themselves who just happened to have a knack for exposing the decadence of others. This is consistent with his analysis in *Twilight of the Idols* that Socrates' "own case, his idiosyncrasy, was no longer exceptional," that the "same kind of degeneration was quietly developing everywhere" (*TI* "Socrates" 9). Decadence in fifth-century Athens was a spreading menace much worse, if less evident, than the plague that overwhelmed the city's population early in the Peloponnesian War. The problem, speaking broadly and somewhat loosely, was evolutionary: the species was simply declining. The root cause was deeply physiological, so no modification of beliefs or of lifestyle could have reversed it. Yet Socrates appeared to many to have a cure (*TI* "Socrates" 9), or at least to be one of the few men with insight into the danger who might serve as a physician. The problem is that as a decadent himself Socrates was doomed to misdiagnose the malady and to prescribe a treatment that only exacerbated the disorder. His diagnosis, as we have seen, was that his fellow Athenians were suffering from a lack of virtue, for which he prescribed the application of reason. His idea was that reason properly employed would provide insight into the good, which men could then embody in the form of virtue, and the result would be health and *eudaimonia*. But with this we have come back to the Socratic equation "reason = virtue = happiness," to which Nietzsche objects on the grounds that it ignores the most essential of the facts at issue, namely, that a healthy organism functions best when it acts unconsciously, as in the case of the dancer I mentioned above. When an animal must think about its actions, it is too late; the rot has set in. If one finds that "concession to the instincts, to the unconscious, leads *downward*" (*TI* "Socrates" 10), then there is no way up; one's organism is corrupt at its base, is decadent, and any move one makes to relieve or to heal oneself will be infected by the decadence and so, inevitably, must fail. This is what Nietzsche has in mind when he declares that

> Socrates was a misunderstanding; *the whole improvement-morality ... was a misunderstanding*. The most blinding daylight; rationality at any price; life, bright, cold, cautious, conscious, without instincts, in opposition to the instincts—all this too was a mere disease, another disease, and by no means a return to "virtue," to "health," to happiness ... [A]s long as life is *ascending*, happiness equals instinct (*TI* "Socrates" 11).

These lines conclude the penultimate section of Nietzsche's analysis of "The Problem of Socrates." In the brief final section Nietzsche paraphrases Plato's report of Socrates' last words, and, as we have seen, the sentiment he puts into the philosopher's mouth is a resigned acknowledgment of his own decadence. By exalting reason over instinct Socrates had denied himself, his only self; he had mistaken his "soul" for his true self and consequently disdained his body as a temporary impediment to all that is true and good. But this is folly, for there is no reality other than the body, and no other way to happiness than the free exercise of healthy instincts. Socrates had lived in flight from the body, in retreat from reality, and his greatest disciple followed him into the metaphysical mists, echoing the old man's call of withdrawal, separation, renunciation. But this call is the siren song of asceticism, a melody appealing only to decadents.

Masters and slaves

Nietzsche is often represented as an ethical or moral relativist, and it is no mystery why in the popular mind he might be regarded this way. He identifies himself as having been the first to attain to the insight that *"there are altogether no moral facts"* (*TI* "Improvers" 1). On the other hand, he regularly issues declarations to the effect that some particular action or mode of life is superior to some other, and he seems both to take himself to be correct and to intend that his readers so take him as well. Is he, then, inconsistent? Is he confused? When he is not represented as a relativist, he is often characterized as having adopted at best an ambiguous position on ethical or moral matters. But to speak for a moment in Nietzsche's defense, the ambiguity of his position may be only apparent, and the appearance may have less to do with Nietzsche's ideas than with our own vague conceptions of the terms "ethics" and "morality."[53] It is true that Nietzsche on occasion refers to himself as an "immoralist," and that with this label he intends to announce his opposition to morality. But there are various senses of the word morality—anyway Nietzsche himself uses the word in at least two different senses. In the narrow sense, which Nietzsche rejects, "morality" refers to a code of conduct characterized by two particularly objectionable features: its prescriptions and proscriptions are meant to apply to everyone equally, despite significant differences between and among human beings; and it is thought to be grounded in the metaphysical, for example in the intellect or will of a deity. Christian morality is the obvious example, and it is to Christian morality that Nietzsche intends to oppose his own position when he labels himself an "immoralist" (*EH* "Destiny" 4, 6). Different people will define morality differently; but this account is relatively unexceptional. In any case, this is what Nietzsche often has in mind when he condemns or rejects morality, and this is our only present concern. But this is not *all* Nietzsche has in mind, and his addition illuminates other aspects of his opposition to morality narrowly conceived. In *Ecce Homo* he defines morality as "the idiosyncrasy of decadents, with the ulterior motive of revenging oneself against life" (*EH* "Destiny" 7). In the previous section I explicated Nietzsche's notion of decadence in the context of the exaggerated value that Socrates and Plato ascribe to reason as opposed to instinct; but when Nietzsche conceptualizes *morality* as a weapon wielded by decadents to revenge themselves against their betters, he usually has Christians in mind.

We may think of morality more broadly defined by taking the word to indicate merely a code of conduct, any code of conduct, whether or not it implies universality of application or a metaphysical foundation. Taking morality in this broad sense, then, one might morally approve of all acts performed by adults over six feet tall while condemning those performed by shorter adults, or by children of any height. Or one might act kindly to every second person one encounters but rudely or cruelly to everyone else, taking this numerical arrangement for one's moral ground. These are preposterous examples, no doubt; but they are codes of conduct that have nothing to do with morality narrowly defined; they are certainly contrary to Christian morality. Now consider a more plausible code: *help friends and harm enemies*. However brutish this may sound to our ears, it was a popular code of conduct among the Greeks.[54] Polemarchus in the *Republic* proposes and defends the maxim as a definition of justice (331d–335e). Socrates rejects it, but he is well acquainted with the principle, as all Greeks would have been.[55] This code, as the Greeks themselves understood it, violates the principles of the narrow conception of morality; yet for all that, it is a code of conduct that not only might, but in many cases once actually did, regulate men's behavior and determine their judgments of the behavior of others. This one example, then, suffices to demonstrate the viability of codes of conduct that we ourselves might classify as "immoral."

One such code of conduct—which would never count as morality according to the narrow sense of the word, but which is nonetheless a code of conduct and so may be regarded as an immoralist morality—is that to which, according to Nietzsche, "the nobility of ancient Greece" adhered (*BGE* 260). The nobility Nietzsche has in mind is roughly coextensive with the class of men I introduced in the first section of this chapter as aspirants to *kalokagathia* (to whom we may refer collectively as the *kaloi kagathoi*), and these are the very men among whom the principle "help friends and harm enemies" was common. These were the warriors, men of influence and power, active members of clubs or associations of like-minded men, known as *hetaireiai*, who worked together to control the social, political, and legal affairs of their city—they were, in short, members of the higher orders (by birth or by marriage, sometimes by military or commercial success) who in many instances behaved as you might imagine followers of Gorgias and Callicles would behave. But we need not dwell on the minutiae of ancient Greek life, for although Nietzsche intends to ground in historical reality those of his moral speculations that presently concern us, he often goes beyond the facts, or anyway beyond the available facts. This is not to say that his analysis is mistaken, but only to recognize it for what it is, an extrapolation from the evidential record. Having been trained as a philologist, his knowledge of the record was broad and deep, and his philosophical-artistic brilliance enabled him to transform his knowledge into a sort of legislative creativity, which is precisely what he did to generate the provocative idea of a "master morality."

We may explain Nietzsche's notion of master morality by concentrating first on two terms, good and bad. Good, the more central of the two, has less a specific content or meaning than a twofold function: self-identification and self-affirmation. Rather than pick out and esteem or recommend any particular quality, habit, or trait, "good" simply indicates "I" or "we" while simultaneously expressing admiration and respect for the subject or subjects who think, speak, or write it. In short, the word is something like a term of endearment or praise that noble men apply to themselves. These nobles may well ground their self-regard in their possession of this or that property or set of properties, yet it is not the properties that give value to the men but rather the other way round. "Courage is good because we good men are courageous." Or consider the designations "powerful," "wealthy," or "honest": these are the features that stand out to the nobles when they observe themselves. Some of these terms may with time come to designate qualities of soul, as has honesty among ourselves, for example; but even in such cases the original designation centers on social-political superiority.

As for the word "bad," among the nobles this is an afterthought. If "good" means *us and all who resemble us*, then bad means simply *everyone else*. Whoever they are and however they are—the specifics are irrelevant; so long as they are not like us, they are bad. I write that the word is an afterthought because the people to whom it applies occupy only the periphery of the nobles' consciousness. Of course they know that other men dwell among them, men who draw the water and hew the wood, the poor, the debased, the slaves; yet these men are too insignificant to attract the nobles' concentrated attention. They are the common men, impoverished, uncultured, and weak. When it occurs to the nobles to contrast their own "goodness" with an opposite, these are the men to whom they refer; but it is worth stressing that there is no urgency to this contrast: the nobles do not derive their value from their superiority to lesser men; they are simply good, period. The fact that there are others whom they may designate "bad" is to them a matter of indifference.

That master morality originates in an act of self-affirmation may be taken to represent its active and affirmative qualities in general. The master type acts sponta- neously, which is to say on his own initiative; he is an originator, a creator of deeds, which flow from him and him alone—he acts rather than *re*acts. If he seeks an other, an opposite, an *enemy*, then he does so the more triumphantly to affirm himself. Thus he desires great and noble opponents, in true Homeric fashion: to defeat in compe- tition or combat a base or a vile man is no mark of distinction—to the contrary, it is degrading even to engage with inferior types. The *kaloi kagathoi* are eminently healthy, vigorous, and robust, and they recognize the fact, even celebrate themselves for it; thus they avoid, and in some cases even *ritually* avoid, situations in which, and contact with people by whom, their wellbeing might be undermined and they themselves corrupted. Overflowing with vitality as they are, these master types thrive on adventure, war, athletic competition, and the hunt—any activity in which they might give vent to their power and their delight in power. Among themselves—among *equals*—these men may display "consideration, self-control, delicacy, loyalty, pride, and friendship," but among others, among strangers, "they go *back* to the innocent conscience of the beast of prey" and are terrible, "monsters" even (*GM* 1.11). It is not that they hate the stranger; they are indifferent to him, simply fail to take stock of him in their accounting of those features of the world that matter. They act as they do also because they are naturally powerful and strong, and power and strength exist in and through their expression and discharge. In other words, these men are not "free" to restrain or check their outflow of force, for they themselves just *are* an outflowing of force.

I stress that these conceptions of "good" and "bad" are, according to the narrow sense of the word "morality," thoroughly immoral. Nietzsche intends to load them with the exclusively social-political significance of their ancient Greek counterparts, *kalos* and *agathos* being the originals of "good," *kakos* the original of "bad." I have used these Greek words throughout this chapter, and I expect that by now it has become clear that *kalos* and *agathos* (Nietzsche's "good") indicate the noble warrior elite, and *kakos* (Nietzsche's "bad") indicates the base lower orders. With this in mind, I suggest that readers make every effort to drain the words "good" and "bad" in this context of whatever moral content they generally read into them and to take them instead to mean nothing other than "noble" and "base" as social-political designations (in the context of ancient Greek social and political life).

It is Nietzsche's contention that master morality was the dominant morality of the ancient world, with particular emphasis on the Greeks and Romans. Ancient society was radically hierarchical, and the men on top were "masters," all of them metaphorically speaking and many of them quite literally. But whether or not these men were slaveholders is peripheral to Nietzsche's point. He certainly writes of a "slave" class among the ancients, but here, too, the stress is on the metaphor, the term "slave" serving as a shorthand designation for the lower orders, whether free or enslaved. This is the sense of the word that Nietzsche has in mind when he labels the morality adhered to by the lower orders of men among the ancients a "slave morality."

As I introduced master morality by way of an analysis of the terms "good" and "bad," so I shall explicate slave morality beginning with its central evaluative terms, "good" and "evil." The first point to make here is that in slave morality the term "good" applies to everyone and everything that in master morality is designated "bad," and the term "evil" applies to all that is "good" according to master morality. So the two systems' central evaluative pairs have precisely and thoroughly opposed denotations. Their connotations are opposed as well, and this is particularly and significantly so with respect to the terms "bad" and "evil." We may begin by exploring this difference, for according to Nietzsche the notion of "evil" is at the center of slave morality. It is in fact the originary principle of slave morality, precisely as "good" is the core around which the whole of master morality is constructed. But whereas "good" with the masters functions as a term of self-affirmation, "evil" with the slaves is a radical denial of the other; and whereas the other is a second thought and a matter of indifference among the masters, among the slaves the other is an obsession.

I have noted that Nietzsche's use of the word "slave" in this context is primarily a metaphor for the lower orders, as inclusive of freemen as of the enslaved—*more* inclusive of freemen than of slaves, with whom as a group as such Nietzsche was not especially concerned. In any case, the lower orders, as the expression suggests, occupied the bottom rungs of the ancient social-political hierarchy. These men were neither beautiful nor noble, neither influential nor strong. In Greece they were the cobblers, blacksmiths, stonemasons, farmhands, and the oarsmen of the fleet. They were the men to whom jury duty appealed as a real source of income. In a later day, in the Roman world, they were the petty vendors, fishermen, vagabonds, women, and slaves. They were, in short, the poor and powerless of the ancient world, the oppressed.

It takes no great leap of imagination to picture these men as having been discontented with their status and the social, political, existential, and even the psychological consequences of that status. Discontented, but with no means to improve their lot. Having no productive outlet for their dissatisfaction, they internalized it, and the roiling blend of their unhappiness and impotence emitted fumes of rage, which in some men were so potent, so heady, so intoxicating that the men in their frenzy became for one horrible moment creative. Their issue was the notion of Evil. "I am unhappy. I am pained. I suffer. Why? Something must be to blame—*someone* must be to blame! But look: *that* man is better off than I; he seems almost to shine, smiling in his beauty and might. Oh, this is all too unfair, and here am I on the wrong side of the imbalance, on the other side from *him*. From *him*—oh, yes, that's it now: *he* is to blame for my condition. *He* has done this to me; *he* has thwarted me and injured me. And *he*, therefore, is cold, cruel, pitiless, and vile—he is, in a word, *evil*." This sort of thinking was the labor that gave birth to slave morality.

So the slave type looks to the "good" man of master morality and sees in him all that he himself is not, and compelled as he is to *blame* someone for his condition, but being unable or unwilling to hold himself responsible, he charges and condemns other men. He packs all of his bitterness, helplessness, frustration, and fury into the concept "evil" and spits it at them. Then, and only then, he formulates the concept of the good man as one like himself, the opposite of this other, one who is weak, timid, harmless, cringing, anxious, and submissive. He does not use *these* words, of course, for they would expose the ugly truth of his condition. Rather, he outfits his vices in the finery of virtue: he labels himself and his type gentle, humble, patient, forgiving, and mild.[56] Moreover, he reckons himself meritorious for possessing these qualities, for, he insists, he *could* be otherwise if he chose, but he *elects* to be as he is. Similarly, the evil ones *could* be caring and supportive if they wanted, but since they *choose* to be cruel they are culpable not only for their actions but for the malice in their hearts as well. Thus does the idea of freedom enter into moral schemes. The invention of free will undergirds the slaves' system of praise and blame: it enables them to deny the truth about themselves (that they are too weak to behave otherwise than they do) and to adopt an attitude of self-respect; and it justifies their condemnation of the masters.[57]

Slave morality is essentially passive and reactive, for the slave type lacks spontaneous assertive force. And his reactions are inextricably entwined with the actions that evoke them: the slave, in short, can only mimic or contradict. He knows himself and defines himself only in relation to an other, and more often than not this other is an enemy whom he regards as wicked. He has no conception of the noble enemy, the beautiful combat, of honor in opposition. He must hate when he fights; he must despise the enemy; he must lay waste to evil. This sort of man makes everything ugly, soils every field of battle. He degrades his environment. Here we have the origin of every Armageddon, of every great conflict that must at all costs result in the elimination of Evil—yea, even if the universe itself be destroyed in the process.

Here also is the origin of morality in the narrow sense. Slave morality teaches that all men are alike as men, and that as a consequence we must all of us treat one another as peers and equals. In practice this means that no man should have more of the good things in life than his fellows; that no man should be markedly superior; that prosperity and happiness ought by right to be distributed "fairly." Let no difference make a difference—this is the cry of the men among whom slave morality flourishes. These men know all too well that in this world as it is the differences often make all the difference. How could they not understand this? They suffer from the phenomenon daily. Nevertheless, they are committed to the idea (which is not to say that all of them sincerely *believe* it) that this is not as it should be, that in this world something has gone awry; and to maintain this position they gesture vaguely toward another realm, a superior realm in which equality and fairness enjoy the status of eternal demands. In the precincts of the divine each soul is as valuable as each, and on earth it should be as it is in heaven.

Earlier I identified universality of application and metaphysical grounding as the two principal features of morality narrowly defined, in particular of Christian morality as Nietzsche understood and opposed it. I then quoted from *Ecce Homo* a definition according to which morality is a means whereby decadent men revenge themselves against life. These decadent men are the "slaves" we have just now inspected, and the life against which they would exact revenge is life as embodied in the "proud and well-turned-out human being who says Yes, who is sure of the future, who guarantees the future" (*EH* "Destiny" 8)—as embodied, in short, in the "masters" of the earth. This great act of vengeance, a turning point in western history, Nietzsche refers to as "the slave revolt in morality."

Revaluation of values

The slave revolt in morality was not waged by force of arms. It was no skirmish between two factions within an ancient culture, nor even a large-scale war between entire antagonistic cultures. The slave revolt Nietzsche has in mind was an event much greater than any military conflict, ancient or modern. It was a seismic upheaval that wrecked the ancient world itself. Civilizational epochs do not collapse and expire from physical wounds alone; far more devastating are corruptions of their intellectual and spiritual systems of belief, radical alterations of, for example, their shared ideas concerning the nature and goal of individual and collective life, and the various presuppositions and implications of these ideas. So the slave revolt had nothing to do with tactics premised on armor, weapons, or man-power. Rather, it proceeded by way of a phenomenon Nietzsche calls the "revaluation of values." The revaluation is primarily a *moral* event, or rather a *meta*-moral event, for it was not an adjustment within a moral system but, what is much more portentous, the substitution of one morality (and the various ideas associated with it) by another.[58]

We can grasp the phenomenon Nietzsche means to indicate by analyzing his expression for it, "revaluation of values." Take each of the two terms, "good" and "bad," as a distinct moral value or set of values, and take "valuation" as you would if we were considering the monetary worth of coins. A quarter has the valuation of twenty five cents; one dollar has the valuation of one hundred cents. Similarly, the value-term "good" in master morality has the valuation of "noble, beautiful, powerful, etc.," and the value-term "bad" has the valuation of "base, ugly, weak, etc." To revalue financial values is to change the worth of a quarter to, say, fifty cents, or of a dollar to twenty five cents. The process is parallel with moral values: if a value-term changes meaning by coming to be used to designate different properties, actions, or types of people than it had previously designated, it has been revalued. If, for example, the value-term "good" transitions from connoting "noble, beautiful, and powerful" to connoting "base, ugly, and weak," it has been revalued. It is no longer "worth" what it once was—it no longer means, no longer indicates the same set of properties.

According to Nietzsche, the shift in meaning of value-terms was a central feature of the movement from the ancient (pagan) to the medieval (Christian) world. The ancient slave class managed somehow to revalue the values of the master class, which is to say that the oppressed lower orders of society gradually altered the way the higher orders thought about good and bad, right and wrong, just and unjust, etc. The alteration was no random variation, but a very specific change: slave morality was everywhere substituted for master morality. The masters abandoned their traditional understanding of good and bad—abandoned their traditional *valuations* of these terms—and adopted the slaves' moral perspective, which included the terminological transformation of "bad" into "evil." Now the masters thought, precisely as the slaves had thought all along, that it is good to be humble and meek, whereas it is evil to be proud and aggressive. But this is the opposite of the masters' traditional way of thinking, and by definition anyone who lives according to these values is not a "master." So master morality itself came to be regarded as evil, and slave morality—which was, in contrast, "good," and which in time came to be identified with morality *as such*—was adopted by everyone nearly without exception. The result, predictably, was that the masters died out as a distinct class—which is not to say that the individuals themselves perished (though eventually they did, of course), but rather that by abandoning the moral beliefs that had made them masters they abrogated their rank and degenerated to the level of slaves; there were then all around only slaves, known thereafter as the "good" common men in contrast with a minority of criminal outcasts and villains.

Spiritual-psychological warfare can be, in the appropriate circumstances, far more effective than any traditional military campaign, for with little expenditure of energy one causes one's enemy to turn against himself, to defeat himself by abandoning those qualities that would otherwise contribute to his victory. Consider, for example, the revaluation on a smaller, and therefore perhaps a more readily comprehensible, scale. Imagine a schoolboy mercilessly bullied. He is weak, unable to defend himself. He is scared and suffering. The older, stronger bully evidently thinks it good that he should harass those weaker than himself, torment them, and take their lunch money. What can the weak child do? I am not writing a screenplay for an after-school special, so the boy's father will not teach him to fight; the boy will not one day punch out the bully before a lunchroom of cheering students. But if he cannot conquer through physical strength, perhaps he can attack the bully psychologically. Let's imagine that over time the child somehow affects the bully's thinking about good and bad, changes the bully's mind about the value of his thuggish ways. How he does this is not our concern; the point is to stress the effectiveness of the strategy.[59] To fight the bully, to fight him and even to defeat him, would be only a temporary solution, for the bully might dismiss his defeat as a fluke and continue his assaults without respite; he might exercise, train, and return to fight another day; he might recruit a gang of hoodlums to fight by his side. But if the bully should no longer *want* to be a bully, if he should come to believe that it is evil to bully others—not just believe that *others* consider it evil, but actually believe this for himself—well, then, he would cease his bullying for good. And what if the child could convince the bully not only that tormenting the weak is evil, but that it is good to befriend the weak, to succor them and relieve them of their burdens? More, imagine the child's convincing the bully that to live a good life the powerful must exalt the weak, kneel down before them, and even, perhaps, turn over to them their own lunch money. If our schoolboy could manage to inspire some such conversion in the mind of his brutish bully, he would no longer suffer. He would, in fact, have conquered his former oppressor—and he, then, would have the power.[60]

Recall Nietzsche's idea that morality is a weapon wielded by decadents to revenge themselves against their superiors. His meaning should now be clear. The lower orders among the ancients were unhappy with their situation in society, but they were unable either to improve their lot or to displace by force those whom they regarded as their oppressors. Impotent to affect any substantive change, they longed at least to inflict retributory pain on those who made them suffer. They sought their revenge by undermining the nobles' self-confidence, their delight in their power, health, and overabundant lives. They taught the masters to regard as evil all those qualities for which hitherto they had celebrated themselves. But these were the very qualities that had made them *masters*. So the masters began to doubt themselves, to regard themselves with a bad conscience. They became sick—psychologically compromised—and consequently they became weak, and so they ceased to be masters. Now the slaves not only had their revenge, they even acquired a sort of power over those who had formerly dominated them.

Does this strike you as fanciful, just a little too improbable? But something like this *must* have happened in the course of those long centuries during which European man gradually adopted the principles of Christian morality. No self-respecting Greek or Roman would have admired the moral assumptions upon which the Sermon on the Mount is grounded. Peleus enjoined his son Achilles always to be the best and preeminent among other men (*Iliad* 11.783–4), and the ancients took this command to heart. Theirs was an agonistic society, thriving on conflict, competition, and war. Christian morality was altogether different. It descended from the teachings of the ancient Israelites who, according to Nietzsche, formulated their distinctive morality in opposition to their oppressors, the Romans in particular. Developed and refined as it was in this context, and later adapted to the existential and social conditions of the poor and the suffering of the Empire, Jewish morality was tailor-made for the lower orders: it commended cooperation, charity, and pity for the downtrodden and weak; not Achilles, but the Good Samaritan was its ideal representative. It was, in short, a slave morality.

Judea against Rome: with this expression Nietzsche sums up the struggle at issue in the slave revolt and its revaluation of values (*GM* 1.16). He might just have well have written *St. Peter's against Athens* or *Christ against Achilles*. The substance of his phrase, in familiar terms, is *Slaves against Masters*. For Nietzsche this conflict is at the heart of "all human history" so far (*GM* 1.16), of western history in particular. Does he exaggerate? Perhaps he does, but consider: if he were not at least partially correct, if the ancient pagans in their prime would all have nodded in ready assent to Jewish and Christian morality, then Jesus and the religion he (or his followers) founded would hardly have been revolutionary; he would have been just one more moralist in the Hellenistic philosophical tradition. But be all this as it may, we need not explore every branch of Nietzsche's cavernous disdain for Christianity, for Plato was no Christian. He certainly did not advocate the sort of pity that Nietzsche locates at the core of Christian morality, the pity that "makes suffering contagious," pity as "the *practice* of nihilism" (*A* 7).[61] Suffice it to say with respect to Christianity that Nietzsche hoped for—and perhaps even intended to *provoke*—a new revaluation of values, which is to say a root rejection of slave morality, of *Christian* morality.[62] He makes it clear that this is "the aim of [his] dangerous slogan … *Beyond Good and Evil*," which slogan serves as the title of the book in which he first identifies and distinguishes the master and slave moralities (*GM* 1.17).

To transcend good and evil is to reject in general the moral interpretation of the world, according to which evaluative judgments are metaphysically grounded (and therefore somehow woven into the fabric of reality) and universally applicable, but it is also to reject, more specifically, the decadence and nihilism of *slave* morality, according to which the peaceful, harmless, and benevolent man is "good" whereas the warlike, daring, and dangerous man is "evil." This is the position Nietzsche has in mind when he labels himself an "immoralist." But as he indicates, his slogan "does *not* mean 'Beyond Good and Bad'" (*GM* 1.17). In other words, he does not reject all codes of conduct or modes of evaluation; he does not reject morality in the broad sense of the term. To the contrary, he means to *affirm* one brand of morality, *master* morality, according to which "good" and "bad" are synonyms for "noble" and "base" as these words would have been understood among the higher orders of ancient Greeks and Romans.

I do not mean to suggest that Nietzsche imagined it possible to resurrect the ancient world on modern European soil. He was sufficiently historicist to regard any such notion as romantically naive. Yet he did foresee a day when a modern variation on the theme of master morality might flourish in the west. To this extent an ancient mentality might live again at least in spirit. What is needed is the rejection of Christianity—not merely the superficial rejection of theological dogma common among those contemporary atheists who remain attached to a morality of harmony, peace, and equality, but the rejection of this morality itself, which is unsustainable without the grounding assumptions of Christian theology, or so Nietzsche believed. Not that religions at the heart of civilizations die quickly or quietly—the phenomenon of our moralistic atheists thoroughly demonstrates that they do not. But they do die, and civilizations end. And if to go down Christianity must drag the modern west with it, then Nietzsche would watch them both go under with great satisfaction. As much as he liked to refer to himself as a "good European," for modern, democratic Europe he had nothing but contempt.

Order and necessity

Despite Nietzsche's assertion that Plato is "pre-existently Christian" because he is "so moralistic," and this because he "takes the concept 'good' for the highest concept" (*TI* "Ancients" 2), Plato would have had as little taste for Christian morality as Nietzsche would have for the many philosophical movements that claim him as their ancestor. As true as it undoubtedly is that Plato's understanding of the soul and the Good contributed to the development of Christian theology and morality, it is equally true that Nietzsche's criticisms of the will to truth and knowledge contributed to the rise of twentieth-century Postmodernism, for example, which movement (or loosely associated collection of movements) Nietzsche would disown for many reasons, not least for the nihilist, anarchist, or generally leftist social and political tendencies of those who fancy themselves "post"-modern. Every argument one might make to relieve Nietzsche of responsibility for the ideas of those who have thought in his wake and with his concepts can be used just as well to dissociate Plato from Christianity.

Therefore, I say, either Nietzsche is guilty for his intellectual pseudo-progeny or Plato is innocent of his.[63]

In 1887, a European academic, Georg Brandes, wrote to Nietzsche in praise of what he referred to as the philosopher's "aristocratic radicalism." Nietzsche was well pleased with the expression, and he hastened to say so in reply.[64] Brandes' formulation brilliantly encapsulates all that separates Nietzsche from the majority of those who like to invoke the authority, or the aura, of his name. The well-known, but regularly ignored, truth is that Nietzsche despised the sort of cultural and political egalitarianism that is popular today with those intellectuals for whom cosmopolitan tolerance and global democracy are sacrosanct orthodoxies. When he writes that "[o]ne has no right to existence or to work, to say nothing of a right to 'happiness'" (*WP* 759); when he dismisses the proponents of modern morality as "the descendants of every kind of European and non-European slavery" who "represent the *regression* of mankind" (*GM* 1.11); when he condemns the "tolerance ... which 'forgives' all because it 'understands' all" (*A* 1)—when he expresses these sentiments, as so often he does, he is merely articulating the spirit of "every aristocratic morality," which is "intolerant," which, moreover, considers "intolerance itself a virtue, calling it 'justice'" (*BGE* 262). So as popular as Nietzsche has become with some thinkers on the left, there just is no escaping the fact that he cared little for humanity *en masse*. He consistently adopted the very perspective that he attributed to "a good and healthy aristocracy," namely, that the proper function of the masses is to serve "as the foundation and scaffolding on which a choice type of being is able to raise itself to its higher task and to a higher state of *being*" (*BGE* 258).

To Nietzsche's mind a great culture is like a pyramid, with a massive base of "slaves" laboring in support of a minority of gifted thinkers and artists who occupy the pinnacle of the structure (*A* 57; *BGE* 257, 258). The democratic urge for equality necessarily undermines this pyramid, unsettles and dislodges its upper courses until there remains only a level base surrounded by a chaos of scattered and broken stones. But this is slave morality at work, a morality that stands with every base against every summit, even at the expense of the nobility and beauty whose existence depends on the rarified air of the heights. What could motivate so pernicious an attitude? First and foremost, as I mentioned above, a specific set of theological beliefs—in particular belief in the equality of souls before God, which Nietzsche condemns as "this falsehood ... this explosive of a concept which eventually became revolution, modern idea, and the principle of decline of the whole order of society" (*A* 62). When Nietzsche writes that "[t]he *democratic* movement is the heir of the Christian movement" (*BGE* 202), he has in mind the "poison of the doctrine of 'equal rights for all,'" which, he says, "Christianity ... spread ... most fundamentally" (*A* 43). But the Christian belief in equality is no mere arbitrary preference, for the Christians ground their notion of equal rights on specific beliefs about the nature of souls and their relation to the deity.

At this point Nietzsche brings Plato into his story. You will recall that he characterizes Christianity as "Platonism for 'the people'" (*BGE* "Preface"). He does so in part because he believes that Plato's "invention" of "the pure spirit" contributed to the Christian conception of soul, and thereby to the doctrine of equality of souls before God, which ultimately led to the false, ignoble, and toxic notions of equal rights and democracy. There is something to Nietzsche's idea, but only a little something. Although Plato in fact inherited his concept of spirit (soul) from earlier thinkers, and from the Pythagorean tradition in particular, it would nevertheless be foolish to deny his role in elaborating and popularizing the notion of an immaterial soul. It is also true that he everywhere stresses a connection between the soul's virtue (or vice) and divine judgment. So we can at least make sense of Nietzsche's reasoning when he concludes that Plato bears some responsibility for Christian theology and, thereby, for Christian morality as well. Yet, as he sometimes does when grappling with Plato, Nietzsche pushes his evidence (or his rhetoric) too far, for Plato himself was no egalitarian democrat. He was every bit as aristocratically inclined as Nietzsche, if not always for the same reasons or in precisely the same sense. Nor is there anything in the relevant Platonic ideas that necessitates their being employed in the service of a doctrine of the natural equality of souls.

Far from being an advocate of anything like a slave morality, Plato recognizes the authority of the noble to rule over the ignoble.[65] It is true that even in this context he ranks those who know and are virtuous above those who are ignorant and vicious, yet he never displays any special favor in the name of equality to the social or political aspirations of citizens of low birth as against members of his own class. And although he believes it is difficult for the powerful (*hoi dunamenoi*) to resist the temptations of easy injustice, to which many master types (*hoi dunastai*) succumb, he readily acknowledges that from among this elite group may come those who are *kaloi kagathoi* (*Grg.* 525e–526b). These men will be "noble and good" with respect to conducting themselves justly, which qualification Nietzsche himself would not have introduced; but since for Plato the virtue of justice preserves a structural hierarchy of rulers and warriors atop a large laboring class, there is no need to read slavish, anti-aristocratic, or "pre-existently Christian" implications into this qualification.

All this is evident in the *Republic*, and though in other dialogues Plato amends this or that point, the anti-democratic inegalitarianism is always present. Nietzsche could not have been unaware of this, so one wonders what motivated him constantly to ignore the manifest dissimilarities between Plato's aristocratic social-political philosophy and Christian slave morality, and at times even to assimilate the two. It is downright baffling, for example, that in *The Antichrist* he should contrast the "law of Manu" and its "*order of castes*" to the Christian, socialist, and anarchist "claim of 'equal rights'" with no hint of an acknowledgment that his description of the society founded on these laws reads like a précis of the ideal city of Plato's *Republic*. Governed as it is by "the most spiritual human beings," to whom asceticism (including knowledge as "a form of asceticism") belongs by "nature, need, and instinct"; protected by warriors as "guardians of the law"; supported by a base of laborers and farmers; and, finally, justified by a "holy lie" that claims for the laws the authority of revelation and tradition, Nietzsche's version of Manu's "high culture" might as well be called *Kallipolis*, which name Plato gives to the three-tiered city he secures in the *Republic* by means of the "noble lie."[66]

It is worth noting that Plato is not responsible for the title "Republic." The word derives from the Latin translation of the Greek noun at the head of the ancient manuscripts, *Politeia*, which in this context means the organization or constitution of a city-state. Although we cannot be sure that Plato gave the work this name himself, we *can* be sure that he did *not* name it after a system of government that recognizes *the people* as the ultimate political authority (as does a republic). In this great work Plato argues that democracy—rule by the *dêmos*, the people—is worse than every other form of government but tyranny (576c–580c). Democracy makes a better showing in the *Statesman* and the *Laws*, but still it is inferior to rule by a single wise and good man, or by a few such men.[67] Plato's extensive critique of democracy in Book 8 of the *Republic* is stunningly prescient, for he exposes in detail the disintegrative consequences of precisely the sort of excessive freedom and tolerance that from a Platonic (as well as from a Nietzschean) perspective characterize our own democratic age, namely, the mockery of virtue and the stimulation and promotion of unnecessary desires, financial irresponsibility resulting in widespread debt and poverty, promiscuous hedonism and existential aimlessness, the collapse of traditional pedagogical standards, the rise of indiscriminate anti-authoritarianism, and, inevitably, the unchallenged sovereignty of youth culture (555b–562a). Democracies, it seems, inculcate in their citizens the character of a hot-blooded and short-sighted adolescent, which is why they are ripe to be taken over and dominated by strong-willed and resolute tyrants (563e–569c).

In a surprisingly Nietzschean turn of phrase, Plato says of the life of the democratic man, for whom all laws are equal, that it lacks *order and necessity* (*taxis* and *anagkê*, R. 561d6). The man who lives this way—to interweave in what follows a Nietzschean with a Platonic analysis—gives free reign to every transient impulse and desire (R. 561a–b) because he lacks "mastery over himself" and so has no "*measure of value*" (GM 2.2); he vacillates randomly between lives of debauchery and moderation, physical fitness and laziness, study and neglect of the intellect, taking up politics one day and soldiering or money-making the next (R. 561b–d), for he lacks "a Yes, a No, a straight line, a goal" (TI "Maxims" 44; cf. A 1); and containing within himself a manifold of various character types, he cultivates them all equally (R. 561e) and thereby neglects the "great and rare art" of giving style to his character (GS 290).

Plato is contemptuous of democratic culture even in his last great political treatise, the *Laws*, which he wrote in his old age. The Athenian in this work insists that the granting of equality to unequal men results in inequality and civil discord. Masters will never be friends with slaves, nor men of low birth with excellent men, even if by law honor is distributed equally (756e–758a). Here Plato is giving voice to sentiments common among men of his class. This is true too of his denigration of cities dependent, as was Athens, on maritime trade and naval power. Market influences render men unstable, faithless, and mutually hostile (704e–705b), and reliance on the navy turns the safety of the city over to every type of anonymous and ignoble man, which subverts the proper distribution of honors (706a–707b). This last point was popular among Athenians of the higher orders who typically equated the rise of Athens' naval power with radical democracy and the city's social and cultural decline. These men shared the Athenian's opinion in the *Laws* that the hoplite battles of Marathon and Plataea made the Greeks better, whereas naval battles made them worse, presumably even granting that their victory on the sea at Salamis, for example, contributed to the Greeks' ultimate triumph over the Persians. The relevant end is not mere victory and survival but political excellence, which is to say all that improves the natural character of a country and the order of its customs and laws (707b–d). The goal, from this perspective, is the preservation of the ideal of *kalokagathia* as understood and lived by those Athenian nobles who longed for a return of the so-called *patrios politeia*, the constitution of the fathers. Depending on the speaker, this phrase might refer to any number of earlier social-political arrangements, but always only to those that had in common a non- or even an anti-democratic structure.

In the *Laws*, then, as in the *Republic* and elsewhere, Plato joins ranks with the traditional, conservative, martial *kaloi kagathoi*. And if he sees himself as standing with the nobles *for the benefit of* the lower orders rather than strictly *against* them, then he does not express himself precisely in Nietzsche's preferred terms. But when it comes to the substance of his cultural, social, political, and moral positions, his differences with Nietzsche are minor relative to their common divergences from the modern perspective, so minor that the typical modern would likely designate Plato's philosophy no less than Nietzsche's a form of *aristocratic radicalism*.

Sophia and Philosophia

Plato as a creative writer

The Byzantine orator Themistius reports that a young woman named Axiothea was so moved by Plato's *Republic* that she travelled from Phlius in the Peloponnese to study with Plato in Athens.[1] Themistius is our sole source for this particular anecdote, but we do know from others that Axiothea was for years a student at the Academy.[2] In any case, I am not now interested in the historical accuracy of this story; I would like rather to appropriate the tale for use in a thought experiment. The *Republic* would probably serve for my purpose, as would most any of Plato's dialogues, but the *Phaedrus*, which I have called a prose poem, will do especially well. Imagine, then, Axiothea reading this dialogue and thinking to herself, "Oh, this *Phaedrus* is a wonderful thing! I want to learn to do *this*!" Now ask yourself: what is the "this" that Axiothea intends here? Is it that which today we would term "philosophy"? Is it, for example, the argument from self-motion to the conclusion that the soul is immortal (245c–246a)? Is it the brief account of dialectical method involving collection and division (265c–266d) or the more elaborate, but less strictly philosophical, analysis of rhetoric (266d–274b)? As interesting as these elements of the dialogue unquestionably are, I doubt they would inspire a young woman to abandon her family and dedicate her life to study with Plato, all the while disguised as a man (as we are told that Axiothea did). I myself cannot imagine anyone putting down the *Phaedrus* and thinking, "I must leave home right away to learn the essential components and the proper arrangement of an oratorical *logos*!" Whatever motivated Axiothea's daring and arduous undertaking, it must have stirred her deeply. I can see the *Phaedrus* accomplishing this, but only by way of its creative, poetic qualities. When Axiothea says, "I want to learn to do *this*," I imagine she means, "I want to learn to write like the man who wrote this charming scene by the river, to dream like the man who dreamt the image of souls in their chariots revolving on the rim of heaven, to think like the man whose wild ideas enkindled in him ecstatic insights into the benefits of god-given madness, and to compose like the man who wove all these elements into so polymorphous and thrilling a work of art." In short, I cannot believe that Axiothea's adventure was motivated by a desire (eros) to master the *technê* of dialectic or philosophy in our usual sense of this word, which hardly turn up in the *Phaedrus*. No, I hear her saying to herself, "I want to learn to create like this, to combine intellect and artistry in this way." I hear her saying, in short, "I want to be a *thinker-artist*."

Few scholars today attend to the fact that Plato was an artist. Or rather, the majority of those who identify Plato as a creative writer of dialogues neglect to consider the implications of his artistry and of his being a prolific author.[3] Michael Frede, for example, begins his "Plato's Arguments and the Dialogue Form" with the assertion that "Plato's dialogues are works of art," which is true.[4] But despite his recognition that the dialogues are "pieces of powerful dramatic fiction,"[5] Frede's interest is not in the artistry of Plato's fiction, but only in his arguments. He may be right in his estimate that "in sheer bulk the dialogues primarily consist of arguments,"[6] but this does not apply to a work like the *Phaedrus*; and even if it does apply to most of the other dialogues, there is still more to them than arguments, more that is often fascinating and significant. To me this suggests that it would be worthwhile to follow the literary trail of Plato's dialogues in a direction other than the dialectical, for it may be that Plato's conception of the philosopher and the proper practice of philosophy is bound up with his art in some way other than as an influence on his arguments. Frede writes that "Plato has certain views about the value and status of philosophical theses and philosophical arguments, as a result of which he thinks that the only responsible way to put forth such views and arguments in writing is in the form of a fictional dialogue … ."[7] This is no doubt true, but I would like to expand the perspective and propose that "Plato has certain views about the value and status of *philosophy* (rather than only those subdivisions of philosophy that concern the articulation and justification of theses and the formulation and defense of arguments), as a result of which he thinks that one absolutely essential way of practicing philosophy is *in writing* (writing in which the 'philosophical' content of the dialogue is only one component—and not necessarily the most important component—of the overall philosophical whole)." Frede expresses what is today a common position when he concludes his piece by noting of the dialogues that a "good part of their lesson does not consist in what gets said or argued, but in what they show."[8] But what do they show? According to Frede they show us the way to truth through dialectic, for "they make us think about the arguments they present."[9] There is nothing wrong with this observation in itself. But I believe we may come to a deeper appreciation of Plato, and in this way to a broader conception of philosophy, if we consider the implications of the dialogues' showing us something else, of their revealing, for example, Plato as an author, and thereby Plato's conception of the philosopher as a creative thinker and writer rather than a dialectical conversationalist. For they do show us this, and most insistently too.

Joanne Waugh looks to "Plato's choice to write dialogues" for insight into his "conception of the activity in which philosophy must consist,"[10] yet she has nothing to say about *Plato's writing* but only about his *characters' talking*. "The events and action of the Platonic dialogue consist of talk," she writes,[11] and only the talk interests her. That Plato was a prolific author does not attract her attention. Her position perhaps is motivated by her belief that "speech and not written language is Plato's prototype for philosophy."[12] But how does she know this? The same way many scholars believe that they know this, namely, because "we are told [this] in the *Phaedrus*."[13] In another essay Waugh writes that "Socrates claims" that this is so (in the *Phaedrus* of course), which is supposed to explain the apparent fact that even when Plato is writing, his mind is on spoken discourse.[14] Waugh contends, following Gilbert Ryle, that one learns to think through speaking, or through encounters with representations of speech. Plato's dialogues are such representations, and the philosopher composed them in order that his students might "learn to speak and think philosophically, for there appears to be no other way in which they could do this."[15] This may be so, but surely this is not all that Plato meant to accomplish with his dialogues. He was a philosopher, after all, and not just a teacher of philosophy. But Waugh, like so many scholars, sees only Plato the professor, and thus for her the dialogues have no significance *as writings*, but only as images and "representations of philosophical speech" composed for pedagogical purposes.[16] As to philosophy having anything to do with writing performed privately in silence through the creative composition of texts, well, again, Socrates tells us in the *Phaedrus* that this is not philosophy.[17] Socrates tells us? Or is it that Ammon tells us through Socrates, one *written character* through another? In any case, are we to take Socrates here as Plato's "mouthpiece"? It is standard to do so, ironically even among those who are conscious of the problems involved in attributing any character's views to Plato.[18]

Kenneth Sayre is another scholar interested in all the talk that occurs in Plato's dialogues.[19] The conversations attract his attention because they are unexpected, apparently even out of place according to the account of philosophical methodology as provided in the dialogues themselves. The late works that interest Sayre deal with methodological matters to such an extent that he labels them "the methodological dialogues."[20] These dialogues both express and exemplify methodological principles, yet they do so by way of characters engaged in conversation, which activity is nowhere mentioned in these works as having anything to do with proper methodology. As Sayre repeatedly points out, there is "no mention of conversation," "no role" nor even a "hint of a role" provided for conversation in the methodological works.[21] This "disparity" between form and content Sayre finds "puzzling,"[22] and he deals with this puzzle by attending to the fact that the conversations are written. Carefully noting that spoken discourse is not actually identified in the *Phaedrus* as the proper vehicle of philosophical insight,[23] Sayre contends that the dialogues' written exchanges between a master dialectician and an inexperienced student enable an auditor (if the dialogues were read aloud) or a reader to learn through a form of indirect participation. Neither the auditor nor the reader actually engages directly with the master; but he may nevertheless benefit as much as the student involved, perhaps even more than the student, for given the evident care with which Plato composed his written lessons, it is "possible that we as readers are better served by Plato's art than were most respondents in conversations with the historical Socrates."[24]

Sayre understands that this will not do as an approach to the broad corpus of Plato's work; his is a reading of the *late* dialogues. Perhaps it will apply with modifications to the aporetic works as well, though I doubt it will apply to the *Phaedrus*, which contains very little dialectical exchange. But my real objection to Sayre's understanding of the dialogues is identical to my objection to Waugh's: both reduce the dialogues' significance as writings to their representations of conversation. If Sayre is right, then like Waugh he has demonstrated something about Plato's conception of the proper method of *teaching* philosophy. But he sheds no light on Plato's conception of the proper method of *practicing* philosophy—assuming, as I think we must, that Plato believed there is more to philosophical activity than teaching.

So it seems to me that Sayre, having overlooked the matter of Plato's practice of philosophy, has overlooked the deeper puzzle. If the methodological dialogues do not mention conversation, they do at least depict it taking place, and to that extent they provide a conversational model of philosophy that is not easily overlooked. Philosophy is commonly understood to proceed maieutically, and this method is termed "Socratic," precisely because of the unmistakably conversational style of the dialogues. The conversations, *as conversations*, have over the years received their fair share of attention. This is the result of our fixation on the character Socrates' words to the neglect of the philosopher Plato's actual practice of philosophy: by reducing the dialogues' significance to what *Socrates* (or the other "main" speaker) *says in* them, we ignore what *Plato* himself *does with* them. Is it not a discrepancy as puzzling as Sayre's that in the methodological dialogues there is no mention, *nor even any enactment of* philosophical *writing*? Sayre analyzes the dialogues as written artifacts in order to render one aspect of their form—they are written conversations—consistent with their content. But here the stress is exclusively on the "conversations," to the total neglect of the "written." Where, then, does Plato the writer fit into Sayre's account of the proper practice of philosophy? According to Sayre he fits in (by implication) as a teacher of philosophy: the character Socrates teaches through conversation; Plato the author teaches by way of the composition of ideal conversations. But this strikes me as odd, for since there is nothing in these conversations to suggest that the philosopher is identical to the teacher of philosophy, to judge by Sayre's reading of the dialogues Plato was not a philosopher, not anyway when writing the dialogues. Surely this cannot be right. Here we touch on the puzzle of Plato himself, which, as I say, is deeper than the puzzle of his dialogues.

A. G. Long understands that Plato was more than a teacher of philosophy, and that he conceived of philosophy more broadly than as a merely pedagogical pursuit. In the first chapter of his *Conversation and Self-Sufficiency in Plato*, Long demonstrates that the criticism of writing in the *Phaedrus* is not meant to apply to the practice of philosophy in general, but rather to the *teaching* of philosophy and to attempts at *converting* others to philosophical eros.[25] To *these* activities conversation may be indispensable, but education and conversion do not exhaust the content of philosophy. There is also original philosophical inquiry, which may be conducted internally in thought, not necessarily through face-to-face conversation. By a close and often ingenious reading of seven dialogues, Long tracks Plato's gradual realization of this fact.[26] "[Q]uestioning oneself," he shows Plato coming to see, is "a satisfactory alternative to conversation."[27]

This is all very good, and Long calls attention to important distinctions in Plato's conceptions of philosophical activity and conversation. But it turns out that like so many others he takes Plato ultimately to be devoted to a conception of philosophy as centered on conversation, his modification of the general consensus being only (which is not to say "merely") that for the mature Plato this conversation may be conducted by a single individual through internal dialogue. So the practice of philosophy is not limited to talking; it may at times be an exclusively mental activity. But this philosophy-as-thinking is still an "activity that results in *judgment*,"[28] and according to Long the thinking that interests Plato is "the thinking that leads to a decision or to a verdict."[29] In other words, philosophy for Plato is in the end a matter of dialectical argumentation aimed at the discovery of truth—inquiry as conversation, even if the question-and-answer exchanges proceed internally. Long nowhere addresses in any detail the fact of Plato's being a writer, much less his being a wildly creative writer; and it is clear from his argument that he regards the dialogues primarily as representations of conversation, conversation conducted with others or within one's own mind.

It would be foolish to dispute Long's claim that "reflection in a conversational format held a particular significance or fascination for [Plato]."[30] His election to write dialogues (rather than, say, lyric poems) proves his fascination. But there is proof of something more here too, proof in the fact that he elected *to write* rather than to spend his time conversing or reflecting in a conversational format, and proof in the fact that the dialogues he elected to write are themselves much more than written conversations or reflections in a conversational format. So when considering Plato as a philosopher, and his dialogues as philosophical art, I have found it intellectually fruitful to regard the conversations less as the core or the heart of his philosophical activity than as the skeleton on which he hangs his philosophy, or as the brush strokes he employs to shape his composition and to apply his philosophical colors. The dialogues as wholes, and as *creatively written* wholes, are Plato's ultimate philosophical productions.

Eric Havelock famously stresses the literacy of Plato in distinction to the orality of Socrates. In this context he tracks the Greeks' transition from an oral to a literate culture and speculates as to how the associated changes affected their conception of individual words, particularly in philosophical discourse. Pre-platonic oral discourse is dynamic. The "absence of any linguistic framework for the statement of abstract principle" puts the stress on personal subjects acting and being acted on. The result is poetic narrative and drama.[31] But with the shift to literacy impersonal nouns ("justice," for example, or "goodness") are identified, isolated, reflected on, and finally made the subject of statements centered on the copula "is," an intransitive verb that freezes these abstractions in static relationships. This new stress on the verb "to be" in association with general and impersonal nouns results in a fixed eternality of abstract conceptual entities like Plato's Forms.[32]

I do not intend to develop Havelock's account in any systematic way, nor do I mean to presume the accuracy of his theories regarding the history and consequences of the Greek transition from oral to literate culture; I only borrow from his work to conjure an image of Plato as a thinker and a writer.[33] If, then, we apply Havelock's ideas to *texts* as well as to words,[34] we may regard Plato's *dialogues* as depending on his taking language as an artifact no less than his Forms so depend. It strikes me that a new kind of art may be revealed to the creative mind that takes language as an artifact in Havelock's sense, as centering on abstraction and the "is" of being, also as divisible into elements to be arranged and rearranged according to an artist's will.[35] Plato describes the process as "turning (the work) up and down over a long period of time, fitting (the parts) to one another and separating them."[36] Working this way with a written text as with an artifact, an author is free to spread out and examine a thought, unravel and unroll it while maintaining its unified integrity, analyzing the thought into its component elements without losing sight of the whole. He may then, if he likes, reassemble the elements on a new pattern, reorder the parts while reconstituting the whole, and experimenting thus with novel ways of structuring the whole he may discover novel wholes. And quite apart from such episodes of accidental creativity, this exploration of the elements of a thought provides one the opportunity to enter into the thought mentally, to rummage around in its appendages and potential for interconnections with other thoughts, to burrow down to explore its root systems. This produces *depth*.

When I conceive of writing in this way—as something static in the foreground or on the surface, but buzzing with intricacies behind or beneath—I imagine a form of philosophical art that in the hands of a master is productive of works with elaborate substructures and infrastructures, which despite their internal density are fronted with lyrical facades. I imagine works descending from Homer and the poets with the difference that they lack traditional dramatic content: there is no stress on agency and action because the focus remains unwaveringly on the "is" and its impersonal concept-subjects. But despite the dialogues' lack of conventional plotting, the play of their ideas proceeds in something like a narrative form from Plato's development and skillful use of their internal networks of reference and allusion, their patterned systems in which each section depends on each, the early on the later no less than the late on the earlier, and the mid-sections on both and vice versa. Homer's poems move forward always in the context of past events; and they are structured with sophisticated complexity.[37] The tragedians push the possibilities of meaning and reference even further, manipulating ambiguities until in a work like Sophocles' *Oedipus Tyrannus* the import of words and phrases changes from moment to moment as the plot unfolds. Plato's dialogues, too, are throughout densely intra-referential; one reads them well only by moving forward and backward through the text, constantly on the hunt for ambiguity and irony, humor and misdirection.[38] In a sense nothing "happens" in a Platonic dialogue. In another sense a dialogue is a moving series of explorations of a question or idea from an intricately varied plurality of angles, and this can generate an impression of narrative action, as can the gradual unfolding of an argument. We may, therefore, imagine a Platonic dialogue as a static being spread out in the field of becoming, as—and here I borrow from Schopenhauer's description of his own book—as a single thought divided according to the measures of space and time. It is, in short, the sort of combination of being and becoming that one encounters in a lively but literally motionless painting or sculpture. The development of a dialogue's ideas provides movement, but it does so in the context of a singular unwavering focus on these ideas; and the multiple forward and backward intra-textual cross-references and allusions stitch together the various parts of the whole, providing unity and stability through the constantly vibrating tension in lines stretched taut by the unrelaxing pull of contrary forces.

Now consider the time that Plato must have devoted to writing the dialogues, and when not actively writing to deciding what to write, then refining his subject and considering how best to structure it, how to frame and to plot it, dreaming up metaphors, analogies, and allegories, taking notes, drawing up and revising outlines, even occasionally dropping all this to rethink and rework the entire project from scratch. Consider that even when speaking with his colleagues and students in the Academy he must have been, in one capacious corner of his mind, collecting and storing up ideas, images, and turns of phrase, developing trains of thought for incorporation into the work laid out on his table at home. We have no evidence that Plato taught in the Academy, but I am willing to allow that he did.[39] Even so, I am sure that he spent at least as much time walking alone and thinking about, then sitting alone and writing, his dialogues. I myself believe that he must have spent *much more time* engaged this way than engaged in dialectical conversation with others,[40] but I admit that such estimates are matters of personal judgment. In any case, it is clear that Plato did not himself practice philosophy exclusively in the manner and mode that in his dialogues he depicts Socrates and his associates philosophizing.

We are often told that Socrates wrote nothing; but we are rarely told that Plato wrote prolifically. We are informed that he wrote dialogues, but (as we have seen) the stress is almost always on the "dialogues" rather than on the "wrote," which emphasis directs us away from Plato's creative activity as a writer and toward the conversational activity of the characters he created. Hence we have no sustained investigation into the facts and implications of Plato as a writer, of *Plato as a philosopher, as a creative writer*. In the dark as we are about the bearing of Plato's authorial activity on his conception of philosophy, and judging according to the standard account (with its constant appeals to the disparagement of writing in the *Phaedrus*[41]), we are led to conclude that Plato devoted as much time to an activity he regarded as trivial play as he devoted to philosophy in the way he believed it ought to be practiced. But surely this conclusion indicates that something is wrong with our premises.

I have noted that my remarks are not meant as a theory (nor even as the beginning of a theory) of the origins of complex, creative textual wholes in early literate culture. Nor am I committed to any particular thesis about either the structural possibilities of oral poetry or the necessary influences on the intellect of writing. I intend only to call attention to some aspects of Plato's activity as a creative author, to prompt my readers to imagine Plato as something other than either an oral dialectician or a literate teacher. Plato was a philosopher, and his practice of philosophy included thinking about and engaging in artistic activities of the sort I have just gone through.

A final qualification before I move on from this subject: although I have gone out of my way to call attention to Plato's authorial activities, I do not mean to stress any particular details that distinguish writing in a radical way from other forms of art (I have in fact *compared* it to painting and sculpture). I mean to emphasize Plato's *artistry*, and it happens that this is manifested most immediately in his writings. Paul Friedländer was attentive to the fact that Plato "wrote books throughout his long life" and that his "need to write" demonstrates "how irresistibly he was drawn to creative form."[42] Friedländer thought it a Platonic principle that "philosophy is possible only as an exchange between two people,"[43] which claim I believe the dialogues themselves— the dialogues *as philosophy*—falsify; and he like most took Plato at Socrates' word in the *Phaedrus* and so inferred that Plato must have regarded the dialogues as play.[44] But unlike most he understood how seriously Plato took this play,[45] as the following quotation makes clear: "Literature, the new form of art, the whole set of dramatic philosophical dialogues a play—what aesthetic passion and seriousness went into this play for half a century."[46]

Now what do you imagine that Plato was doing when Axiothea arrived in Athens? I imagine him writing, or thinking about his writing, or—and this is really the point—thinking about, thinking through, and ruminating on ideas under the influence (even if only the subconscious influence) of the fact that he would eventually express his thoughts creatively in writing. Surely the example he set for his students was of a man who for hours every day gave himself over to thinking and writing in private. He may have been their teacher, but he was unmistakably also an artist, an artist whose medium was the play of ideas developed, refined, and interrelated in a way that only writing, thinking, and thinking about writing make possible. Call this play if you will, but do not forget the "aesthetic passion and seriousness." This is the image of Plato I wish to take from his activities as a writer. It is an image he has in common with Nietzsche.

Plato and philosophy

In each of the two late dialogues, the *Sophist* (216c–217b) and the *Statesman* (257a–c), we are led to expect a third dialogue providing an account of the philosopher. As far as we know, however, Plato wrote no such work. But the Stranger in the *Sophist* does at one point suggest that in the course of their conversation they may have inadvertently defined the philosopher. According to this account, the philosopher is one who through dialectic can identify the Forms and specify their interrelations (253b–254b). And since the Stranger himself identifies the Forms (the "greatest" of them anyway) and specifies their interrelations, some have concluded that *he* is the philosopher. The idea, in brief, is that Plato never intended to write a third dialogue in which to define the philosopher, for the philosopher is manifest in the person of the Stranger as he appears in the two dialogues that we have. But if we must define the philosopher as one who engages in this activity, what are we to call Plato? He does not quite act in accord with this definition in any dialogues other than the *Sophist* and the *Statesman*, and even in these works he does much else besides this. We might therefore note the discrepancy between philosophy as *defined* by the Stranger *in* the dialogues and philosophy as *practiced* by Plato *through* the dialogues, and infer that the philosopher is one who possesses not only the Stranger's dialectical skills but Plato's much wider array of talents as well. Plato provides a broader account of the philosopher in the *Phaedrus*, and this account could seem to apply to him.[47] But if we apply to the *Phaedrus* the distinction between what Socrates says in the dialogues and what Plato does through them, we might take the claims in the *Phaedrus* to apply only within the borders of the world of this dialogue and to indicate something greater beyond this world—this something greater being Plato himself, Plato and his intellectual-creative activities. Now since Plato possesses—if not existentially, then at least intellectually or imaginatively—all of the properties of the characters that appear in the *Phaedrus* and then some, we shall have to find for him a designation more expansive than, and superior to, "philosopher." Perhaps we should call him a *sage*. It is true that at the close of the *Phaedrus* Socrates says that the term "wise" is fitting only for god.[48] But this is Socrates, or the character "Socrates," speaking. What did Plato think? With every dialogue he wrote Plato showed himself greater than any character he portrayed, for he encompasses all of them. Socrates is the man who says *x*; the Stranger is the man who says *z*. But Plato is the man who says *x*, *z*, and literally everything else said in every one of the dialogues. As impressive as Socrates and the Stranger are, Plato is more impressive, for he is their creator. May we not conclude, then, that Plato was wise, his characters' reservations notwithstanding?

In the *Republic* Plato defines wisdom as belonging to the small reasoning (*logistikos*) part of the soul that has forethought for the whole based on knowledge of what is good for each of the soul's parts as well as for the totality (441e, 442c). Wisdom is attainable only by the few, for it depends on knowledge of Being, which itself requires years of the right sort of education (as outlined in Book 7). Nevertheless, according to this account wisdom is indeed available to mortals. In other words, taking the collection of the dialogues as a whole, we cannot rule out the possibility that Plato believed that mortal men may be wise, and that their wisdom may have more substance than the merely "human wisdom" of the man who knows that "with respect to wisdom he is in truth worth nothing," as Socrates puts it in the *Apology* (23a–b).

We are running up against the distinction between the philosopher and the sage, which Plato nowhere treats at length. But as one goal of this chapter is to reflect on wisdom and the love of wisdom in the light of Plato's and Nietzsche's works and ideas, it is worth exploring this distinction for ourselves. But first, as a preliminary, we should examine competing conceptions of philosophy and the philosopher.

The word "philosophy" is today the name of an academic discipline, and the title "philosopher" is the aspiration of a certain small subset of university students. The philosopher thus understood is a certain type, namely, one who studies a particular subject and who shares his knowledge with others through teaching and publications. Here I am using "type" to designate a permanent condition, or at least an end-state. One who is a type according to this sense of the word no longer moves toward a goal; he has reached it. If he ceases to be this type, it will not be due to his having transcended it on his way to its natural *telos*; it will be because he has decided to do something else, to make himself over into a different type. It is true that some are wary of the title "philosopher," as many are of the title "poet," believing that one must attain to the status of acknowledged and influential master of the discipline before applying to oneself so exalted a denomination. According to this way of thinking, the "philosophers" today are those who speak at the major conferences, who publish articles in the best journals and write books for the most prestigious presses. But even admitting this qualification, it remains the case that the philosopher today is conceived by many (including many philosophers) as someone bound up with a particular academic discipline and professional activity. In this discipline there is a canon of books, ideas, arguments and counter-arguments studied by the professional or aspiring professional. In this context the proposition "I want to study philosophy" means, "I want to read and write about *these* books and *these* ideas in *this particular* academic setting," with, perhaps, the addition that "I hope one day to deliver papers at *these* conferences, to place my work with *that* publisher, and to be cited as an authority by others speaking and writing in my special area of the discipline." Whoever accomplishes this has accomplished his goal, attained his *telos*. This is not to say that he may now relax, for he must keep active in the field and even work to refine his skills. But as to becoming a particular *type*, this he has achieved; he has earned the appellation "philosopher."

This conception of philosophy and the philosopher differs considerably from the central ancient conception, according to which the philosopher is not a type but temporarily a bearer of a linguistic designation. In short, the word "philosopher" is just that, a word, and only that. It is a linguistic label employed to designate a man or a woman who aspires to a condition beyond philosophy. This condition is *wisdom*. Attaining to this condition may well involve reading a certain canon of books and mastering certain ideas and arguments; one may even study these matters in an academic environment. But the point is that such activity is not a goal in itself. This sort of philosopher is not one who says, "I want to study philosophy," as if he were expressing his highest aspiration. He is, rather, one who says, "I want to be wise." If he calls himself a philosopher, or acquiesces in others so naming him, he takes the term for nothing more than a convenient label for one who is on his way to a condition beyond anything properly designated by the term. The word "philosopher," to him, designates not a type as defined above, but rather one who aspires to be the type properly designated *sage*.

There is, then, a fundamental distinction between the word "philosopher" as used to designate a type, a type as an end, and the word "philosopher" as applied to a man passing through one mode of being on his way to another, and a higher, way of life. I have remarked that there are those who, in accord with the first conception of philosophy, distinguish between the student or teacher of philosophy and the genuine philosopher as an influential academic. But according to the conception presently under consideration, even this so-called genuine philosopher is more often than not a *mere* academic or, worse, an intellectual.[49] Plato calls these types lovers of sights and sounds, or lovers of opinion (*philodoxoi*). Nietzsche applies to them a number of labels he takes to be disparaging—"scholars," for example, or "philosophical laborers."[50] Such men not only are not wise: they do not even aspire to wisdom. They may even dismiss the very idea that there is or ever has been such a type as a sage. The famed seven *sophoi* of ancient Greece, after all, were so pitifully ignorant of so much that we know to be true. At best, then, they only appeared to be wise to their even more ignorant contemporaries.

The *Symposium* is noteworthy in relation to this distinction, for it has influenced a popular understanding of the philosopher as a type and of philosophy, therefore, as an end-state. This reading is standard despite the fact that the dialogue culminates in a depiction of the lover of wisdom actually transcending philosophy, which to me suggests that Plato regarded "philosopher" not as the designation of a type, but rather as merely a term by which to refer to a man during one transient stage of his ascent to wisdom. Or perhaps (a third option) to one mode or manifestation of a man's wisdom. But I shall come back to these points; for now I return to the *Symposium*. The core of this dialogue consists of a series of speeches delivered in praise of Eros during a celebratory drinking party for the poet Agathon, recently victorious in the competition of tragedies staged during the annual Athenian festival of Dionysus. Socrates begins his own speech by arguing that anyone who desires (*epithumei*) or loves (*erai*) a thing must necessarily lack it (199e–200e). This is significant for much of the rest of his speech, for the love in philosophy as the love of wisdom (*philia*) will later be associated with this love and desire (*erôs* and *epithumia*) that necessarily imply a lack, and since one and the same Greek word means "to lack" and "to be in need of," the philosopher who lacks wisdom must be in need of it, and so his love and desire for wisdom amount to a search for it, a seeking after it, and all of these points taken together imply that the philosopher loves wisdom by forever pursuing without ever acquiring it.

Socrates develops this account of philosophy in the course of relating a conversation he claims once to have had with Diotima, a woman from the Peloponnesian town of Mantinea. For all we know this woman is Socrates'—or, rather, Plato's—invention, but in any case Socrates claims that she taught him about the erotic things (*ta erôtika*, 201d5). She was, he says, wise with respect to these matters, and many others besides (201d).[51] Diotima begins her account (as reported by Socrates) by relating Eros's parentage and, thereby, indicating something of his nature. She demonstrates in particular that Eros is an intermediate kind of being, for he is neither god nor mortal, but something in between the two, namely, a "great *daimôn*" (202b–e). Related to this ontological status is his cognitive status, for Eros is neither wise nor ignorant, but something in between, namely—a philosopher. This is the element of Diotima's discourse of particular interest to us.

Diotima lists among Eros's traits his "philosophizing through all his life" (203d). His inclination to philosophy is the result of his intermediate nature as I have just described it. According to Diotima, none of the gods philosophizes, nor does any desire to become wise, for the gods *are* wise, and no one who is wise philosophizes.[52] Nor does any mortal who is ignorant philosophize or desire to become wise, for being ignorant he knows nothing of wisdom, not even as a possibility. Only someone in the state between ignorance and wisdom knows enough to know both that he is not wise and that wisdom is a good to be desired. Such a one is Eros, who is thus necessarily a philosopher (204a–b). Conversely, the philosopher necessarily resembles Eros in being neither wise nor ignorant but in an intermediate cognitive state. So the philosopher lacks wisdom by definition; the lack, as I have said, is entailed by his love. But this means that the philosopher, so long as he is a philosopher, can never be wise.

This has become for us a standard way to describe the nature of philosophy. The philosopher is moved by eros, one says, and this means that the philosopher is seeking, searching, constantly on the hunt for—for what? For the truth, of course. Not wisdom; we no longer believe in wisdom. We have modified the *Symposium* at least to this extent: we desire, not wisdom, but the truth. The truth about what? That usually depends on the interests of the person one asks. A fine approximation to the most general sort of reply in this category of answers is this one, from Stanley Rosen: "Philosophy is the pursuit of truth about *phusis*."[53] Rosen formulates this definition as a Platonic contrast to the goal that Nietzsche, "in his persona as antiphilosopher," sets for himself of replacing discovery and truth with production and creativity.[54] I am not now concerned to evaluate Rosen's argument that Nietzschean creation is inextricably bound up with the very given of *phusis* (nature) it would like to deny. I am, however, interested in his definition of philosophy. The pursuit of truth about *phusis* may well be a noble activity, and it may for some count as the essence of philosophy; but I would not like to attribute the idea to Plato. Aristotle might approve, for Rosen's definition fits nicely with his account of wisdom as (to paraphrase) *knowledge* of truth about *phusis*.[55] But even if Plato in some of his moods would acknowledge, and even if he might insist on, the value of Rosen's pursuit, the evidence of his dialogues suggests that he was interested in much more than this, and that he was interested in this more precisely *as a philosopher*.

Seth Benardete once observed that "what philosophy is seems to be inseparable from the question of how to read Plato," and although I cannot say precisely what Benardete himself had in mind when he formulated this thought, it strikes me as more fruitful, and as more faithful to the spirit of Plato's work, than any simple definition, certainly than any definition that omits altogether to include wisdom or that rules out the possibility of the philosopher's attaining it.[56]

But to return to the *Symposium*, try to imagine the man who aspires to be a philosopher on the model supplied by the standard reading of this work. I myself cannot imagine a man who knowingly wills to be a type whose highest aspiration is necessarily unattainable. But if this is not plausible—and I believe that it isn't—then the true lover of wisdom, the true *philosopher*, must not aspire to be a philosopher; he must rather want to be wise. He may consent to the label "philosopher" as a designation, but if so, not as a designation of himself as a type, but only as a temporary designation of himself as passing through a phase on his gradual progress toward wisdom. Diotima, I believe, implies this much, for although she brings up philosophy throughout her discourse, when she comes to describe "the ultimate rites and mysteries" of erotic desire,[57] she says that the man who "begets many beautiful and magnificent discourses and ideas in bounteous philosophy" is at last on the threshold of his highest *telos* (209e–210e), and after this she never again mentions philosophy. Nor does she mention wisdom. And though she does speak of giving birth to true virtue, the real *telos* seems to be neither truth nor virtue but the spiritual-intellectual contemplation of the Form of *beauty*, which here is likely a stand in for, a useful but inadequate name for, the ultimately unnamable principle (*archê*) that is simultaneously the source and center of all things (like the Good beyond Being from *R.* 509b). The pure individual who beholds this in its purity is neither a philosopher nor a sage but a type higher still, he is beloved of god (*theophilês*, 212a6).

But this conception of philosophy as a stage to be transcended is the character Diotima's conception. This may be the highest conception of philosophy expressed *in* the dialogues, but if it is, it is nevertheless necessarily confined to the world of the dialogues. Plato himself transcends this world as its creator, and it may be that *he* intends to *reveal* something other—and something more—*through* the dialogues than his *characters* ever *say*, or even show, *in* them.

In the past it was common to assume (as some still assume today) that Plato's thoughts on a particular topic (or at least all that he intended to share of his thoughts) were exhausted by what Socrates says (also perhaps by what he suggests or implies) about the matter in the relevant dialogue. Today more scholars find Plato's view in the dialogue as a whole, not just in Socrates' words but in the words of all the characters, their insights and their questions, and not only in the remarks of the totality of characters but in all that is intimated by their relations to one another and to the setting in which the dialogue takes place as well. Now this may be the correct approach for those concerned with Plato's thoughts about *sôphrosunê* as expressed in the *Charmides*, for example, or about eros as expressed in the *Symposium*. But what shall we do to understand Plato's conceptions of philosophy and of the philosopher? For this I think we must broaden our perspective even further. Let's remember that Plato was a philosopher, and let's at least consider the possibility that he judged his own creative-intellectual activities as author of the dialogues to flow from the nature of philosophy.

With this last thought in mind, consider that there is the model of philosophy as presented *in* the *Symposium*, but there is also the model of philosophy *as* the *Symposium*, which by implication is simultaneously a model of the philosopher as one who creates and composes the *Symposium*. As author of the dialogues Plato always does much more than his characters say, so the content of his characters' words can never by itself amount to a portrait of the man who formed this content. Where, then, should we look to find the philosopher? Before coming out with my own answer, I present for contrast a response that is today more and more common but that is also, to my mind, too narrow. Roslyn Weiss has attempted to specify Plato's conception of the philosopher in the *Republic*.[58] She finds in the text two primary accounts, namely, "the philosopher by nature" of Books 5 and 6, and "the philosopher by design" of Book 7. Other varieties of philosopher appear as well, but these two Socrates describes explicitly and at some length. In the fourth chapter of her book, however, Weiss argues that Socrates himself exemplifies a third type of philosopher, a type that Plato "prefers to any of those outlined in the *Republic*."[59] But Plato's preference is only implicit, and we readers must look beyond Socrates' words to his nature and his actions to identify him as Plato's ideal. As Weiss puts it in her Introduction, Socrates "represents a third paradigm—but one that lies outside the confines of the *Republic*: none of the philosophers described *in* the *Republic* can meet his standard."[60] We have encountered this move before, as when Kenneth Sayre, puzzled at not finding conversation described in the methodological dialogues, found it in the dialogue form itself. Similarly, according to Weiss, although no one discusses Socrates as a philosophical type in the *Republic*, his type is enacted by and through the man (the character) himself. And just as Sayre believes that conversation reveals something essential about Plato's practice of philosophy, Weiss believes that Socrates reveals something about Plato's ideal of the philosopher. But to my mind both these scholars are looking in the wrong place, and Weiss is as confined within the work as is Sayre. Conceptually she acknowledges a distinction between Socrates' message and Plato's,[61] but like most everyone else she reads Plato's messages as always being about Socrates, never about himself. It is true that Socrates as a philosophical type is not *described* in the *Republic*; but it is not the case that he does not appear as such *in* the work. That Socrates is an admirable model of the philosopher is as hard to miss as is the fact that conversation is essential to his conception of philosophy.

It will not do merely to look away from what Socrates says to what he is or does. This perspective is still too restricted, and whoever adopts it treats Plato as reductively as did previous generations of scholars, interpreting his ideas always and exclusively as having to do only with Socrates. But did Plato not regard *himself* as a philosopher, and *his own activities* as philosophy? Did he not recognize that his nature as a philosopher and his practice of philosophy differ dramatically from Socrates' nature and practice? Surely he must have, and *really* outside the confines of his dialogues one finds, not Socrates, but *Plato himself*—and Plato was no Socratic conversationalist. Weiss has overlooked Plato precisely as Sayre and so many others have done, and for the same reason too: they are all of them distracted by Socrates— so distracted they can see only him and are, ironically, blinded to the man who made him so distracting.

These remarks might suffice to communicate my own proposal for identifying the philosopher by way of Plato's dialogues. But to be explicit, and returning to our original example of the *Symposium*, I note that if by producing this dialogue Plato is practicing philosophy—as I think he must be—then the philosopher as Plato, creator of this dialogue, is not at all identical to the philosopher as Socrates, or as Socrates informed by Diotima, or as Socrates-Diotima in relation to the other characters, or even as all these characters in relation to one another and also to the setting in which they appear. But since the conversation *in* this dialogue (as in the *Republic* too) concerns the nature of philosophy, our attention is naturally directed there, *into* the dialogue. But to look into the work is to look in the wrong direction—and this is so whether we look to what the characters say, what they imply through their words and deeds, or even to what they are—for *Plato himself* is the one and only actual example of a philosopher on display here, even if he reveals himself always behind the mask of his work. And here perhaps we should consider as well that Plato may reveal himself also *through* this mask, intimating his identity as one who chooses to communicate *this* way and with *this particular style* of mask. When searching for Plato, then, we should look outside the work—*really* outside the confines of the work—which is to say behind the mask, or through it, toward Plato.

Scholars have rightly adjusted their interpretive focus to encompass not just Socrates' words, but his nature and his actions, and the words of his interlocutors and the dialogues' settings as well. They have broadened their visual frame, as it were, which is good. But one step farther back and we will see even more than the dialogue as a whole; we will see the creator of this whole, whose combined intellectual and creative activities teach lessons beyond those taught by Socrates or even by the whole of any work in which he appears. There is nothing *in* the dialogues to suggest that the philosopher is a thinker-artist; but consider the dialogues *as* philosophy and Plato immediately snaps into focus as just this type.

I suggested above that Plato may have been wise. This is not to say that as an author he wrote straightforwardly *as* a wise man. Wise men, like Solon, typically write poems and laws. But neither did Plato write simply as a philosopher, for philosophers write treatises or (rarely) dialogues that are treatises in all but the most superficial form. I would, therefore, like to propose that *Plato was a sage writing as an artist writing as a philosopher*. I do not say simply that he *wrote as a philosopher*, for sage or artist, if he wrote solely *as* a philosopher, his dialogues would be works of philosophy and nothing more. But it seems to me that the dialogues *are* something more than philosophy, and that Plato was engaged in a pursuit that he ranked *higher* than philosophy. Plato, I believe, was an original type among the wise men and philosophers of his day. He composed poems and legislation, as had his ancestor Solon; but unlike the traditional sage he *combined* these activities, wove them together into a new intellectual-art form. The result is his philosophy, which unlike traditional philosophy is not itself a search for wisdom but is instead an emanation of it. In short, Platonic philosophy is a particular mode or manifestation of Plato's wisdom.

This, anyway, is the story I sometimes tell myself when I think on these things. And to situate the idea in the context of my earlier remarks on philosophy and wisdom in relation to the *Symposium*, I would say that Plato transcended philosophy and attained wisdom, which movement Diotima hints at in her discourse in the *Symposium*; and when he expresses his wisdom creatively in writing he produces philosophy, as he intimates himself *through* the *Symposium* as a whole (and the whole of his other dialogues as well).

Another way to put this point is to say that Plato employed his prodigious— and prodigiously varied—gifts to produce creative works that on the surface are philosophy, but that deep inside are infused with wisdom. Considering the dialogues from this perspective I imagine them on the model of Alcibiades' description of Socrates in the *Symposium*—as works resembling statues of Silenus that open up to reveal images of the gods inside (215a–b). I imagine, too, that Nietzsche may have had some intimation of this, which prompted him to reflect in *Beyond Good and Evil* on Plato's "secrecy and sphinx nature," particularly in association with an ancient anecdote that Plato slept with a copy of Aristophanes' comedies beneath his pillow, Aristophanes that great presence in the *Symposium* (*BGE* 28). And when later in this same work Nietzsche writes of philosophers having caves behind their caves in which to conceal their true philosophy (*BGE* 289), I am sure he was aware that his words apply to Plato every bit as much as they describe himself.

Nietzsche and Plato

In his account of the philosopher in sections 7 and 8 of the Third Essay of the *Genealogy of Morals* Nietzsche alludes throughout to Plato's *Symposium* and *Phaedrus*, though he is careful to conceal his intentions.[62] The fact has yet to be noted in the literature, but that it is a fact strikes me as undeniable. Each of these works has to do with the taming, sublimating, or transfiguration of desire for the sake of a calling higher than the experience of bodily pleasure, than sexual excitation in particular. In the *Symposium* Diotima speaks of the desire for the beautiful throughout her speech; this desire is her main concern, and she never loses sight of it. Her account of the so-called "ladder of love" begins with the ascent away from lust for beautiful physical bodies.[63] Similarly, in the *Phaedrus* Socrates describes the soul's internal struggle to master the desire for sexual gratification when in the presence of beauty.[64] For his part, Nietzsche begins his discussion by questioning Schopenhauer's account of "the nature of the beautiful" (*GM* 3.6), and he concludes with the assertion that upon "the sight of the beautiful" sensuality is "transfigured and no longer enters consciousness as sexual excitement" (*GM* 3.8). The discussions in Plato's works center on the philosopher's self-control and ultimate transcendence of desire; in Nietzsche the focus is on the philosopher's mastery of desire through various ascetic tendencies and practices.[65] Both discussions examine the nature and effects of the desire for beauty in order to address, quite specifically and explicitly, philosophy and the proper activities of the true philosopher.[66]

The discussion in the *Symposium* begins with Diotima explaining to Socrates that the desire for the beautiful and the good is ultimately a desire for happiness (*eudaimonia*). This, she says, is the real *telos* of the desire in question (204c–205a). Nietzsche intervenes in this very discussion, while stressing his opposition to its specifics, by early on contradicting this account of the philosopher's goal. The philosopher does *not* seek happiness, but rather "an optimum of favorable conditions under which it can expend all its strength and achieve its maximal feeling of power." He insists as well that virtue is not relevant here, a fact that he "must say again and again," whereas for Diotima this striving toward the goal of happiness is directly bound up with wisdom, justice, moderation, and the other virtues, a fact she repeats throughout her discourse (209aff.).

Despite these specific disagreements, there is agreement as to general subject matter. The condition for which Nietzsche's philosopher strives is optimal for a particular expression of power, namely, "for the highest and boldest spirituality" (*höchster und kühnster Geistigkeit*), which is directly related to his "periods of great pregnancy" and his concern for "that which is growing in him." It is for this that he saves up his love. I read these expressions as allusions to the *Symposium*, particularly to Diotima's claim that those who are "pregnant in their souls" go around in search of "the beautiful in which [they] might beget" (208e–209e). Moreover, Nietzsche writes that as every animal strives for its highest state, just so does the philosophical animal strive for that state in which "all animal being becomes more spiritual and acquires wings" (*geistiger wird und Flügel bekommt*), and it regards self-mastery as "the cheerful asceticism of an animal become fledged and divine" (*vergöttlichten und flügge gewordnen*). Since the "fledged" here means "winged" I note the repetition of the imagery (*Flügel*, *flügge*) and think of the *Phaedrus*, in which the philosopher in particular is portrayed as the man who grows wings and whose soul is like, and longs for, the divine (246d–e, 248e–249a, 250c–253c). In Nietzsche this winged and divine condition leads to the philosopher's "fairest fruitfulness," which looks "somewhere else than in children" for "its little immortality," precisely as Plato's philosopher seeks not the immortality of mortal progeny but of higher and more spiritual offspring (*Smp.* 207c–209e).

Nietzsche's account of the spiritually pregnant philosopher, then, is modeled on— or modeled *against*—Diotima's discourse from 208e to 209e. We may even identify parallels between Nietzsche's list of the "three glittering and loud things" the philosopher avoids and the various worldly concerns dismissed or deprioritized by Diotima. The first of these, according to Nietzsche, is fame, which recalls Diotima's contrasting the philosophers with those who desire honor, notoriety, and fame (*philotimia*, *onomastoi genesthai*, *kleos*, *eukleos*, 208c–d). Nietzsche's second item is princes, which corresponds to Diotima's treatment of the lawgivers Lycurgus and Solon, whose works (their laws) were noble and worthy of reverence, to be sure, but nonetheless inferior to the object of the philosopher's higher love (209d–e). The final item on Nietzsche's list is "women," avoided also by Diotima's philosophers, who associate with noble and philosophically inclined young men and who, besides, have no interest in either sexual gratification[67] or reproduction (208e–209a).[68]

If spiritual pregnancy is the dominant theme in both Plato and Nietzsche,[69] what can we say of their accounts of the philosopher's offspring, his spiritual child? Diotima's philosopher, like the philosopher as described in the *Phaedrus*, aims through the practice of self-mastery to ascend to a vision of the Form of *beauty*; he aims to behold and to be with it.[70] Beauty itself, like all Forms, is "unalloyed, pure, and unmixed, not infected with human flesh and coloring and so much other mortal nonsense" (*Smp.* 211e1–3). Nietzsche's philosopher, too, escapes from "the noise and democratic chatter" of typical human concerns; he seeks that which is "still, cold, noble, distant, past, and in general everything in the face of which the soul does not have to defend itself and wrap itself up." This passage calls to mind an image of Nietzsche in his beloved Sils-Maria, a crisp sky gleaming over towering mountains, walking alone absorbed by thoughts of the ancients.[71] It reminds one as well of the Platonic philosopher's experience of the Forms, for in *Beyond Good and Evil* Nietzsche describes the Platonic way of thinking as "noble," in part for its opposition to a plebian mob mentality, which for Plato means a democratic mentality; and of course the Platonist's soul need not defend itself from the one true object of its desire.

But to return to the matter of the philosopher's spiritual offspring: according to Diotima it is true virtue (*aretê alêthê*), and the man who begets virtue is loved by the gods and may at least hope for immortality (212a). Similarly, in the *Phaedrus*, those who attain to the spiritual-intellectual vision of the Forms by transfiguring their desire for physical beauty win for themselves immortality and philosophical friendship (256a–257a). In short, then, in Plato the goal of philosophical ascent is eternal life as a virtuous philosopher, or as a type superior even to the philosopher. Nietzsche's goal seems to be philosophy itself, or more immediately perhaps the philosopher himself, whose "little immortality" is "the evolving work" forming in the womb of his mind. The philosopher's work is most obviously his philosophy as written in a book, but it is also, and more deeply, his philosophy as manifested existentially in himself as a philosopher. Hence the philosopher's "impious wish," in its way a wish for immortality, that the world might perish while philosophy, the philosopher, and *he himself* remain.[72]

Throughout his discussion Nietzsche masks the associations with Plato, particularly by adverting to Indian philosophy and the Buddha when one might expect a reference to Plato or Socrates,[73] though he does mention these two in connection with well-known unmarried philosophers and the single most famous exception, which I suppose was unavoidable. But Nietzsche is rarely guided by what might appear unavoidable to others; he is among the most intentional of writers. We may, therefore, take his passing attention to Socrates as an indication of his true intentions, especially considering that his remark that a married philosopher belongs in comedy recalls the married Socrates at the end of the *Symposium* attempting to convince a tragedian and a comic poet that one and the same artist should be able to compose tragedies and comedies both—a remark that some have read as Plato's allusion to himself as author of this very dialogue, which itself contains elements of the tragic and comic. There is perhaps another indication of Nietzsche's intentions in the matter of the "impious wish." The line has more than one source, but it is most likely an allusion to the beginning of Schopenhauer's "On Religion." I trace it to Schopenhauer's work, first, because Nietzsche structures his discussion around an analysis of Schopenhauer's aesthetics; and second because Nietzsche's stress on philosophy and the philosopher (*fiat philosophia, fiat philosophus*) is a notable, and typically Nietzschean, alteration of the emphasis in Schopenhauer's dialogue on truth (*vigeat veritas*) and justice (*fiat justitia*).[74]

Despite Nietzsche's sleight of hand, then, there is in fact a covert connection between his treatment of the philosopher in the *Genealogy* and the accounts of the type in the *Phaedrus* and *Symposium*. A noteworthy difference, beyond those I have already mentioned, is the absence in Nietzsche's work of any indication of a state higher than philosophy. Diotima's philosophers rise above the obsessions of this world, and eventually they transcend even philosophy itself. For Nietzsche philosophy seems to be an end-state. Even with the model of Zarathustra before us, I see no path to wisdom laid out in Nietzsche's reflections on the nature of the philosopher. Needless to say, however, his philosopher has nothing in common with the philosopher as academic type described above. It may be that a philosopher must at some point have passed through the stage of being a scholar (*BGE* 211, *EH* "UM" 3), but one who is by nature a scholar "can never become a philosopher" (*SE* 7; cf. *BGE* 204–7).

Nietzsche and philosophy

Nietzsche devotes no book, nor even the chapter of a book, to providing a sustained analysis, account, or description of the philosopher. He does, however, reflect on the nature of philosophy and the intellectual and existential habits of the philosopher throughout his career, particularly in *Beyond Good and Evil*, to which work he gave the telling subtitle, *Prelude to a Philosophy of the Future*. His early essay on the man whose work turned him decisively toward philosophy, "Schopenhauer as Educator" (from 1874), is something of a portrait of the ideal philosophical personality.[75] But for his longest systematic treatment of this subject one must look back even further, back to his notes of 1872, the year his *Birth of Tragedy* appeared. These and other notes written through to 1875, collected today under the title *Philosophy and Truth*, introduce themes that Nietzsche would play on, with variations, for years.[76] Consider, for example, the first entry to the earliest collection of these notes, entitled by the editor (after one of the many headings Nietzsche himself tried out) "The Philosopher: Reflections on the Struggle Between Art and Knowledge." Here Nietzsche writes that "from the right height everything comes together: the thoughts of the philosopher, the work of the artist, and good deeds" (*P* 16). The last phrase indicates something of Schopenhauer's influence, and in later years Nietzsche would not express himself this way. Yet he would most likely include a moral (or immoralist) reflection alongside a pairing of philosophy and art, for he did maintain that "moral (or immoral) intentions" are at the core of every philosophy (*BGE* 6). Instead of "good deeds" he might write "moral legislation," "value creation," or "deeds beyond good and evil," but the point is that for Nietzsche philosophy is always an artistic enterprise, and the philosopher reserves his creative energies for the formation and ranking of values. In his early notes Nietzsche imagines a "*philosopher-artist*" whose work is a worldview designed to replace the extinct pagan myths and the moribund western religions (*P* 44;

cf. *WP* 795). When Christianity has passed away for good, only the philosopher, the philosopher as the boldest and grandest variety of artist, will have the will to invent, "beyond the limits of experience," a new image of the world and of the whither and wherefore of existence (*P* 53). In short, the philosopher engraves the supreme tablets of value for man, which is to say that in his nature are combined the roles of thinker, artist, and lawgiver.

If, then, we may describe the philosopher as a chimera—artist in front, thinker behind, and lawgiver in the middle—it will be good to examine more closely the complex nature of the beast. The philosopher's task involves formation, formation as creation as well as organization. In Nietzsche's earliest notes these two activities are often combined: the philosopher creates (*P* 53), and what he creates is an organizing image of life to guide his mastering and molding of the scientist's "indiscriminate knowledge drive" (e.g. *P* 28, 30, 37, 48). The man of science seeks knowledge for its own sake; he pays no heed to the good or ill effects of the "truths" he uncovers and exhibits to the world. Lacking "selectivity," he is motivated by "the blind desire to know." The philosopher, on the other hand, with his eye ever trained on "the great and the important insights," is concerned with "legislating greatness" (*PTG* 43). The philosopher, then, stands above the scientist, and he receives or dismisses the deliverances of the scientific mind as guided by his creative-legislative goals.

Nietzsche suspects that the aimless accumulation of knowledge is a mark of cultural decline, and not just a mark but an aggravating condition as well (*P* 125, 137, 138). Something has gone awry with a people among whom *la science pour la science* is the norm, and the pursuit of this ideal only exacerbates the original disorder. Recall, from the first chapter of this book, Nietzsche's account of the degenerative effects that Socrates' scientific-theoretical optimism worked on the healthy and unified culture of the Greeks.[77] A concern with the health and integrity of a culture is always with Nietzsche, but it is especially prominent in his earliest period, when he was under the powerful influence of Wagner, who intended through his own work to affect the rehabilitation of German *Kultur* by infusing it with the spirit of an ancient tragic mentality. This theme comes out at length in *The Birth of Tragedy*, but it is present also in Nietzsche's conception of "the philosopher as physician of culture," which expression he considered around this time for the title of a book on Greek philosophy.[78]

When Nietzsche writes in *The Gay Science* of the need to give style to one's character, what he says of a man he means to apply also to a culture. A culture, like an individual, is a collection of disparate elements; and a high culture, like a healthy individual, is one whose elements are unified by, and bear the stamp of, a singular will. Until now this will has manifested typically as myth or religion, but as these forces have exhausted themselves, philosophy and art, or both as united in the philosopher-artist, must take their place. It is not likely a coincidence that Nietzsche's praise of the "constraint of style" follows his call, "Embark, philosophers!"[79] The drive to gather and collect knowledge, disconnected from an overarching vision and goal, is necessarily hostile to the integrity of a culture; therefore the philosopher, by controlling this drive, is "an instrument of culture" (*P* "Appendix" 1). And this is true whether we regard a culture as the unity of an individual or of a people. Nor is this all. In the preface to the second edition of *The Gay Science*, Nietzsche writes that he is "still waiting for a philosophical *physician* in the exceptional sense of that word—one who has to pursue the problem of the total health of a people, time, race, or of humanity" (*GS* "Preface" 2). So Nietzsche's philosopher is always a physician, but ultimately he lays under his knife not just a single individual or a culture, but all of mankind.

In his early work Nietzsche often ties the role of physician of culture to the philosopher's estimation of the value of existence, which is part of his function as lawgiver. Informed by his observation of man, the philosopher legislates "the measure, stamp, and weight of things" (*SE* 3). In doing so he models and molds his culture, if not the culture of his today, then the culture of tomorrow and the day after tomorrow. There is, therefore, a danger for the philosopher who lives in a motley and discordant age like our own, an age when neither individuals nor peoples are unified, whole, and healthy. The great peril for such unfortunate philosophers, as Nietzsche declared respecting himself, is "[*n*]*ausea* at man" (*EH* "Destiny" 6).[80] A modern philosopher of refined tastes will have to withdraw from his contemporaries or risk suffering from the sight of man, and thereby from life, as a result of which he may *under*-estimate the value of existence. But withdrawal is the way to decline, to self-induced depressive states that debilitate a man and so render him morose and useless, to himself as well as to others, as a philosopher. How different, and how beneficial, the judgment of thinkers surrounded by a healthy and cheerful nobility! The philosophers who lived among the Greeks of the highest period, for example, "had life itself before and around them in luxuriant perfection." Therefore, their "verdict … on the value of existence" will always be significant, not only as an accurate estimation of the worth of man at his best, but also as a reminder of human potential, and thereby as a stimulant to life (*SE* 3).

In *Beyond Good and Evil* Nietzsche writes that the philosopher "demands of himself a judgment, a Yes or No … about life and the value of life" (*BGE* 205). Later he will claim to count it an objection if a philosopher considers the value of life a problem, for "judgments of value, concerning life, for it or against it, can, in the end, never be true" (*TI* "Socrates" 2). If we are to take him at his word (for it is possible to read this remark in context as a rhetorical broadside aimed for effect at Socrates), then when he declares in two of his last works that his happiness depends on a Yes and a No (*TI* "Maxims" 44 and *A* 1), we must understand him to have in mind something other than affirmative and negative judgments of the value of life. We know that Nietzsche in his maturity consistently condemns the denial of life: the affirmation of human existence, even in its ugliest, most nauseating aspects, is among the highest of philosophical conditions. This is not to say that the philosopher should yield uncritically to the squalid reality surrounding him, for his very act of affirmation, noble in itself, may well transfigure this reality, or at a minimum initiate the transfiguring work to be carried on by future philosophers. We should, then, read Nietzsche as directing his Yes and No, not at the value of life itself, but rather at present and future personal and cultural conditions and the life they make possible, necessitate even. This is why he associates, in the two late works I have just mentioned, the Yes and the No with "a straight line, a goal." The philosopher's gaze is on the summit of the future and his feet seek a path up its slopes, direct if not necessarily smooth.

As a physician in the strict sense acts on the basis of knowledge of anatomy and physiology, we might wonder to what extent Nietzsche's cultural physician is a knower of men and society. In his earliest notes Nietzsche more often than not is dismissive of all claims to knowledge, as to both their reliability and their value. This is the period of "On Truth and Lies in a Nonmoral Sense," according to which knowledge is merely the invention, grounded upon self-delusion, of a haughty and ephemeral species.[81] Our desire to know, then, is unrealizable, perhaps even self-contradictory (*P* 114); but even if we could make sense of the idea, it remains true that we gain much more from creating than from knowing (*P* 84). Science and knowledge must be controlled by philosophy as "a form of artistic invention" (*P* 53), and the "poorly demonstrated philosophy of Heraclitus possesses far more artistic value than do all the propositions of Aristotle" (*P* 61). This last thought contains in sum the insight and approach of the thinker-artist.

In his later work Nietzsche is somewhat more respectful of knowledge, but his attitude is, at best, ambivalent, and many have gone further and dismissed it as inconsistent. The charge of inconsistency may be facile, but it is understandable given the ambiguity of Nietzsche's remarks. In the fifth book of *The Gay Science*, for example, he associates the philosopher with "the seeker after knowledge" but then observes, in the same section, that philosophers "simply do not believe in any 'men of knowledge'" (*GS* 351). In *Beyond Good and Evil* 210 he reflects on the philosophers' "passion for knowledge," but in the following section he defines genuine philosophers as legislators whose "'knowing' is *creating*," which expression is reminiscent of his early formulation that the philosopher "knows in that he invents, and he invents in that he knows" (*P* 53). Then there is the preface to the *Genealogy*, in the first sentence of which Nietzsche refers to "we men of knowledge" (*GM* "Preface" 1), though later in the book he surrounds this same phrase with quotation marks, which ought not to surprise us given that he questions not only the value but even the justification of the will to truth and claims that those who "*still have faith in truth*" are "far from being *free* spirits" (*GM* 3.24). But can there be knowledge if there is no truth? In any case, my point is not that there is no explaining such remarks, but only that Nietzsche is no friend of knowledge or truth in the simple, straightforward fashion of the typical philosopher, scholar, or scientist.

Sometime in the spring of 1888 Nietzsche referred to himself in a notebook entry as "half artist, half bird and metaphysician" (*KSA* 13:14[1]), which is reminiscent of a note from the time he was busy with *Beyond Good and Evil* in which he seems to describe himself as having "an anti-metaphysical but artistic worldview" (*KSA* 12:2[186]). These two notes are unusual, admittedly; but they call to mind Nietzsche's many remarks associating the philosopher with the artist, and more than merely associating the two. I have already mentioned his early conception of the philosopher-artist, the type who following the withdrawal of metaphysics "returns to art its rights" (*P* 37). The philosopher conceived in these terms recognizes the value even of "*indemonstrable* philosophizing," which may generate ideas unverifiable (and unfalsifiable) by the methods of science that are nevertheless worth more than any scientific proposition (*P* 61). I take this insight from an early note, but it is not the expression of a mere passing fancy. In *Philosophy in the Tragic Age of the Greeks*, which he eventually abandoned but to which he devoted serious attention for some time, Nietzsche insists that philosophy is propelled by the "illogical power ... of creative imagination," and that "non-provable philosophic thinking has its value" (*PTG* 40–1). Nor is it difficult to detect the continuing influence of these ideas on Nietzsche's mature thought, on, for example, his conceptions of the will to power, the eternal return, and the wisdom of Zarathustra, all of which—and even whatever there may be of "truth" in them—are the result of Nietzsche's own creativity and interpretation.[82]

The creative-interpretive task of the philosopher is a recurrent theme in *Beyond Good and Evil*; philosophy itself is depicted in this book as the will to world creation (*BGE* 9). If the philosopher is a friend of "truth," he is so in a most privately personal sense, sufficiently idiosyncratic to justify the scare quotes (*BGE* 43). And when Nietzsche characterizes his philosophers of the future as tempters or attempters (*Versucher*, *BGE* 42), he thereby associates them with Dionysus, "the great … tempter (*Versucher*) god," and so also with himself, the "disciple and initiate" of this god (*BGE* 295). As the god of tragedy Dionysus is an art-deity, and according to Nietzsche this philosopher-god would like to make humans "more beautiful" (*BGE* 295). As a Dionysian philosopher Nietzsche admires in particular the beauty of his own philosophical reflections, a beauty that is truth only after aging and growing stale (*BGE* 296).[83]

Even on those occasions when Nietzsche concedes (whether sincerely or merely for the sake of argument) that scholarship and science may discover the truth about this or that matter, he is clear that the discovery does not settle all questions. The philosopher need not humbly submit to the findings of the *wissenschaftlicher Mensch* (the scholarly-scientific man). The judgment in this context that "the truth is inestimable and cannot be criticized" is an "overestimation of truth" (*GM* 3.25), which is to say an overestimation of the *value* of truth. There may be higher values than truth, and it is the supreme task of philosophy and art, of *the philosopher as artist*, to determine which *truths or untruths* are most valuable. It just is not the case, then, that Nietzsche "thinks that whenever a scientific explanation is available, one should accept that explanation."[84] The scholars, the scientists, and the philosophical laborers perhaps, the unfree spirits constrained by the "unconditional will to truth"—yes, perhaps these types should revere the truth and the consensus of their day concerning the proper method for discovering it. But the philosopher has a different goal, a higher task, and those who would make of him a lackey of science reveal thereby their own impoverished conception of philosophy. Or so I imagine Nietzsche would say.

I have referenced the reading of Nietzsche as a Pyrrhonian philosopher, or at least as a philosopher deeply indebted to this tradition.[85] Though I myself am not inclined to classify Nietzsche as a skeptic, I do believe he found a certain significant value in skepticism, a value allied with his conception of philosophy as a creative endeavor. In *Beyond Good and Evil* he writes of a vigorous form of skepticism that "does not believe but does not lose itself in the process." Here Nietzsche's eye is on the social-political use one can make of skepticism, but the general idea is that skepticism clears the ground of accepted (and fashionably acceptable) "truths" and thereby "gives the spirit dangerous freedom" (*BGE* 209). When I read this in the context of Nietzsche's suggestion that the philosophers of the future will be skeptics in this sense (*BGE* 210), and when in turn I read this in the context of his insistence that the philosopher's "knowing" is creating (*BGE* 211), and this in association with his early identification of philosophy, art, and "the *mythical drive*" (*P* 53), then I cannot help remarking how closely Nietzsche's own philosophical practice exemplifies his early conception of the philosopher as one whose intellectual-spiritual *creations* are unconstrained by the constricting canons of scientific empiricism (*P* 53). In short, I believe that Nietzsche occasionally employs skepticism to underwrite, motivate, or to accompany and illuminate the thought that there are no inviolable truths to which the philosopher must conform his speculations on pain of being convicted of uttering demonstrable falsehoods, or that the uttering of falsehoods is anyway not the most offensive of philosophical acts. This insight liberated Nietzsche to think as he pleased, to proclaim as his "truths" those ideas that moved him most deeply. Thus he once wondered in a notebook, "Why should one not be allowed to *play metaphysically*? and to expend on this a wholly enormous energy of creativity?"[86]

Here then we have one side of Nietzsche's life as a free spirit, free to rank anything that strikes him as noble or beautiful higher than everything other men call truth—free to formulate, teach, and believe even *indemonstrable* ideas. To give this attitude a name, we might call it "Creative-Pyrrhonism." The Creative-Pyrrhonist understands that (or, to employ a Pyrrhonian formula, it seems to him now that) no one knows the truth, if such a beast even exists, but he "nevertheless seizes" (*BGE* 209) on the thoughts that move him and, shunning the lure of religious, philosophical, or scientific dogmatism on one side, and of nihilistic-skeptical idleness and indecision on the other, he creates his own values, indeed his own world. And by following the trail of the fact that the world's creator has the freedom and power to be its destroyer as well, we may come to the root of Nietzsche's experimentalism. In the end this amounts to a form of self-experimentation, for more than all else he experiments with, and on, *his own mind*.[87]

Wisdom and the love of wisdom

Plato and Nietzsche were intellectual experimentalists—thinkers who drew and developed ideas from the deepest wells of creativity, and artists whose medium was the collection of these ideas taken as raw material. Their unconstrained creativity distinguishes them from most thinkers, as their informed and serious intellectuality distinguishes them from most artists. Their ideas center on subjects traditionally associated with philosophy, but given their artistic mode of thought I am reluctant to designate them with a word—"philosopher"—so laden with a confusion of meanings. I prefer to employ the intentionally untraditional expression, *thinker-artist*.

Recall that Plato erected a shrine to the Muses on the grounds of the Academy. Whether or not he wrote dithyrambs, lyric poems, and tragedies as a young man, as Diogenes reports (3.5), he was surely as inspired as any poet, and it is only through him that we have the conception of an artistic Socrates, a conception that captivated Nietzsche. The idea derives explicitly from Socrates' report in the *Phaedo* of the dream that urged him to practice *mousikê*, but it is implicit in Plato even apart from this report, for Plato himself was the artistic Socrates, the thoroughly artistic philosopher. In what other thinker does one find art as "a necessary correlative of, and supplement for science" (*BT* 14)? In none; only in Plato. In no other, that is, until Nietzsche himself.

Nietzsche's conception of the philosopher as a free spirit is an image of a man "practiced in maintaining himself on insubstantial ropes and possibilities and dancing even near abysses" (*GS* 347). If it is regrettable that he cannot keep pace with the scientists' ceaseless accumulation of knowledge, it would be even worse if he could, for the philosopher must not know too much; he is unfree when stuffed with knowledge (*GS* 381). These characterizations of the philosopher no doubt descend from Nietzsche's early notion of *indemonstrable* philosophizing, as must his similar thoughts about the nature of the sage. In his early notes he alludes to the possibility of wisdom "independent of any knowledge of science" (*PHT* 39); in *The Birth of Tragedy* he imagines "a realm of wisdom from which the logician is exiled" (*BT* 14); and much later in *Twilight of the Idols* he observes that "[w]isdom sets limits to knowledge too" (*TI* "Maxims" 5). One cannot emphasize often enough that although Nietzsche was thankful for science and scholarship, he envisioned the philosopher and the sage alike as superior to the products of any and every knowledge industry, as individuals who, when engaged in their highest and most characteristic activities, regard scholarly-scientific knowledge as valuable only to the extent that they might take it up, along with much other matter besides, into their creative experimentings with abysmally ungrounded possibilities. Knowledge is just one of the many colors on their palette.

The line from the ancients that runs to Nietzsche as a creative philosopher may begin with Heraclitus and pass through Socrates, but Plato decisively altered its trajectory. We have seen that Nietzsche's notion of Becoming is closer to Plato's radicalization of Heraclitus than to the surviving fragments of Heraclitus himself. And although, like Nietzsche, Socrates battered the popular sentiments of his age, he lacked the soul of the artist. Plato leveled the idols of his day with his own sort of hammer—Socrates' critical spirit comes to us primarily through Plato, author of the aporetic dialogues—but he combined this work with a boundlessly creative and inventive imagination. Despite Nietzsche's occasional eruptions to the contrary, Platonic philosophy is literary in the deepest possible sense, and will stand forever among the greatest *poetic* achievements of the west. Imagine a man in Athens, 425 BCE, asking a friend, "What is this practice I've been hearing such chatter about lately, this *philosophy*?" In reply his friend might point out Socrates, standing near the Agora or strolling in a palaestra, surrounded by a group of young men talking, talking, talking. Now imagine the same question 50 years later. This time the friend might level a finger in the direction of the shaded grove of Hekadêmos, out beyond the city walls, where Plato most likely was walking alone absorbed in thought, or sitting in his home nearby in silence, writing. Nietzsche was no Socrates on the prowl for public disputation. He was, like Plato, a quiet contemplative and a writer, a thinker and an artist.

But the question remains whether Plato and Nietzsche were wise or only lovers of wisdom, for the denomination "thinker-artist" may apply to the one type as well as to the other, characterizing either the expression of a man's wisdom or the mode of his philosophizing. My first inclination is to reply, as I have already, that Plato was a sage and Nietzsche a philosopher. But the precise course of the dividing line between these types is hard to plot, and neither Plato nor Nietzsche offers us sufficient guidance: they do not often address the distinction explicitly, and they never discuss the matter in detail. We have seen that Plato's Socrates says both that wisdom belongs only to the gods and also that humans may be wise. Humans may even become like god (*homoiôsis theôi*). May we assume that Plato intends to insinuate a distinction between Socrates and himself? We may assume; but we will never know. For his part, Nietzsche confesses in his early notes to being ashamed at the thought of describing himself as "one who is becoming wise" (*PHT* 47), which sentiment foreshadows his observation, recorded in the fifth book of *The Gay Science*, that "*modesty* ... invented the word 'philosopher' in Greece and left the magnificent overweening presumption in calling oneself wise to the actors of the spirit" (*GS* 351).[88] In this same book he claims that for some philosophers wisdom (*weisheit*) is merely a screen behind which they hide from spirit (*GS* 359); yet he is not an utter skeptic in this regard, for he refers to his own *gaya scienza* as a "secret wisdom (*weisheit*)" (*GS* 377).[89]

Plato and Nietzsche are more forthcoming about the nature of the philosopher, as we have seen. This is particularly true of Nietzsche, and one characterization of the type recurs as a leitmotif in most all of the works in which he addresses the matter directly. Nietzsche's philosopher is, above all, *untimely*. The idea comes through powerfully in his early essay on Schopenhauer (included in a collection aptly entitled *Untimely Meditations*), and recurs even in his last work, *Ecce Homo*, when in his account of this essay he describes the ideal philosopher (himself, really) as "a terrible explosive, endangering everything" (*EH* "UM" 3). *Beyond Good and Evil* is at heart a sustained assault on timeliness in every field of culture and thought, and the reference to the future in the subtitle confirms the point. In the fifth book of *The Gay Science* Nietzsche recommends his ideas to all those who, like him, are "untimely" (*GS* 377). With *Twilight of the Idols* he declares war against present and eternal idols alike, as he explains in the preface; he contrasts himself with timely men in "Maxims" 15; and he gives to one chapter the title "Skirmishes of an Untimely Man." As for the book that followed this, *The Antichrist*—the title says it all, I think. The book is so thoroughly untimely that there may not be ears to hear its message until after Nietzsche's death, as he suggests in the preface; and the subtitle of the work, *Revaluation of All Values*, stresses his opposition to the tendencies of his age.

Nietzsche often associates his idea of untimeliness with images of distance, height, and isolation obviously drawn after the model of his own life. In *Twilight of the Idols* we read:

> To live alone one must be a beast or a god, says Aristotle. Leaving out the third case: one must be both—a philosopher (*TI* "Maxims" 3).

I have offset this quote because for me it sums up Nietzsche's self-understanding, his conception of his task and of his life as well. From his earliest period he understood that a philosopher's mode of existence is more fully a manifestation of his philosophy than even his books (*P* 48), and his demand that philosophers live beyond good and evil (*TI* "Improvers" 1) is simultaneously a demand that they separate themselves from the judgment of their time and its cramped majorities. In *Ecce Homo* he calls his *Zarathustra* a "dithyramb on solitude" (*EH* "Wise" 8), and although he means to stress an intellectual solitude and cleanliness, he tends throughout his corpus to illustrate this mental state with descriptions of his preferred physical surroundings. In the mountains around Sils-Maria, the small Swiss town he discovered in 1881,[90] and to which he returned every summer from 1883 to 1888, Nietzsche felt at home. Here there was "no limit to the quiet, the altitude, the solitude" he required to think and to write. Here, he wrote, "*my* muses live."[91] The idea of the eternal return came to Nietzsche while walking beside a lake near Sils during his first stay in the town, and when he wrote in his notebook beneath his initial expression of the thought, "6000 feet above the sea and much higher above all human things" (*KSA* 9:11[141]), although he intended to communicate something of his intellectual-spiritual mood, he was writing quite literally as well: the Upper Engadine, in which Sils-Maria is situated, is very nearly 6,000 feet above sea level. The untimely men in *The Gay Science* "prefer to live on mountains, apart" (*GS* 377), and the philosopher in the *Genealogy* enjoys "mountains for company," mountains, like those surrounding Sils-Maria, "with *eyes* (that is, with lakes)" (*GM* 3.8). Whoever would understand the untimely message of *The Antichrist* "must be skilled in living on mountains" (*A* "Preface"), as was Nietzsche himself, who "understood and lived" philosophy "among ice and high mountains" (*EH* "Preface" 3).

Nietzsche's characterization of the philosopher as untimely bears on the question whether he himself was philosopher or sage. If the untimely philosopher is necessarily "the bad conscience of [his] time" (*BGE* 212), then he must be bound to his time and, therefore, unable to transcend it on his way toward wisdom. Even if he is necessarily "a man of tomorrow and the day after tomorrow" (*BGE* 212), if his task is the enhancement of man then he is still bound. As I have already mentioned, even with the image of Zarathustra before me I find it hard to imagine Nietzsche a sage. His model of the philosopher is not a man who aspires to wisdom, but rather a ploughshare uprooting the intellectual weeds of his day, or a miner who tunnels beneath the foundations of a culture, setting charges beneath every cornerstone. In accord with this model Nietzsche may be, as I have written in the Introduction, *the eternal philosopher*.

This distinction between Plato as a sage and Nietzsche as a philosopher depends of course on there being a difference between philosophy and wisdom, but there are reasons to doubt that there must always be such a difference. Cicero relates a story told by Plato's student Heraclides that may be taken to assimilate philosophy to wisdom. It seems that Pythagoras when passing through Phlius[92] was asked by the local tyrant what it is to be a philosopher. Pythagoras replied that some men attend the Olympic Games to buy and sell among the gathered crowds and thereby to earn a profit; others come to compete, and through victory to acquire honor and fame; but then there are those who attend in order to watch, the curious souls eager to observe the festivities. The philosophers, Pythagoras concluded, are like these curious observers, for they long to know and to contemplate the nature of things. These are the best sort of men.[93] In this account of the philosopher I detect a resemblance to the sage. The philosopher here is not lacking and seeking a thing; he is admiring the object of his love, which is present before him. This account is compatible with an aspect of Socrates' description of desire in the *Symposium* that I have yet to mention. Socrates argues that even the lover who possesses his beloved still lacks it in a way, for he desires its continued presence into the future, which, as not yet actual, may still be counted a lack and therefore an object of desire (200b–e). But this at least implies that the philosopher as a lover of wisdom may after all possess wisdom, which is to say that the philosopher may be wise. What he lacks, and therefore desires, is not wisdom itself but the permanent retention of his wisdom. It is true that Diotima describes Eros, and by implication the philosopher, as lacking wisdom, but in light of this account of what it is to lack and to desire, we might take her use of "wise" to mean "assuredly permanently wise," in which case we would be free to designate the philosopher as wise even while admitting our uncertainty as to the permanence of his state. Here we have a glimpse, even *within* the *Symposium*, of the possibility of the philosopher as sage, a type I suggested above that Plato intimates *through* this work, and that Plato himself instantiated.

Diogenes Laertius reports that Pythagoras called himself a philosopher, a lover of wisdom, because no mortal may claim to be wise, which designation must be reserved for God.[94] This, too, comes to us by way of Plato's student Heraclides, and we have seen that Plato himself sometimes reserves wisdom for the divine. But we have seen as well that on occasion he allows that mortals may be wise. He may even allude in the *Symposium* to Pythagoras's account of philosophy-as-wisdom when he has Socrates mention those who love money, those who love sport, and those who love wisdom just prior to elaborating his earlier point that whoever desires a thing desires to possess it forever (205d–206a). So, again, perhaps we may take the lover of wisdom, the philosopher, to be a sage who desires to remain wise forever. In this case the "philosopher" would be a wise man seen through the limiting prism of time—wise in fact, even if cognitive restrictions on our temporal perception preclude subjective certainty—whereas the "sage" would be the same man regarded *sub specie aeternitatis*.

In his account of philosophy in the *Republic*, Plato associates the "love" in the "love of wisdom" with desire (*epithumein*, 475b5), as he does in the *Symposium*, but he does not gloss desire as indicating a lack that generates a (perhaps endless) search. To the contrary, he relates the philosopher's love (*philein*) to the mutual love among family members (*stergonta*, 474c10), also to being glad at the sight of someone (*aspazesthai*, 479e9). The philosopher is glad when contemplating that which is (479e), and the philosopher thus conceived is not lacking and in pursuit of the object of his love. He has attained his beloved; he beholds it, cherishes it, and takes delight in it. The philosopher, in a word, is wise.

If we may associate the philosopher and the sage in this way, then we may translate the φιλεῖν implicit in *philosophia* as "to admire," as one admires something or someone present. One may be said to admire the flowers in a garden through which one wanders lost in thought, and lost as well in the beauty of the flora. The wise man is such a wanderer, and all things real and imagined are the flowers in his garden. So if we dismiss the constricted accounts of the philosopher as eternal seeker or as a student of the discipline of philosophy, we may characterize the type either as a "philosopher" who aspires to transcend philosophy and become wise, or as a sage who wanders in admiration through all the gardens of his wisdom. In both cases we shall have in mind an existential-metaphysical experimentalist, a creatively pondering man, a thinker-artist.

None of this, by the way, has necessarily to do with knowledge or the will to truth. Solon appears on every known list of the Greeks' Seven Sages, yet he believed much that today we dismiss as false. The thunderbolt steers all things, bafflingly declares the sagacious Heraclitus. If Plato is wise, his wisdom is manifest in his dialogues, which is to say in prose-poetic assemblages of dramatic encounters, exploratory flights of fancy, arguments, allegories, myths, and the jostling together of irreconcilable sentiments. The dialogues may contain expressions of the truth, but their wisdom resides in the whole rather than in any particular proposition. The wise man, then, need not know the truth; and if he does know the truth, he need not care; and if he cares, he may nevertheless have higher values; and even if on occasion he recognizes truth as the supreme value, this is only on occasion and in some contexts. Nietzsche once wrote in a letter to a friend: "Knowledge, art, and philosophy are now growing into one another so much in me that I shall in any case give birth to a centaur one day."[95] In this context I denominate the polymorphous offspring Nietzsche has in mind—*wisdom*.

I have suggested that the philosopher and the wise man in some cases may be identical. I have even suggested that Plato himself may have been such a man. But whether Plato or Nietzsche was in fact a philosopher-sage I cannot determine with confidence. These men are just too difficult to know. Still, as I have said, I am on occasion inclined to regard Plato rather than Nietzsche as wise. There is a serenity in Plato that one rarely detects in Nietzsche, who so often comes across as agitated. This distinction corresponds to the fact—anyway this seems to me to be a fact—that whereas Nietzsche is profound, Plato is sublime. Is one of these states superior to the other? I would not like to say, or rather I prefer to imagine a condition in which the two align and come together, the condition of a mind well accustomed to deep diving that remains undisturbed by its gloomy insights, a mind that can gaze into the abyss without the abyss glaring back. The man possessed of such a mind would be both profound and sublimely serene, and he would echo Nietzsche's remark that "whatever one casts into us, we take down into our depth—for we are deep, we do not forget— *and become bright again*" (*GS* 378). By rights these words belong to the man who can pose to himself the accursed questions without regarding them *as* accursed. This is the philosopher-sage or, in my terms, the thinker-artist.[96]

* * *

Finally, I end by recalling Nietzsche's Heraclitean image of the world as two wrestlers, locked so in eternal struggle that their entwined bodies intermingle, interpenetrate, and finally interfuse, becoming one while retaining their plurality, and blending as well with the referees and judges who are themselves participating combatants. The chaos of this melee generates an ordered cosmos, as from the ceaseless tension of opposition there arises the harmony of the All. This is the real.

What, then, is philosophy? What is wisdom? And what must we be, how must we live, as lovers of wisdom? To answer these questions it will help, I believe, to regard Plato and Nietzsche as the entangled wrestlers and ourselves as the officials caught up in the fight. As active participants we must never call the match, never declare a victor, and in fact our role is to keep the contest live, acting if necessary even as goads and instigators. Our minds are the dust churned up by the fray; they grow deeper and more expansive with every escalation of the conflict.

To me this image suggests that we must never take sides in the struggle between Plato and Nietzsche. We should engage energetically in the action, to be sure, but not for the sake of helping either man to win. We should in fact do all that we can to prolong the agon. The contest serves *our* needs only if the antagonists remain forever unreconciled, neither one crowned with laurel, neither ever lifeless in the dust. Superficially Plato and Nietzsche are opposed, their specific ideas distinctly identifiable and distinguishable one from the other. But at bottom, in the depths beneath the surface, they are one in spirit, united as the *artists* of their ideas. Their creativity binds them even as the colors of their creations set them apart. But these colors are merely the surface features of their masks, and we who would learn from them—would learn from both of them at once, and thereby learn at last about *ourselves*—we must look through the differences between the two masks to see the one great thing behind them.

Notes

Introduction

1   The details in this brief biography are uncertain. Was Plato a wrestler? Did he write tragedies and later burn them? We do not know. We cannot even be sure of the facts of his involvement in Italian and Syracusan affairs. Our biographical information comes for the most part from late sources and the dubious "Seventh Letter."

2   If Nietzsche's final madness resulted from syphilis, which was the original diagnosis, then we could attribute his collapse to decisions he made himself; but these would have been innocent decisions resulting from a near virginal ignorance of erotic matters. However, there is today no clear agreement that the cause of his illness was syphilis in fact. For a diagnosis of bipolar affective disorder with psychotic features, see Cybulska 2000. For a review of the case in general, including a diagnosis of retro-orbital meningioma, see Huenemann 2013.

3   What I am here calling a "creation" story would more accurately be termed a "construction" story, for the deity in Plato's *Timaeus* does not create the world *ex nihilo* but rather fashions it into its present form from preexistent material.

4   Despite the popular legend, Socrates nowhere asserts unambiguously that he knows that he knows nothing. On this, see Fine 2008.

5   The *Theaetetus* may be such a work.

6   Zuckert 2009 organizes the dialogues according to their dramatic dates, which for the most part are more secure than any dates of composition. See her rationale in the Introduction ("Platonic Dramatology"). Anderson and Osborn 2009 also follows the dramatic dates. Lampert 2010 follows the dramatic dates as well. See his Introduction, which includes a brief critical comment on Zuckert's dating (p. 15 n. 22).

7   Assuming here that the standard dating is correct, among the early dialogues are the *Apology*, *Euthyphro*, and *Crito*; among the middle are the *Republic*, *Symposium*, and *Phaedrus*; and among the late are the *Sophist*, *Statesman*, and *Philebus*.

8   Nietzsche, by the way, shared this opinion, or so it seems from his early lectures on Plato (*KGW* II.4: 98–9 and 168).

9   For an exception to the contemporary consensus, see Tomin 1997.

10 A "*ripened* freedom of spirit … permits one to take the paths of many varied and opposed ways of thinking" (*HH* "Preface" 4).

11 Letter to Peter Gast (Heinrich Köselitz), 5 October 1879 (Middleton 1996, 169).

12 See, for example, Cate 2002, 451 and Marie von Bradke's reminiscence in Gilman and Parent 1987, especially pages 189–90.

13 Magnus 1986, 83–4.

14 Ibid., 84–5.

15 Breazeale 1990, xvii–xxiii. For similar accounts of Nietzsche's hectic authorial activities during his late period, see Brobjer 2010 (especially pp. 20–2) and 2011, and Endres and Pichler 2013.

16   Montinari 2003, 97–9.

17   All serious thinkers have levels and layers, but none has so many as do Plato and Nietzsche. The fewer the layers the more easily a philosopher may be understood with the assistance of secondary sources. Kant, for example, is difficult in the extreme, but his ideas are thoroughly communicable through commentary and analysis. It might actually be *easier* to come to know Kant in this way. A book such as the one you are now reading may illuminate some aspects of Plato's and Nietzsche's ideas, especially as they relate to one another, but with these two it is always advisable to read their works and to read them again, and then to read them many more times in addition. For secondary sources it is best, I think, to study philologists on Plato's use of language, his style and technical vocabulary, and to acquaint oneself with ancient Greek history and culture, for so much of Plato is set in and refers or alludes to his (or Socrates') contemporary world. For Nietzsche it is best, again, to know the ancients well, and also to know those of his contemporaries or near contemporaries by whom he was most profoundly influenced, including not only the greats such as Goethe, Schopenhauer, and Wagner, but also the many philosophers and scientists whose names are largely forgotten today but who affected Nietzsche by evoking from him either consent or disagreement.

18   It is true that Nietzsche refers to *Zarathustra* as "the Yes-saying part of [his] task" (*EH* "BGE" 1); but that he knew that he must sustain and perhaps even expand his program of affirmation may be indicated by his several references to *Zarathustra* as the "entrance hall" to his philosophy. (On these matters, see Brobjer 2006, 285; and for a related point regarding Nietzsche's program of affirmation, see Brobjer 2011, 254–5. Loeb 2010, 213–14n. 13 is skeptical of Brobjer's interpretation of Nietzsche's remarks, but with my "sustain and perhaps even expand" just above I make a point more modest than Brobjer's.)

Chapter 1: Art and Reason

1   See, for example, *The Birth of Tragedy*, in which work Nietzsche writes that "we cannot fail to see in Socrates the one turning point and vortex of so-called world history" (*BT* 15).

2   Socrates appears as the lead character in Aristophanes' comedy *The Clouds*, and he is the protagonist as well of Xenophon's *Memorabilia, Apology, Symposium,* and *Oeconomicus*; he appears briefly also in Xenophon's *Anabasis* (3.1).

3   Gregory Vlastos was the dean of this approach. See, for example, Vlastos 1991. For more recent work in this tradition, see Brickhouse and Smith 2000.

4   Yet Nietzsche once hoped for a time "when we will, in seeking to advance ourselves morally and rationally, prefer to take in our hands the memorabilia of Socrates, rather than the Bible … " (*WS* 86). Though Nietzsche does not refer to Xenophon by name here, his mention of "die Memorabilien des Sokrates" is likely an allusion to Xenophon's Socratic *Apomnêmoneumata*.

5   Ever the old philologist, Nietzsche wrote this line in Greek. It is a play on Homer's description of the Chimaera at *Iliad* 6.181.

6   Marsilio Ficino (1433–99) was a Florentine humanist scholar, translator, and philosopher. He was the first to translate into Latin the complete works of Plato and Plotinus (and much else besides—the Hermetica, for example).

7 The first volume of the series, in which the "General Introduction" appears, was published in 1804. For more on this, see Lamm 2000.

8 On this subject see the very good collection of essays in Press 2000. See also Klagge and Smith 1992.

9 Socrates occasionally speaks in private with a small group of friends, but this fact does not obscure the contrast with Plato that I intend to stress here.

10 As John Dillon once remarked, "we really do not know … why Plato composed his dialogues, or what role they were designed to play in the social or intellectual life of his school" (Dillon 1999, 207).

11 Nehamas 1985, 30.

12 Ibid., 29.

13 Ibid., 26.

14 Ibid., 41.

15 Woodruff 2002 and 2007 urge points similar to my own concerning the distinction between Plato and Socrates and similarities between Plato's and Nietzsche's conceptions of philosophy.

16 Breazeale 1990, 127.

17 See the approving reference to science also in *TI* "Reason" 3. (From *TI* "Reason" 2 and, especially, 5 it is clear that Nietzsche did not imagine that natural science can attain to unvarnished truth.)

18 See note 4 above, and consider that at *HH* 433 Nietzsche calls Socrates a "free spirit" (cf. *HH* 437). The classic account of Nietzsche as an admirer of Socrates is Kaufmann 1974, 391–411.

19 Magee 2000 exaggerates Wagner's anticipation of Nietzsche's thesis that Greek tragedy grew out of the interplay of Apollinian and Dionysian forces (pp. 296–301), as one can see for oneself by reading the relevant passage near the beginning of "Art and Revolution" (in Wagner 1993, 23–65; see pp. 32–3 in particular) and as is made clear in Silk and Stern 1981, 214–16.

20 I explain these Kantian ideas with attention to Schopenhauer's concerns and in his preferred terminology.

21 Here I oversimplify somewhat Schopenhauer's more technical-historical objection, which may be found in *WWR* 1: "Appendix: Criticism of the Kantian Philosophy" (see in particular pp. 473–7).

22 Nietzsche dedicated the book (his first) to Wagner, as he announced in his "Preface to Richard Wagner."

23 Nietzsche uses the word "*Apollinischen*," hence the English "Apollinian," with an "i," rather than the seemingly more natural "Apollonian," with an "o."

24 Although it is true that in his preface to the second edition of *The Gay Science* Nietzsche calls the Greeks "superficial," he attributes their superficiality to their profundity (*GS* "Preface" 4); and in *The Birth of Tragedy* he calls the Greeks "profound" (*BT* 9) and refers to the greatest of their artists as deep abysses (*BT* 13).

25 The phrase echoes an only slightly less concise expression of the same idea at *BT* 13.

26 The equation does not appear in these terms in *The Birth of Tragedy* (I take it from *TI* "Socrates" 4), but its content is identical to "the three basic forms of optimism" embodied in the "Socratic maxims" that Nietzsche analyzes in *BT* 14.

27 Kaufmann 1974 maintains that Nietzsche's late conception of Dionysus incorporates the relevant elements of his early conception of the Apollinian (p. 129).

28 See, for example, *WWR* 1:17, 24, and 27.

29 In *EH* "Destiny" Nietzsche writes throughout as if he has successfully attained to this condition.

30 I take Nietzsche's notion of *amor fati* (the love of fate), which appears in this same section of *The Gay Science* and recurs in *Ecce Homo* (*EH* "Clever" 10), as well as his "formula for happiness" ("a Yes, a No, a straight line, a goal") as expressed in *Twilight of the Idols* ("Maxims" 44) and *The Antichrist* (1), to be instances and reminders of this same aspiration.

31 Suffering as a theme is explicit in *GM* 3.20 and 28.

32 Quoted in Frank 2010, 720.

33 In a late note on the tragic artist, for example, Nietzsche writes that it is "a question of *strength* (of an individual or of a people), *whether* and *where* the judgment 'beautiful' is applied. The feeling of plenitude, of *dammed-up strength* … the feeling of *power* applies the judgment 'beautiful' even to things and conditions that the instinct of impotence could only find *hateful* and 'ugly'" (*WP* 852).

34 Socrates' last words: "O Crito, we owe a rooster to Asclepius. So offer it (to him) and don't neglect it" (118a). For more on decadence, see pp. 138–41.

35 At *HH* 261 Nietzsche wonders whether "Plato, had he remained free of the Socratic enchantment, might not have discovered a still higher type of philosophic being." To my mind Plato himself *was* this higher type. Halliwell 2011 notes that Plato's writing "at certain key junctures claims for *itself* nothing less than the status of a new kind of philosophical poetry and art: the status, indeed, of 'the greatest music' and even of 'the finest and best tragedy'" (p. 241; the quotations in Halliwell's text are from *Phd.* 61a, which I discuss on p. 44, and *Lg.* 817b, which I discuss on p. 29).

36 Postcard to Paul Deussen, 16 November 1887 (*KGB* 954).

37 The expression is reminiscent of Diotima's speech in the *Symposium*, but here in the *Republic* Plato does *not* appear to intend a metaphysical aim like the love of the Form of *beauty*.

38 For an account of the sophistication of Plato's engagement with the poets, see Halliwell 2000.

39 *KGW* II.4, 161 (translated by Andrew Davis).

40 *De Demosthene* 7.

41 Ibid., 6.

42 Ibid., 7.

43 Ibid.

44 Ibid., 23.

45 *On the Sublime* 4.6.

46 Ibid., 13.3–4.

47 Quoted from Thesleff's Introduction to his *Studies in the Styles of Plato*. See page 7, note 1 of the collection in Thesleff (2009).

48 See, for example, *Men.* 76c–e.

49 Tarrant 1955 declares the *Symposium* "a *tour-de-force* of oblique narration" (p. 22). The dialogue is Apollodorus's narration to an unnamed friend of speeches and conversations overheard at a symposium not by himself but by Aristodemus, who was present at the event but could not recall all that was said (as Apollodorus cannot recall all that Aristodemus told him). Among these speeches was Socrates' retelling of a conversation he once had with a woman named Diotima. So Diotima's speech, which is the philosophical core of the work, comes to us by way of Socrates as recounted by Aristodemus as retold by Apollodorus (and as written by Plato). With its multi-layered framing and extensive indirect discourse, the dialogue calls

attention to its form, thereby demanding that readers take account of the formal elements when reflecting on the work's philosophical import.

50   But see the discussion of Plato's prose meter, specifically the clausulae, in Brandwood 1992 (pp. 103–7 in particular). The end of the line at *Phdr.* 241d1 scans as dactylic hexameter, the epic meter, as Socrates himself points out.

51   Scholars tend to divide Plato's works into the imitative, like the *Euthyphro*, and the mixed type (the reported dialogue), like the *Republic*. But strictly speaking *all* of Plato's works are pure imitations. The distinction among the types as presented in the *Republic* is based on the *author's* mode of presentation, not the characters'. Plato always purely imitates, even when his character Socrates is delivering a mixed discourse. Socrates himself never purely imitates; the closest he comes to pure imitation is in the imitative parts of his mixed reports, and even then, in truth, it is *Plato* who is imitating *through* his imitation of Socrates imitating.

52   See Nietzsche's reflections on his own dependence on art in, for example, *HH* "Preface" 1 and 2.

53   Nietzsche prefers to view art from the perspective of the creator rather than from that of the spectator, as his critique of Kant's aesthetics at *GM* 3.6 makes clear.

54   On this episode of Nietzsche's life, see Small 2005. For a more detailed and fully biographical account, see Cate 2002 (especially Chapters 26–9, pp. 320–91).

55   Middleton 1996. For "suffering excessively" and "unendurable solitude" (which are my paraphrases of Nietzsche's words), see pp. 240–1; for "black despair," see p. 282; for "absurdly alone," see p. 283; for " … solitude too long," see p. 199. Nietzsche occasionally employs the language of isolation and solitude to represent his philosophical originality and uncanniness, and there may be a shade of this in the "absurdly alone" I have quoted. There is also, however, a clear indication of his personal loneliness, as there are similar indications throughout his correspondence.

56   Nietzsche's hymns in praise of pain and suffering (as, for example, at *GS* 19, *BGE* 225, and *TI* "Maxims" 8) read at times and at least in part as words of encouragement addressed to himself. In this regard the preface to the second edition of *The Gay Science* is most revealing.

57   *KGW* II.4, 8 (translated by Andrew Davis).

58   All references in this section are to the *Republic*.

59   The procedure is not "roundabout" in fact. The approach, which is meticulously structured and obviously intentional, permits Plato to write about ethical and political philosophy simultaneously.

60   *Kallipolis* (which means, literally, noble or beautiful city-state): *R.* 527c2.

61   For more on the vexed question of whether there actually was any such ancient quarrel, see Most 2011.

62   For much more on Platonic Forms, see pp. 51–61. Throughout this work I capitalize the word "Form" and italicize the name of the Form itself to emphasize the Forms' metaphysical (and therefore from our usual perspective, peculiar) status.

63   Socrates' assertions that (a) there are Forms of artifacts like tables (596b), and (b) that the Forms are created (597b–d) are anomalous in the Platonic corpus (though Forms of *shuttle* and other tools may be indicated at *Cra.* 389c–390a). According to the standard account, there are Forms only of naturally occurring kinds of things and these Forms exist eternally, independent of the creative activity of any god or gods.

64   For more on the meaning of the verb *to be* in this connection, see pp. 48–51.

65 Tragedians portray human beings and human actions, which obviously are not produced by craftsmen in the way that tables are. But humans are generated by other humans (through reproduction), and they and some of their actions (just acts, for example) participate in the Form of *human* and, for example, the Form of *justice*.

66 *R.* 598d8–9, 607a2–3. At *Tht.* 152e Socrates calls Homer the supreme practitioner of tragedy.

67 Plato makes a similar point about the ignorance of poets in the *Ion*, but in this dialogue he mentions only briefly the consequences for the audience of citizen spectators (at 535d–e). He makes the same point with respect to the activities of the sophists throughout the dialogues. Sophists are ignorant of the just and unjust, yet they frequently work their persuasive magic on individuals and cities alike in arenas in which justice is the issue at hand. This is a major theme of the *Gorgias* (see pp. 129–31). Book 2 of the *Laws* is dedicated almost exclusively to the education of citizens through the proper employment of music (which includes poetry).

68 pp. 28–9.

69 Halliwell 2002 (the quotation is from p. 74, and Halliwell expands on his use of the label "romantic puritan" on pp. 94–7). Halliwell 2011 labels the all too common claim that Plato "banished the poets" a "reductive slogan" (p. 244). Halliwell 2012 is quite good on Plato's ideas about, and relation to, poetry, both in the *Republic* and in general (pp. 155–207).

70 I call Athens small relative to the contemporary United States and the major European nations. Relative to other ancient Greek *poleis* Athens was immense, and not actually a *polis* but rather an *ethnos* (a "nation") according to Cohen 2000. Cohen cites "300,000 or more" as an estimate of the total population of Attica (p. 17). The number of free men regularly active in the social-political life of Athens itself would have been smaller; but even if we opt for the largest plausible estimate of this class of men, their numbers would be sufficiently small that Plato might worry *legitimately* about the effects of their character and conduct on Athenian traditions and institutions. Consider the turmoil stirred up in Athens by Alcibiades and his friends, and of the harm done by Alcibiades alone during the Peloponnesian War.

71 At *HH* 261 Nietzsche calls Plato "the incarnate desire to become the supreme philosophical giver of laws and founder of states."

72 All following references are to the *Laws*. Very good on this work in its social, political, and historical context is Morrow 1993.

73 Later it is implied that this third group will not sing in public but only among a few intimate friends (*Lg.* 665d–666d).

74 Plato's expression is "approaching 40 years," but I assume he means to include everyone in the third chorus and thus all men at least 30 years of age.

75 *Sussitia*, as were standard in Crete and Sparta. On the common meals in Sparta, see Plutarch's *Lycurgus* 10–12.

76 For Plato's interest in the cultural practices related to the symposium, see Tecuşan 1990.

77 *technêi … epistêmêi*, 532c6.

78 *ouk emphrones*, 534a2; *ekphrôn*, 534b5; *ho nous mêketi en autôi enêi*, 534b6.

79 *mania*, 245a2; *tôn mainomenôn*, 245a8.

80 *Nicomachean Ethics* 10.7 (1177b26–1178a1).

81 Socrates' linguistic history may be incorrect, but "mantis" and "mania" do in fact descend from the same Indo-European root. See Flower 2008, 23.

82 *teletôn*, 244e2; *telestikên*, 265b4.

83 *prosepaisamen ... paidiai pepaisthai*, 265c1–9.

84 *tês philosophou manias te kai bakcheias*, 218b3–4.

85 *tôn dianoêmatôn hê ek tou nou pheromenê dunamis*, 71b3–4.

86 This part of the soul is referred to as *to theion* at 69d6. At 69c5–6 it is described as the "immortal principle (*archê*) of soul."

87 *alêtheias pêi prosaptoito*, 71e1.

88 The "immortal *archê* of soul," the human soul's divine part encased in the head, also called *nous*, is Apollo; the power of the thoughts borne down from *nous* into the lowest cavity of the torso is Apollo's divine communication; the liver is the oracular seat (Apollo's temple or the adyton inside); the visual images the liver reflects like a mirror from the impressions received from *nous* are the Pythia's inspired utterances; the part of the mortal soul dwelling around the liver that has no share in reason or wisdom (*logos*, *phronêsis*), and that consults the liver-oracle while asleep after having been made gentle and serene by a soothing inspiration (*epipnoia*) from *dianoia*, is the inquirer who has entered Apollo's temple after having purified himself and offered a sacrifice to the god; the fact that the oracular session begins when the "power of *phronêsis*" is fettered in sleep or altered through illness or divine enthusiasm corresponds to the Pythia in her mad mantic state when possessed by Apollo; and the *emphrôn* prophet who deciphers the enigmas of the sounds heard and the appearances seen during the consultation is the priest who understands and translates the Pythia's pronouncements.

89 Here it is ambiguous whether Socrates refers to everything he has said up to this point or only to his description of the afterlife.

90 Compare the *phaula* at 278c7 to the *phaulên* at 276e1.

91 On the irrational in Plato, see Dodds 1951, 207–35. See also Dodds 1945.

92 *Basic Writings of Nietzsche*, p. 98n. 10.

93 DL 4.1. Plato's shrine may have been located on his personal property nearby. On this, see Dillon 2005, 2–3 (including note 6).

Chapter 2: Being

1 Plato writes of wondering why something exists (*dia ti esti*) at, for example, *Phd.* 96a9.

2 This abstraction is thought by many to have been Thomas Aquinas's great conceptual achievement, though everyone admits that his Pagan, Christian, and Muslim predecessors contributed to the development of the Thomistic *esse*. On this, see Dewan 2000, Bradshaw 1999, and Gilson 2005. For remarks at least indirectly related, see the closing pages of "On the Terminology for *Copula* and *Existence*" and the opening pages of "Why Existence Does Not Emerge as a Distinct Concept in Greek Philosophy" in Kahn 2009.

3 This is not to say that Plato never employs the existential "is," but only that "in conceptualizing Being" he does not draw on a conception of Existence as such.

4 *On the Heavens* 3.1 (298b21).

5 Plato doubtless believed that he improved on Parmenides' account of nonbeing in the *Sophist* (237a–259b).

6   Even when his assertions that "it is" are not obviously construable as shorthand for
       a predicative use of "to be," they still may not be existential but rather veridical or
       locative. See Kahn 2009.

7   We can see the same point in positive terms when Socrates at *Phd.* 101b–c speaks of
       something coming to be (*gignomenon*, 101c3) but clearly has in mind its coming to
       be *x*, in this case its coming to be one or two.

8   The same holds for words like "real" and "reality." The "real" or the "fully real" is
       not that which exists as opposed to that which does not exist, but rather that which
       exists invariably as itself as opposed to that which exists at variance from self.

9   For more on this, see pp. 57–8.

10   On the possibility that the "is" of existence is isolated in the *Sophist*, and that Being
       is there identified as an independent Form, see the account of the *Sophist* in Chapter
       Five of Silverman 2002. In "The Greek Verb 'To Be' and the Concept of Being,"
       Charles H. Kahn writes that he has seen "exegetes furrowing their brow over the
       question whether Plato in a given passage of the *Sophist* means us to take *einai* in
       the existential or the copulative sense, whereas in fact he shows no sign of wishing
       to confront us with any such choice." See Kahn 2009, 19.

11   There is confusion (or at least ambiguity) about these matters even in the dialogues.
       For example, in the *Parmenides* (130a–c), Socrates (as a young man) explicitly
       affirms that there are essences (under the technical term "Form," on which see pp.
       51–61 of Chapter 2) of *justice, beauty*, and *goodness*, but is unsure about *human
       being, fire* and *water*. He denies that there are Forms of *hair, mud*, and *dirt*. *Phlb.*
       15a seems at least to imply a Form of *human being*, as *Men.* 72a–b suggests a Form
       of *bee*. At *R.* 596a–b Forms of *table* and *bed* are mentioned.

12   In my defense I appeal to the precedent of Plato's use of a craftsman deity (the
       Demiurge) in the *Timaeus*.

13   Even in the *Timaeus*, which dialogue includes a craftsman deity who models
       his work on eternal paradigms, the paradigms do not obviously exist in the deity's
       mind.

14   The notion that Forms are ideas in the divine mind goes back prior to the advent of
       either Christianity or Neoplatonism—back, for example, to the Hellenized Jew Philo
       of Alexandria (c. 20 BCE–c. 50 CE). Neoplatonism is so named from its following
       chronologically on an earlier development of Platonism referred to by scholars as
       "Middle Platonism."

15   The precise nature of this dependence relation, standardly summed up in the word
       "emanation," does not concern us here. For as basic an account as one is likely to
       find in Plotinus's always complex treatises, see *Ennead* 5.1. For general introductions
       to Plotinus, see Rist 1977, O'Meara 1995, and Hadot 1998.

16   For more on this subject see *Ennead* 5.5 (particularly sections 1–3), 5.9 (particularly
       sections 5–8), and 6.4 (for example sections 2–4).

17   Plotinus's account of participation is none too clear, and for the sake of simplicity
       I have ignored what may be a distinction between two different ways in which,
       according to Plotinus, Forms act causally on matter. For a more expansive treatment,
       see Strange 1992.

18   Keep in mind that, once we have set aside the existential connotations of the term,
       we may take Being as a synonym for "what-is." It is only for the sake of consistency
       that I employ "what-is" when writing of Parmenides and Being when writing of
       Plato.

19   Not a *creator* God, for the deity works with preexistent material.

20 *Physics* 8.1 (251b14–26).

21 This, I believe, is the straightforward reading of Plato's texts. But see Fine 1990.

22 In his lecture course now published as *The Pre-Platonic Philosophers*, Nietzsche refers (p. 84) to a passage near the end of Plato's *Cratylus* (439d–440a) in which Socrates argues that whatever is always changing never is any particular type of thing, for in every moment it is becoming different, with the consequence that whenever a would-be knower attempts to acquire knowledge of this (pseudo-) thing, it is at that very moment changing into something else.

23 This is sometimes referred to as the "argument from knowledge," or the "epistemological argument," for the existence of Forms. There are other arguments, the "semantic argument" for example, but this one will do for our purposes here. I should add that by employing as it does a mathematical object, this argument raises the question whether in Plato's metaphysics such objects are similar to, but technically distinct from, Forms. But this controversy need not detract from the general force of the argument.

24 At *Sph.* 253b–e the Stranger attributes expertise in this procedure to the philosopher. His own account of the "greatest kinds" and their interrelations does not proceed by collection and division as straightforwardly as does his account of the angler. Some scholars argue that these "kinds" (*genê*) are not Forms. See, for example, Teloh 1981 (in particular pp. 174–99). Holger Thesleff deals with this matter throughout the later chapters of his *Studies in Plato's Two-Level Model*, which is included in Thesleff 2009 (pp. 383–506).

25 On this subject, contrast *Sph.* 248c–249d with, for example, *Phd.* 78c–80b.

26 *Metaphysics* 1.6 (987b18ff.).

27 Aristotle himself refers to Plato's *agrapha dogmata* at *Physics* 4.2 (209b13–16). The notion of unwritten doctrines is most closely associated with the Milan-Tübingen school of Plato interpretation, in particular with the work of Hans Joachim Krämer and Konrad Gaiser. The most accessible works in this tradition are Krämer 1990, Reale 1997, and Szlezák 1999.

28 The most important work in this tradition is Cherniss 1945. There is also Vlastos 1963, a critical review of the original German version of Krämer's book (see previous note).

29 Sayre 2005.

30 In the *Timaeus* the Demiurge is introduced at 28a. This deity appears in other late dialogues as well, for example at *Sts.* 270a and *Phlb.* 27b.

31 *Ti.* 34b–37c. The World Soul appears in other late dialogues, for example at *Phlb.* 30a–d.

32 At *Ti.* 52a8 and 52d3 the Receptacle is called *chôra*, which indicates a place or the space in which something is situated.

33 The correct interpretation of just what it is that comes to be in the Receptacle is much disputed.

34 See, for example, *Phd.* 81d–82c, *Phdr.* 248b–249c, and *R.* 617d–618b.

35 At *R.* 389b Plato writes that "for the rulers of the *polis* … it is fitting to lie with respect to either enemies or citizens for the benefit of the *polis*." See also 382a–e and, for *the* noble lie, 414b–415d.

36 For example, the creation of humans in the *Timaeus* (40e–43a), and in the *Critias* the founding of Athens (109c–d) and of Atlantis (113b–114c).

37 *duscherôs pôs apodechomai*, *Euthphr.* 6a8.

38 See Else 1949.

39   This reading of Xenophanes is somewhat controversial, but if he was not strictly a monotheist, he was at least a critic of traditional anthropomorphic polytheism.

40   It is clear from *Euthphr.* 7a–8a that multiple gods in conflict and disagreement cannot serve as a standard or measure.

41   See Dillon 1996, 7.

42   The history of this identification is disputed. For a flavor of the debate see Dodds 1928 and Rist 1962. Also interesting in this connection is Gaiser 1980.

43   *Noêsis noêseôs noêsis, Metaphysics* 12.9 (1074b34).

44   In the *Symposium* Eros is called a great *daimôn*, and Socrates seems to have been notorious for claiming occasionally to hear a voice in his head that he referred to as his *daimonion*.

45   For Christians this assertion is true under only certain interpretations.

46   For more on Becoming, see the next chapter.

47   Nietzsche reformulates some of the attributes traditionally ascribed to Becoming, others he outright rejects.

48   The plurality is implicit in the previous section, in which Nietzsche refers to God's shadow being shown in multiple caves.

49   Recall that Parmenides hailed from the southern Italian town of Elea.

50   *Z*:I "On the Gift-Giving Virtue" 3.

51   " … nor does one ever say 'idol,' especially not in the most distinguished instance" (*TI* "Preface").

52   See, for example, *TI* "Reason" 1.

53   Similarly, the holy hermit in *Zarathustra* has not heard that God is dead (*Z*:I "Prologue" 2).

54   For more on this theme see, for example, *BGE* "What is Noble" and *WP* Book 4, section 1.

55   Cf. *Z*:IV "On the Higher Man" 1–2.

56   *GM* 1.14.

57   In *Beyond Good and Evil* Nietzsche marvels at the "enormous abundance of gratitude" manifest in the Greeks' religious spirit. "It is," he writes, "a very noble type of man that confronts nature and life in *this* way" (*BGE* 49).

58   For an extended treatment, see Gillespie 1995.

59   Frank 2010, 483.

60   Ibid., 790 (emphasis removed from "its").

61   See *GM* 3.24, *Z*:IV "The Shadow," and various notes in *WP*, for example 602 and 15. I do not mean to suggest that the proposition is an expression of Nietzsche's own position (though neither would I like to rule this out); I merely note his abiding interest in it.

62   Cate 2002, 492.

63   In fact, Nietzsche likely read first "The Landlady," which, in the French translation (*L'esprit souterrain*) that he discovered by chance in a bookstore, was grafted onto *Notes from Underground* as its first part.

64   Frank 1961 argues that Dostoevsky intended the underground man as depicted in Part 1 to be a nihilist.

65   He also claims, perhaps more obviously, that our abolition of ourselves would be nihilism too (*GS* 346).

66   This is the first appearance of the word "nihilism" or its cognates in Nietzsche's published works.

67   This is the period during which Nietzsche discovered Dostoevsky.

68 In *The Will to Power* these notes have been separated into sections numbered 4, 5, 114, and 55 of Book 1 (see Kaufmann's footnote to entry number 4, p. 9). For the original, see *KSA* 12:5[71].

69 "Being" here is employed as a synonym for "truth" or "true world" as these terms are used earlier in the note.

70 See, for example, Schacht 1973.

71 When you are dead, moreover, you will have no awareness of time's passing among the living, and so will experience no respite from life. As far as you will ever be consciously aware, you are living this life. Nietzsche once put the matter this way in a note: "Between the last moment of consciousness and the first appearance of [your] new life there is 'no time'" (*KSA* 9:11[318]).

72 Zarathustra, the teacher of the eternal return, refers to himself as "the advocate of the circle" in Z:III "The Convalescent" 1. On the eternal return as implying circular time, see Loeb 2010, 51–60.

73 Z:III "The Convalescent" 2.

74 For the allusion to Pythagoras, see *HL* 2, and for the eternal return in association with Heraclitus and the Stoics, see *EH* "BT" 3. A. A. Long 1985 is very good on the Stoics and the eternal return.

75 See Resa von Schirnhofer's recollections in Gilman and Parent 1987, pp. 157 and 161–2 in particular.

76 In *Ecce Homo* Nietzsche observes that this section of *The Gay Science* "offers ... the basic idea of *Zarathustra*" (*EH* "Z" 1).

77 Loeb 2013 has good coverage of this and related interpretations (pp. 662–9).

78 Loeb 2013, 667. On the compatibility of Nietzsche's believing in the truth of the eternal return with his reflections on its existential and psychological implications, see also Loeb 2010, 18–29.

79 For a thorough and, to my mind, persuasive defense of the eternal return as a cosmological doctrine, see Loeb 2010, Chapter 1, and 2013, 652–62.

80 Loeb 2013, 659–62.

81 I address the question whether Nietzsche may consistently employ a concept like causality on p. 111.

82 In this section I have made much use of Paul Loeb's work, which I consider the best work done of late on *Zarathustra* and the eternal return. Among other readers of *Zarathustra* with an interest in Plato, Lampert 1986 and Rosen 2004 stand out.

83 For this characterization of Heraclitus, see p. 81.

84 Z:III "The Other Dancing Song" 3; Z:IV "The Drunken Song" 10–12.

85 *KSA* 7:7[156].

Chapter 3: Becoming

1 DL 9.1.1–6.

2 Regarding the number of times Nietzsche offered the course, and for his work on the manuscript, see the "Translator's Preface" in Whitlock 2001.

3 Here I only state the fact, without making any claims as to influence. For a study of Nietzsche's early work on Heraclitus, see Jensen 2010.

4 Or, in *PTG*, "mere semblance and illusion" (p. 79).

5 See, for example, *PTG* 52–4.

6   Physicists would balk at most of what follows if I intended it as an accurate
      description of physical reality. But I do not so intend it. I merely employ a few
      concepts of physics as they are understood by the educated non-specialist in order to
      generate an image before my reader's mind's eye. I simplify and omit as many details
      as did Plato in his allegory of the cave.

7   See the direct quote to this effect at *KSA* 11:26[432], in which passage Nietzsche
      comments on his own "philosophical genealogy." Whitlock 1999 cites this and other
      relevant material (see pp. 191–3 in particular).

8   Many contemporary scholars are embarrassed on Nietzsche's behalf at the will to
      power taken as an ontological doctrine, and they expend much energy attempting
      to liberate him from it (primarily by way of discounting the evidentiary value
      of the *Nachlass* material). Brian Leiter, for example, labels it "a piece of crackpot
      metaphysical speculation" (Leiter 2002, 252). This is an exaggeration, to be sure;
      but as I note at the end of this section, I myself doubt that Nietzsche was at his best,
      or most interesting, when writing about the will to power. I do not consider it the
      foundation of Nietzsche's philosophy, as some have done. I discuss will to power
      because the idea is part of his heritage, and although it does not appear often in the
      published writings, it does appear, and as an ontology. For our purposes, we may
      take it broadly as synonymous with Becoming.

9   I refer to *WP* 1067 only as an aid to our picturing what Nietzsche himself may
      have regarded before his mind's eye when he reflected on the will to power as
      a cosmological or metaphysical principle; I do not claim that it represents his
      final, considered account of the nature of things. Having acknowledged this, I
      do think it worthwhile to note that although it is popular to dismiss this passage,
      the rationale for doing so is less conclusive than some scholars make it out to be.
      Bernd Magnus claims that Nietzsche "had set aside [this passage] by February
      1888 as material for which he had no further use" (Magnus 1986, 88), and Brian
      Leiter claims that Mazzino Montinari "conclusively discredited" the passage by
      showing that Nietzsche's "literary intentions" involved "discarding" it (Leiter
      2002, 139; the "literary intentions" is Leiter's quotation from Montinari). But
      all that Montinari has actually shown, and all that the evidence will bear, is that
      in the spring of 1887 Nietzsche selected from among his notes 53 passages to
      remember and, presumably, revise for publication (or at least to consider for
      publication). There is nothing to rule out the possibility of his later reading this
      note and judging it "usable" after all, for it surely is not the case, as Montinari
      claims, that Nietzsche published "another version" of the passage in *Beyond
      Good and Evil* (Montinari 2003, 88–90); rather, he merely adapted a closing
      phrase from this note ("*This world is the will to power—and nothing besides*")
      for the conclusion of *BGE* 36. Moreover, even if we were to count this another
      version of the note, a comparison of, for example, *BGE* 191 with *TI* "Socrates"
      5–7 reveals that Nietzsche was not in principle against recycling good ideas. In
      any case, Montinari's point has nothing to do with whether Nietzsche believed or
      "ultimately accepted" the content and implications of this passage (Leiter appeals
      to Montinari to support his claim that Nietzsche did not accept it), but only with
      whether he intended to publish it in a particular book. (For the many difficulties
      involved in determining Nietzsche's literary intentions during his last active
      years, see Brobjer 2010 [pp. 20–2 in particular] and 2011, and Endres and Pichler
      2013.)

10   Keeping in mind the qualifications expressed in note 8 above.

11 Against the notion that Nietzsche intends to associate his ideas here with Schopenhauer's metaphysics, see Loeb 2014, which also makes a case for taking the will to power more seriously than recent scholars have been inclined to do. Loeb has convinced me that the will to power and eternal return are much more significant than I have recognized. I have never explicitly denied this (as some scholars have done); but I now see that I must attend to these ideas very closely indeed, and I suggest that my readers do so as well.

12 There is disagreement in the tradition about whether all the atoms are so small. Democritus may have believed in atoms of many different sizes, some of them quite large.

13 Nietzsche associates Democritean atomism with the later skeptical tradition of Pyrrhonism, on which see Swift 2005, 22 and 39n. 43. For a somewhat fuller treatment of this same topic, and for a thorough account of Nietzsche's early work on Democritus, see Porter 2000 (for Democritus and Pyrrhonism, see in particular pp. 92–3 and pp. 321–2n. 32). McEvilley 2002 traces Pyrrho's ideas to "the Democritean tradition" (p. 492).

14 This idea is rejected in both the *Republic* and the *Laws* (see p. 62 in the text above). Plato seems to have been particularly opposed to atomism—or so it would appear from the fact that he nowhere mentions Democritus. Nietzsche refers to an ancient legend that Plato wanted to burn Democritus's writings, on which see Swift 2005, 26–30 and Porter 2000, 43–4.

15 Nietzsche cites Augustine's claim that the Academics were dogmatic Platonists who employed skepticism as a propaedeutic to traditional Platonism at *KSA* 12:9[3].

16 For a thorough account of Nietzsche's relation to Pyrrhonism, see Berry 2011.

17 There are those who doubt the legitimacy of the very idea of the Scientific Revolution. For a fine collection of essays on the subject, see Osler 2000.

18 " 'Tis all in pieces, all coherence gone," John Donne wrote in this connection in 1611.

19 See Bakewell 2010, 127–8 (incl. illustration).

20 Berry 2004. See also Berry 2010, 77ff.

21 Descartes' contemporary, Gassendi, advocated a mitigated skepticism, grounded in atomism, against the more extreme tendencies of the Pyrrhonists: Scientific knowledge is available, but it does not amount to knowledge of the world as it is in itself. For an accessible account of Gassendi's contribution to early modern debates about skepticism, see Popkin 2003, 120–7.

22 Please note that I shall keep to general terms and loose expressions. Technical precision is not necessary for our purposes here and, besides, Nietzsche himself appears to have been uninterested in the minutiae and abstruse technicalities of Kant's philosophy.

23 Many contemporary scholars believe that too much has been made of "On Truth and Lies," particularly by various postmodern readers of Nietzsche. They are probably right. I introduce the piece here *not* because I consider it central to Nietzsche's development or an encapsulation of a position he never abandoned or altered, but only to provide chronological context and to demonstrate a continuity of general tendencies in his thoughts on knowledge and truth.

24 I omit many stages of a complex process to track Nietzsche's own streamlined account.

25 Specifically Schopenhauer's account of perception in *The Fourfold Root of the Principle of Sufficient Reason*, which, unlike Kant's account, draws on medical knowledge of the physiology of the eye and optic system.

26   See *GM* 3.24, *Z*:IV "The Shadow," and *WP* 540 and 602.

27   A classic text in this regard is Nehamas 1985. For a more recent work, see Hales and Welshon 2000.

28   Clark 1990 set the contemporary agenda in this regard.

29   In *TI* "Reason" 5 and "Errors" 3 Nietzsche writes as if this movement from ego to being to thing were the result of faulty introspection and flawed reasoning, as if it were an intellectual process occurring in time. If he does mean this, if he believes that our view of reality as composed of relatively enduring substances (things, doers) is the result of a series of inferences, then *TI* "Errors" 3 suggests that these were the inferences of our ancestors ("the most ancient and enduring psychology was at work here") that long ago hardened into a second nature that now operates in us (through the activity of our cognitive-perceptual apparatus) immediately, without inference. If the problem were merely our own unsound reasoning, then we could perhaps overcome it; but in *TI* "Reason" 5 Nietzsche insists that we cannot correct our erroneous perception *even if* we know it to be erroneous. Present rational inferences, then, do not seem to be at issue. Of course it may also be that Nietzsche does not mean to suggest that any such inferential process has ever actually occurred, and that he is only analyzing the conceptual components of our substance-view of reality by way of a heuristically convenient narrative, precisely as some interpret Plato's narrative account of "creation" in the *Timaeus* to be only an aid to formulating an analysis that otherwise would be overly abstract and dense.

30   We have no access to an objective standard or there just is no such standard. In *The Gay Science* Nietzsche is more tentative; in the passage I have quoted from *The Will to Power*, written in 1888, he outright denies the existence of an objective standard/ world.

31   He has this idea in mind when, while discussing the will in *Beyond Good and Evil*, he writes that "our body is but a social structure composed of many souls" (*BGE* 19), an allusion to an earlier mention of "soul as social structure of the drives and affects" (*BGE* 12).

32   In this same section (*GS* 112) Nietzsche equates the continuum with the "flux" of Becoming, and in the immediately preceding section he claims that nothing real corresponds to the concept of substance, which, he says, we believe in only because our perceptual systems are too imprecise to reveal to us that everything is "in flux" (*GS* 111); and in the section before this last one he characterizes as "erroneous articles of faith" the ideas that "there are enduring things; that there are equal things; that there are things, substances, bodies" (*GS* 110), to which list he soon adds the idea that there are "lines, planes, *causes and effects*, motion and rest, form and content" (*GS* 121, my emphasis).

33   At *TI* "Reason" 2 Nietzsche insists that the senses do not lie; the problem is with what "we *make* of their testimony." But given his insistence in *TI* "Reason" 5 that in our view of reality we are "compelled into error," I take it that raw sense input does not amount to experience, that the input of our honest senses is always worked over by reason in such a way that our actual experience is necessarily falsified.

34   Nietzsche portrays Plato as an optimist whenever he associates him with the Socratic notion that "reason = virtue = happiness" (see the section "Decadence" on pp. 138–41); others have found pronounced pessimistic tendencies in the *Laws* (see pp. 39–40). Popper 1971 famously identifies Plato as a totalitarian; Wallach 2001 and Roochnik 2003 both portray Plato as sympathetic to democratic culture. Plato as a dreamy metaphysician is perhaps the common notion; the idea that he was, or

became in his late period, something of a philosopher of language was introduced by Ryle 1939.

35   Mencken 1908, 156.

36   Ibid., 155.

37   Ibid., 157.

38   Ibid., 156–7.

39   This account of Nietzsche's development is most closely associated with Clark 1990.

40   Brian Leiter I think is right to insist that the "dominant misreadings [of Nietzsche] of the past fifty years go wrong" by, among other mistakes, "treating him as a proto-postmodernist or by erasing his naturalism" (Leiter 2002, 289–90). Rosen 2004 expresses a related objection (pp. vii–viii).

41   Consider the following, from Leiter 2002: " … in his later works Nietzsche's skepticism [with respect to science] vanishes and he repeatedly endorses a *scientific* perspective as the correct and true one" (p. 21). Consider also this, from Clark and Dudrick 2012: "Nietzsche's naturalism is methodological, in the sense that he thinks that whenever a scientific explanation is available, one should accept that explanation. And this naturalism has ontological consequences: it refuses to posit entities invoked by explanations that compete with such empirical explanations" (p. 130). For a more balanced and, I think, reliable reading of Nietzsche on these matters, Schacht 2012 is very good.

42   For a similar position, see R. L. Anderson 1999.

43   Clark 1990 adopts this last view (see, for example, pp. 109–17).

44   This is all quite clear from Nietzsche's *Nachlass*, which fact in this case seems to me significant. Is there disagreement as to the meaning and implications of Nietzsche's published remarks on falsification? If only we had some way to supplement our knowledge of his thoughts about this subject. But we do, in his notebooks; and the arguments that scholars devise to discount them strike me as motivated by their desire to believe that Nietzsche did *not* think these thoughts, a desire they "defend with reasons they have sought after the fact" (*BGE* 5). In any case, Nietzsche's commitment to falsification is demonstrated to my satisfaction by R. L. Anderson 1996.

45   Berry 2010.

46   See, for just one among many available examples, *BGE* 208.

47   See Small 2001; Green 2002 and forthcoming; Hussain 2004a and 2004b. Also relevant here is R. L. Anderson 1996.

48   See, for example, *BGE* 22. *GM* 3.24 is relevant here as well.

49   Brann 2011 insists that "the picture of Heraclitus as the philosopher of ultimate instability, of radical mutability, is just ludicrous." See section III, T: "That Flux" (pp. 96–100; the quotation is from p. 100).

50   Strictly speaking, in the *Theaetetus* Socrates associates proposition (b) with Protagoras, author of the famous dictum that "of all things the measure is the human being: of the things that are, that they are, and of the things that are not, that they are not" (DK B1). This idea he then associates with the more strictly Heraclitean propositions (a) and (c), his point being that Heraclitus's ontology is necessary to make sense of Protagoras's epistemology. But since at *Tht.* 160d–e he claims that these theories "fall together into the same thing," and since we are primarily concerned with Heraclitus, I will resist the urge constantly to refer to propositions of the form of (b) as "Protagorean."

51   DL 3.5–6. Aristotle is less specific, but generally confirms Diogenes' history at *Metaphysics* 1.6 (987a).

52 DL 3.8–10.

53 Unless otherwise indicated, all references in this section are to the *Theaetetus*.

54 Scholars disagree whether this is Plato's account of Becoming or a *reductio* of any such account. Irwin 1997 denies that Plato accepts so radical an ontology. For a detailed argument on the other side, see Nakhnikian 1955a and 1955b.

55 In point of fact Socrates refers to this as a truth taught in secret by Protagoras, but he immediately attributes the thought to Heraclitus (and others) as well. See note 50 above.

56 We need not worry over the details of the theory Socrates is here expounding. Suffice it to say that by the active he means, for example, a stone and its whiteness, and by the passive, an eye and its sight of the white stone.

57 That this is true of the whiteness of the stone and the perceiver's quale of whiteness is uncontroversial. Whether it is true as well of the stone and the eye themselves is less clear, but Socrates at times suggests as much. He does refer to physical objects as slow motions (156c), and Burnyeat 1990 has this in mind when he writes that in Plato's version of Heraclitus "there are no *things*, only processes" (p. 16). Compare Nietzsche's observation that "all scientific procedures have pursued the task of dissolving everything thinglike (material) into movements" (*HH* 19).

58 Plato's account of the particulars (i.e. physical, material objects) in the *Timaeus* (49a–50a) is as radical as that in the *Theaetetus*, though scholars disagree as to how best to characterize it. Cornford maintains that "Plato's position was nearer to that of Heraclitus" than to the other Presocratics, who conceived the four elements as "permanent things with an unchanging character." See Cornford 1997, 177–81 (the two quotations are from p. 178 and p. 180). For sustained treatments of the controversy itself, see Zeyl 2000, lvi–lxiv and Silverman 2002, 246–65.

Chapter 4: Noble and Good

1 For our purposes we may distinguish the ethical (from the Greek *êthos*, which in the plural designates a person's character or disposition) from the moral by noting that the former has to do with the various character traits and habits of different, and different sorts of, individuals while the latter concerns universally applicable prescriptions and proscriptions grounded in metaphysical or theological principles.

2 Socrates compares this to the behavior of dogs (*R.* 376a), which is perhaps an allusion to Heraclitus's "dogs bark at whomever they do not know" (DK B97). The idea may go back even to the *Odyssey* 16.4–10.

3 For more on Socrates' military activities, including the implications of his service for Nietzsche's characterization of him, see M. Anderson 2005.

4 See, for example, *R.* 475e–480a.

5 In the *Sophist* Plato famously argues, against claims to the contrary derived from Parmenides, that false belief is possible (240d–264b).

6 Plato probably held that at least some beliefs are both true and false simultaneously, for the objects of some beliefs (namely, the many particulars) possess contrary properties. In this section, however, we are not concerned with specifically Platonic ideas.

7 I find in my classes that most students, after hearing a brief account of the differences between objectivism and relativism, will identify as ethical relativists, for

the reasons mentioned in the text, even those who after further clarification realize that their belief in a creator-deity who has issued universally binding ethical decrees qualifies them as objectivists.

8   *Nicomachean Ethics* 1.4 (1095a16–20). Many later philosophers will aim instead at freedom from disturbance (*ataraxia*) or moderate (or no) emotions (*apatheia*).

9   See, for example. *Tht.* 176e–177a.

10 I qualify the claim that happiness attends *eudaimonia* with the expression "in normal circumstances" because, however virtuously one may live, external factors can always depress or otherwise interfere with one's psychic wellbeing. For instance, the death of a loved one may cause even the *eudaimôn* man to feel sad.

11 See *R.* 344a–b, 352d, 354a–c, 361d, 365c–d, 576c–580d, 619d–e.

12 The division, developed at length in the *Republic* from 435b to 441c, is probably only heuristic, for at 611b1–3 Socrates says that "in its truest nature" the soul is not "full of much variety," and at b5 he at least implies that it is not "compounded of many (things or parts)." His point is consistent with the argument in the *Phaedo* that the soul is eternal because incomposite (78b–80c).

13 On *eudaimonia* in particular, see 472c–d, 507c–d, 523b, 527c; on the best way of life more generally, see 458a–b, 487e–488a, 500c–d.

14 On this point see Callicles' remarks at 482c–d.

15 For more on likeness to God and the related idea of purification, see M. Anderson 2009, 75–84 and Miller 2011, 78–113.

16 Schopenhauer 1995, 49.

17 On this see the Introduction and notes in Burnet 1911.

18 Burnet 1911 denies that the myth is Pythagorean (p. 127, note on 108c8), but for a detailed argument to the contrary see Kingsley 1995, 79–111.

19 67c–d. Cf. *R.* 515c4–5 and 532b6.

20 *pantôn megiston ... kakôn* (83c1–2); *ouk estin ... meizon ... kakon* (89d2–3).

21 Purification of the senses is associated with misology in the *Republic* at 411d. For more on purification as it relates to empiricism, materialism, and misology, see the account of "intellectual purification" in M. Anderson 2009, 93–101.

22 For convenient collections of interpretations, see McPherran 2003 and Peterson 2003.

23 The one near-exception is Most 1993 (specifically p. 110, note 85).

24 Although it will not be apparent to readers without Greek, every transliterated occurrence of "to touch" in this section comes from the same verb. The same holds for "to cover" and "to uncover," though with these two words the similarities are easier to detect by sight.

25 For references see Cairns 2001, 30n. 22.

26 *egkalupsômai* (8.7.26); *enekalupsato* (8.7.28).

27 Plutarch: *olophuromenon ouk ekeinon, all' heauton* (16.7); Plato: *apeklaon emauton— ou gar dê ekeinon ge, alla tên emautou tuchên* (117c8–10).

28 *Pericles*, 16.7. We know nothing of Plutarch's source for this story, but it might have predated Socrates' death or Plato's narrative of the event. But even if this were so, we cannot rule out the possibility, to which I have called attention in the text, that Plutarch intentionally told his tale in language borrowed from the *Phaedo*.

29 *Demosthenes*, 29.3–7. Pausanias tells the story of Aristomenes the Messenian, whom the Spartans gravely wounded in battle and tossed into a pit to die. Aristomenes miraculously survived the fall, but fully expecting to die he covered himself over

with his cloak. Two days later he heard a noise (presumably in the interval he had lain unconscious) and uncovering himself (*ekkalupsamenos*) he saw in the pit a fox feeding on his fallen comrades. When the fox left, Aristomenes followed it to safety (Pausanias 4.18.3–7).

30 There is some confusion in the sources as to the time and place of the episode involving Pericles and Anaxagoras, but it may have occurred well before the philosopher's death.

31 Since the verb here is middle/passive we cannot discern from the grammar alone whether Socrates has covered himself (middle) or has been covered by the guard or by someone else (passive). It is standard to translate the verb as middle, and I myself take the context to suggest that Socrates covered himself since (a) we can be confident that Socrates *un*covered himself, for no one else knew that he was about to speak, and the participle indicating this act of uncovering is unquestionably middle, which fact we may reasonably allow to influence our reading of the immediately following verb as also middle; and (b) there is no agent clause attached to the verb (e.g. "by the guard") which, if Plato had intended a passive verb, though not strictly necessary, would have obviated confusion arising from the reader's assuming that the agent of the verb was identical to the agent of the preceding participle (Socrates). In any case, my point throughout depends, not on the fact (if it is a fact) that Socrates covers himself, but rather on his *un*covering himself.

32 We may assume that Phaedo uncovered his eyes after covering them, for the end of the dialogue just is his eye-witness report of subsequent events. We may also assume that Socrates covered himself again after speaking, for the guard must uncover him to verify that he is dead. Finally, it is only natural that the guard would cover Socrates again after Crito closed his mouth and eyes.

33 LiDonnici 1995 (B11, pp. 108–9).

34 On *ta strômata* as burial shrouds or "bier-cloths," see Garland 1985, 24ff.

35 The slave's reply to the question put to him at 714 clarifies that he was covered by a little threadbare cloak (*tou tribôniou*, 714). The play includes no explicit information as to whether he employed his *strôma* for covering as well.

36 My thanks to Bronwen Wickkhiser for directing me to the two items in this paragraph.

37 On veiling and shame in ancient Greek culture, see Cairns 1993 and 1996.

38 Socrates says *apodounai*, from the same verb he employs when asking Crito to offer (*apodote*) a rooster to Asclepius.

39 These associations ought not surprise us given that among the ancient Greeks "the deprivation of vision signifie[d] the loss of life" (Tatti-Gartziou 2010, 182).

40 In an article in which he associates the oppositions of purity and impurity with the oppositions of light and darkness, Richard Seaford writes that "[m]ystic initiation was a rehearsal for death, and designed to remove the fear of death" (Seaford 2010, 204).

41 For more on covering/veiling in this connection, see Burkert 1983, 265–72; 1985, 285–9; and 1987, 94–102.

42 Dyer 1964, 32. The Proto-Indo-European name for the goddess of death has been reconstructed as "*Kolyo, 'the coverer,'" on which see Lincoln 1991, 78.

43 On two of the "Orphic" gold tablets Hades itself seems to be characterized by the "darkness *covering* it all around" (*skotos amphikalupsas*, Edmonds 2004, 49 and Graf and Johnston 2013, 6 [line 14] and 16 [line 3]).

44 For a discussion of "Plato's indebtedness to Orphic ... tradition," see Kingsley 1995, 112–32 (the quote is from p. 132), and for mention of the *Phaedo* as a "meeting

point of the Bacchic, the Orphic, and the Pythagorean" specifically in connection with the gold plates, see ibid., 262–3. For a concise account of scholars who have stressed divergences among these three traditions, see Edmonds 2004, 39–40; and see Edmonds' "Sacred scripture or oracles for the dead? The semiotic situation of the 'Orphic' gold tablets" (Edmonds 2011, 257–70) for an argument against the existence of an organized Orphic tradition in antiquity.

45 *nun ethanes kai nun egenou … amati tôide*. See Edmonds 2011, 36–7.

46 See Graf and Johnston 2013, pp. 122, 129–34, 143–50, 165–6. See also Riedweg 2011 (pp. 230–1 in particular).

47 See p. 43 of this text and M. Anderson 2009, 75–9 and 93–101. For a discussion of covering in the context of death, bonds, and release or loosing (all themes in the *Phaedo*), see Onians 2000, 420–42.

48 Edmonds, too, argues with specific reference to the *Phaedo* and the gold tablets that "Plato takes the traditional idea of an initiation that qualifies the deceased for a favorable afterlife and transforms it into a way of referring to philosophy" (2004, 180–207; the quotation is from p. 206).

49 If I am not correct, I hope at least to have made a case for the significance of the covering-uncovering opposition in the *Phaedo*, and for its relevance to any interpretation of Socrates' last words.

50 Loeb 2010, Chapter 2, includes a lengthy and persuasive account of the connections between the *Phaedo* and both *Thus Spoke Zarathustra* and the final three aphorisms of Book 4 of *The Gay Science*.

51 See notes 56 and 60 below, in which I indicate similarities between Callicles and Nietzsche (without making any claims as to identity of position or influence).

52 I discuss this and the next two examples (involving Callicles and the tripartite soul of the *Republic*) in greater detail on pp. 127–31.

53 We need not explore the niceties of distinction between "ethics" and "morals" any further than I have done in the first note to this chapter; and unless I have good reason to do otherwise, I will follow Nietzsche's usage and employ "moral," "morals," and "morality" throughout.

54 "The dictum 'help friends and harm enemies' pervades the whole of Greek literature from Homer to Alexander, and was a basic moral principle for determining behavior" (Mitchell and Rhodes 1996, 11). For a more specialized work on this subject, see Blundell 1989.

55 Although Socrates declines to accept "help friends and harm enemies" as a definition of justice, he himself offers up a version of the principle as a description of the guardians of his ideal city (as I have noted on pp. 119–20).

56 Callicles argues that the weak transpose the meaning of moral categories at *Grg.* 483a–d.

57 For more on freedom in this context, see *GM* 1.13.

58 For an account of the revaluation theme in the context of the development of Nietzsche's thought, see Brobjer 2010.

59 Nietzsche nowhere provides a clear, extended account of how the slave revolt succeeded. The gradual decline into decadence of the master class must have played a role. His suggestion at *GM* 1.8 that the Jews rejected Jesus, the embodiment of their own slave morality, so that their enemies would embrace him and thereby unknowingly adopt their morality, is unusual and implausible, to say the least.

60 Compare this to Callicles' account of weak men manipulating law and custom to subvert the natural rule of the powerful at *Grg.* 482e–484c.

61   Nietzsche admits as much regarding Plato at *HH* 50.
62   See, for example, *A* 62.
63   Here I do not have the Nazis in mind, for to appropriate Nietzsche the Nazis
     had to ignore or misconstrue much of his work. The Christians did not so
     much misunderstand the ideas they borrowed from Plato as use them to move
     philosophically in directions that Plato himself did not travel; and I think it fair
     to characterize similarly the relation between, say, a Foucault, Derrida, or Rorty
     and Nietzsche. (Rorty, by the way, was happy to admit that Nietzsche would have
     disapproved of the uses to which he put the ideas he borrowed from him.)
64   Cate 2002, 510–11. For a study of Nietzsche's politics from this perspective, see
     Detwiler 1990.
65   See, for example, *Lg.* 690a and 714e.
66   *Kallipolis*: *R.* 527c2. For Nietzsche's characterization of Manu's "high culture,"
     see *A* 57. Nietzsche associates Plato with the holy lie of the law of Manu at *A* 55,
     and in a notebook he remarks that "Plato is quite in the spirit of Manu" (*KSA*
     13:14[191]). I make no claims as to whether a society based on Manu's law
     represents Nietzsche's political ideal. Brobjer 1998 argues that it does not, and
     he may be right if we take "political" and "ideal" in the strictest sense. But when
     Brobjer admits that "Nietzsche's view of man (and society) was hierarchical, elitist
     and antidemocratic, and it is therefore, apparently, not wholly incompatible with a
     caste-society á la Manu or Plato" (p. 313), I believe he concedes the broader point
     of interest to most scholars. The "apparently" in the foregoing quotation indicates
     only the qualification that Nietzsche prefers a hierarchy and order of rank among
     men to a strict caste system. But this still leaves us with a Nietzsche who approves
     a radically hierarchical social-cultural regime, as is evident from "What is Noble"
     in *Beyond Good and Evil*, which chapter Brobjer surprisingly neglects altogether to
     mention.
67   *Sts.* 291d–303b; *Lg.* 709e–712a.

Chapter 5: Sophia and Philosophia

1   Themistius: *Orations* 23 (295c). I infer the *Republic* from Themistius's statement that
     Axiothea read one of Plato's writings concerning a constitution (*huper politeias*) and
     supply the Phlius from DL 3.46 (Themistius names only the region, Arcadia).
2   DL 3.46.
3   The most outstanding exception to this rule is Stephen Halliwell, who is always
     attentive to Plato's authorial creativity, as exemplified, for example, in his 2007 study
     of the Myth of Er as "an elaborate piece of philosophical *writing*, rather than as the
     vehicle for a set of putative authorial beliefs" (p. 445; the stress is Halliwell's own).
4   Frede 1992, 201.
5   Ibid.
6   Ibid., 202.
7   Ibid.
8   Ibid., 219.
9   Ibid.
10   Waugh 2000, 46.
11   Ibid., 48.

12 Ibid., 49.

13 Ibid. Some scholars appeal as well to the testimony of the "Seventh Letter," but the authenticity of this letter is disputed. I myself am not persuaded that Plato wrote it, nor am I swayed by the contention that even if Plato was not the author, its contents must reflect his views accurately enough to be successful as a forgery. This sort of appeal to what strikes one as plausible is notoriously unreliable. In biblical criticism, for example, it produces arguments of two incompatible forms, one (the criterion of coherence) that reasons that Jesus likely said x if x is consistent with his theology as we know it as well as with the times in which he lived, and another (the criterion of dissimilarity) that reasons that Jesus probably said z if z is strikingly unlike anything we might imagine him saying in the context of the Judaism of his day or of the early church founded in his name.

14 Waugh 1995, 75.

15 Ibid., 73.

16 Ibid., 75.

17 When I write of philosophy enacted "privately in silence" I do not mean to imply anything about the *initial* development of thought and the "intellectualist legend" to which Waugh objects on p. 74 of her essay.

18 The first essay I have quoted from Waugh appears in a collection dedicated to just this topic. See note 10 above.

19 Sayre 1992.

20 Ibid., 221.

21 Ibid., 221–3.

22 Ibid., 221.

23 Ibid., 231. Sayre may push this point further than the text will support, for when he claims that Socrates' "admonition that prepared speeches like those of Lysias, whether 'spoken or written' (λέγειν τε καὶ γράφειν, 277D 2), serve at best as crutches to memory ... " (p. 231), he runs together Socrates' *question* concerning 'spoken and written' discourse with his *assertions* as to the value of certain types of discourse. Socrates does tend to stress the inadequacies of *writing* in these critical passages, and it is at least plausible to take his praise of the 'living and vital' discourse to refer to *spoken* discourse, especially considering that, for example, it is through speech that a man who knows responds to an inquirer's questions, as a written text cannot.

24 Ibid., 235.

25 Long 2013, Chapter 1.

26 In his book Long covers eight Platonic dialogues, but the aspect of his account to which I refer is complete before his final chapter.

27 Long 2013, 51.

28 Ibid., 112.

29 Ibid., 113.

30 Ibid., 1.

31 Havelock 1984 (in particular pp. 69–72) and 1986 (the quotation in the text is from p. 94). Havelock 1963 covers all these matters in greater detail (Chapters 12–14).

32 See Havelock 1984, 72–7 and 79–80, and 1986, 94–7.

33 For criticism of Havelock's work, see Halverson 1992.

34 As Havelock does himself, for example in 1986, 102ff.

35 See Havelock 1984, 76 and 80, and 1986, 103.

36 *Phdr.* 278d9–e1.

37 The manipulation of chronology and narrative linearity is evident in the *Odyssey*. For structural complexity in the *Iliad*, see Heiden 2000 and 2008.

38 The *Republic* is full of such elaborate webs of interconnection. For an easily overlooked example of this phenomenon, see M. Anderson 2010 (specifically pp. 258–9). Havelock 1986 refers to the words in a written text as susceptible of being "looked at, read, and 'backward-scanned'" (p. 103).

39 But recall John Dillon's observation, quoted on page 187, note 10.

40 I suspect that Nietzsche had this side of Plato's personality in mind when he attributed to him "the features of the regal exclusive and self-contained Heraclitus" (*PTG* 35).

41 For an extended and accessible argument that we should take this disparagement of writing seriously, and an account of the implications of this for Plato's philosophical practice, see Szlezák 1999.

42 Friedländer 1964, 110.

43 Ibid., 113.

44 Ibid., 121–2.

45 Ibid., 119 and 123–5.

46 Ibid., 124–5.

47 See my remarks on p. 45.

48 The same idea is expressed, famously, at *Ap.* 23a–b.

49 Nietzsche on the type of our contemporary intellectual: "Such men have lost the last remnant not only of a philosophical but also of a religious mode of thinking, and in their place have acquired not even optimism but journalism, the spirit and spiritlessness of our day and our daily papers. Every philosophy which believes that the problem of existence is touched on, not to say solved, by a political event is a joke- and pseudo-philosophy" (*SE* 4).

50 See, for example, *BGE* 206–7 and 211.

51 Socrates calls Diotima wise also at 206b6 and 208b8, and in some translations he refers to her even as a "prophetess." Now there are manuscripts that at 201d2 read *gunaikos mantikês*, which would translate as "(from) a prophetic woman," but Burnet's edition has *Mantinikê*, which means "from Mantinea" (Dover 1980 has the same). Of course, even if this latter is textually correct, the play on *mantis* and *mantikê* is obvious. On the other hand, Plato might well have intended a reference to Mantinea, for at the conclusion of Socrates' speech a drunken Alcibiades bursts into the party and proceeds to dominate the scene. This is the same Alcibiades who persuaded the Athenians to wage what has since become known as the first Battle of Mantinea (418) just two years before the dramatic date of the *Symposium*, which battle the Spartans won and so recovered from the terrible consequences of their humiliation at Pylos in 425. In any case, it is worth keeping in mind the textual uncertainties here.

52 In *Beyond Good and Evil* Nietzsche introduces the novel and "far from innocuous" idea, in connection with Dionysus and Nietzsche himself as "the last disciple and initiate" of this god, that "gods, too … do philosophy" (*BGE* 295).

53 Rosen 2004, 8.

54 Ibid., 8–9.

55 See, for example, *Nicomachean Ethics* 6.1, 3, and 7.

56 The quotation is from Benardete 2000, 407. Its meaning is unclear to me not least because Benardete concludes his essay by quoting Strauss's seemingly incompatible assertion that "[t]o articulate the problem of cosmology means to answer the question of what philosophy is or what a philosopher is" (p. 416).

57 Compare the initiatory language at *Phdr.* 249c and 250c.

58 Weiss 2012.

59 Ibid., 135.

60 Ibid., 10.

61 Ibid., 2.

62 In *Ecce Homo* Nietzsche writes that in "expression, intention, and the art of surprise" the three essays in the *Genealogy* are "perhaps uncannier than anything else written so far" (*EH* "GM").

63 *Smp.* 209e–212a; see in particular 211c–212a.

64 *Phdr.* 249d–256e. I take the "sexual gratification" from the *tês tôn aphrodisiôn charitos* at 254a6–7.

65 Migotti 2013 argues that Nietzsche distinguishes *the* ascetic ideal, which he associates exclusively with priests, from the personal ascetic practices of some philosophers.

66 Unless otherwise noted, all quotations from Nietzsche in the discussion to follow come from *GM* 3.7–8.

67 This is at least implied by Diotima's observation (at 210a–b) that the correct practice of love requires that one slacken the excessive desire for an individual body, also by the *suneinai* at 211d8, which may mean both "to associate with" and "to have sexual intercourse with." Sexual gratification is explicit in the *Phaedrus* (see note 64 above).

68 This is not to deny that the philosophers' avoidance of fame, princes, and women corresponds as well to their rejection of the "three great slogans of the ascetic ideal," namely "poverty, humility, and chastity."

69 Very good on Plato in this connection is Pender 1992.

70 I have rendered the *sunontos autôi* at 212a2 as "be with it," but it comes from the same verb as the *suneinai* in note 67 above and so has the same range of meaning.

71 Nietzsche clearly has himself in mind throughout this paragraph, and in one line he even specifically mentions himself.

72 *GM* 3.7 closes with the line, "*pereat mundus, fiat philosophia, fiat philosophus, fiam!*"

73 Nietzsche might well have made his point about children as "fetters" and the house as "a place of impurity" with reference to Socrates' repeated remarks on purification as liberation from the bonds or fetters of bodily concerns in the *Phaedo*.

74 Schopenhauer 2000, 324.

75 In *Ecce Homo* Nietzsche all but declares this essay to be a *self*-portrait (*EH* "UM" 3).

76 Breazeale 1979.

77 In later works, *Twilight of the Idols* most notably, Nietzsche acknowledges that the Greeks succumbed to Socrates only because they had already begun to decline from independent causes. On this, see the section "Decadence" on pp. 138–41.

78 Breazeale 1979, lv.

79 *GS* 290. To obviate a superficial interpretation of this famous passage it is useful to consult *EH* "Clever" 10, in which we read: "The pathos of poses does *not* belong to greatness; whoever needs poses at all is *false*—Beware of all picturesque men!"

80 See also Nietzsche's quotation from *Zarathustra* at *EH* "Wise" 8. The passage is something of a hymn to overcoming nausea at man.

81 See pp. 100–3.

82 On the cosmic doctrine of the will to power as "only interpretation," see *BGE* 22.

83 The *Versuchern* in *Zarathustra* prefer the dangerous creativity of guesses to easy but cowardly deductions (*Z*:III "Vision and Riddle" 1). "There are many kinds of

eyes. Even the sphinx has eyes—and consequently there are many kinds of 'truths,' and consequently there is no truth" (*WP* 540). Nietzsche headed this note "*Der Versucher*" (not included in *WP*; see *KSA* 11:34[230]).

84 Clark and Dudrick 2012, 130. I quote this in reference to the discussion in Chapter 3, "Nietzsche and Science" (pp. 109–13 above).

85 See p. 197, n. 16.

86 *KSA* 8:29[45].

87 The "master privilege of the free spirit" is "the dangerous privilege of living *for experiments* and of being allowed to offer itself to adventure" (*HH* "Preface" 4).

88 This remark is not as straightforward as it may seem, for the "modesty" Nietzsche has in mind is "the modesty of such *monsters of pride and sovereignty* as Pythagoras, as Plato—." (my emphasis).

89 In the summer of 1878, inspired by the publication of *Human, All Too Human*, Nietzsche writes in letters of his determination to seek wisdom and be a philosopher, whereas formerly he had only admired philosophers and the wise (*KGB* 729 and 734).

90 In 1879 Nietzsche visited and fell in love with St. Moritz, which is a mere six miles from Sils-Maria.

91 Letter to Carl von Gersdorff, 28 June 1883 (Middleton 1996, 214).

92 Phlius, the same Peloponnesian town from which Axiothea was said to have come to study with Plato in the Academy; the same town in which Phaedo relates to Echecrates the events of Socrates' last day in Plato's *Phaedo*.

93 Cicero, *Tusculan Disputations* 5.3.

94 DL "Prooimion" 12.

95 Letter to Erwin Rohde, January and February 1870 (Middleton 1996, 63).

96 Only one name comes to mind as more certainly an example of the type than either Plato or Nietzsche, but it is the name of a fictional character: Melville's Ishmael.

Bibliography

Anderson, M. (2005), "Socrates as Hoplite." *Ancient Philosophy* 25, 273–89.

—(2009), *Pure: Modernity, Philosophy, and the One*. San Rafael: Sophia Perennis.

—(2010), "ἀληθῆ λέγεις: Speaking the Truth in Plato's *Republic*." *Ancient Philosophy* 30, 247–60.

Anderson, M. and Osborn, G. (2009), *Approaching Plato: A Guide to the Early and Middle Dialogues*. Online text (http://campus.belmont.edu/philosophy/Book.pdf).

Anderson, R. L. (1996), "Overcoming charity: the case of Maudemarie Clark's Nietzsche on truth and philosophy." *Nietzsche-Studien* 25, 307–41.

—(1999), "Nietzsche's Views on Truth and the Kantian Background of his Epistemology." In Babich and Cohen (1999), 47–59.

Aristophanes (1901), *Ploutos*. In *Aristophanis Comoediae*, Hall, F. W. and Geldart, W. M. (eds). Oxford: Oxford University Press.

Babich, B. E. and Cohen, R. S. (eds) (1999), *Nietzsche, Epistemology, and Philosophy of Science: Nietzsche and the Sciences II*. Dordrecht: Kluwer Academic Publishers.

Bakewell, S. (2010), *How to Live or A Life of Montaigne*. New York: Other Press.

Benardete, S. (2000), *The Argument of the Action: Essays on Greek Poetry and Philosophy*. Chicago: The University of Chicago Press.

Berry, J. N. (2004), "The pyrrhonian revival in Montaigne and Nietzsche." *Journal of the History of Ideas* 65.3, 497–514.

—(2011), *Nietzsche and the Ancient Skeptical Tradition*. Oxford: Oxford University Press.

Blundell, M. W. (1989), *Helping Friends and Harming Enemies: A Study in Sophocles and Greek Ethics*. Cambridge: Cambridge University Press.

Bradshaw, D. (1999), "Neoplatonic origins of the act of being." *The Review of Metaphysics* 53, 383–401.

Brandwood, L. (1992), "Stylometry and Chronology." In Kraut (1992), 90–120.

Brann, E. (2011), *The Logos of Heraclitus*. Philadelphia: Paul Dry Books.

Breazeale, D. (ed. and tr.) (1990), *Philosophy and Truth: Selections from Nietzsche's Notebooks of the Early 1870s*. Amherst: Humanity Books.

Brickhouse, T. C. and Smith, N. D. (2000), *The Philosophy of Socrates*. Boulder: Westview Press.

Brobjer, T. H. (1998), "The absence of political ideals in Nietzsche's writings: the case of the laws of Manu and the associated caste-society." *Nietzsche-Studien* 27, 300–18.

—(2006), "Nietzsche's *magnum opus*." *History of European Ideas* 32, 278–94.

—(2010), "The origin and early context of the revaluation theme in Nietzsche's thinking." *The Journal of Nietzsche Studies* 39, 12–29.

—(2011), "The place and role of *Der Antichrist* in Nietzsche's four volume project *Umwerthung Aller Werthe*." *Nietzsche-Studien* 40, 244–55.

Burkert, W. (1983), *Homo Necans*. Berkeley: University of California Press.

—(1985), *Greek Religion*. Cambridge: Harvard University Press.

—(1987), *Ancient Mystery Cults*. Cambridge: Harvard University Press.

Burnet, J. (ed.) (1911), *Phaedo*. Oxford: Oxford University Press.

Burnyeat, M., tr. (1990), *The Theaetetus of Plato* (revision of Levett, M. J., trans.). Indianapolis: Hackett.

Cairns, D. L. (1993), *Aidôs: The Psychology and Ethics of Honour and Shame in Ancient Greek Literature*. Oxford: Oxford University Press.

—(1996), "Veiling, *Aidôs*, and a red-figure amphora by Phintias." *Journal of Hellenic Studies* 116, 152–7.

—(2001), "Anger and the veil in ancient Greek culture." *Greece & Rome* 48.1, 18–32.

Cate, C. (2002), *Friedrich Nietzsche*. New York: The Overlook Press.

Cherniss, H. (1945), *The Riddle of the Early Academy*. Berkeley: University of California Press.

Christopoulos, M., Karakantza, E. D., and Levaniouk, O. (eds) (2010), *Light and Darkness in Ancient Greek Myth and Religion*. Lanham: Lexington Books.

Cicero, M. T. (1918), *Tusculanae disputationes*, Pohlenz, M. (ed.). Leipzig: Teubner.

Clark, M. (1990), *Nietzsche on Truth and Philosophy*. Cambridge: Cambridge University Press.

Clark, M. and Dudrick, D. (2012), *The Soul of Nietzsche's Beyond Good and Evil*. Cambridge: Cambridge University Press.

Cohen, E. (2000), *The Athenian Nation*. Princeton: Princeton University Press.

Colli, G. and Montinari, M. (eds) (1967–), *Nietzsche Werke: Kritische Gesamtausgabe*. Berlin and New York: de Gruyter.

—(1975), *Briefwechsel: Kritische Gesamtausgabe*. Berlin and New York: de Gruyter.

—(1980), *Sämtliche Werke: Kritische Studienausgabe*. Berlin and New York: de Gruyter.

Cornford, F. M. (trans.) (1997), *Plato's Cosmology: The Timaeus of Plato*. Indianapolis: Hackett.

Cybulska, E. M. (2000), "The Madness of Nietzsche: A Misdiagnosis of the Millennium?" *Hospital Medicine* 61.8, 571–5.

Destrée, P. and Herrmann, F. (eds) (2011), *Plato and the Poets*. Mnemosyne Supplements: Monographs on Greek and Latin Language and Literature 328. Leiden: Brill.

Detwiler, B. (1990), *Nietzsche and the Politics of Aristocratic Radicalism*. Chicago: The University of Chicago Press.

Dewan, L. (2000), "Aristotle as a Source for St. Thomas's Doctrine of *esse*." Maritain Center, University of Notre Dame website—Summer Thomistic Institute.

Diels, H. (1951–2), *Die Fragmente der Vorsokratiker*, 6th edn, edited and revised by Kranz, W. Berlin: Weidmann.

Dillon, J. (1996), *The Middle Platonists: 80 B.C. to A.D. 220*. Ithaca: Cornell University Press.

—(1999), "A case-study in commentary: the neoplatonic exegesis of the *Prooimia* of Plato's dialogues." In Most (1999), 206–22.

—(2005), *The Heirs of Plato: A Study of the Old Academy (347–274 BC)*. Oxford: Oxford University Press.

Diogenes Laertius (1925), *Lives of Eminent Philosophers*, vols. 1 and 2, Hicks, R. D. (ed.). Cambridge: Harvard University Press.

Dionysius of Halicarnassus (1899), *De Demosthene*. In *Dionysii Halicarnasei Opuscula*, vol. 1, Usener, H. and. Radermacher, L. (eds). Leipzig: Teubner.

Dodds, E. R. (1928), "The *Parmenides* of Plato and the origin of the neoplatonic 'one.'" *The Classical Quarterly* 22, 129–42.

—(1945), "Plato and the irrational." *The Journal of Hellenic Studies* 65, 16–25.

—(1951), *The Greeks and the Irrational*. Berkeley: University of California Press.

Dover, K. (ed.) (1980), *Plato: Symposium*. Cambridge: Cambridge University Press.

Dries, M. and Kail, P. (eds) (2014), *Nietzsche on Mind and Nature*. Oxford: Oxford University Press.

Dyer, R. R. (1964), "The Use of καλύπτω in Homer." *Glotta* 42, 29–38.

Edmonds, R. G. (2004), *Myths of the Underworld Journey: Plato, Aristophanes, and the "Orphic" Gold Tablets*. Cambridge: Cambridge University Press.

—(ed.) (2011), *The "Orphic" Gold Tablets and Greek Religion: Further Along the Path*. Cambridge: Cambridge University Press.

Else, G. F. (1949), "God and Gods in Early Greek Thought." *Transactions and Proceedings of the American Philological Association* 80, 24–36.

Endres, M. and Pichler, A. (2013), " 'Warum ~~ich diesen missrathenen Satz schuf~~': ways of reading Nietzsche in the light of *KGW* IX." *The Journal of Nietzsche Studies* 44.1, 90–109.

Everson, S. (ed.) (1990), *Companions to Ancient Thought 1: Epistemology*. Cambridge: Cambridge University Press.

Ferrari, G. R. F. (ed.) (2007), *The Cambridge Companion to Plato's Republic*. Cambridge: Cambridge University Press.

Fine, G. (1990), "Knowledge and Belief in *Republic* V–VII." In Everson, S. (1990), 85–115.

—(2008), "Does Socrates claim to know that he knows nothing?" *Oxford Studies in Ancient Philosophy* 35, 49–88.

Flower, M. A. (2008), *The Seer in Ancient Greece*. Berkeley: The University of California Press.

Frank, J. (1961), "Nihilism and *Notes from Underground*." *The Sewanee Review* 69, 1–33.

—(2010), *Dostoevsky: A Writer in His Time*, Mary Petrusewicz (ed.). Princeton: Princeton University Press.

Frede, M. (1992), "Plato's Arguments and the Dialogue Form." In Klagge and Smith (1992), 201–19.

Friedländer, P. (1964), *Plato: An Introduction*. New York: Harper and Row.

Gaiser, K. (1980), "Plato's Enigmatic Lecture on the Good." *Phronesis* 25, 5–37.

Garland, R. (1985), *The Greek Way of Death*. Ithaca: Cornell University Press.

Gemes, K. and Richardson, J. (eds) (2013), *The Oxford Handbook of Nietzsche*. Oxford: Oxford University Press.

Gillespie, M. A. (1995), *Nihilism Before Nietzsche*. Chicago: The University of Chicago Press.

Gilman, S. L. (ed.) and Parent, D. J. (trans.) (1987), *Conversations with Nietzsche*. Oxford: Oxford University Press.

Gilson, E. (2005), *Being and Some Philosophers*. Toronto: Pontifical Institute of Mediaeval Studies.

Gonzalez, F. J. (ed.) (1995), *The Third Way: New Directions in Platonic Studies*. Lanham: Rowman and Littlefield.

Graf, F. and Johnston, S. I. (2013), *Ritual Texts for the Afterlife: Orpheus and the Bacchic Gold Tablets*, second edition. London: Routledge.

Green, M. S. (2002), *Nietzsche and the Transcendental Tradition*. Urbana: University of Illinois Press.

—(forthcoming), "Was Afrikan Spir a phenomenalist (and what difference does it make for understanding Nietzsche)?" *Journal of Nietzsche Studies* 45.3.

Hadot, P. (1998), *Plotinus or the Simplicity of Vision*, Chase, M. (trans.). Chicago: University of Chicago Press.

Hales, S. D. and Welshon, R. (2000), *Nietzsche's Perspectivism*. Champaign: University of Illinois Press.

Halliwell, S. (2000), "The Subjection of Muthos to Logos: Plato's Citations of the Poets." *Classical Quarterly* 50.1, 94–112.

—(2002), *The Aesthetics of Mimesis: Ancient Texts and Modern Problems*. Princeton: Princeton University Press.

—(2007), "The Life and Death Journey of the Soul: Interpreting the Myth of Er." In Ferrari (2007), 445–73.

—(2011), "Antidotes and Incantations: Is There a Cure for Poetry in Plato's *Republic*?" In Destrée and Herrmann (2011), 241–66.

—(2012), *Between Ecstasy and Truth: Interpretations of Greek Poetics from Homer to Longinus*. Oxford: Oxford University Press.

Halverson, J. (1993), "Havelock on Greek orality and literacy." *Journal of the History of Ideas* 53, 148–63.

Havelock, E. A. (1963), *Preface to Plato*. Cambridge: The Belknap Press of Harvard University Press.

—(1984), "The Orality of Socrates and the Literacy of Plato: With Some Reflections on the Historical Origins of Moral Philosophy in Europe." In Kelly (1984), 67–93.

—(1986), *The Muse Learns to Write: Reflections on Orality and Literacy from Antiquity to the Present*. New Haven: Yale University Press.

Heiden, B. (2000), "Major systems of thematic resonances in the *Iliad*." *Symbolae Osloenses* 75, 34–55.

—(2008), *Homer's Cosmic Fabrication: Choice and Design in the Iliad*. Oxford: Oxford University Press.

Hollingdale, R. J. (trans.) (1995), *Untimely Meditations*. Cambridge: Cambridge University Press.

Homer (1920), *Iliad*, Munro, D. B. and Allen, T. W. (eds). Oxford: Oxford University Press.

Homeric Hymns (1912), "Hymn to Demeter." In *Homerici Opera*, vol. 5, Allen, T. W., (ed.). Oxford: Oxford University Press.

Huenemann, C. (2013), "Nietzsche's Illness." In Gemes and Richardson (2013), 63–80.

Hussain, N. J. Z. (2004a), "Nietzsche's positivism." *European Journal of Philosophy* 12.3, 326–68.

—(2004b), "Review of Michael S. Green, *Nietzsche and the Transcendental Tradition*." *The Philosophical Review* 113.2, 275–8.

Irwin, T. H. (1977), "Plato's heracleiteanism." *The Philosophical Quarterly* 27.106, 1–13.

Jensen, A. K. (2010), "Nietzsche's interpretation of Heraclitus in its historical context." *Epoché* 14, 335–62.

Kahn, C. H. (2009), *Essays on Being*. Oxford: Oxford University Press.

Kaufmann, W. (ed. and trans.) (1954), *The Portable Nietzsche*. London: Penguin.

—(ed. and trans.) (1967), *The Basic Writings of Nietzsche*. New York: The Modern Library.

—(1974), *Nietzsche: Philosopher, Psychologist, Antichrist*, 4th edn. Princeton: Princeton University Press.

Kelly, E. (ed.) (1984), *New Essays on Socrates*. New York: University Press of America.

Kingsley, P. (1995), *Ancient Philosophy, Mystery, and Magic*. Oxford: Oxford University Press.

Klagge, J. C. and Smith, N. D. (eds) (1992), *Oxford Studies in Ancient Philosophy* 4, Supplementary Volume: *Methods of Interpreting Plato and His Dialogues*. Oxford: Oxford University Press.

Krämer, H. J. (1990), *Plato and the Foundations of Metaphysics: A Work on the Theory of the Principles and Unwritten Doctrines of Plato with a Collection of the Fundamental Documents*, Catan, J. R. (trans.). Albany: SUNY Press.

Kraut, R. (ed.) (1992), *The Cambridge Companion to Plato*. Cambridge: Cambridge University Press.

Lamm, J. A. (2000), "Schleiermacher as Plato Scholar." *Journal of Religion* 80.2, 206–39.

Lampert, L. (1986), *Nietzsche's Teaching: An Interpretation of* Thus Spoke Zarathustra. New Haven: Yale University Press.

—(2010), *How Philosophy Became Socratic: A Study of Plato's* Protagoras, Charmides, *and* Republic. Chicago: The University of Chicago Press.

Leiter, B. (2002), *Routledge Philosophy Guidebook to Nietzsche on Morality*. London: Routledge.

LiDonnici, L. R. (1995), *The Epidaurian Miracle Inscriptions: Text, Translation, and Commentary*. Atlanta: Scholars Press.

Lincoln, B. (1991), *Death, War, and Sacrifice*. Chicago: University of Chicago Press.

Loeb, P. (2010), *The Death of Nietzsche's Zarathustra*. Cambridge: Cambridge University Press.

—(2013), "Eternal Recurrence." In Gemes and Richardson (2013), 645–71.

—(2014), "Will to Power and Panpsychism: A New Exegesis of BGE 36." In Dries and Kail (2014).

Long, A. A. (1985), "The stoics on world-conflagration and everlasting recurrence." *The Southern Journal of Philosophy* 23, 13–37.

Long, A. G. (2013), *Conversation & Self-Sufficiency in Plato*. Oxford: Oxford University Press.

Longinus (1907), *De sublimitate,* Roberts, W. R. (ed.). Cambridge: Cambridge University Press.

Magee, B. (2000), *The Tristan Chord: Wagner and Philosophy*. New York: Henry Holt and Company.

Magnus, B. (1986), "Nietzsche's philosophy in 1888: *The Will to Power* and the *Übermensch*." *Journal of the History of Philosophy* 24.1, 79–98.

McEvilley, T. (2002), *The Shape of Ancient Thought: Comparative Studies in Greek and Indian Philosophies*. New York: Allworth Press.

McPherran, M. L. (2003), "Socrates, Crito, and their debt to Asclepius." *Ancient Philosophy* 23, 71–92.

Mencken, H. L. (1908), *The Philosophy of Friedrich Nietzsche*. Boston: Luce and Company.

Middleton, C. (ed. and trans.) (1996), *Selected Letters of Friedrich Nietzsche*. Indianapolis: Hackett.

Migotti, M. (2013), "Sensuality and its discontents: philosophers, priests, and ascetic ideals in the *Genealogy of Morals*." *The Journal of Nietzsche Studies* 44.2, 314–27.

Miller, P. L. (2011), *Becoming God: Pure Reason in Early Greek Philosophy*. New York: Continuum.

Mitchell, L. G. and Rhodes, P. J. (1996), "Friends and enemies in Athenian politics." *Greece & Rome* 43.1, 11–30.

Montinari, M. (2003), *Reading Nietzsche*, Greg Whitlock (trans.). Urbana: University of Illinois Press.

Morrow, G. R. (1993), *Plato's Cretan City: A Historical Interpretation of the Laws*. Princeton: Princeton University Press.

Most, G. W. (1993), "A cock for Asclepius." *The Classical Review* 43.1, 96–111.

—(ed.) (1999), *Commentaries—Kommentare* (*Aporemata: Kritische Studien zur Philologiegeschichte*, Band 4). Göttingen: Vandenhoeck & Ruprecht.

—(2011), "What Ancient Quarrel Between Philosophy and Poetry?" In Destrée and Herrmann (2011), 1–20.

Murray, O. (ed.) (1990), *Sympotica: A Symposium on the Symposion*. Oxford: Oxford University Press.

Nakhnikian, G. (1955a), "Plato's theory of sensation, I." *The Review of Metaphysics* 9.1, 129–48.

—(1955b), "Plato's theory of sensation, II." *The Review of Metaphysics* 9.2, 306–27.

Nehamas, A. (1985), *Nietzsche: Life as Literature*. Cambridge: Harvard University Press.

Nietzsche, F. (1954a), *Thus Spoke Zarathustra*. In Kaufmann (1954), 121–439.

—(1954b), *Twilight of the Idols*. In Kaufmann (1954), 465–563.

—(1954c), *The Antichrist*. In Kaufmann (1954), 568–656.

—(1967a), *The Birth of Tragedy*. In Kaufmann (1967), 15–144.

—(1967b), *Beyond Good and Evil*. In Kaufmann (1967), 191–435.

—(1967c), *On the Genealogy of Morals*. In Kaufmann (1967), 449–599.

—(1967d), *Ecce Homo*. In Kaufmann (1967), 671–800.

—(1968), *The Will to Power*, Kaufmann, W. and Hollingdale, R. J. (trans.). New York: Vintage.

—(1974), *The Gay Science*, Kaufmann, W. (trans.). New York: Vintage.

—(1990a), "On Truth and Lies in a Nonmoral Sense." In Breazeale, D. (1990), 77–97.

—(1990b), "The Philosopher." In Breazeale, D. (1990), 1–58.

—(1990c), "Philosophy in Hard Times." In Breazeale, D. (1990), 99–123.

—(1995a), "On the Uses and Disadvantages of History for Life." In Hollingdale, R. J. (1995), 57–123.

—(1995b), "Schopenhauer as Educator." In Hollingdale, R. J. (1995), 125–94.

—(1995c), *The Pre-Platonic Philosophers*, Whitlock, G. (trans.). Urbana: University of Illinois Press.

—(1997), *Human, All Too Human* Handwerk, G. (trans.). Stanford: Stanford University Press.

—(1998), *Philosophy in the Tragic Age of the Greeks*, Cowan, M. (trans.). Washington, DC: Regnery.

—(2012), *The Wanderer and His Shadow*, Handwerk, G. (trans.). Stanford: Stanford University Press.

O'Meara, D. J. (1995), *Plotinus: An Introduction to the* Enneads. Oxford: Oxford University Press.

Onians, R. B. (1951, 2000 reprinting), *The Origins of European Thought about the Body, the Mind, the Soul, the World, Time, and Fate*. Cambridge: Cambridge University Press.

Osler, M. J. (2000), *Rethinking the Scientific Revolution*. Cambridge: Cambridge University Press.

Owens, J. (1985), *An Elementary Christian Metaphysics*. Houston: Center for Thomistic Studies.

Pausanias (1926), *Description of Greece*, vol. 2, *Books 3–5*, Jones, W. H. S. and Ormerod, H. A. (eds). Cambridge: Harvard University Press.

Pender, E. E. (1992), "Spiritual Pregnancy in Plato's *Symposium*." *Classical Quarterly* 42, 72–86.

Peterson, S. (2003), "An Authentically Socratic Conclusion in Plato's *Phaedo*: Socrates' Debt to Asclepius." In Reshotko (2003), 33–52.

Plato (1901a), *Philebus*. In *Platonis Opera*, vol. 2, Burnet, J. (ed.). Oxford: Oxford University Press.

—(1901b), *Symposium*. In *Platonis Opera*, vol. 2, Burnet, J. (ed.). Oxford: Oxford University Press.

—(1901c), *Phaedrus*. In *Platonis Opera*, vol. 2, Burnet, J. (ed.). Oxford: Oxford University Press.

—(1902a), *Timaeus*. In *Platonis Opera*, vol. 4, Burnet, J. (ed.). Oxford: Oxford University Press.

—(1902b), *Critias*. In *Platonis Opera*, vol. 4, Burnet, J. (ed.). Oxford: Oxford University Press.

—(1903a), *Meno*. In *Platonis Opera*, vol. 3, Burnet, J. (ed.). Oxford: Oxford University Press.

—(1903b), *Ion*. In *Platonis Opera*, vol. 3, Burnet, J. (ed.). Oxford: Oxford University Press.

—(1907), *Laws*. In *Platonis Opera*, vol. 5, Burnet, J. (ed.). Oxford: Oxford University Press.

—(1959), *Gorgias: A Revised Text with Introduction and Commentary*, Dodds, E. R. (ed.). Oxford: Oxford University Press.

—(1995a), *Euthyphro*. In *Platonis Opera*, vol. 1, Duke, E. A., Hicken, W. F., Nicoll, W. S. M., Robinson, D. B., and Strachan, J. C. G. (eds). Oxford: Oxford University Press.

—(1995b), *Apology*. In *Platonis Opera*, vol. 1, Duke, E. A., Hicken, W. F., Nicoll, W. S. M., Robinson, D. B., and Strachan, J. C. G. (eds). Oxford: Oxford University Press.

—(1995c), *Phaedo*. In *Platonis Opera*, vol. 1, Duke, E. A., Hicken, W. F., Nicoll, W. S. M., Robinson, D. B., and Strachan, J. C. G. (eds). Oxford: Oxford University Press.

—(1995d), *Cratylus*. In *Platonis Opera*, vol. 1, Duke, E. A., Hicken, W. F., Nicoll, W. S. M., Robinson, D. B., and Strachan, J. C. G. (eds). Oxford: Oxford University Press.

—(1995e), *Theaetetus*. In *Platonis Opera*, vol. 1, Duke, E. A., Hicken, W. F., Nicoll, W. S. M., Robinson, D. B., and Strachan, J. C. G. (eds). Oxford: Oxford University Press.

—(1995f), *Sophist*. In *Platonis Opera*, vol. 1, Duke, E. A., Hicken, W. F., Nicoll, W. S. M., Robinson, D. B., and Strachan, J. C. G. (eds). Oxford: Oxford University Press.

—(1995g), *Statesman*. In *Platonis Opera*, vol. 1, Duke, E. A., Hicken, W. F., Nicoll, W. S. M., Robinson, D. B., and Strachan, J. C. G. (eds). Oxford: Oxford University Press.

—(2003), *Republic*, Slings, S. R. (ed.). Oxford: Oxford University Press.

Plutarch (1888), *Septem sapientium convivium*. In *Moralia*, vol. 1, Bernardakis, G. N. (ed.), 358–402. Leipzig: Teubner.

—(1891), *De defectu oraculorum*. In *Moralia*, vol. 3, Bernardakis, G. N. (ed.), 69–142. Leipzig: Teubner.

—(1914), *Lycurgus*. In *Lives*, vol. 1, Perrin, B. (ed.). Cambridge: Harvard University Press.

—(1916), *Pericles*. In *Lives*, vol. 3, Perrin, B. (ed.). Cambridge: Harvard University Press.

—(1919), *Demosthenes*. In *Lives*, vol. 7, Perrin, B. (ed.). Cambridge: Harvard University Press.

Popkin, R. H. (2003), *The History of Scepticism: From Savonarola to Bayle*. Oxford: Oxford University Press.

Popper, K. (1971), *The Open Society and Its Enemies, vol. 1, The Spell of Plato*, 5th edn. Princeton: Princeton University Press.

Porter, J. I. (2000), *Nietzsche and the Philology of the Future*. Stanford: Stanford University Press.

Press, G. A. (ed.) (2000), *Who Speaks for Plato? Studies in Platonic Anonymity*. Lanham: Rowman and Littlefield.

Reale, G. (1997), *Toward a New Interpretation of Plato*, 10th edn, Catan, J. R. and Davies, R. (trans. and eds). Washington, D. C.: Catholic University of America Press.

Reshotko, N. (2003), *Desire, Identity, and Existence: Essays in Honor of T. M. Penner*. Kelowna: Academic Printing & Publishing.

Riedweg, C. (2011), "Initiation – death – underworld: Narrative and ritual in the gold leaves." In Edmonds (2011), 219–56.

Rist, J. M. (1962), "The neoplatonic one and Plato's *Parmenides.*" *Transactions and Proceedings of the American Philological Association* 93, 389–401.

—(1977), *Plotinus: the Road to Reality*. Cambridge: Cambridge University Press.

Roochnik, D. (2003), *Beautiful City: The Dialectical Character of Plato's* Republic. Ithaca: Cornell University Press.

Rosen, S. (2004), *The Mask of Enlightenment: Nietzsche's* Zarathustra, second edition. New Haven: Yale University Press.

Ryle, G. (1939), "Plato's *Parmenides.*" *Mind* 48, 129–51 and 302–25.

Sayre, K. (1992), "A Maieutic View of Five Late Dialogues." In Klagge and Smith (1992), 221–43.

—(2005), *Plato's Late Ontology: A Riddle Resolved*, rev. edn. Las Vegas: Parmenides Publishing.

Schacht, R. (1973), "Nietzsche and nihilism." *Journal of the History of Philosophy* 11, 65–90.

—(2012), "Nietzsche's naturalism." *The Journal of Nietzsche Studies* 43.2, 185–212.

Schopenhauer, A. (1969), *The World as Will and Representation*, vol. 1, E. F. J. Payne (trans.). New York: Dover.

—(1974), *On the Fourfold Root of the Principle of Sufficient Reason*, E. F. J. Payne (trans.). Peru: Open Court.

—(1995), *On the Basis of Morality*, E. F. J. Payne (trans.). Indianapolis: Hackett.

—(2000), *Parerga and Paralipomena*, vol. 2, E. F. J. Payne (trans.). Oxford: Oxford University Press.

Seaford, R. (2010), "Mystic Light and Near-Death Experience." In Menelaos, Karakantza, and Levaniouk (2010), 201–6.

Silk, M. S. and Stern, J. P. (1981), *Nietzsche on Tragedy*. Cambridge: Cambridge University Press.

Silverman, A. (2002), *The Dialectic of Essence: A Study of Plato's Metaphysics*. Princeton: Princeton University Press.

Small, R. (2001), *Nietzsche in Context*. Aldershot: Ashgate.

—(2005), *Nietzsche and Rée: A Star Friendship*. Oxford: Oxford University Press.

Strange, S. K. (1992), "Plotinus' account of participation in *Ennead* VI. 4–5." *Journal of the History of Philosophy* 30, 479–96.

Swift, P. (2005), *Becoming Nietzsche: Early Reflections on Democritus, Schopenhauer, and Kant*. Lanham: Lexington Books.

Szlezák, T. A. (1999), *Reading Plato*, Graham Zanker (trans.). London: Routledge.

Tarrant, D. (1955), "Plato's use of extended oratio obliqua." *Classical Quarterly* 5, 222–4.

Tatti-Gartziou, A. (2010), "Blindness as Punishment." In Menelaos, Karakantza, and Levaniouk (2010), 181–90.

Tecuşan, M. (1990), "*Logos Sympotikos*: Patterns of the Irrational in Philosophical Drinking: Plato Outside the *Symposium.*" In Murray (1990), 238–60.

Teloh, H. (1981), *The Development of Plato's Metaphysics*. University Park: The Pennsylvania State University Press.

Themistius, Or. 23 (*Sophistês*) (1973). In *Themistii Orationes quae supersunt*, vol. 2, Schenkl, H., Downey, G., Norman, A. F. (eds), 75–95. Teubner: Leipzig.

Thesleff, H. (2009), *Platonic Patterns: A Collection of Studies*. Las Vegas: Parmenides Publishing.

Tomin, J. (1997), "Plato's First Dialogue." *Ancient Philosophy* 17, 31–45.

Vlastos, G. (1963), "On Plato's Oral Doctrine." *Gnomon* 41, 641–55.

—(1991), *Socrates, Ironist and Moral Philosopher*. Ithaca: Cornell University Press.

Wagner, Richard (1993), *The Art-Work of the Future and Other Works*, Ellis, W. A. (trans.). Lincoln: University of Nebraska Press.

Wallach, J. R. (2001), *The Platonic Political Art: A Study of Critical Reason and Democracy*. University Park: The Pennsylvania State University Press.

Waugh, J. (1995), "Neither Published Nor Perished: The Dialogues As Speech, Not Text." In Gonzalez (1995), 61–77.

—(2000), "Socrates and the Character of Platonic Dialogue." In Press (2000), 39–52.

Weiss, R. (2012), *Philosophers in the* Republic: *Plato's Two Paradigms*. Ithaca: Cornell University Press.

Whitlock, G. (1999), "Roger J. Boscovich and Friedrich Nietzsche: A Re-examination." In Babich and Cohen (1999), 187–201.

Woodruff, M. K. (2002), "The music-making Socrates: Plato and Nietzsche revisited, philosophy and tragedy rejoined." *International Studies in Philosophy* 34.3, 171–90.

—(2007), "*Untergang* and *Übergang*: the tragic descent of Socrates and Zarathustra." *The Journal of Nietzsche Studies* 34, 61–78.

Xenophon (1914), *Cyropaedia*. In *Xenophon*, vol. 6, *Cyropaedia Books 5–8*, Miller, W. (ed.). Cambridge: Harvard University Press.

Zeyl, D. J. (trans.) (2000), *Timaeus*. Indianapolis: Hackett.

Zuckert, C. H. (2009), *Plato's Philosophers: The Coherence of the Dialogues*. Chicago: The University of Chicago Press.

Index of Names

Subject Index